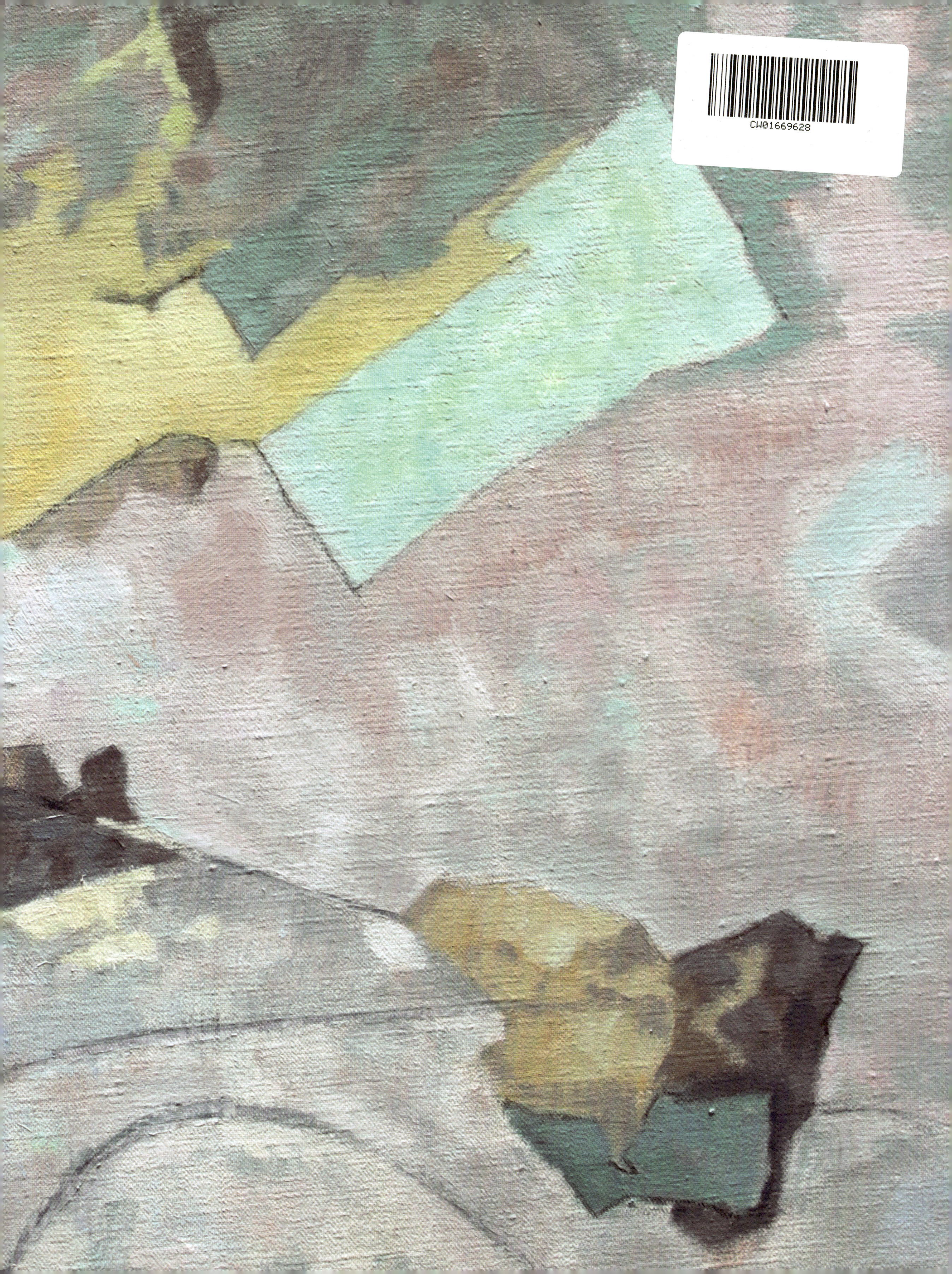

John Busby *Lines from Nature*

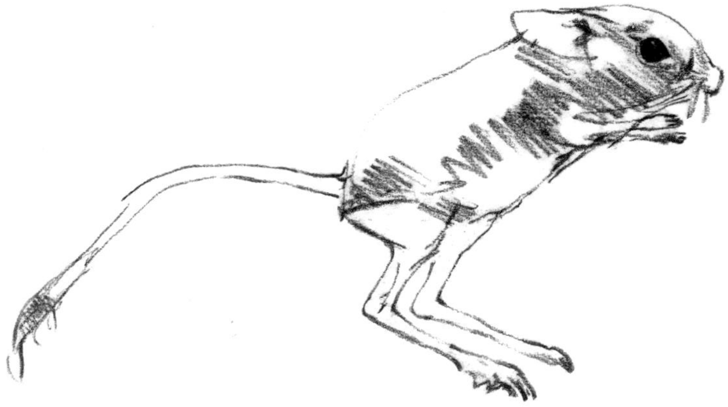

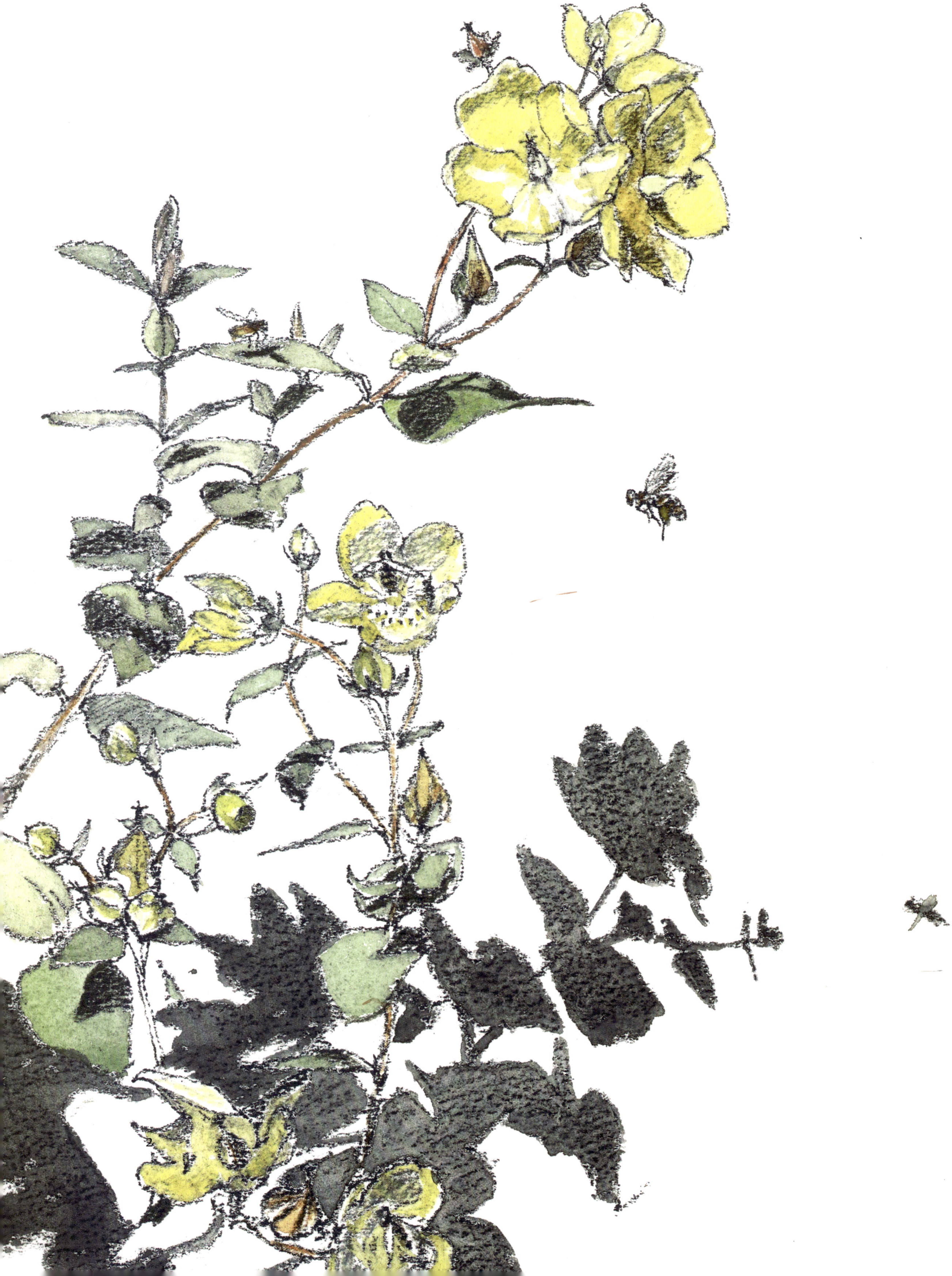

John Busby
Lines from Nature

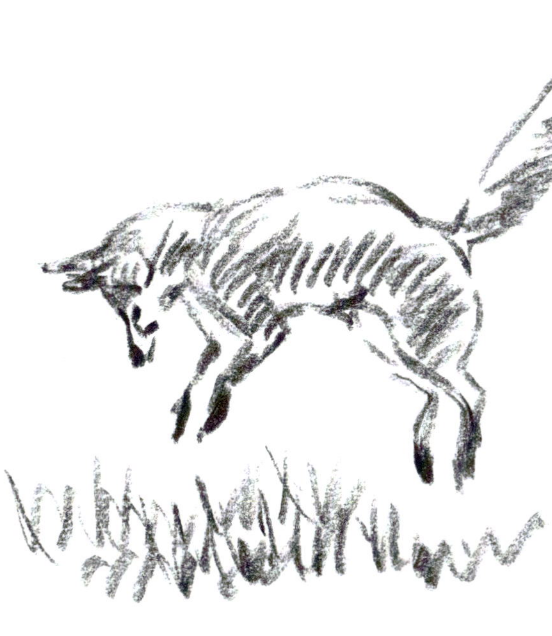

LANGFORD PRESS

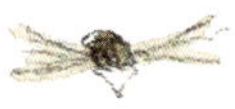

When the flush of newborn sun fell first
On Eden's green and gold
Our Father Adam sat under a tree
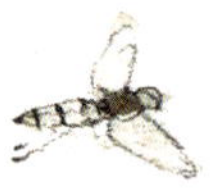
And scratched with a stick in the mould,
And the first rude sketch that the world had seen
Was a joy to his mighty Heart
Till the devil whispered behind the leaves,
"It's pretty, but is it Art?"

From 'The Conundrum of Workshops'
by Rudyard Kipling

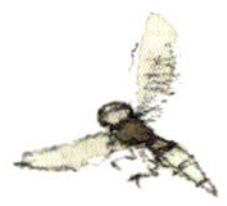

First published in 2016 by
Langford Press, 32 Eastfields, Narborough
King's Lynn, Norfolk PE32 1SS
www.langford-press.co.uk
Email sales@langford-press.co.uk

ISBN 978-1-904078-61-6

A CIP Record for this book is available
from the British Library

Edited by Robert Hume
Designed and typeset in Elena by
Nye Hughes, Dalrymple, Edinburgh
Origination by James Wilson
Photography by John McKenzie and Ian Langford
Printed in Spain

Front cover: Peacock; half title: Jerboa;
frontispiece: Hypericum and Honey Bees.

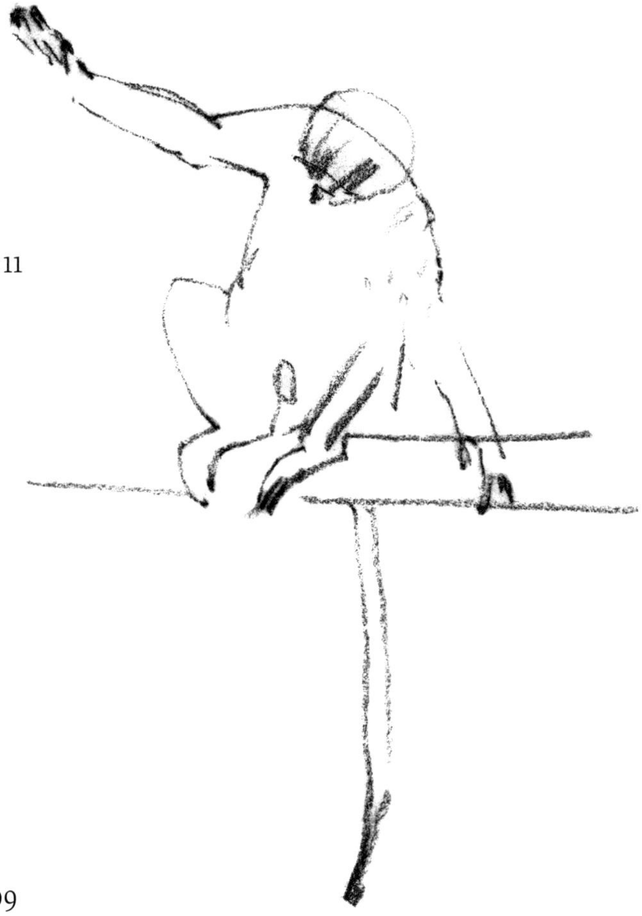

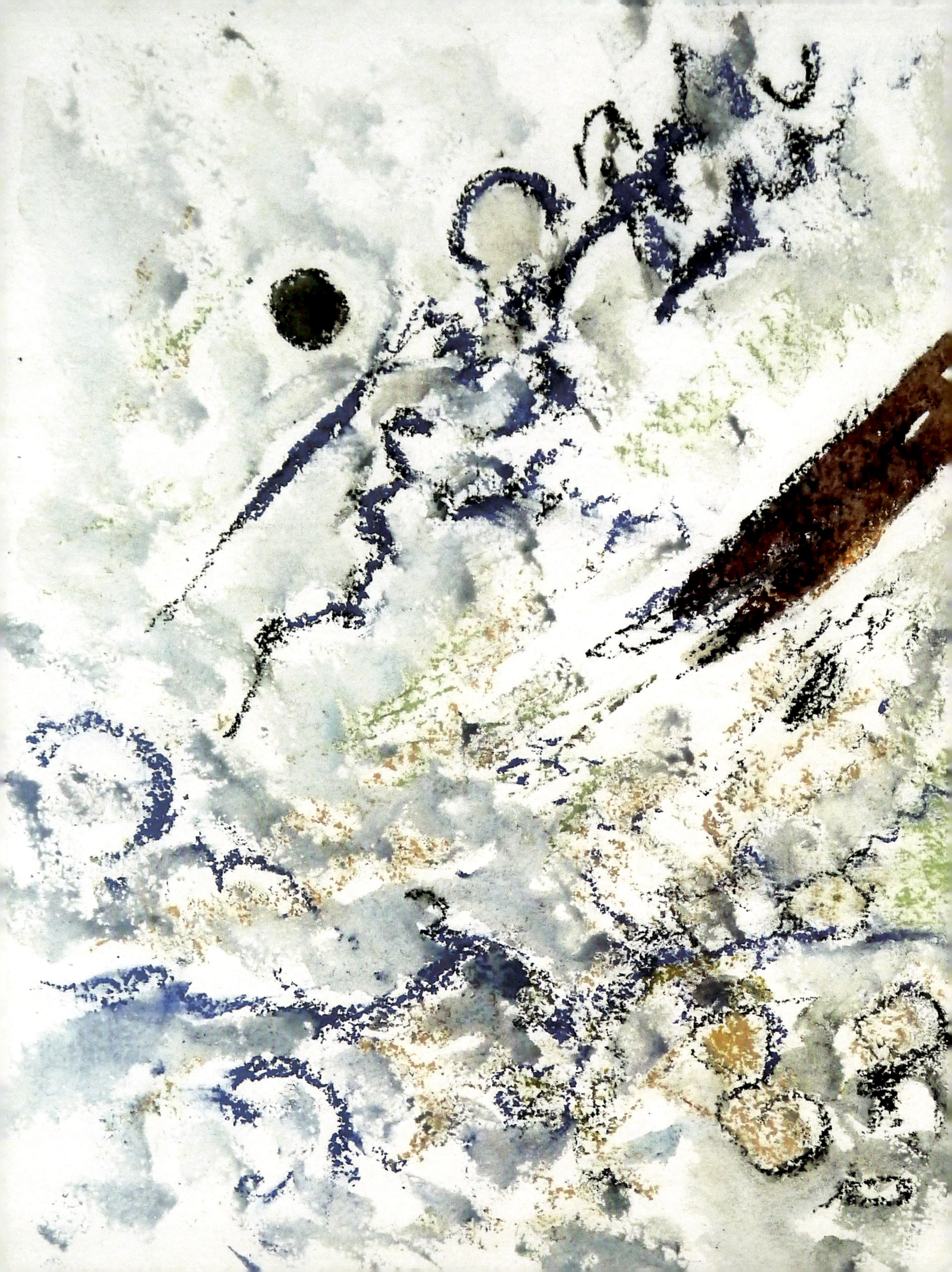

Introduction

My fascination with nature began at an early age when the family moved from the city of Bradford to Menston-in-Wharfedale. The village was surrounded by farmland leading to heather moorland on the hill tops – land where curlews called and skylarks sang.

The view across the valley stretched from Beamsley Beacon in the north-west, along the ridge of Langbar, to Almscliffe Crags and Otley Chevin in the east. It was a spacious landscape of fields and scudding clouds where vision could expand.

A radio programme on *Children's Hour* called *Out with Romany** inspired my childish curiosity to go out and explore nature, and drawing became the natural way of responding to what I saw; the start of a lifetime of discovery.

Since then drawings of wildlife, places and events have filled many sketchbooks and have been made into many paintings. Some of these memorable moments together are collected here.

To draw wildlife, an artist needs a quick eye and a strong visual memory. Animals and birds are nearly always on the move. They don't wait about posing for an artist. Knowing a creature's basic anatomy helps me to see it clearly, as does a growing understanding of its behaviour – background knowledge to add to fresh field experience.

I love to watch nature in action and I try to match the activity I see with energy-creating lines and marks on the sketch book page. The sheet of paper becomes the air the creature breathes and into which it moves, as well as the place where my thoughts can grow.

Often there is only time for a brief mark; a reminder of a quickly changing moment. In such a situation I may draw without taking my eyes off the bird or animal in the process; hand and eye acting as one. At other times the pace slows and there is time to develop new insights as one draws.

When an artist's work is described as 'drawn from life', the implication is that everything is portrayed the moment it happens. That is quite a challenge and a purity of intention, but seeing imaginatively comes into it as well.

Patterns in a rock pool.
Pastel and watercolour

* *The Rev. G. Bramwell Evens, Naturalist, writer and artist*

Direct experience is vital of course, but in practice the sketches I do in the field are often tentative scribbles searching for answers, rather than anything approaching 'works of art'. They are responses that attempt to make me one with the subject – sharing and reflecting its way of life.

After a moment is drawn, it leaves an impression in my mind's eye that can be recalled, developed and re-drawn more than once, without losing that essential truth to a living moment. The more drawing I do, the more I am conscious of the choices I can make in the way of doing it. Just as when finding the right word to convey a clearer meaning when writing, finding the right line can express so much.

A drawing that gets to the heart of things should, perhaps by its economy of means, or sometimes by its complexity, but mostly by how it is composed, communicate the artist's sense of the occasion, and hopefully bring the moment alive.

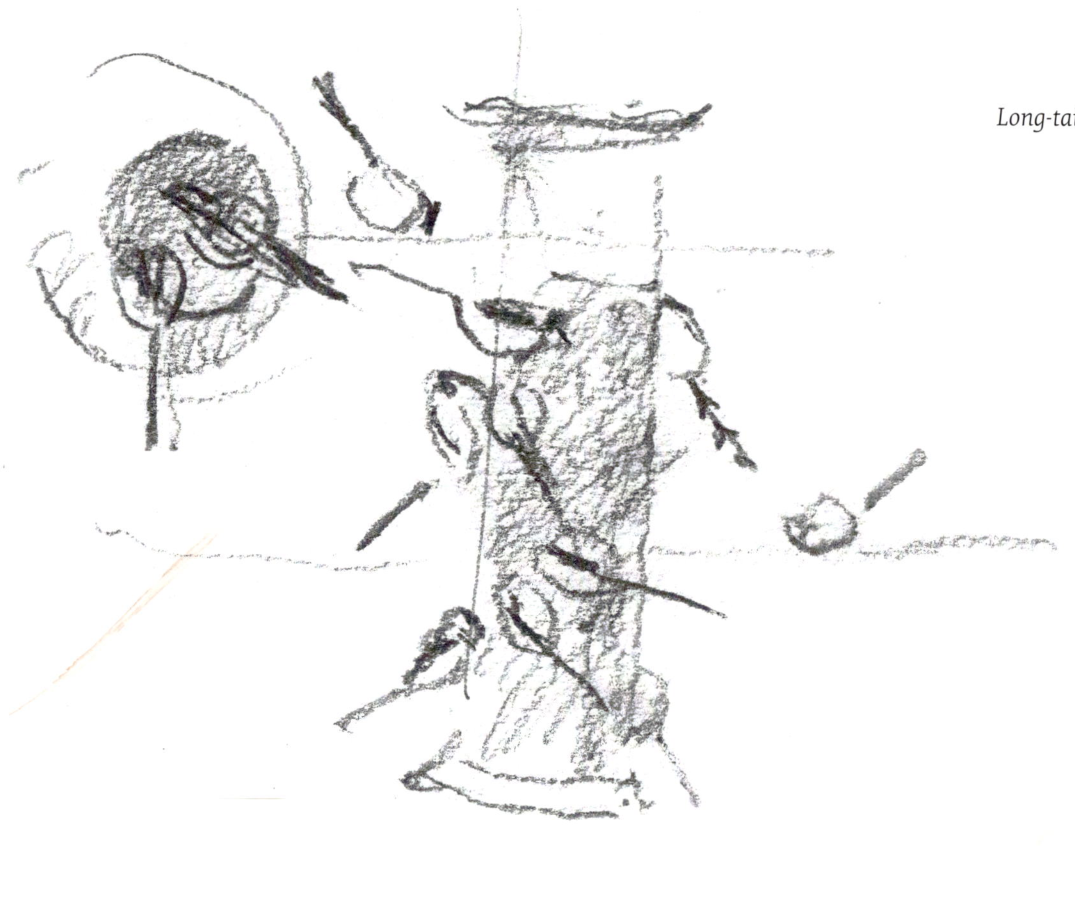

Long-tailed tits on feeders

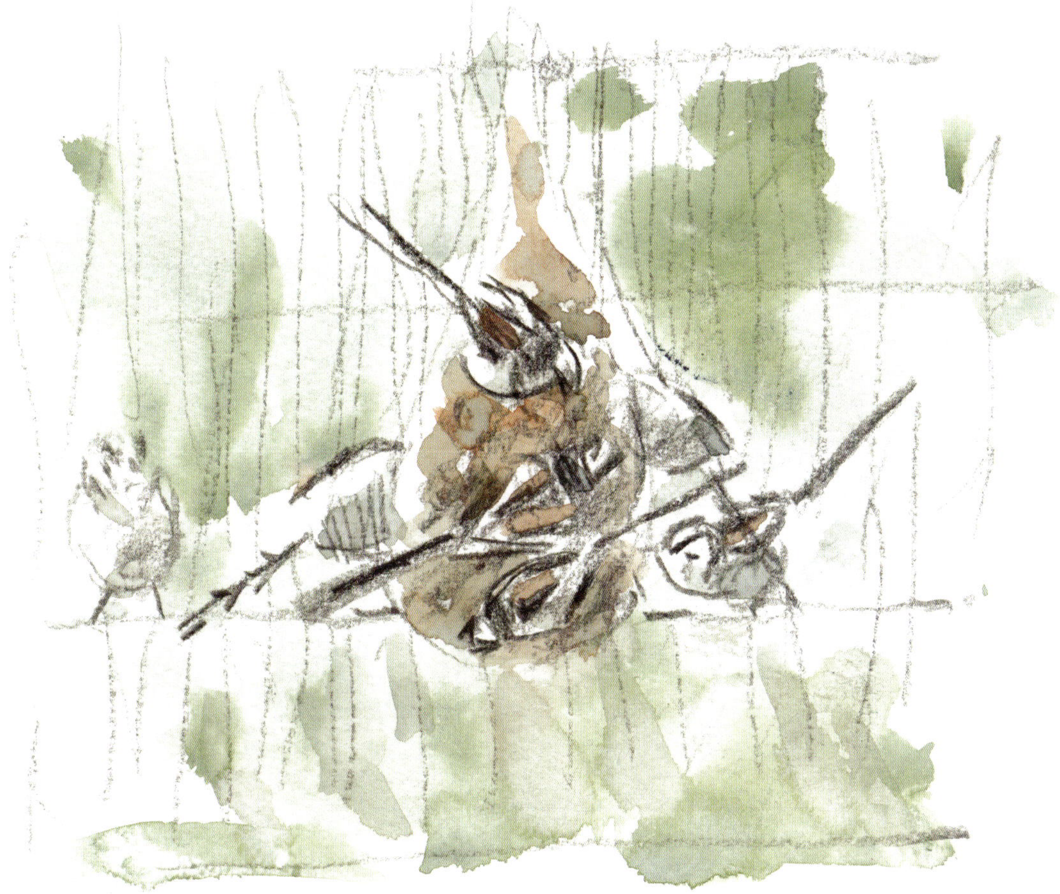

Long-tailed tits on feeder

In my earlier books *Nature Drawings* (Arlequin), *Birds in Mallorca* (Helm), and *Land Marks & Sea Wings* (The Wildlife Art Gallery, Lavenham), the focus was on the landscapes and fauna of special places. Here I have collected some of the moments that gave me great enjoyment to draw and paint – subjects ranging from common garden birds, seabirds and waders to tigers in India; a little-visited part of Australia; Alpine mountains; British native animals; birds of prey; monkeys; cranes; grebes, and glimpses of a few rarities.

Also, I want to share a little of my passion for rock pools – those water-formed miniature landscapes of the sea-shore exposed between the tides: times of stillness, waiting for the changes each incoming sea will bring.

The patterns of rocks and seaweeds are beautiful. They rival anything an abstract artist could possibly invent and their interplay of shapes seems to echo the spiritual searching of the soul for resolutions.

It is a privilege to share such moments with you. JB

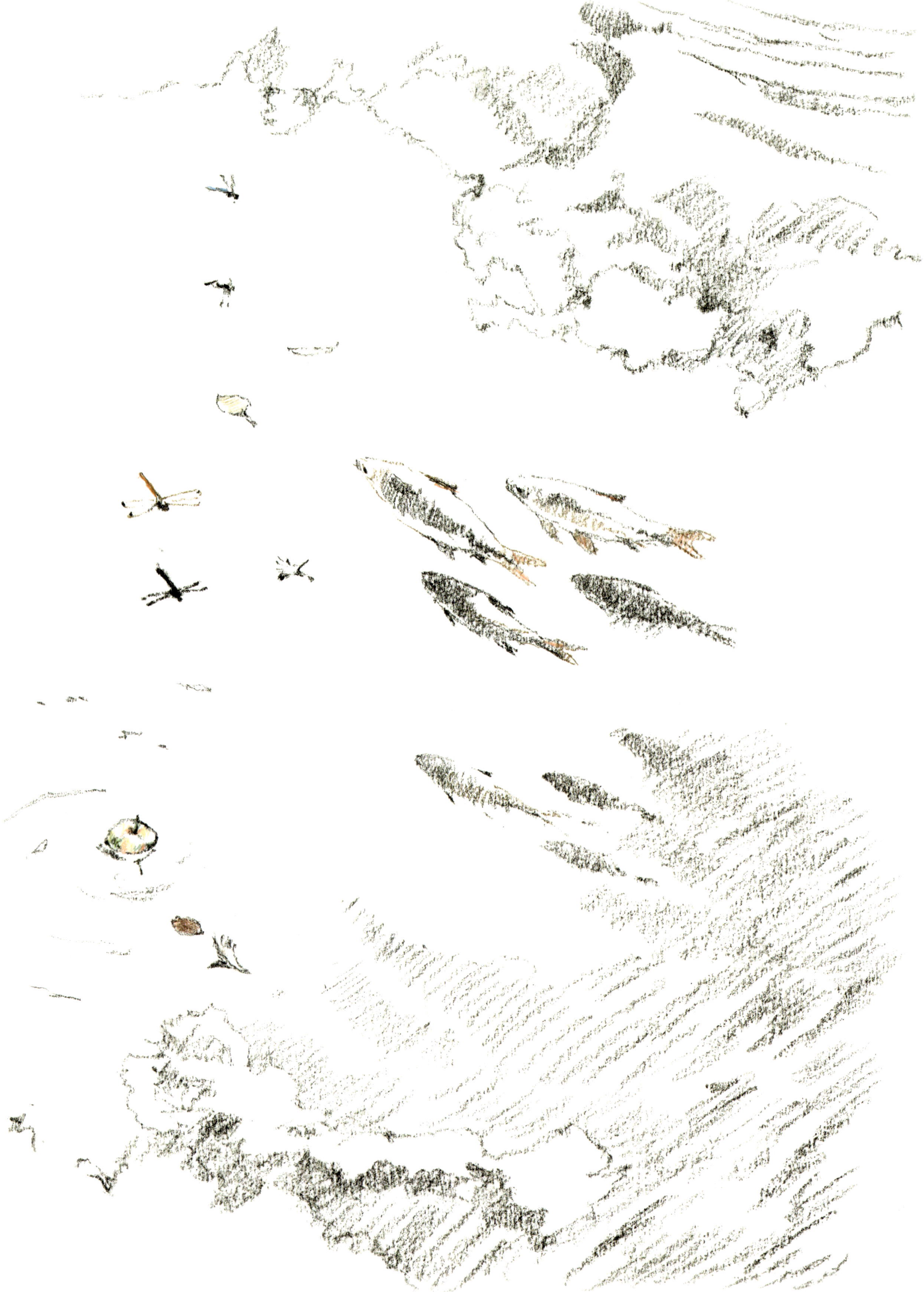

Clouds, dace and dragonflies

A quote from John Ruskin:

> *The greatest thing that a human soul ever does in this world*
> *Is to see something and tell what it saw in a plain way.*
> *Hundreds of people can talk for one who can think*
> *And thousands can think for one who can see.*
> *To see clearly is poetry, philosophy and religion – all in one.*

That is quite a claim. Was Ruskin writing about artists? We all have eyes. Do artists see differently from other people? What he means by 'seeing' goes beyond mere looking at something and copying it.

I am sitting by a pond in Gloucestershire, crayon in hand, eyes at the ready. I see a group of fish with red fins (they are dace); dragonflies skimming the water; a floating apple; duck feathers; fallen leaves, and the reflected sky of cumulus clouds. (Our brains like to identify what we see).

The fish are still; resting; all pointing in the same direction; poised – their streamlined shapes embodying potential energy, ready to dart across the pond. I line them up in my drawing on a diagonal. The dragonflies move in quick jerks as they hawk over the surface. They are unpredictable; never still for more than a split second. The apple used up its gravitational energy when it fell from the tree and the water absorbed it; now it cannot go anywhere and rests with its reflection. The feathers are caught by gusts of wind and sail towards the bank or round in circles. The leaves slowly sink to the bottom of the pond. They echo the fishes' shapes but they cannot generate motion of their own. A towering cumulus cloud is reflected upside down in the water and slowly expands into its watery sky.

Because I use the same crayon to describe in marks everything I see, all are related to each other in a way that can only exist in a drawing. So, clouds live in the same environment as the fish, and the marks I make with my hand float my eyes across the water to discover new relationships.

Artists' drawings define the way things come together. How would a naturalist see?

Clouds, dace and dragonflies (From The Curious Eye *exhibition at the Royal Scottish Academy, Edinburgh 2008)*

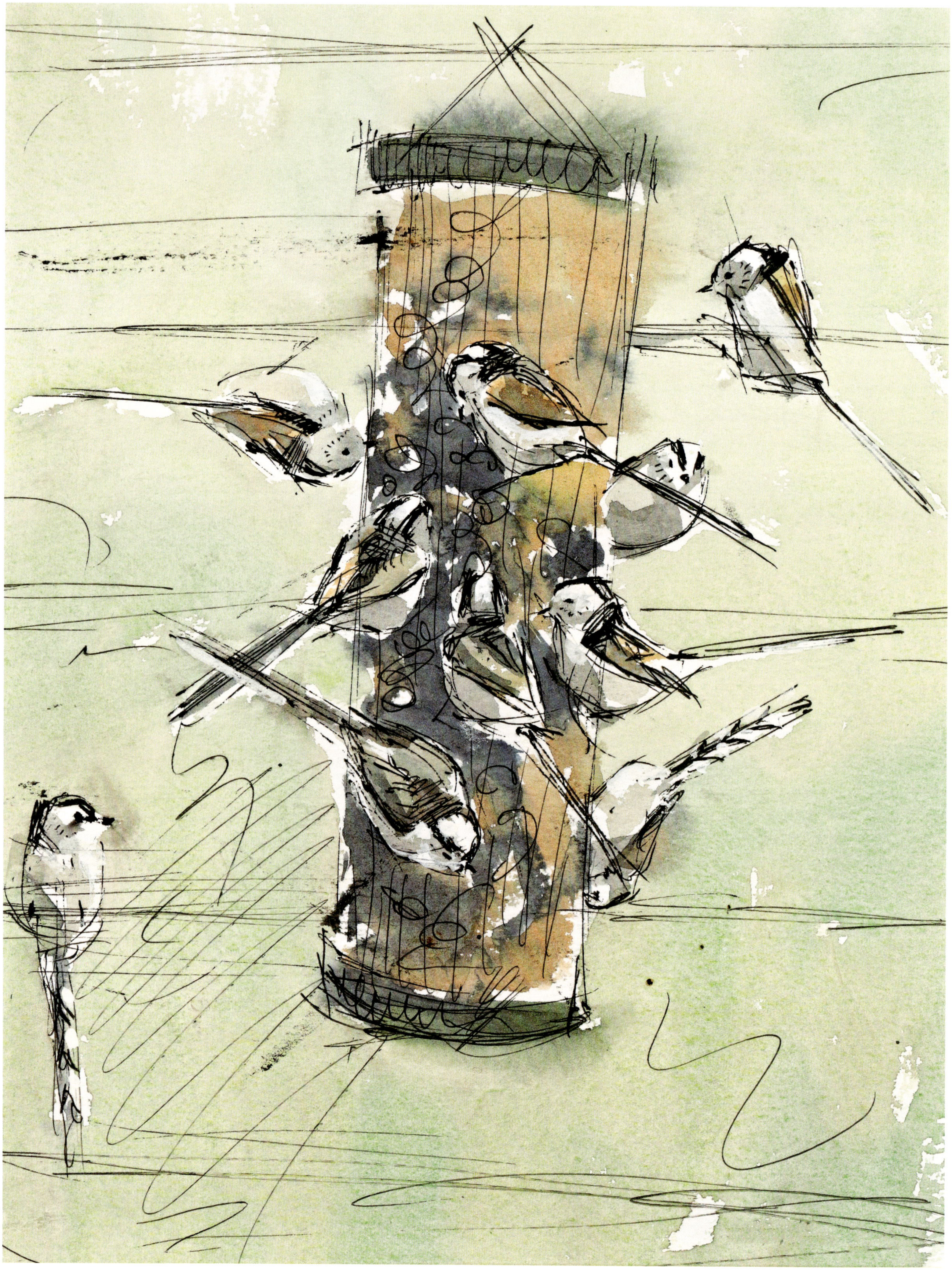

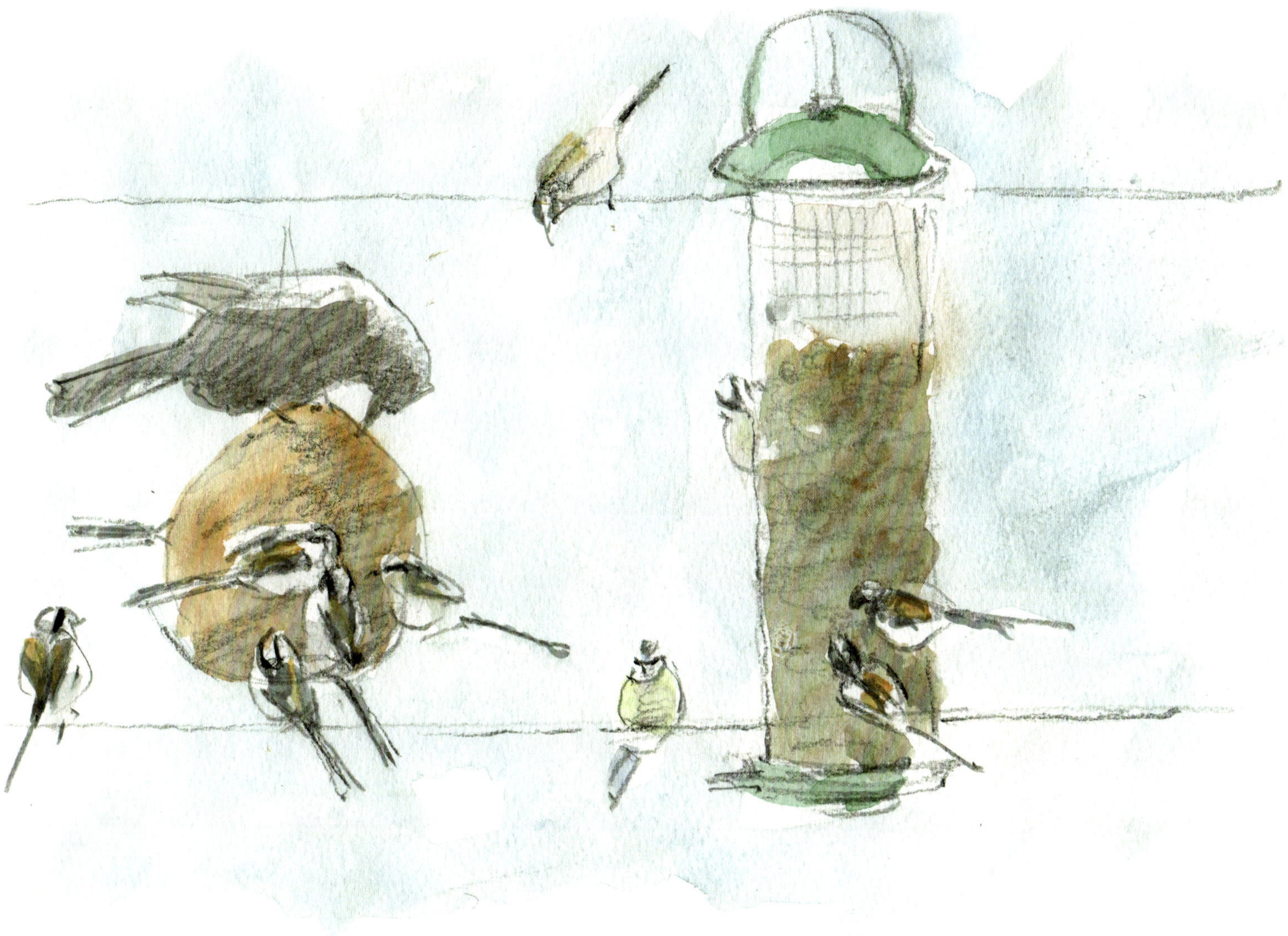

Close encounters

The most accessible wild birds to watch and draw are the ones you can encourage to come close to you. The bird feeder hanging outside the window allows me to sit comfortably indoors before I begin! I hang nut feeders on the wires of our balcony and they attract all our resident tits: great, coal, blue and long-tailed, together with robins, siskins, chaffinches, nuthatches, and a pair of great spotted woodpeckers, while dunnocks and robins forage for bits the other birds drop.

Watching rivalry and the way species relate to each other is entertaining. Only the long-tailed tits allow close feeding together and as I write, there are ten clustered on the nuts, heads touching as they eat, and tails pointing at all angles. When they perch on the wires, they resemble crotchets and quavers on a musical stave. A winter flock of long-tails spends less than a minute

Long-tailed, great and blue tits on the feeders

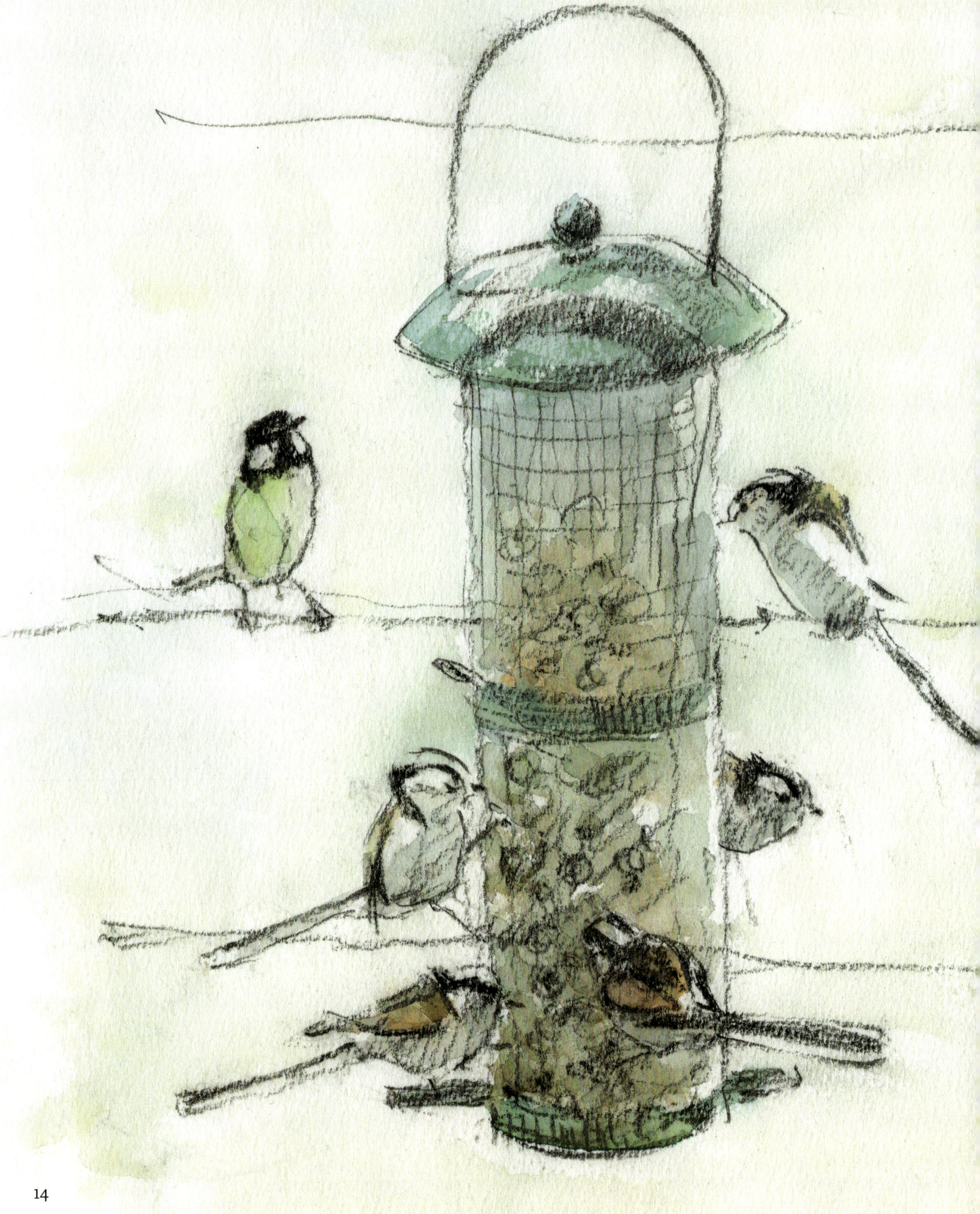

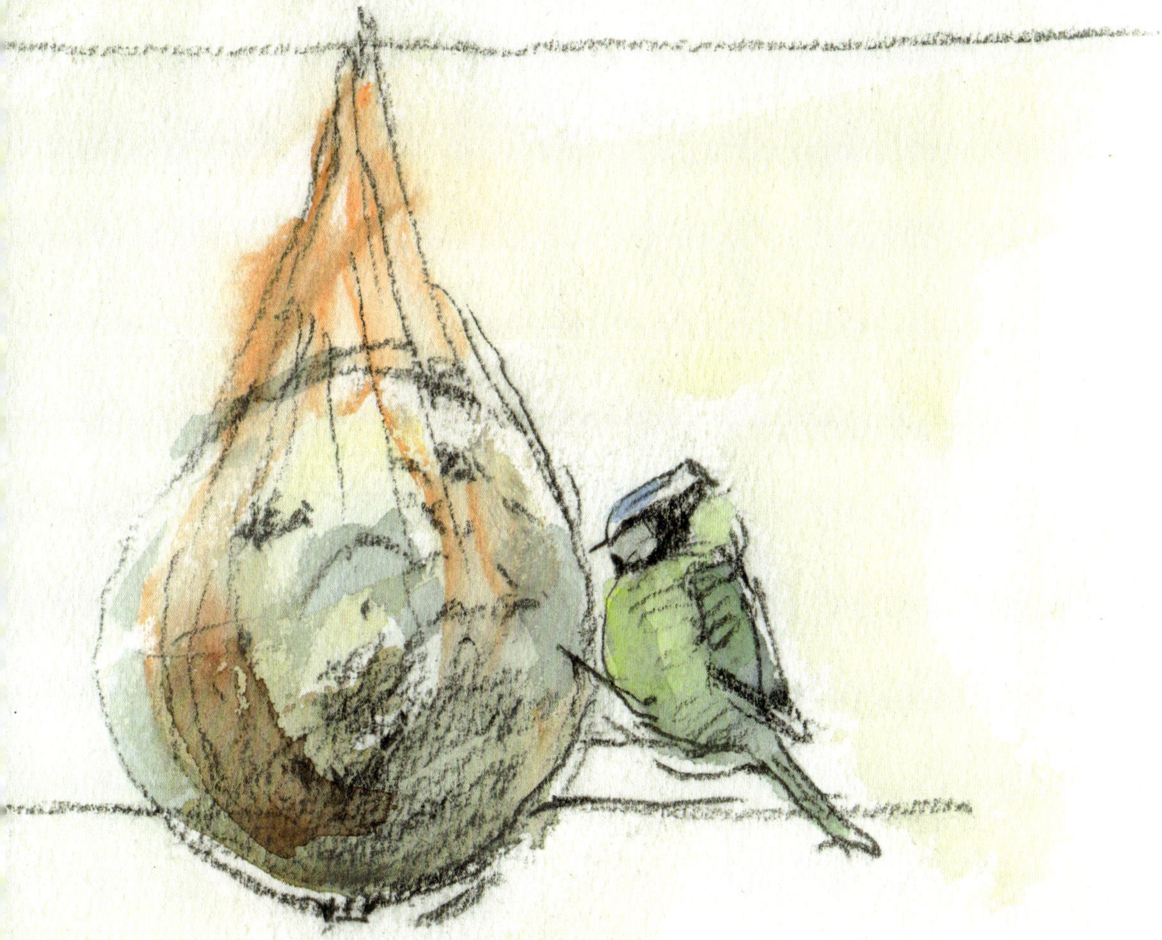

feeding before it moves into the trees, to return maybe an hour later after leaving the nuts to the more persistent birds. I never tire of drawing them.

I like the freedom to draw with the subject there in front of me, without binoculars or a telescope to limit my range of focus. My eyes can quickly relate to events near and far, and to each side of me as I draw. Then, even if the subject is a tiny bird, I do not feel that I have to place it in the centre of the drawing page, as if within the circle of an eye-piece. Although my telescope and binoculars are vital aids for seeing creatures that are wary of any human presence, and have allowed me to draw intimately from a distance, I want to share firstly some moments of close encounter eye-to-eye.

Long-tailed tits on the feeders

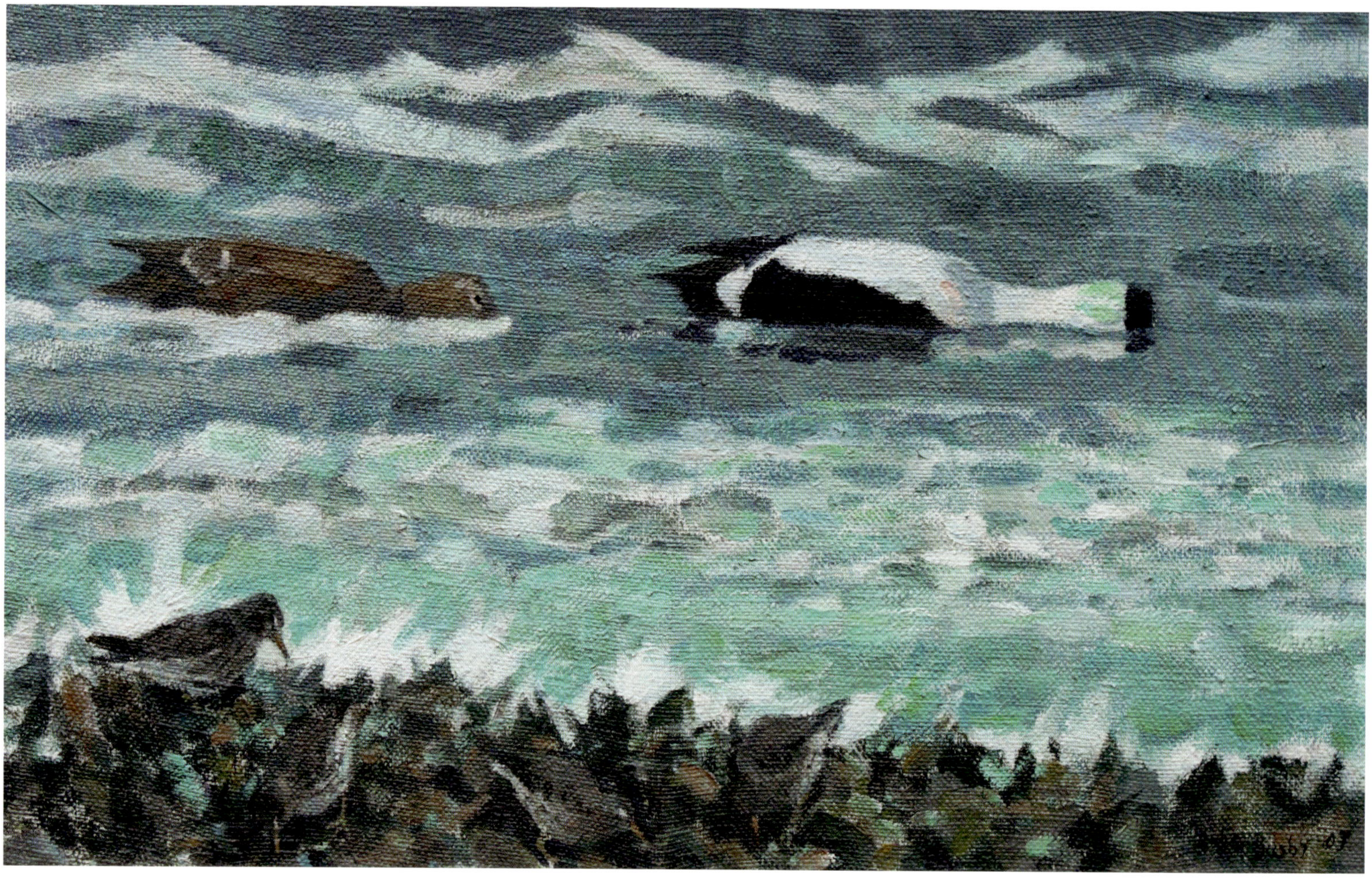

A pair of eiders on the sea looking underwater for food; purple sandpipers on the shore

Mallards resting

There are many places where birds become used to human presence, especially where they are fed; city parks and lakes for example.

Ducks have confidence in the safety of water, and that landlocked humans will provide food for them. They swim hopefully towards anyone standing with children on the bank, and join in the mad dash and splash to get to the food first. With gulls joining the frenzy there is plenty of contrasting behaviour and action for an artist.

Ducks are a delight to artists, whether on land or in water; resting or in action. Their shapely form is very sculptural, and their plumage range is striking, whether in full breeding or eclipse; drake or duck. Eiders are abundant in Scottish coastal waters and a favourite species to watch and draw – males in their black and white finery, tossing their heads and presenting their blush-pink breasts to the ducks – ducklings gathered on the sea under the care of mothering females.

Other ducks visit us in winter from the far north. Scoters and long-tailed ducks turn up regularly, with smews and king eiders occasional winter vagrants in the Firth of Forth, but often on choppy seas at telescope range.

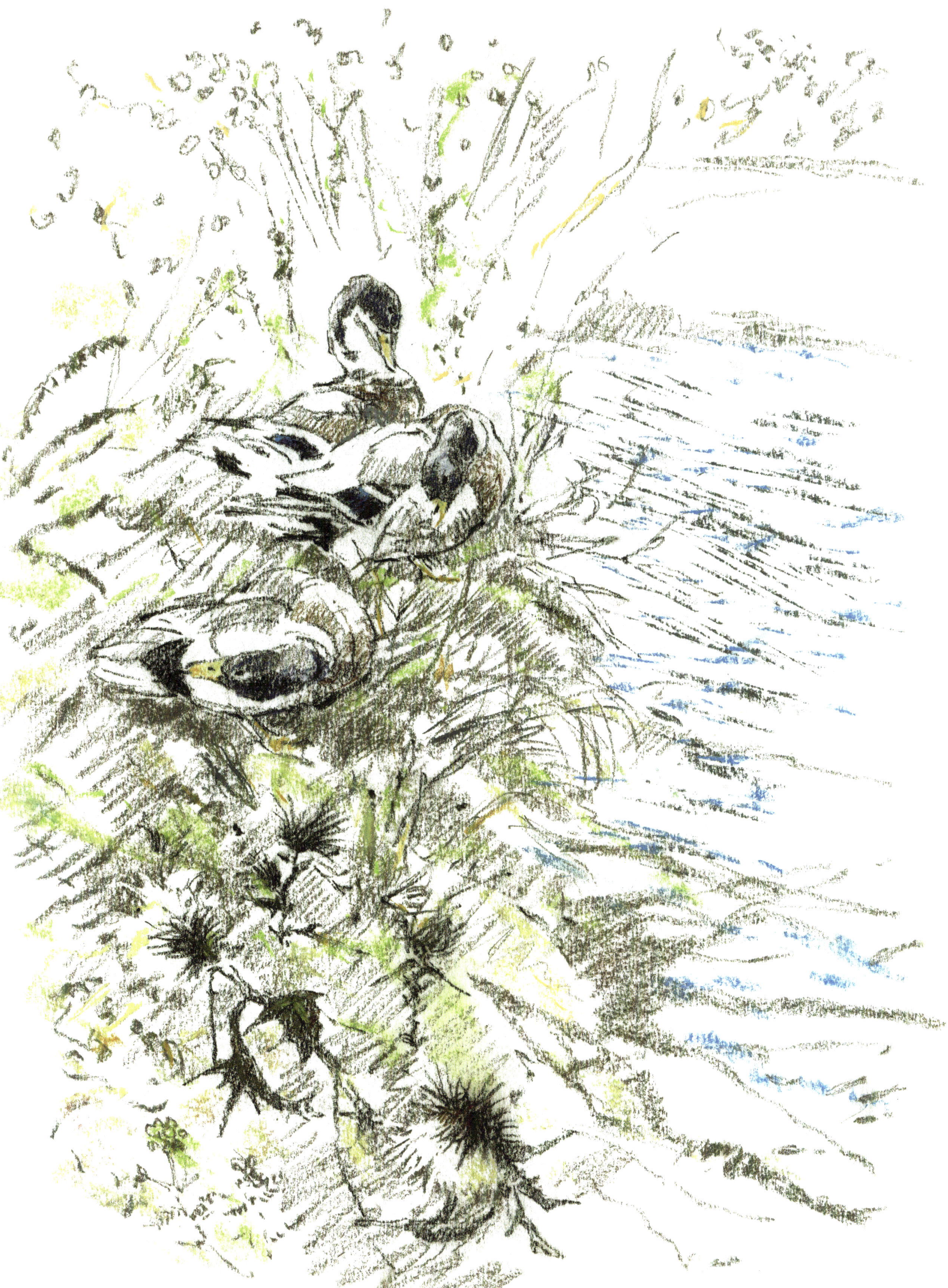

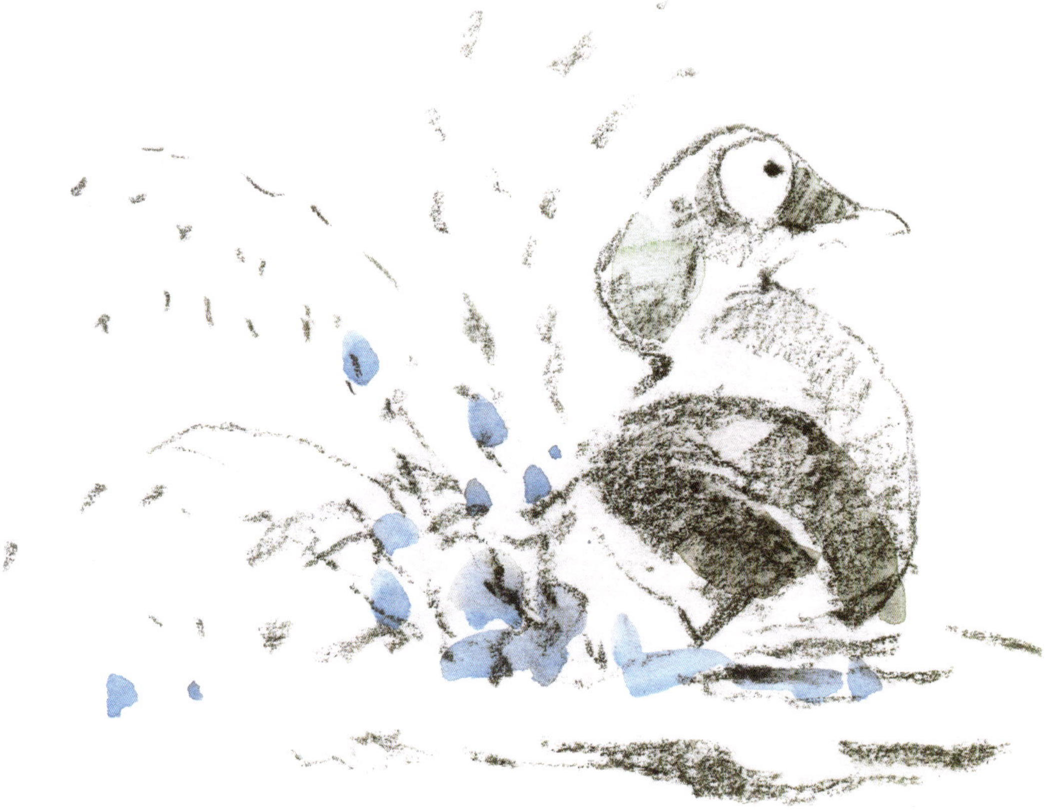

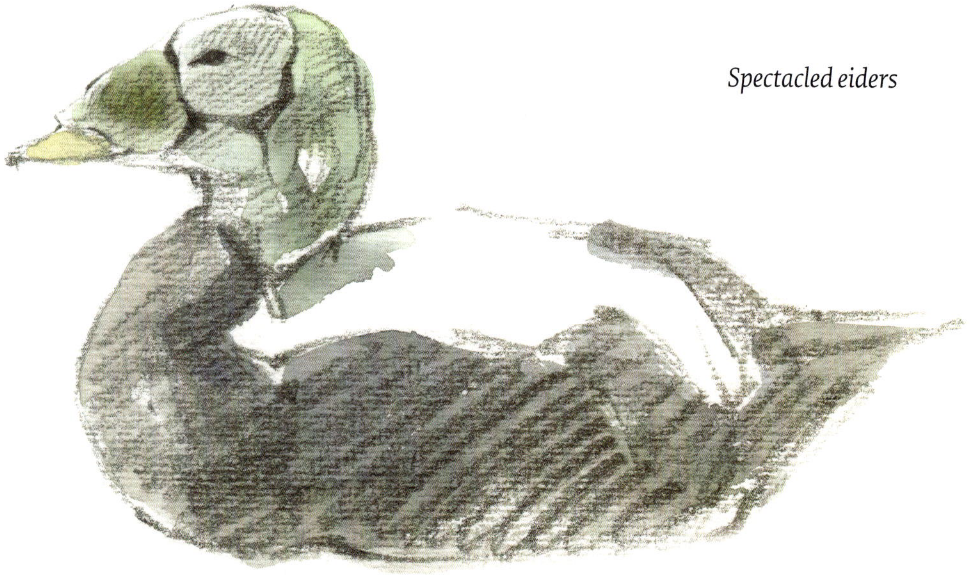

Spectacled eiders

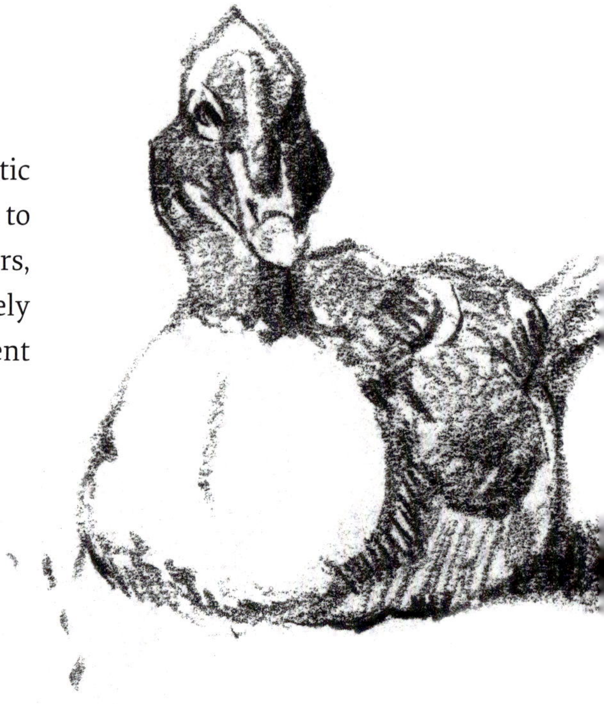

John Prentice, a farmer in Berwickshire, kept a private collection of arctic ducks which he bred successfully on his ponds. He kindly allowed me to draw them. His collection included Steller's, king and spectacled eiders, smew, harlequins, scaup and hooded mergansers: not birds one is likely to see often at our latitudes. It was a treat to find them there in different seasonal plumages and swimming close at hand on the farm ponds.

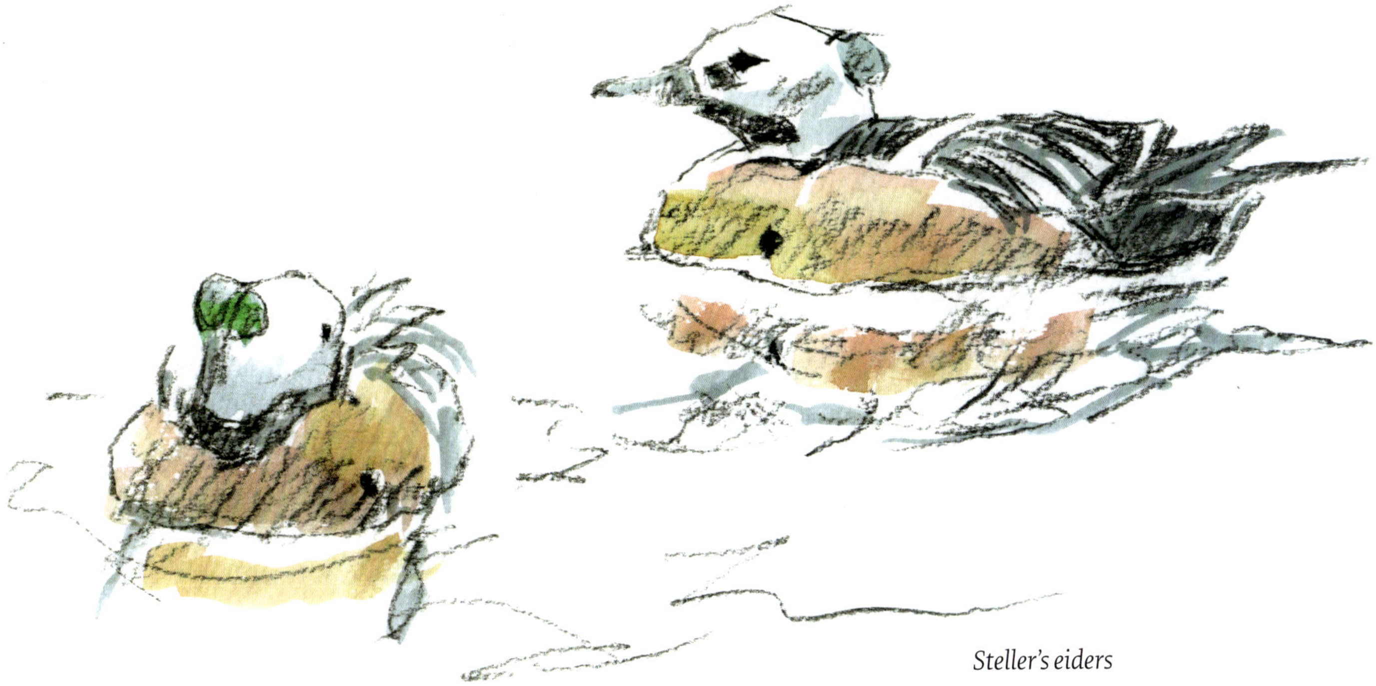

Steller's eiders

King and spectacled eiders in eclipse

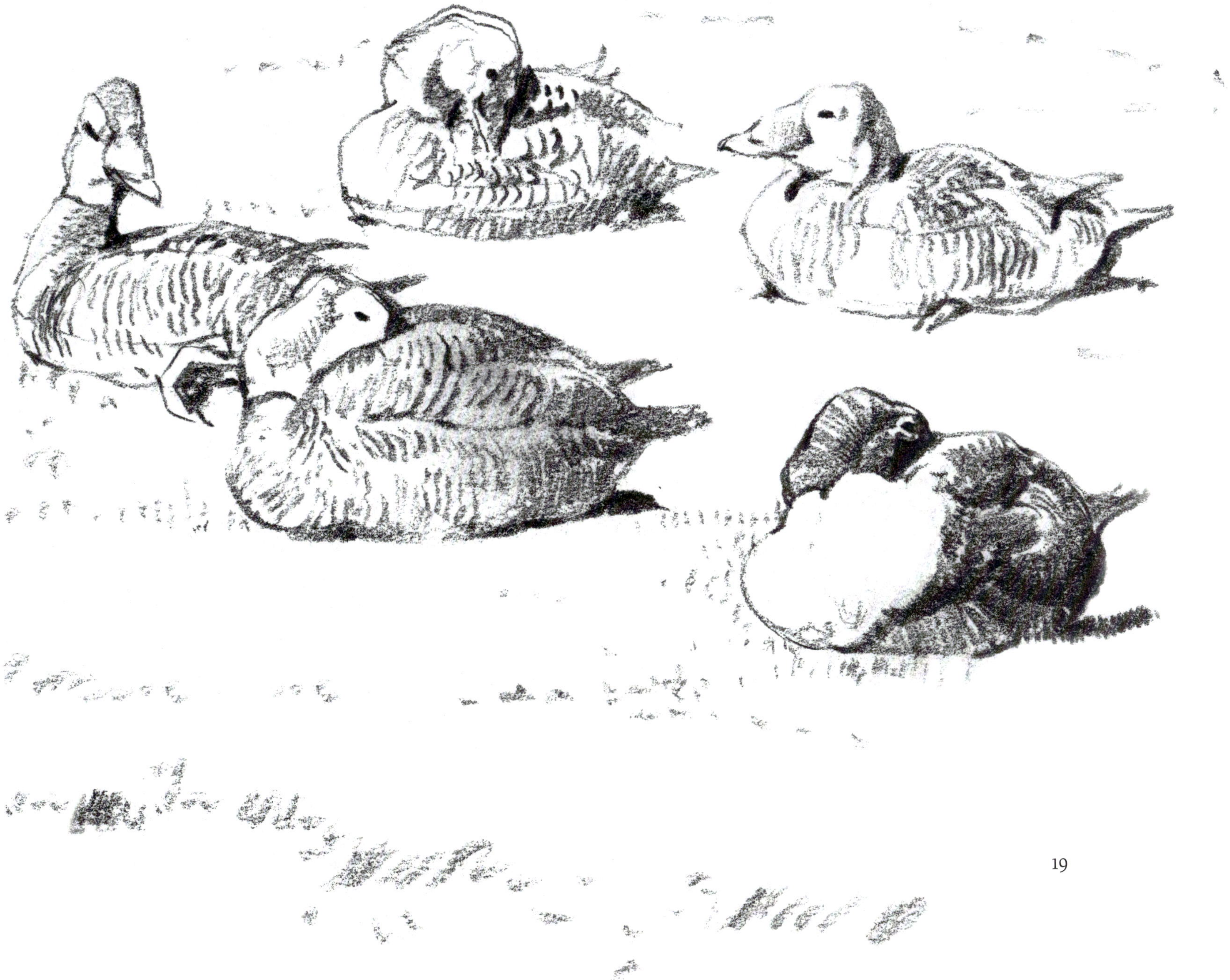

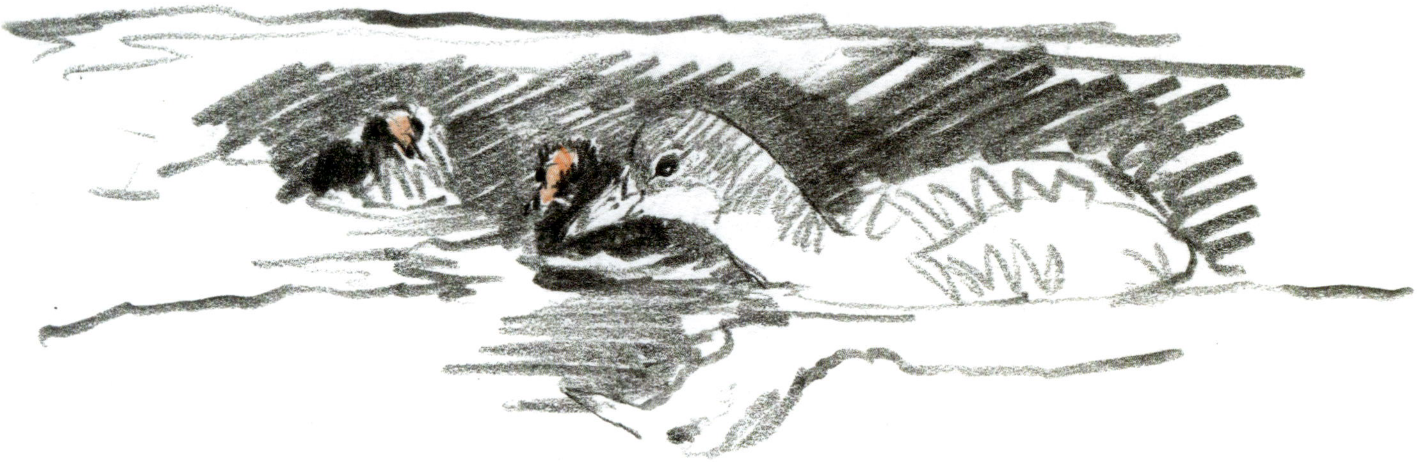

Moorhens

I have enjoyed getting to know the moorhen family which breeds on a pond in our nearby woods, and watching the immature young of the first brood help the parents to feed the chicks of the second. The pond also attracts frogs and toads, and the occasional heron; once a water rail. A butterbur margin gives plenty of cover, and a small island a place to nest safely.

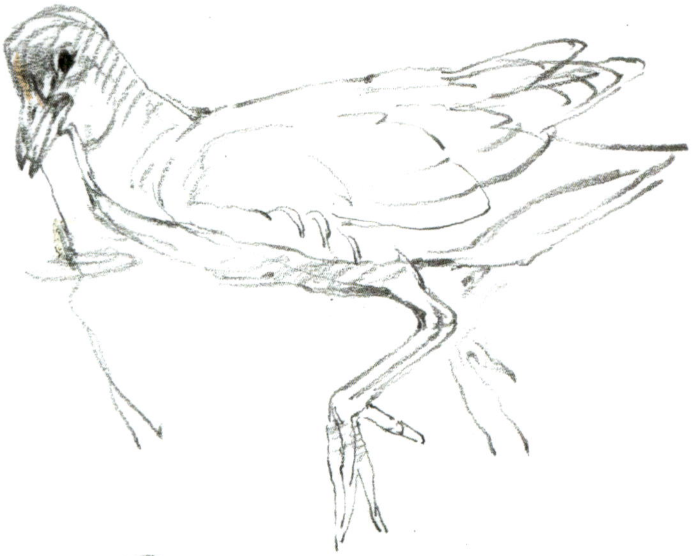

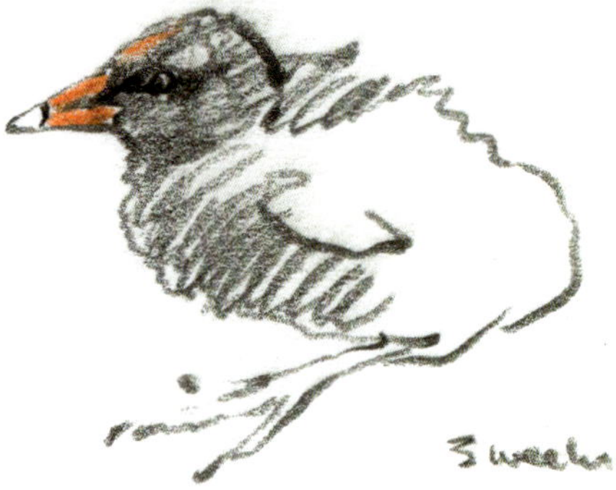

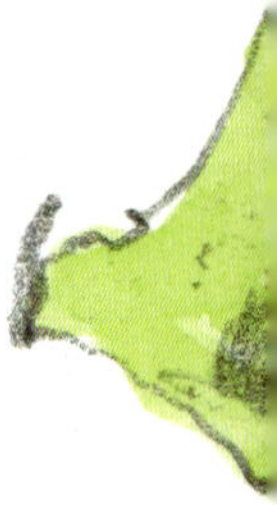

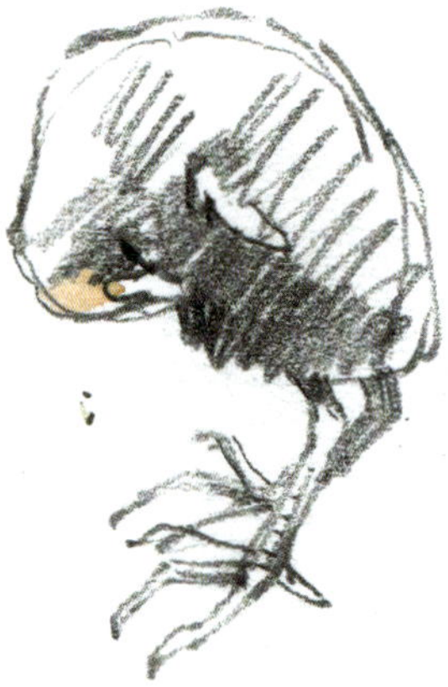

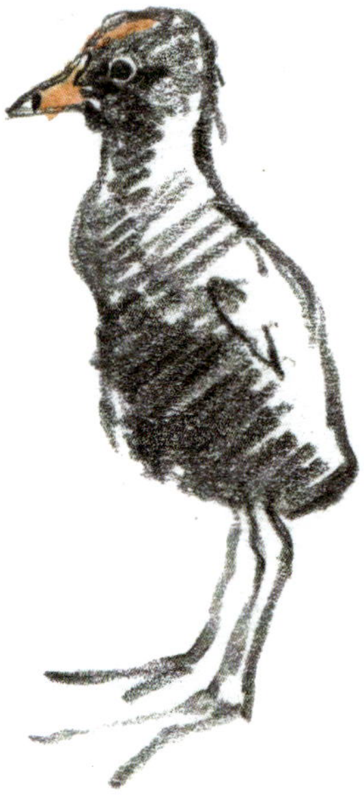

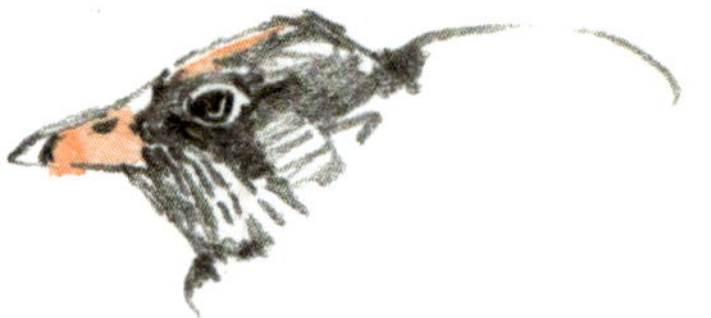

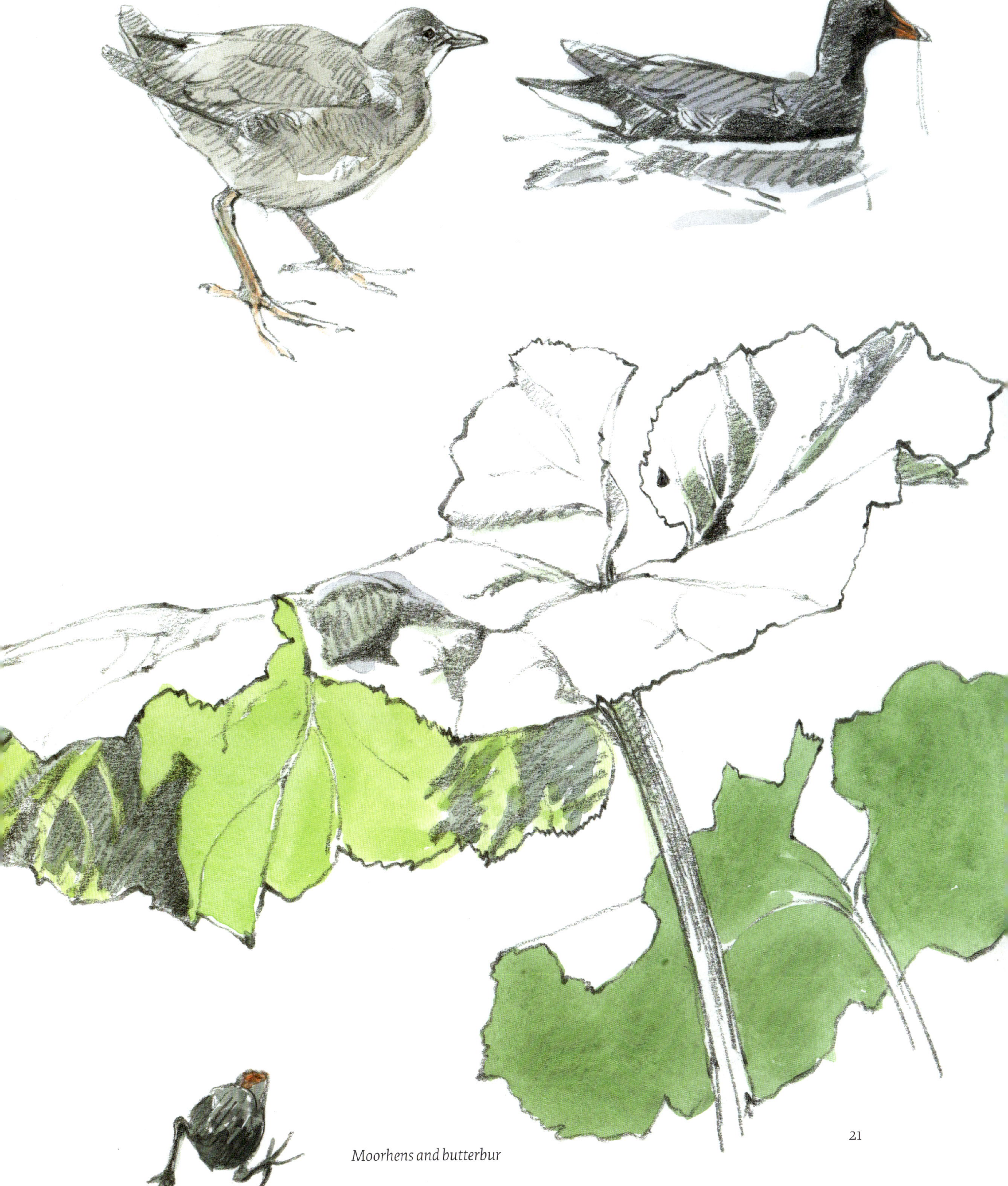

Moorhens and butterbur

It takes more time to get wild animals used to you. I was able to join Hugh Miles when he was filming otters in Shetland. Hugh found that the gulls and other 'alarmists' took no notice of the local shepherd, so he first dressed in the same clothes every day and befriended the gulls with gifts of bread, so the gulls' reactions were less hostile. Getting close to otters was achieved by noting where they mostly came ashore to feed after fishing in the sea; and waiting.

By following Hugh's field craft and keeping still, I saw far more of otters than I thought possible, and watched the progress of a female and her two kittens at Burravoe on the island of Yell in Shetland.

On one occasion, while I was sitting drawing irises by a stream, an otter walked right past me, close enough to touch, only seeing me when I moved my hand to draw.

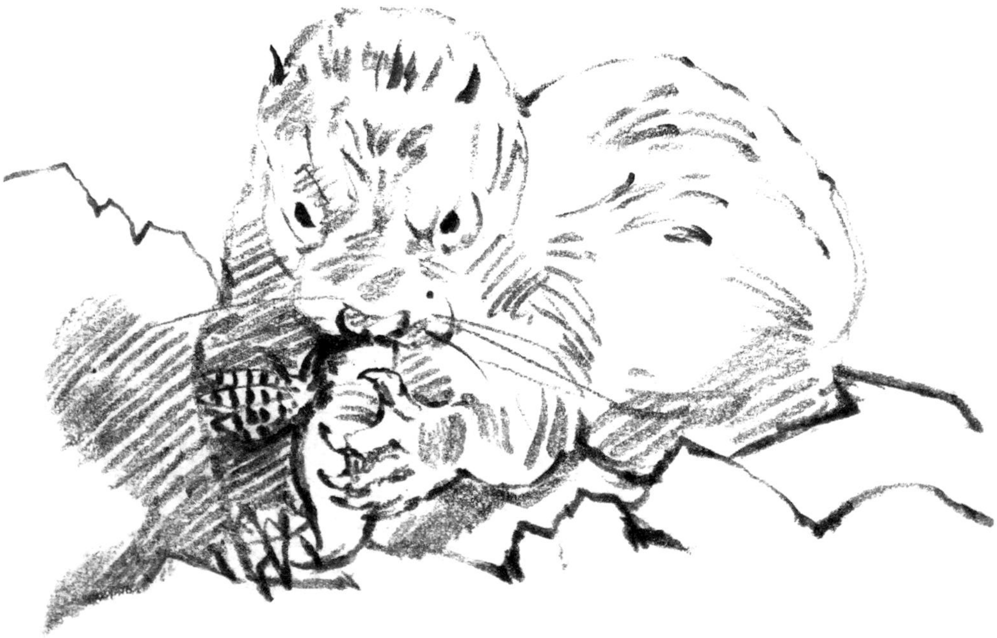

Otter kitten feeding

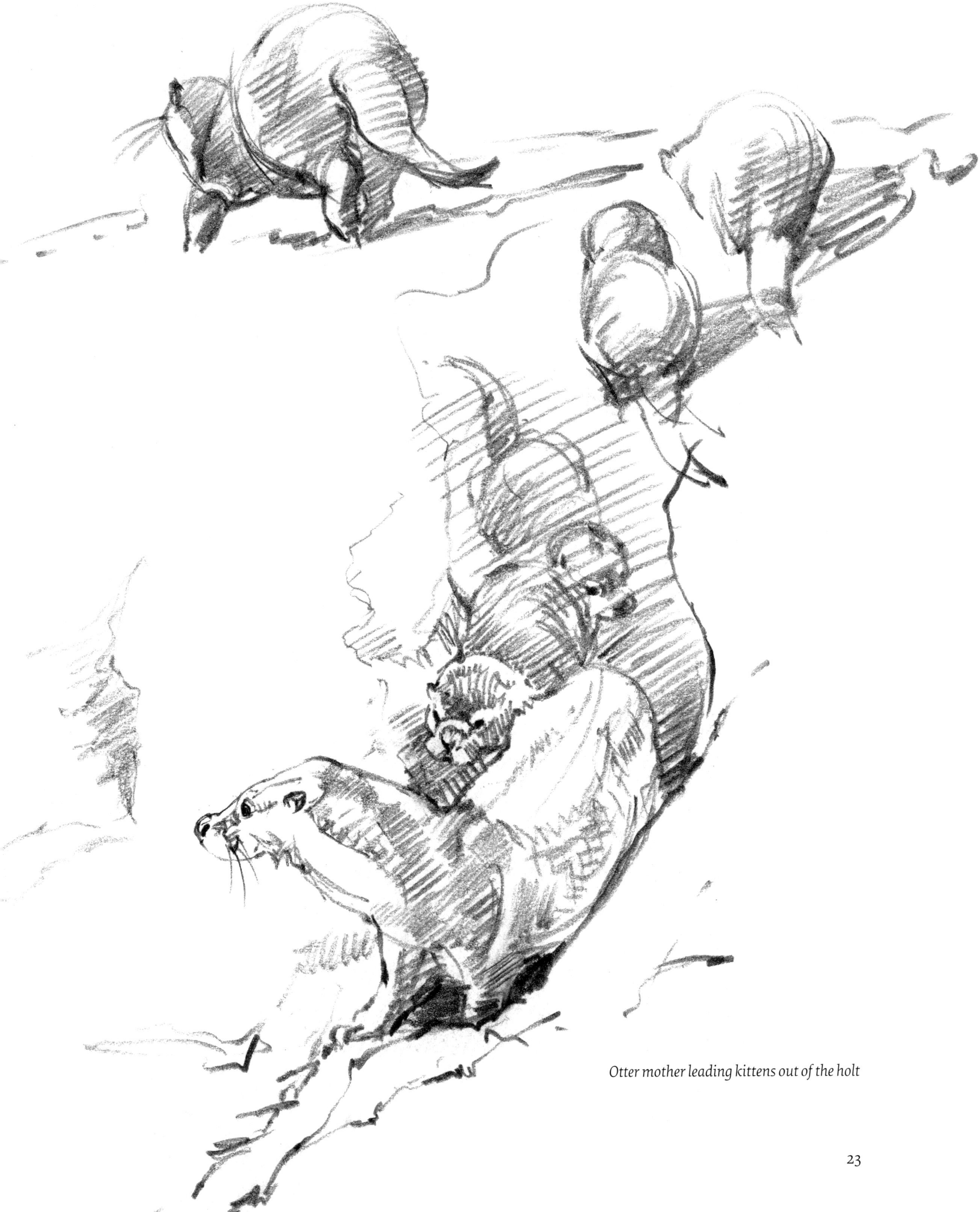

Otter mother leading kittens out of the holt

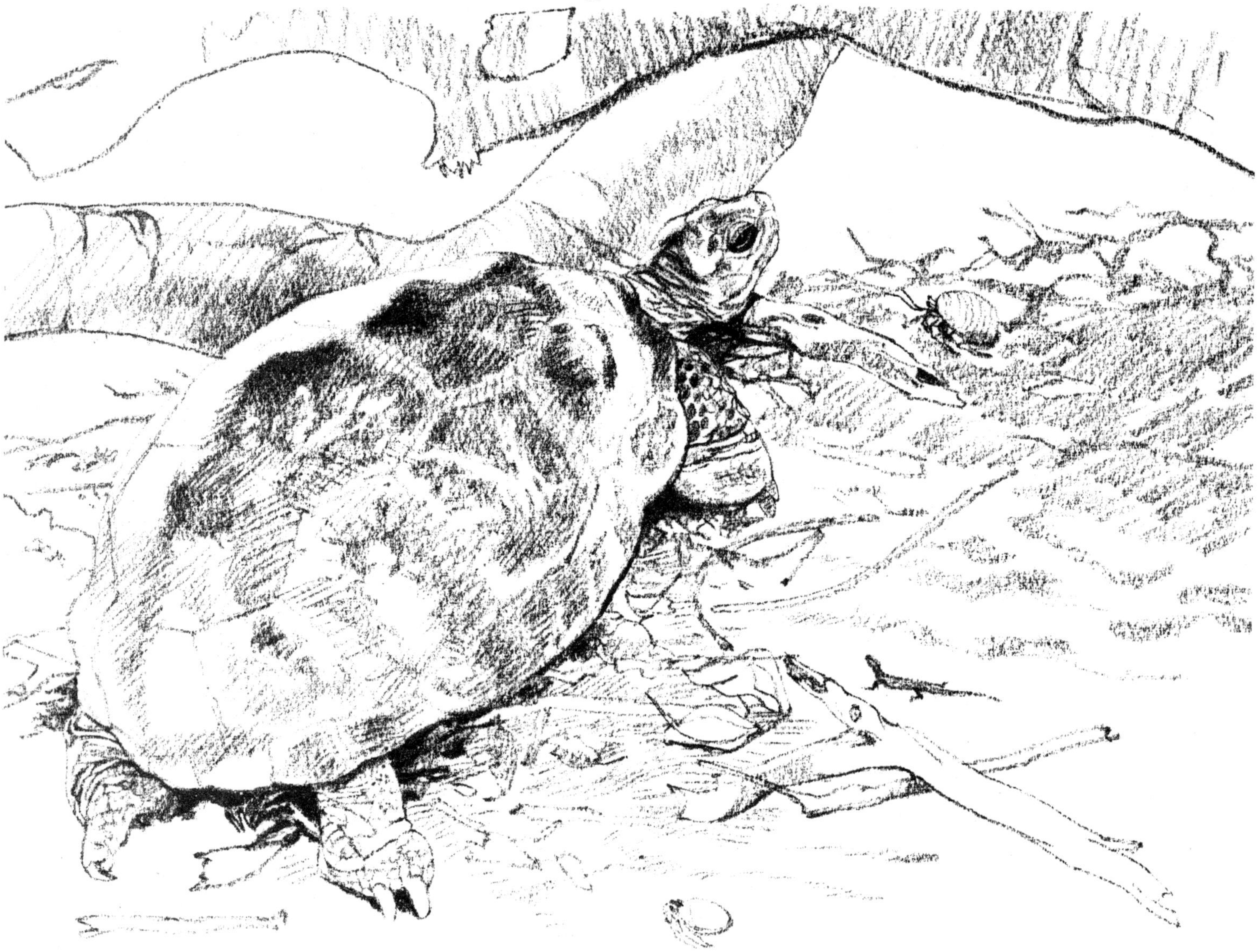

Aldabra giant tortoise

Islands where human presence is too recent to inject fear are noted for the 'tameness' of the wildlife. I have been fortunate to spend time on Aldabra, a coral atoll in the Indian Ocean, and on the Falkland and Galapagos islands, where fear of humans is not in-bred.

On Aldabra one is seen as no more of a threat to wildlife than are the giant tortoises, so you can see the true relationship of species to each other without the 'human element' intruding. In the Falklands I was able to sit among colonies of penguins and even draw alongside a great skua while it sat on its nest. A tussock bird used my shoe as a perch from which to catch insects as I walked by. In the Galapagos, humans can experience a similar close relationship with its unique wildlife. Some of these moments I recorded in my book *Land Marks & Sea Wings* (Lavenham), and in illustrations for Bryan Nelson's *On the Rocks* (Langford Press).

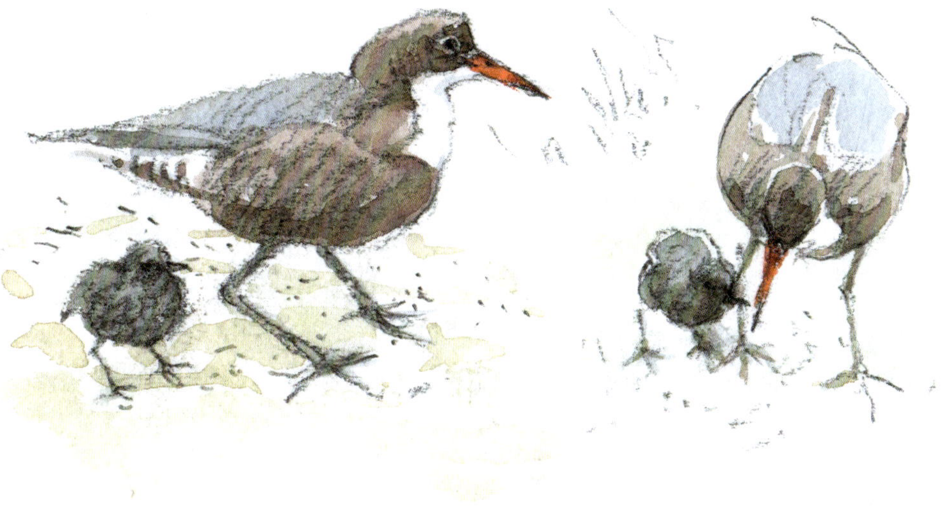

Aldabra flightless rail and young

Here is a giant tortoise from Aldabra, and the flightless Aldabra rail, with a young one who always stayed behind the adult even when being fed, and a group of brown noddy terns on an island in the Aldabra lagoon.

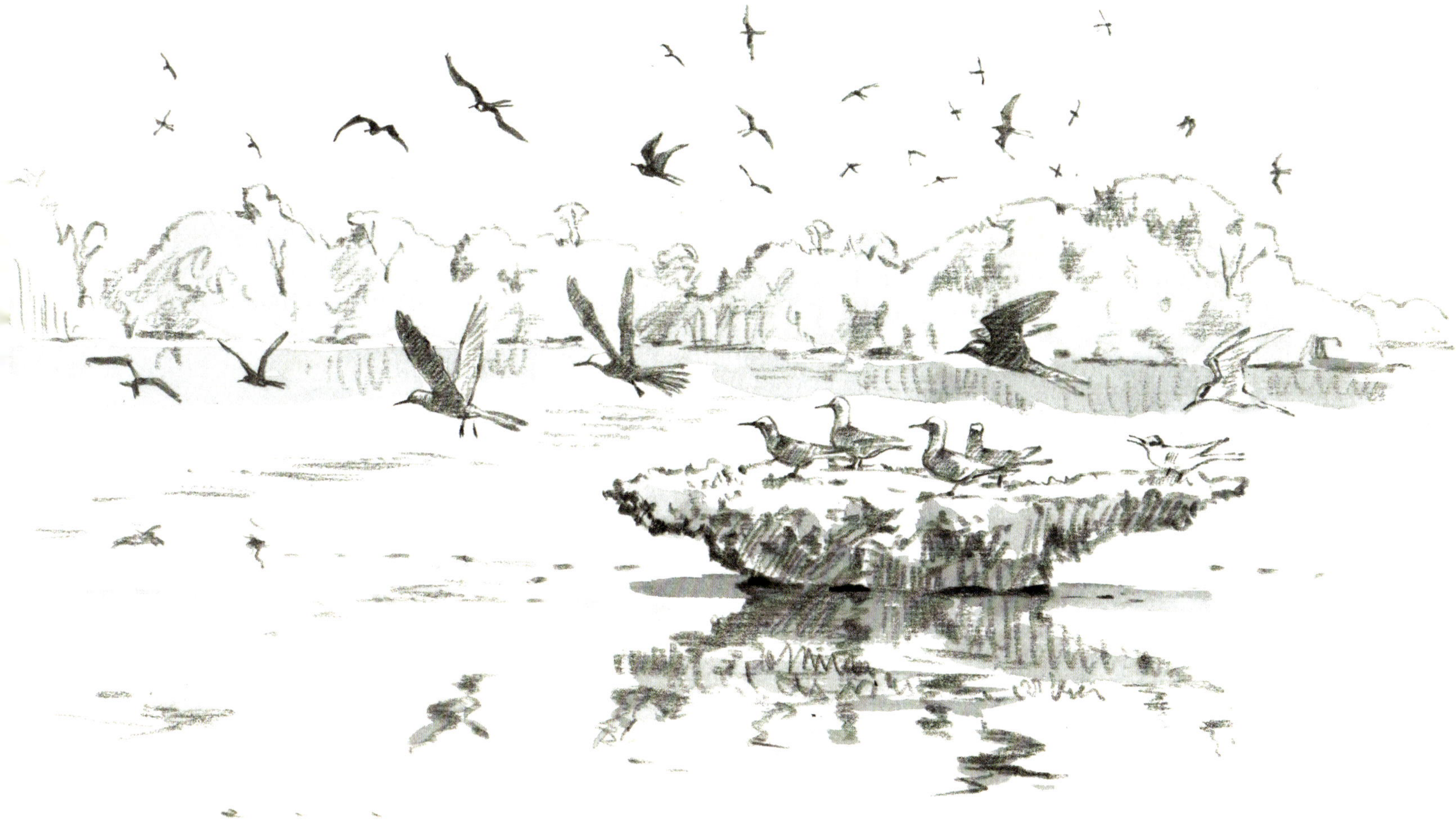

Aldabra lagoon, with brown noddy terns and distant frigates.

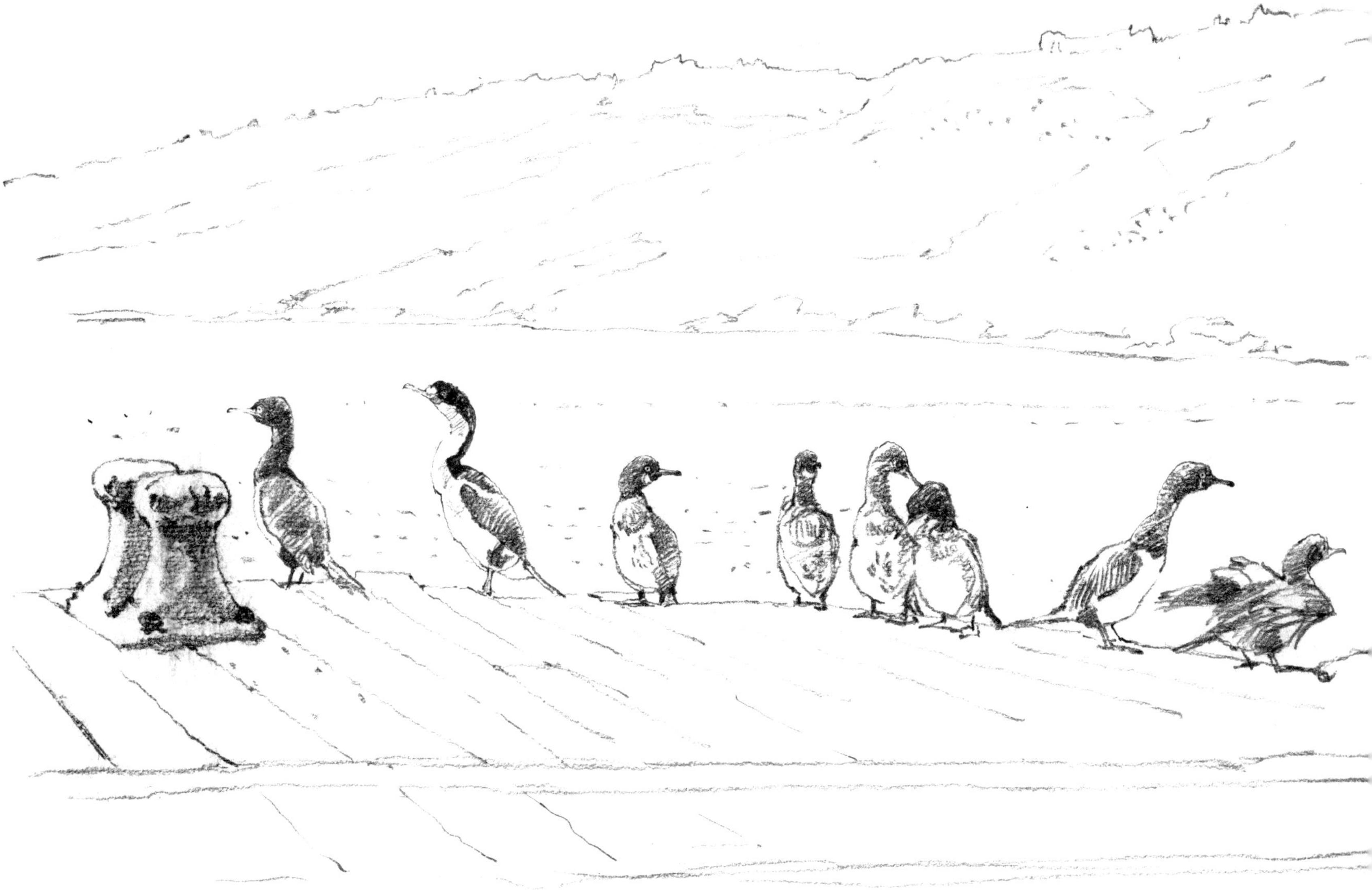

From the Falklands: king penguins at Volunteer Point, imperial and rock shags, and a flightless steamer duck.

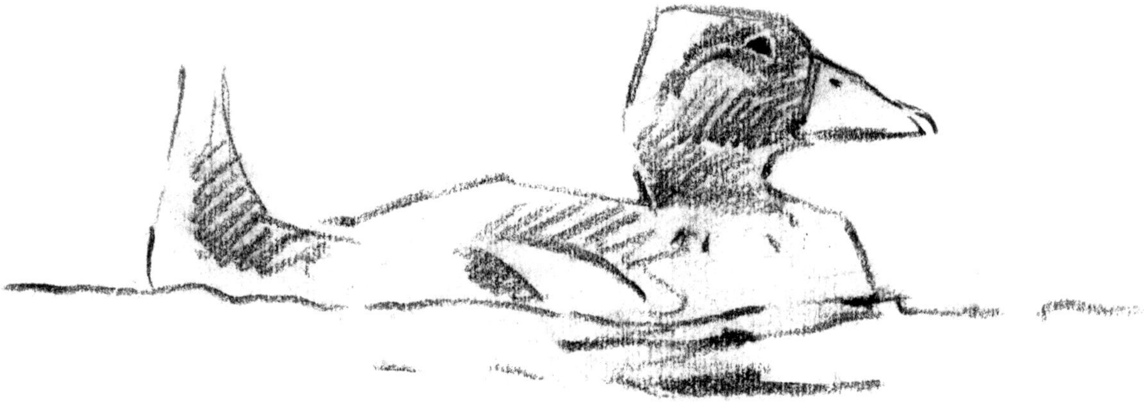

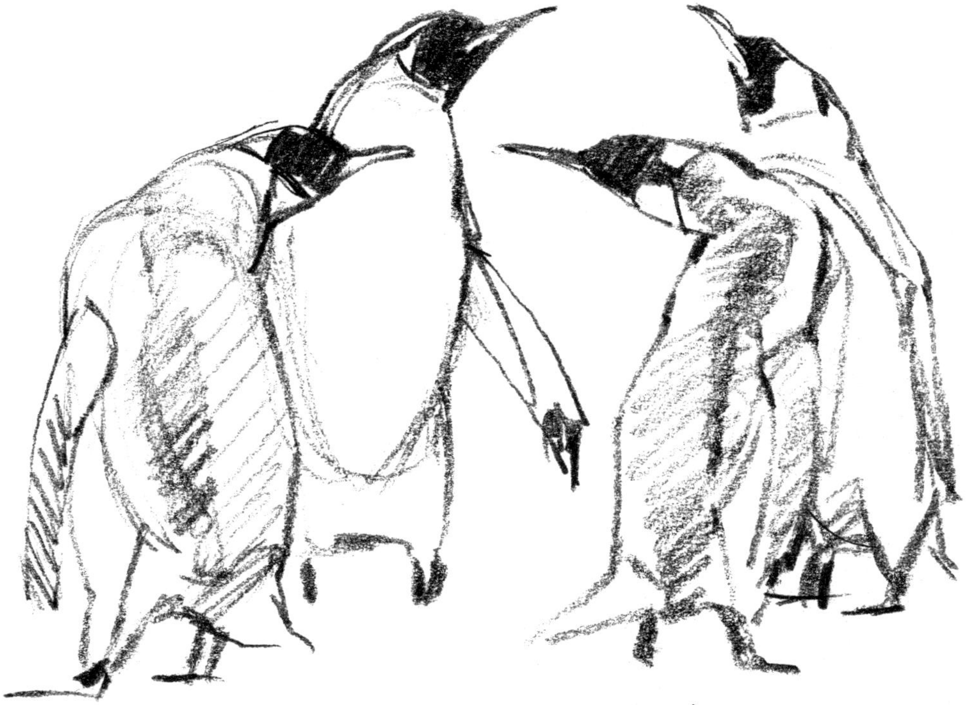

King penguins

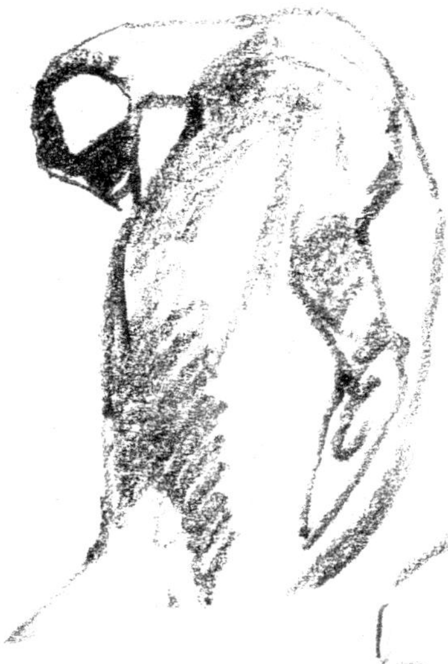

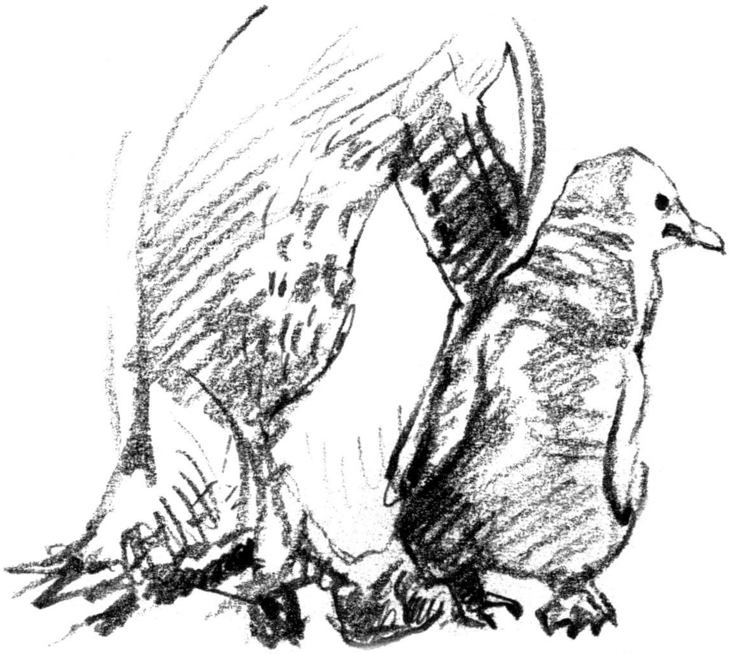

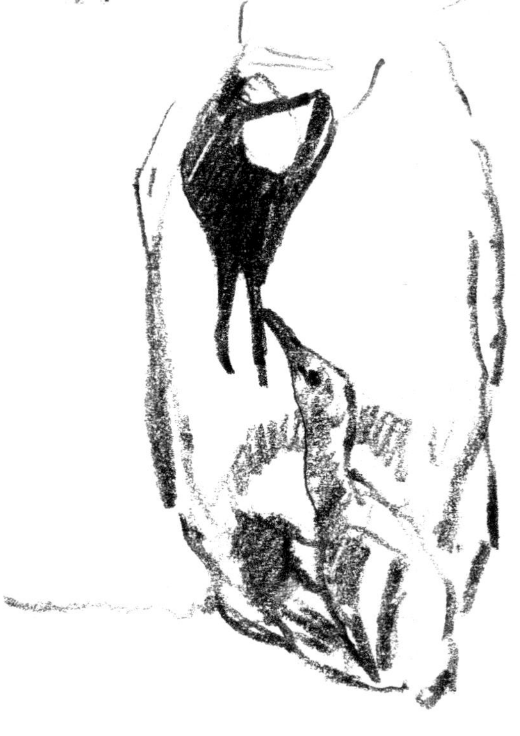

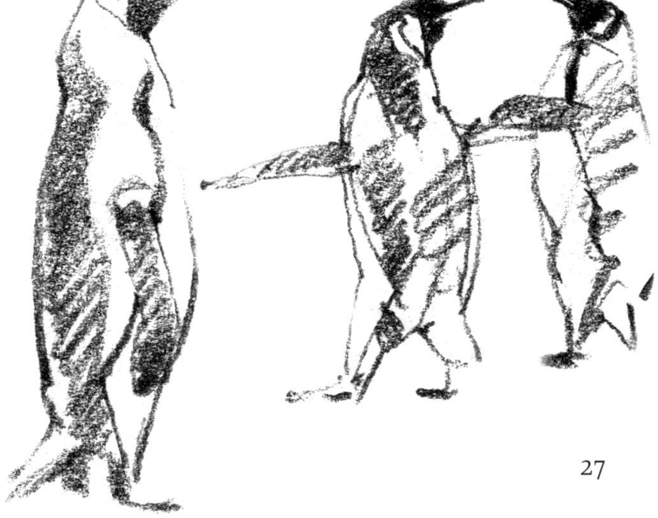

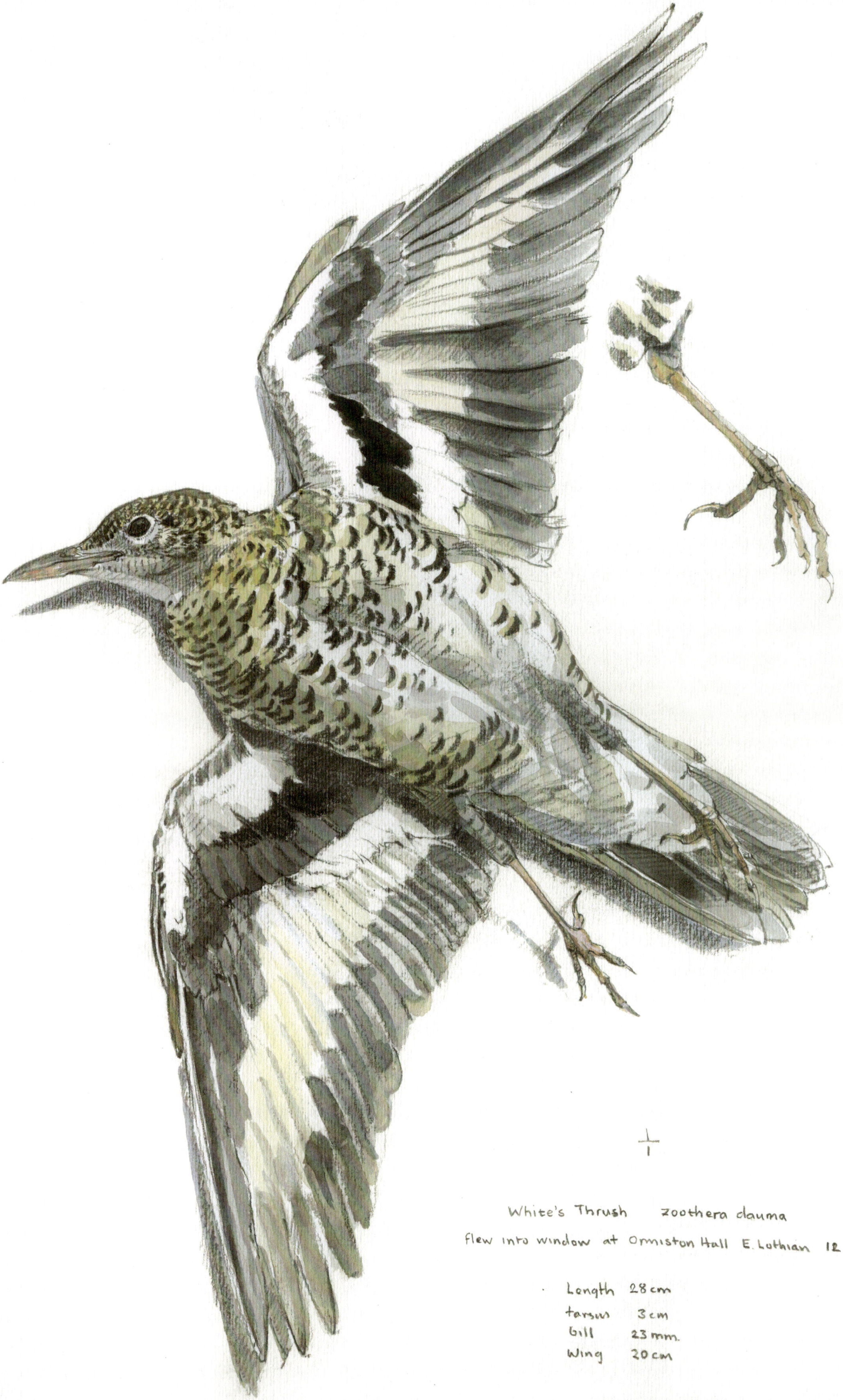

White's Thrush   *Zoothera dauma*

flew into window at Ormiston Hall E. Lothian 12 Oct 1998

Length 28 cm
tarsus 3 cm
Bill 23 mm.
Wing 20 cm

There are close-up moments which give opportunities for study, though life is finished, and I draw all the newly dead birds and animals I find.

One November morning I looked out of the window at home to see a bird lying face down on the flat roof outside. It was obviously a thrush, but not one I had seen before – slightly larger than a mistle thrush, with back markings resembling a golden plover. I turned it over to see crescent shaped spots on its breast and a dark band of feathers running along the centre of each wing. It was a White's thrush, a bird that had reached Scotland from Eastern Europe or the Urals.

I wish I had seen it alive feeding on yew berries with the redwings and fieldfares it most likely travelled with. I was sorry it met its end by hitting our windows.

< dead White's thrush

dead puffin

I include a study of a long dead puffin found on the shore; a very beautiful female merlin found dead in Orkney, and a long-eared bat from a local ruin.

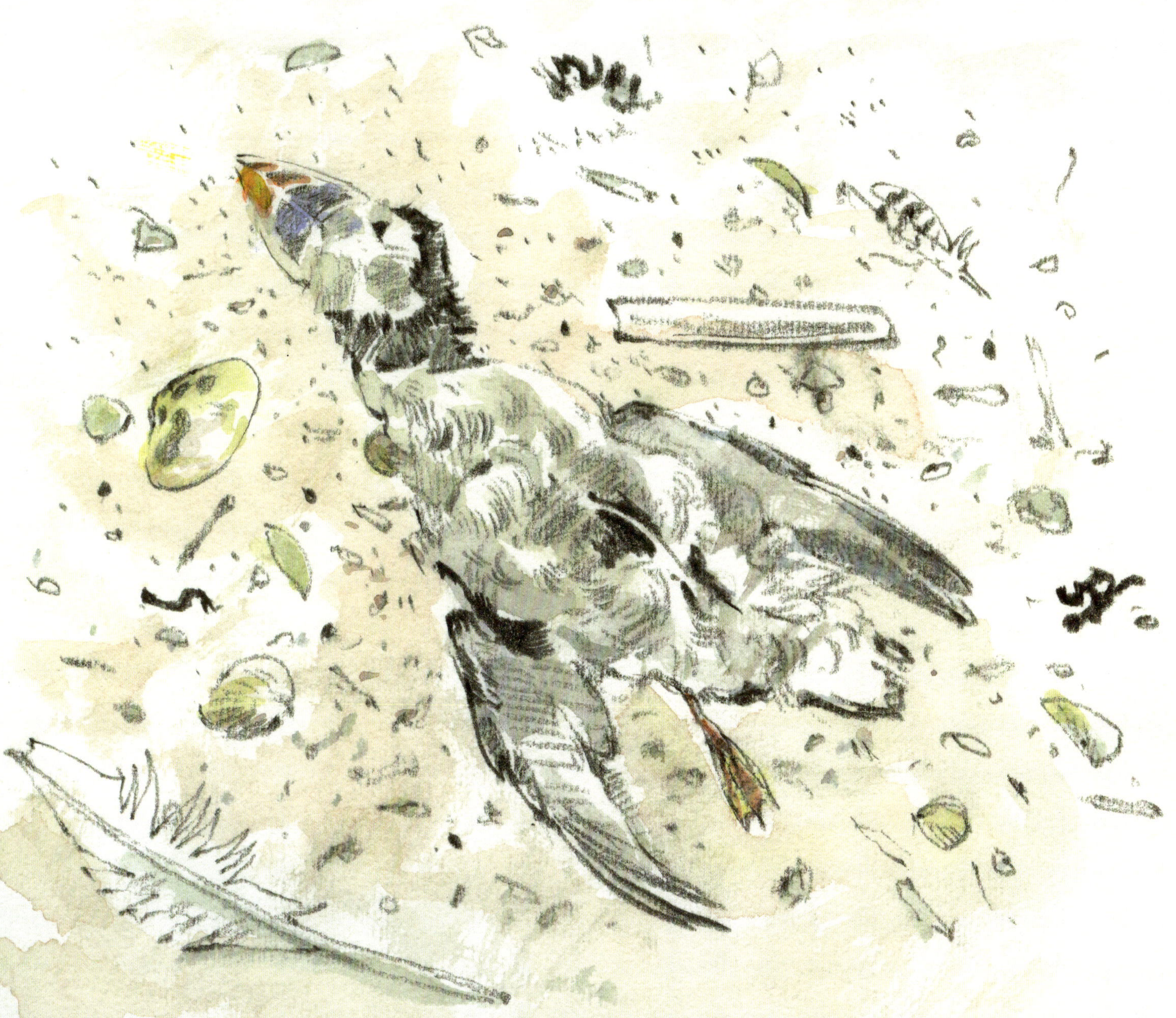

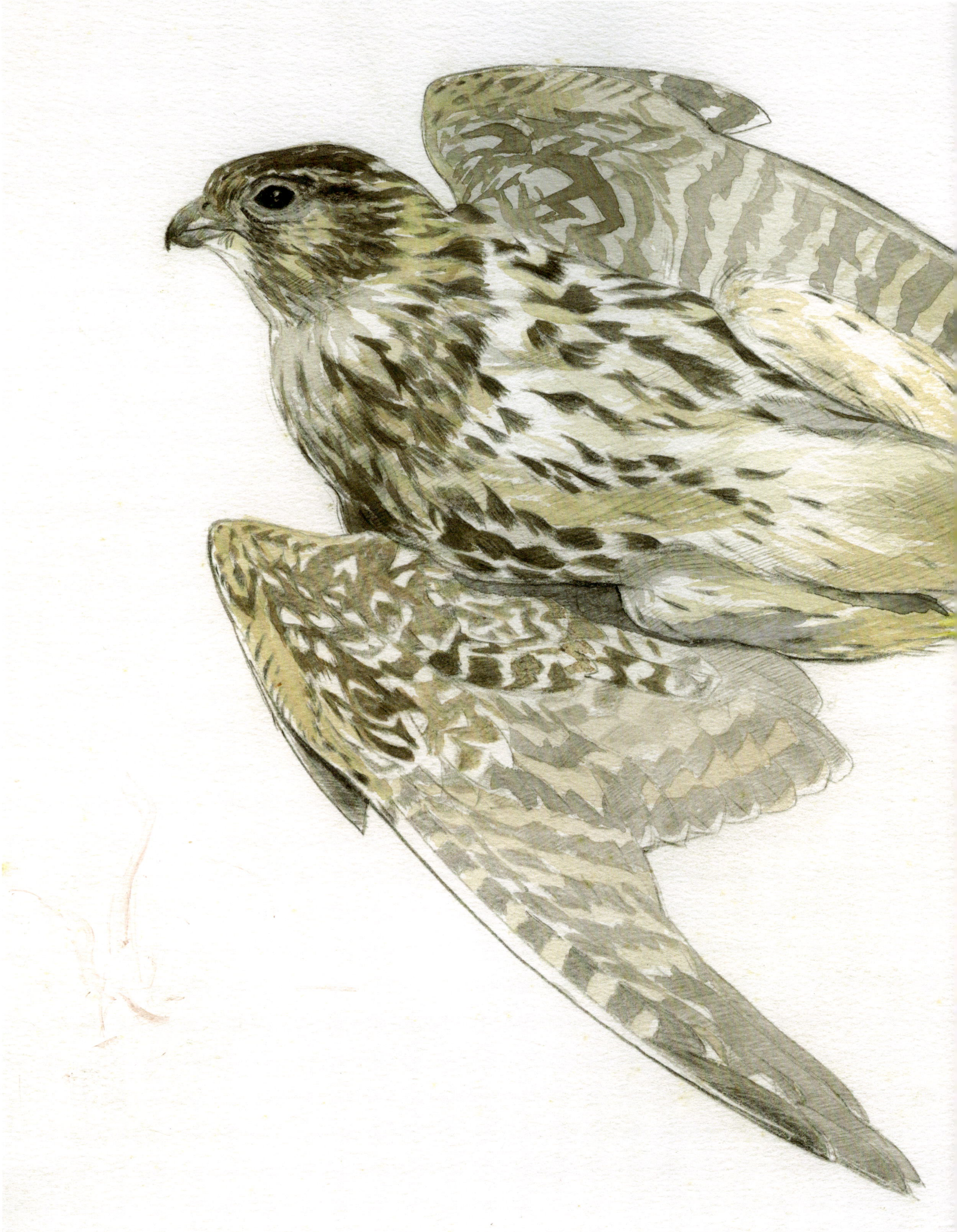

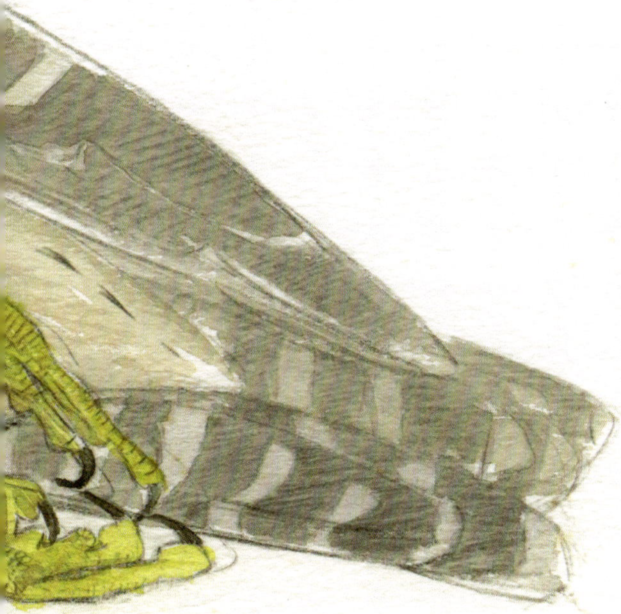

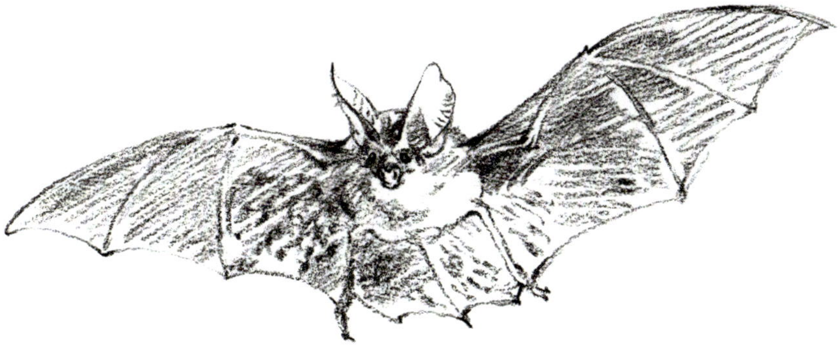

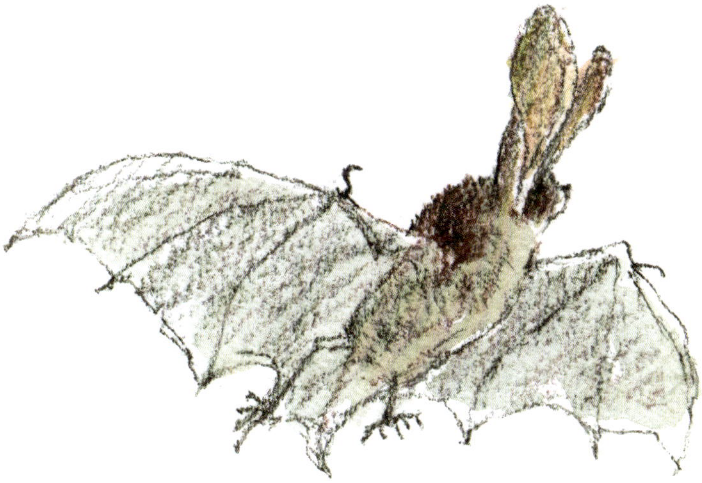

Long-eared bat, studies from a dead one

< Female merlin, found dead in Orkney

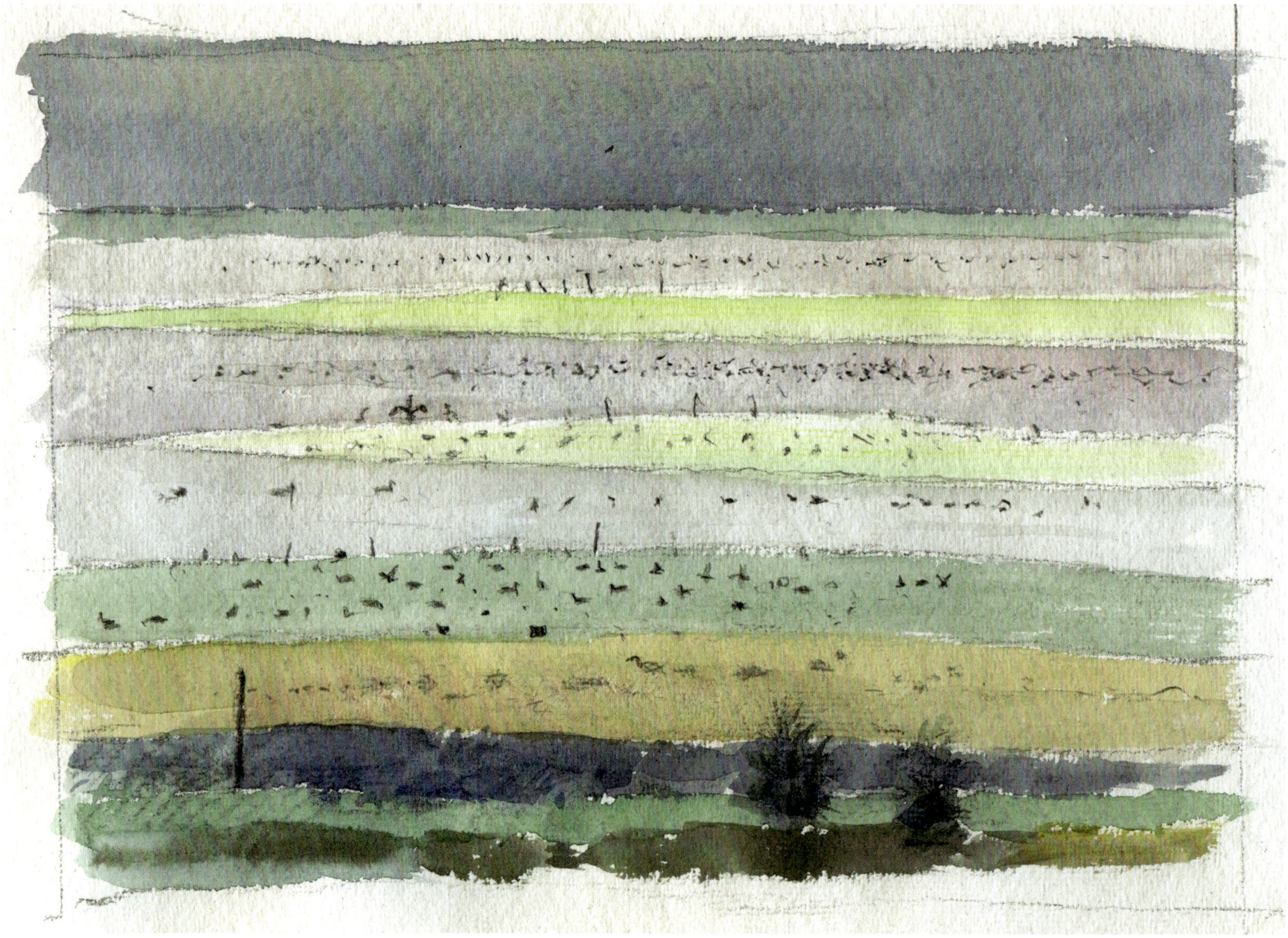

Estuary scene; to the unaided eye

At a distance

I do admit to the excitement of seeing a distant bird close-up through a telescope, especially if it is a 'rarity'. The estuary of Aberlady Bay on the East Lothian shore is my local feeding ground for waders and wildfowl.

This could be the scene with the naked eye before telescope and binoculars are unpacked and the many birds can be changed from mere patterns of dots into species. There may well be an unusual wader among the dunlins and knot, or winter grebes and divers among ducks swimming amongst the waves.

At best a telescope anchors you to one spot. It is a cumbersome beast to carry around, so one needs to choose a view like this, full of possibilities; changing tide lines; a natural food source such as a marsh, or a breeding colony.

Here is a group of brent geese on an estuary on the south-east coast of England. They contrast nicely with old weathered mooring posts sticking up through the mud.

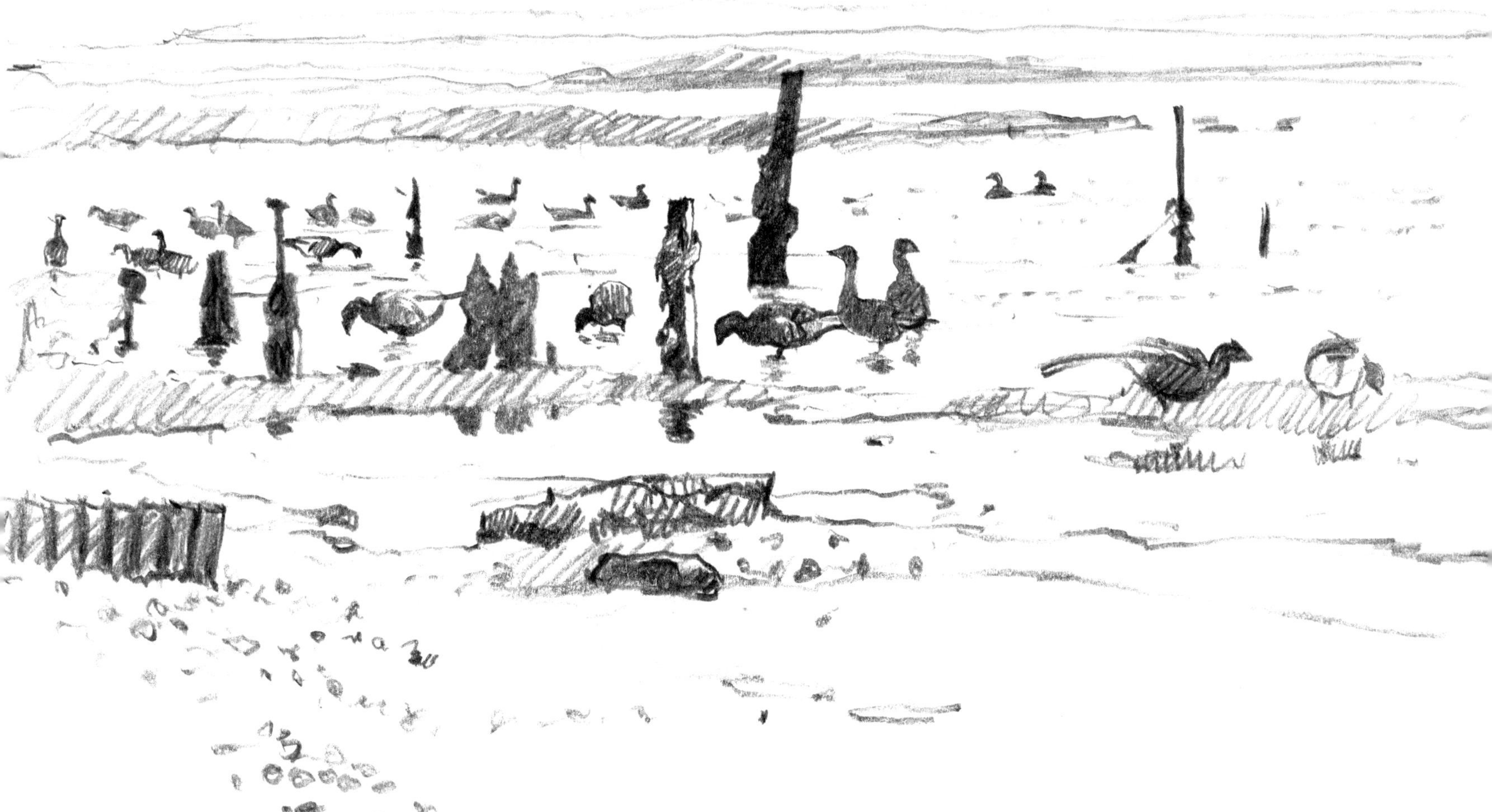

Brent geese

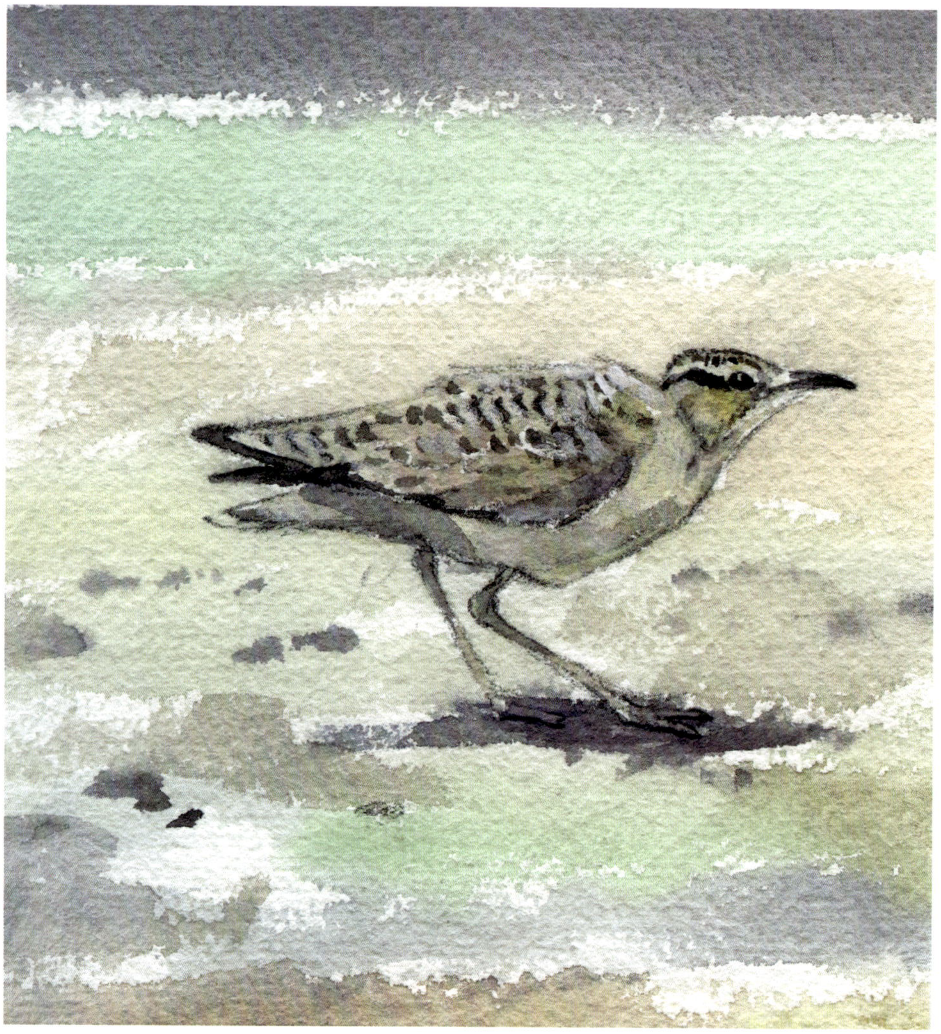

Cream-coloured courser, Aberlady

On the shore in East Lothian I once spotted a cream-coloured courser and watched it feeding with quick dashes after insects in the marram grass on the edge of the sand. Sitting still, I was able to watch and draw without disturbing the bird with a close approach. Next day the courser's presence had become known and the area was crowded with birders with 'scopes, trying to get ever closer for a photo, and the poor bird had no chance to feed. It left for quieter shores.

The bay has attracted a number of rarities. A Caspian plover which landed close to a lapwing I was drawing had me guessing – it was dotterel size, but not right in plumage – identified later by a more knowledgeable watcher.

A buff-breasted sandpiper feeding among starlings on a rocky part of the shore was easier to identify through the telescope by its plumage and small size. It was a very energetic feeder and even looked small next to a starling.

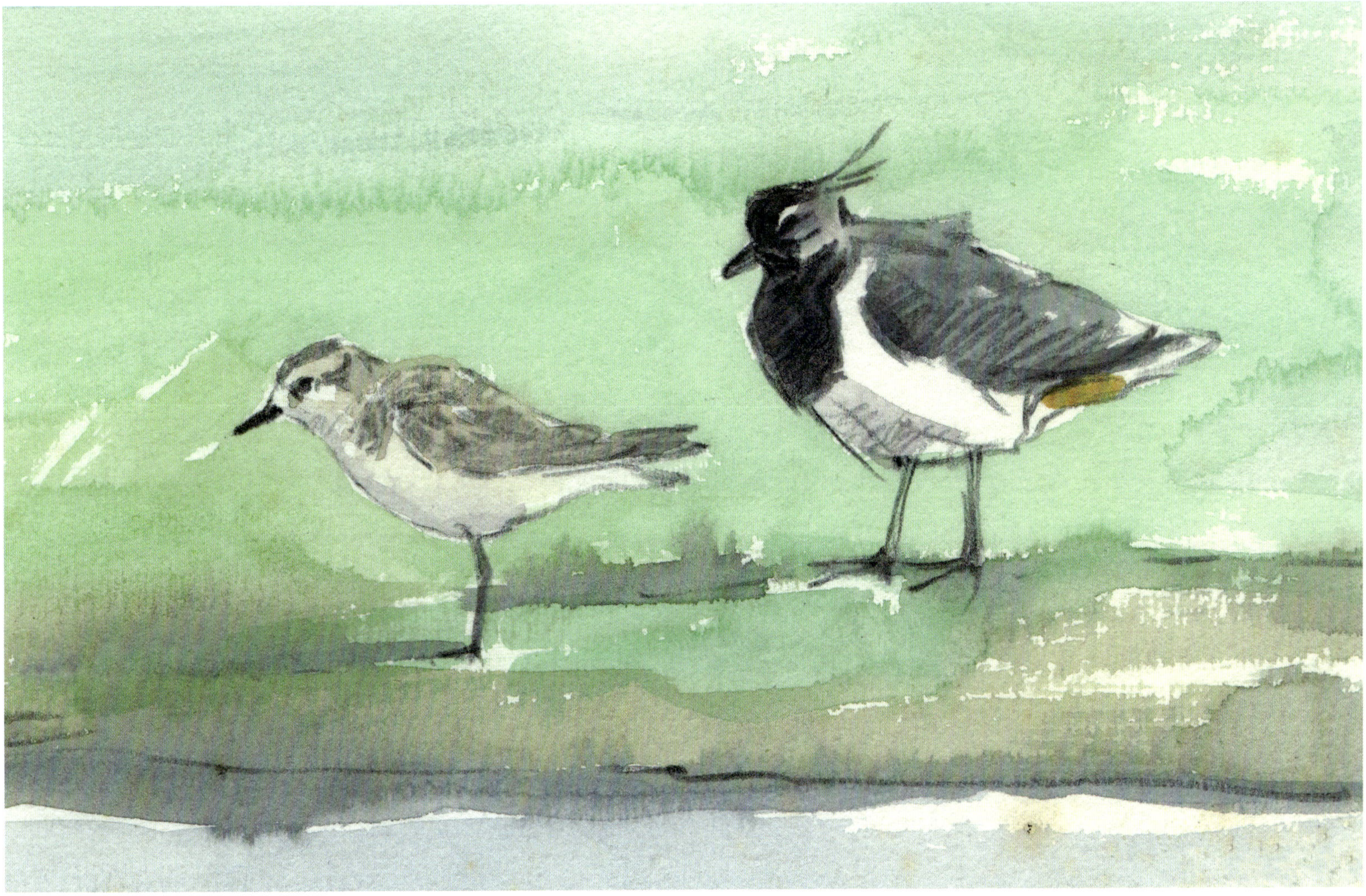

Caspian plover, lapwing

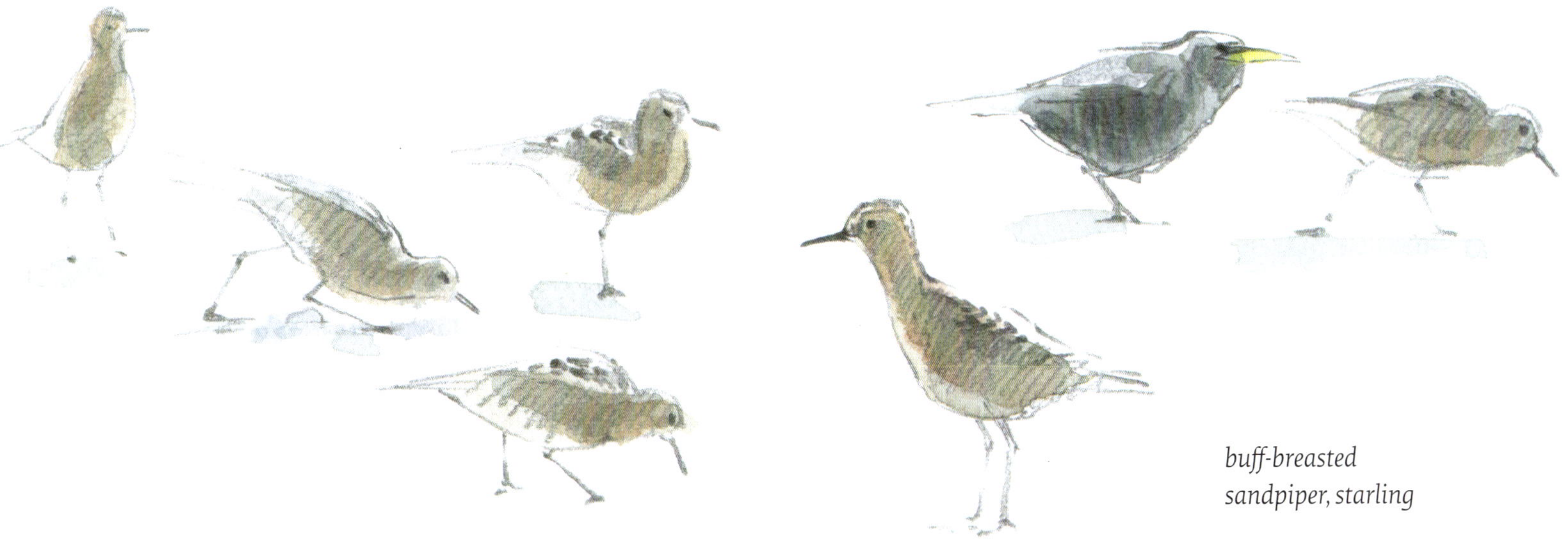

buff-breasted sandpiper, starling

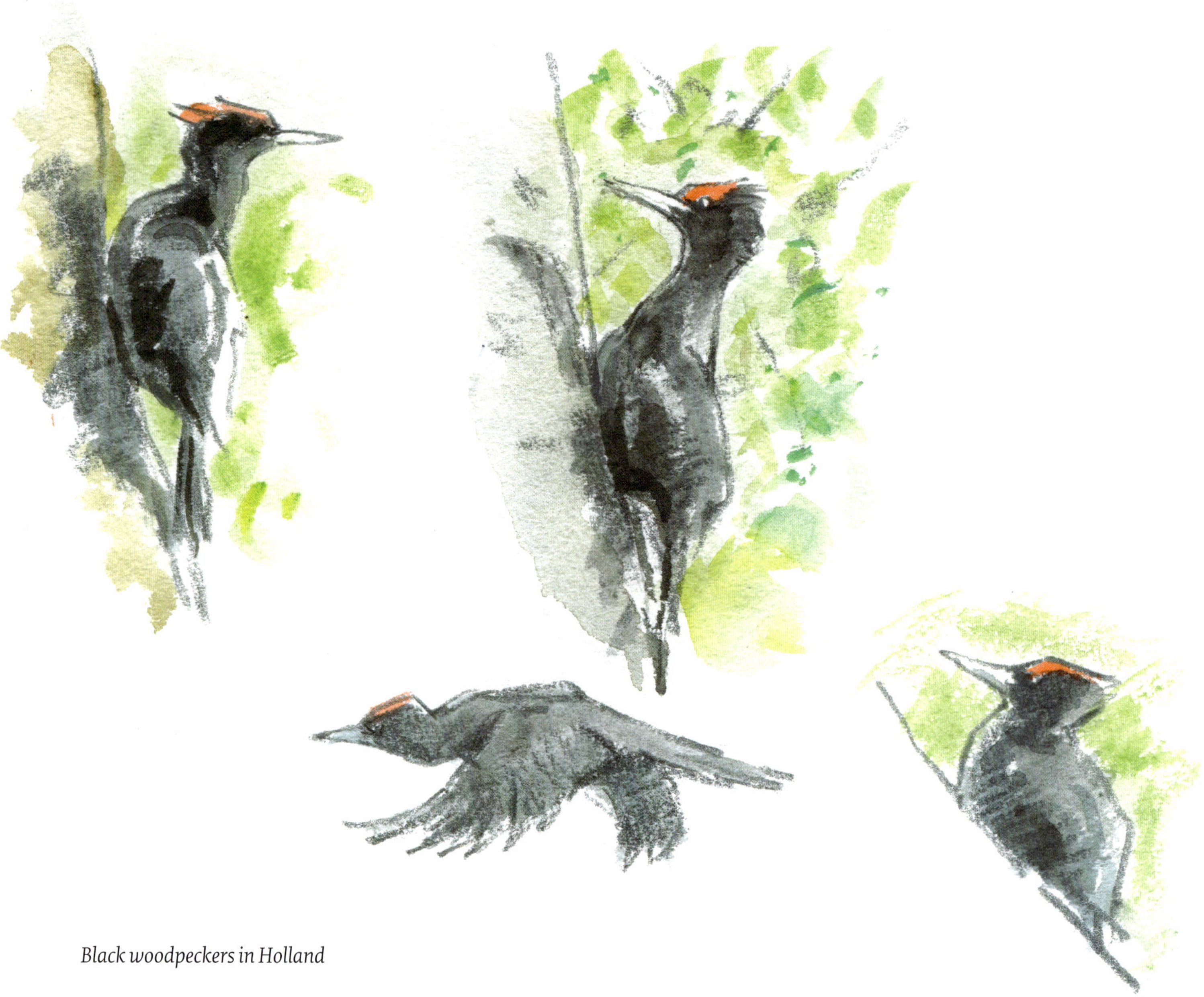

Black woodpeckers in Holland

I prefer binoculars to a telescope in woodland situations where birds are in and out of view among trees. It is easier to focus and change position, and two eye viewing is an advantage, but it is difficult to hold binoculars and draw in a sketch book, at the same time.

It is always stimulating to see unfamiliar birds on a visit to other countries. Here are some which were new to me and a delight to watch and draw.

Black woodpeckers are the largest of the woodpeckers found in Europe, but do not breed in Britain. This striking bird, the size of a crow, was seen in a wood of large mature trees in Holland.

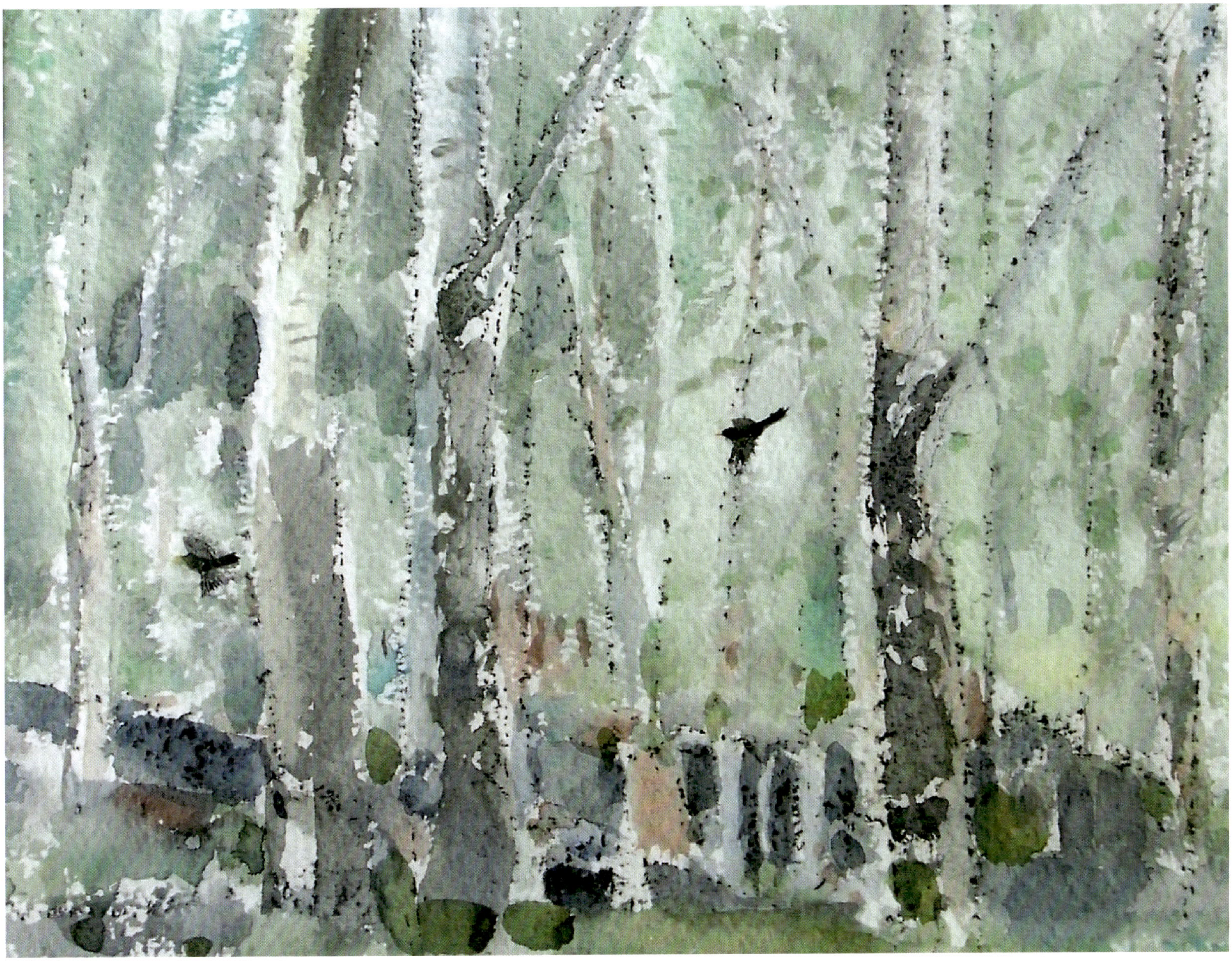

Woodland scene with blackbirds

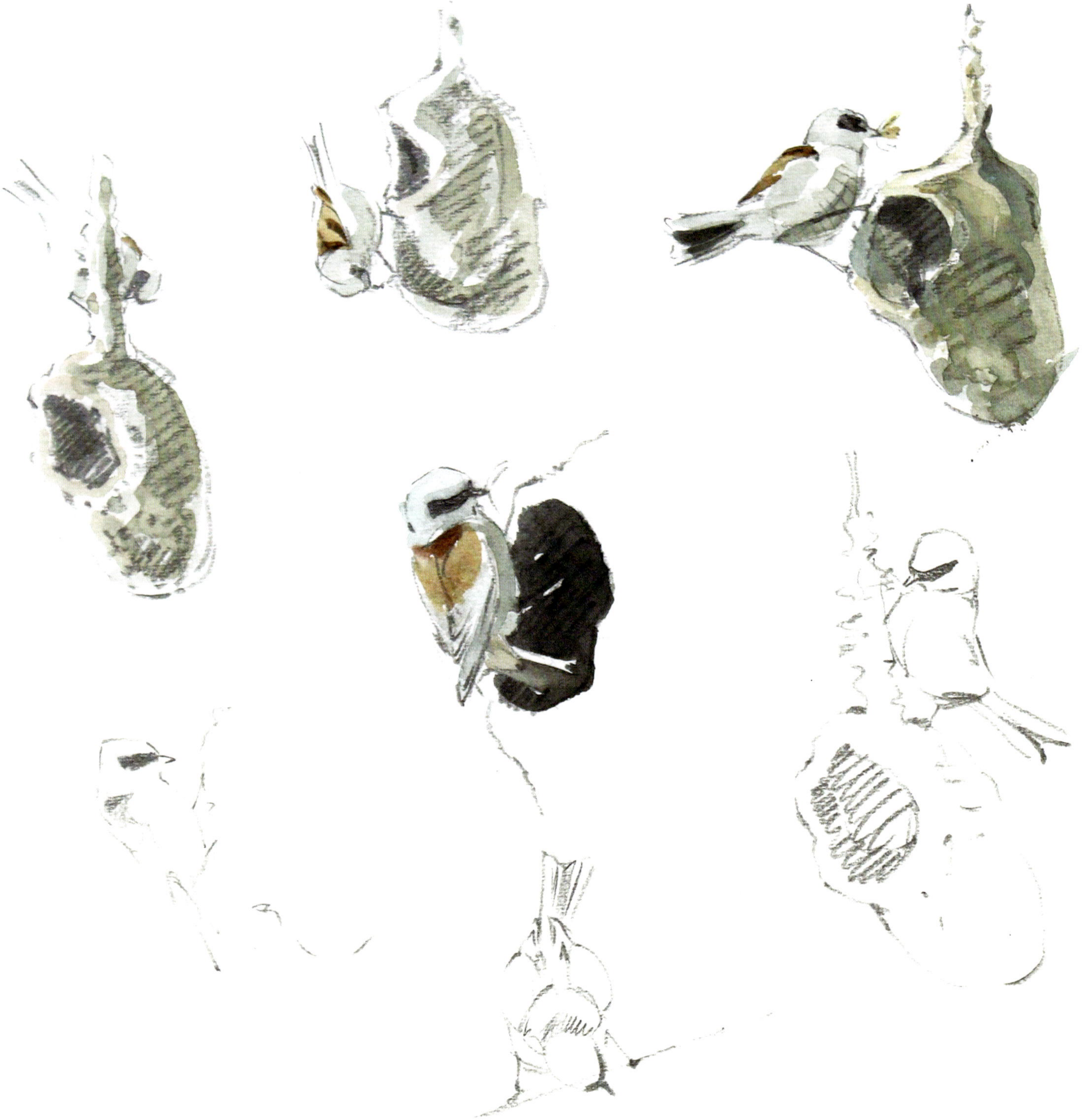

Working alongside other artists in projects organised by the Artists for Nature Foundation (ANF) has taken me to work in many countries to help the cause of wildlife. In the Biebzra marshes of eastern Poland I drew these bearded reedlings and reed warblers. The penduline tit building its nest was drawn from a canoe shared with artist Keith Brockie deep in the same marshes.

Penduline tit nest building, Biebzra marshes, Poland

Reed warblers and bearded reedling, Biebzra

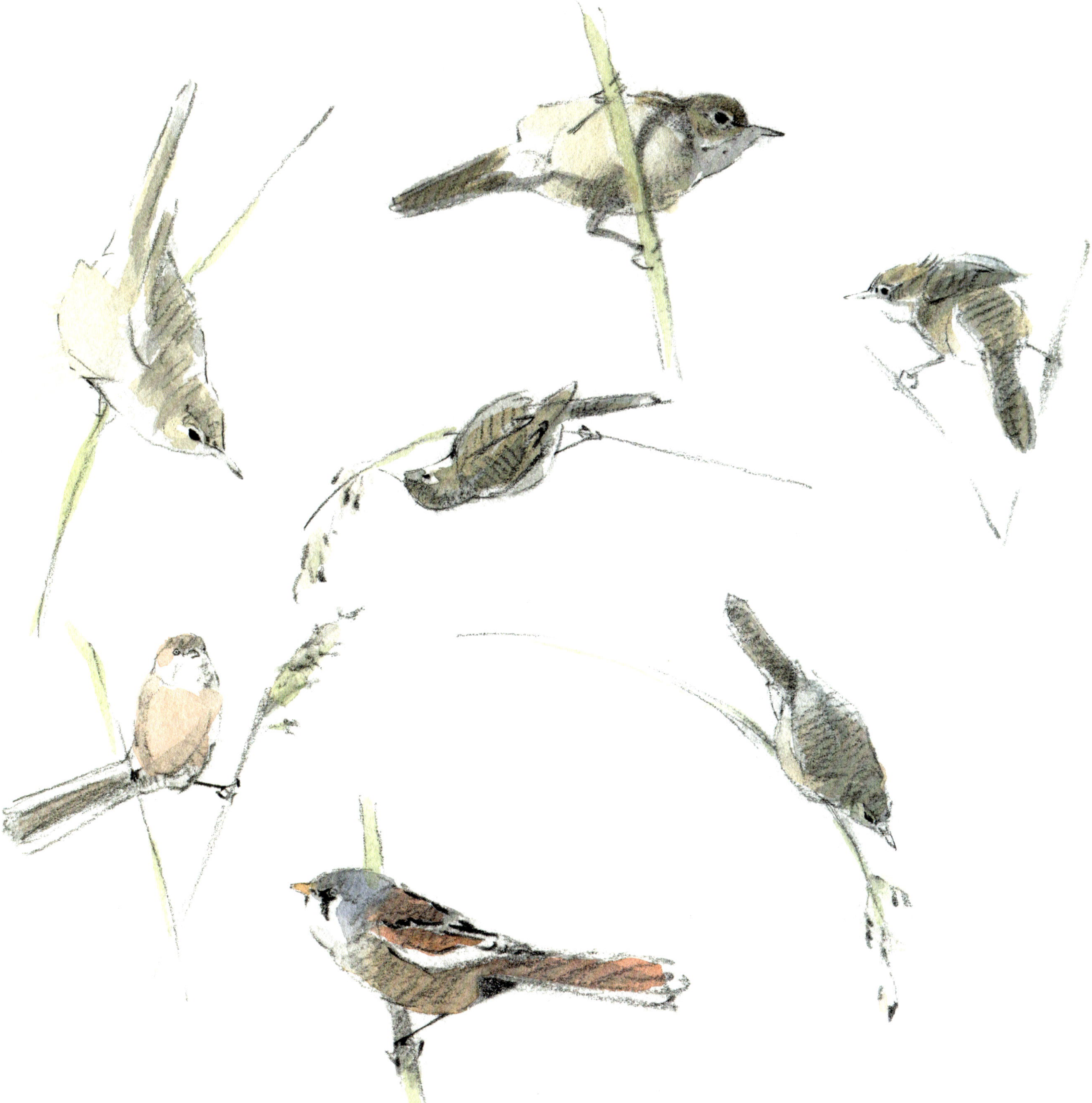

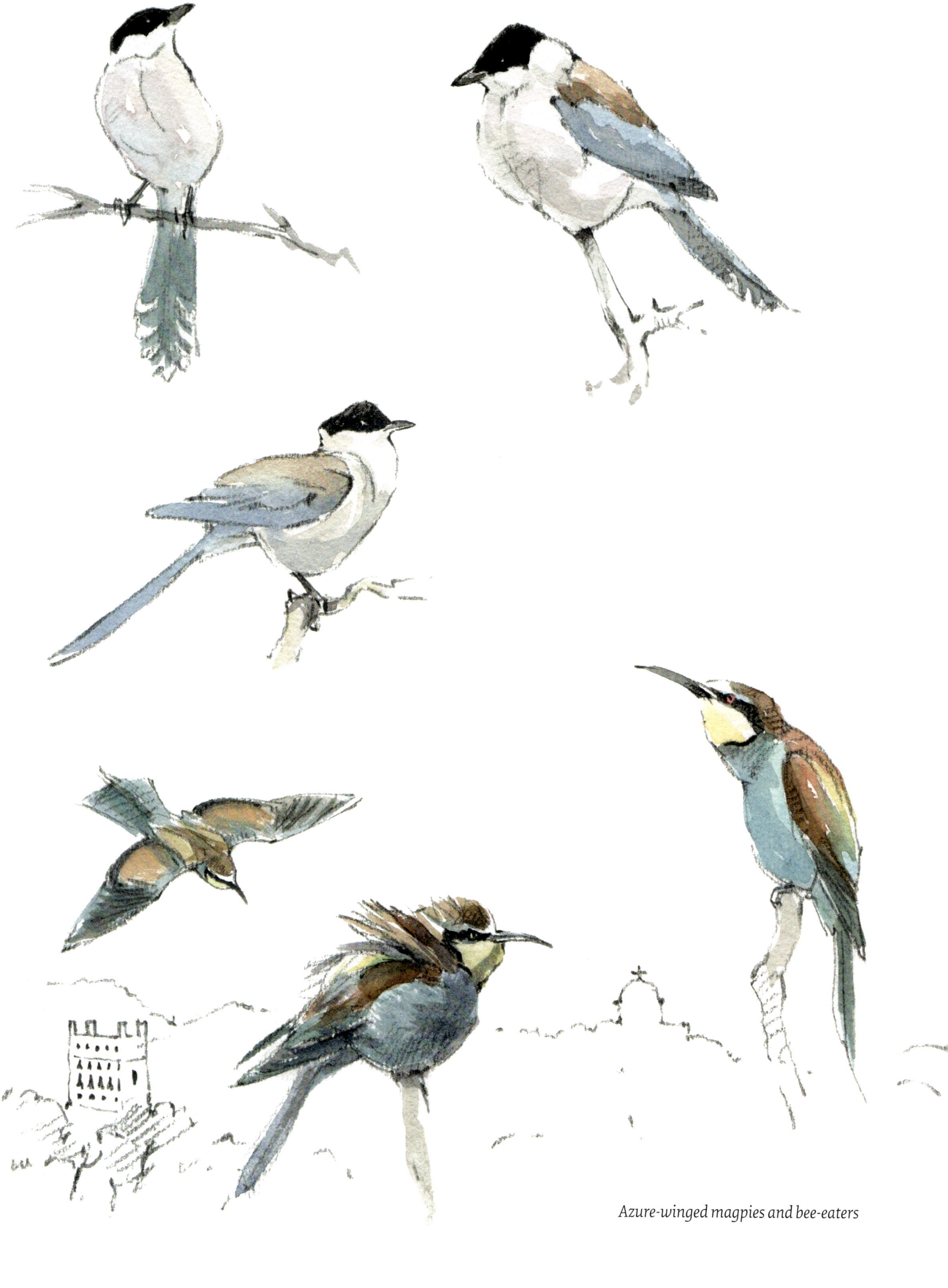

Azure-winged magpies and bee-eaters

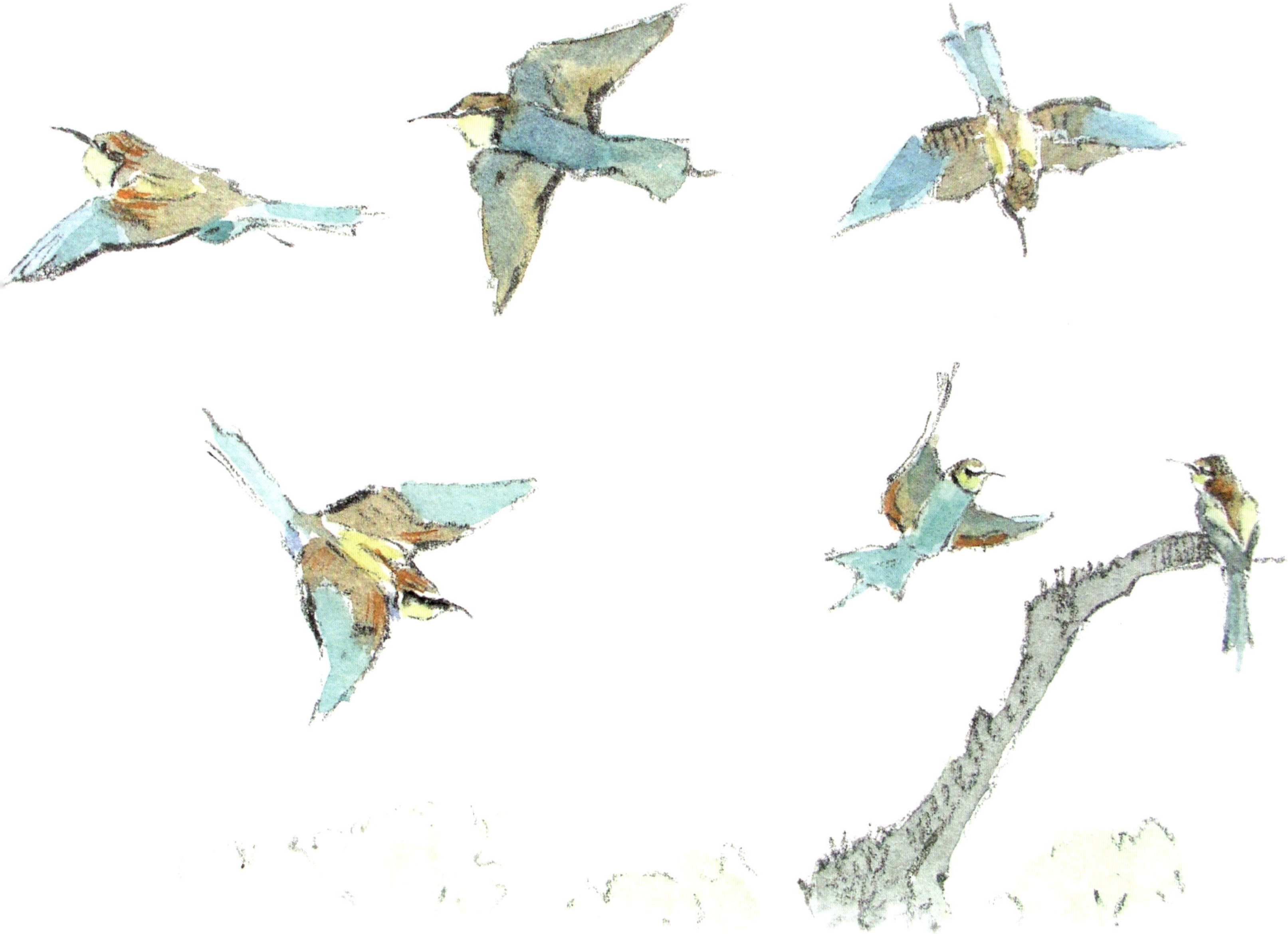

Bee-eaters are widely spread in Europe, mostly in the south, but they have turned up as vagrants as far north as the Hebrides. They are found in more open areas and by river banks. They hawk insects in flight, sometimes flying high in pursuit.

Azure-winged magpies are the most colourful corvids in Europe, and found only in eastern Spain and Portugal. In the orchards and vineyards of the Extremadura they are fairly numerous. They are very characterful birds behaving with a curiosity, much as our own magpies do.

European bee-eaters

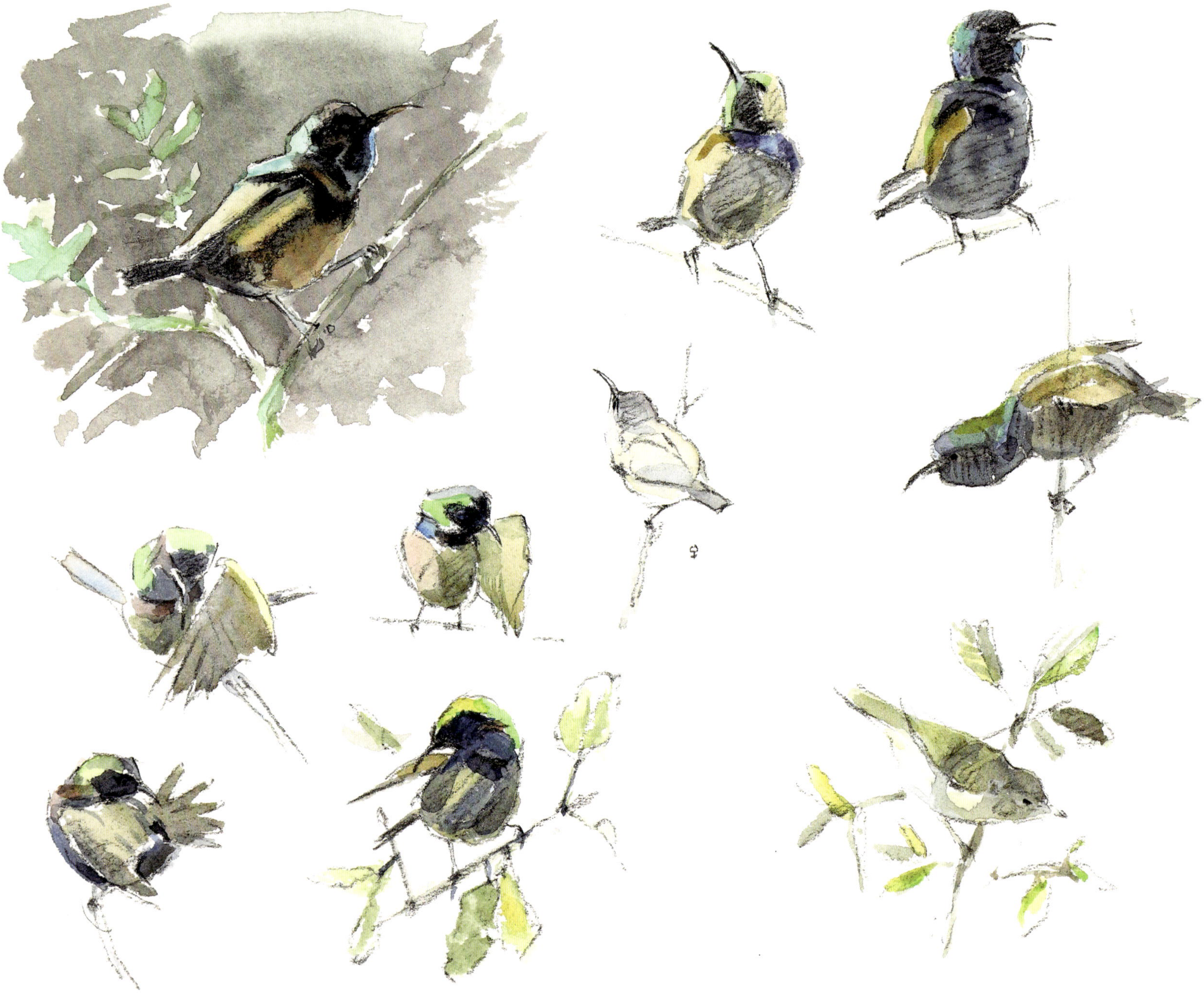

An ANF project to the marshlands in the Hula reserve in Israel in 2010 reintroduced me to the Palestine sunbird. The colourful male reflects metallic blues, greens and reds from its glossy feathers in contrast to the dull brown female. Graceful prinias are long-tailed marshland birds from the Hula reserve in Israel, seen on an ANF project in 2010. My first slender-billed gull was spotted on the shore of the Sea of Galilee.

Brightly coloured male Palestine sunbirds and a dull brown female, plus a garden warbler

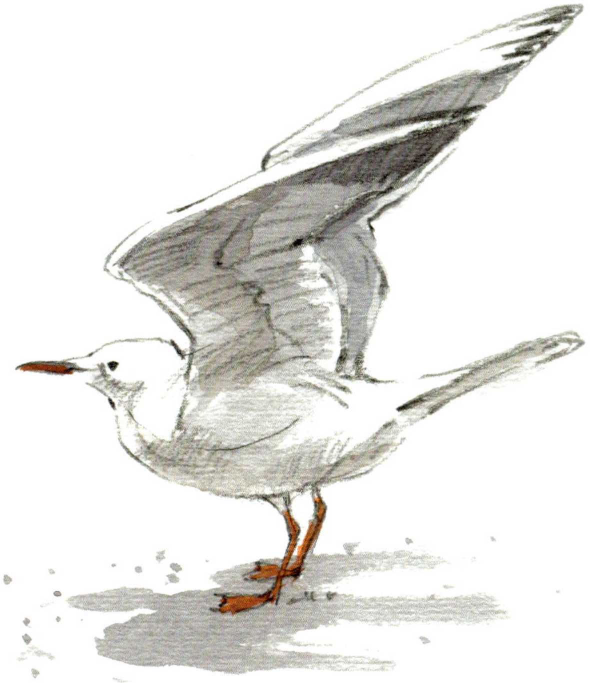

Slender-billed gull

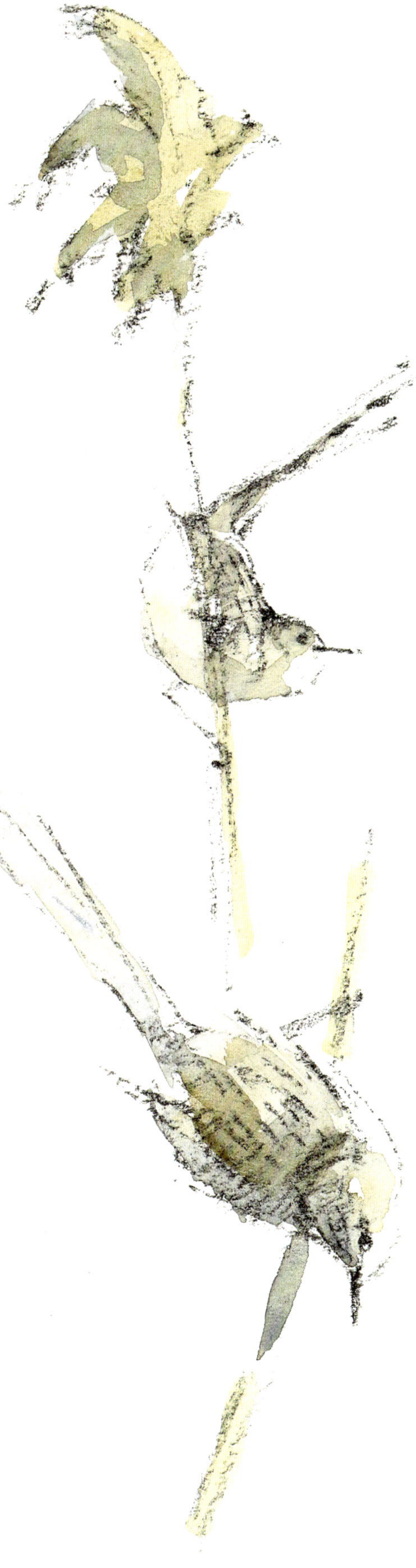

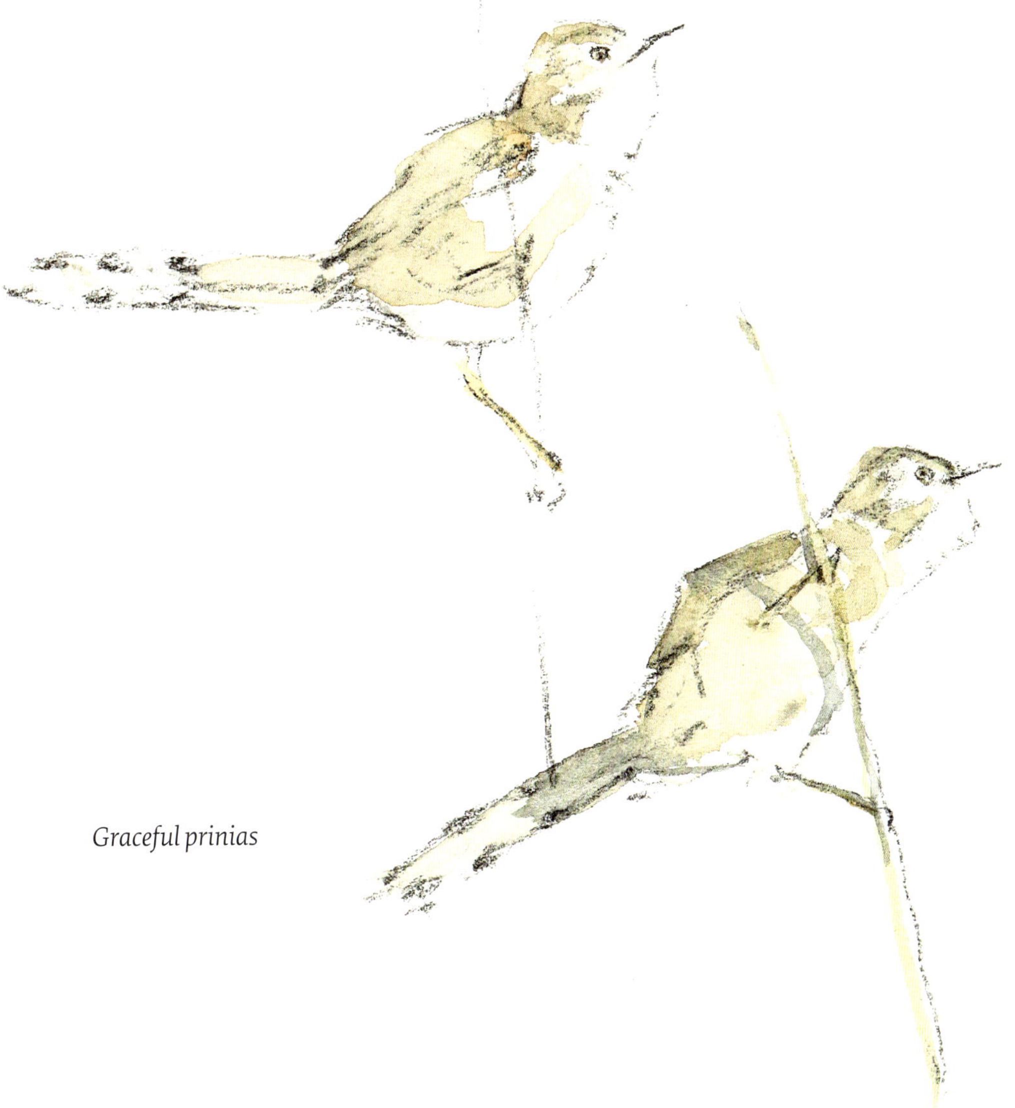

Graceful prinias

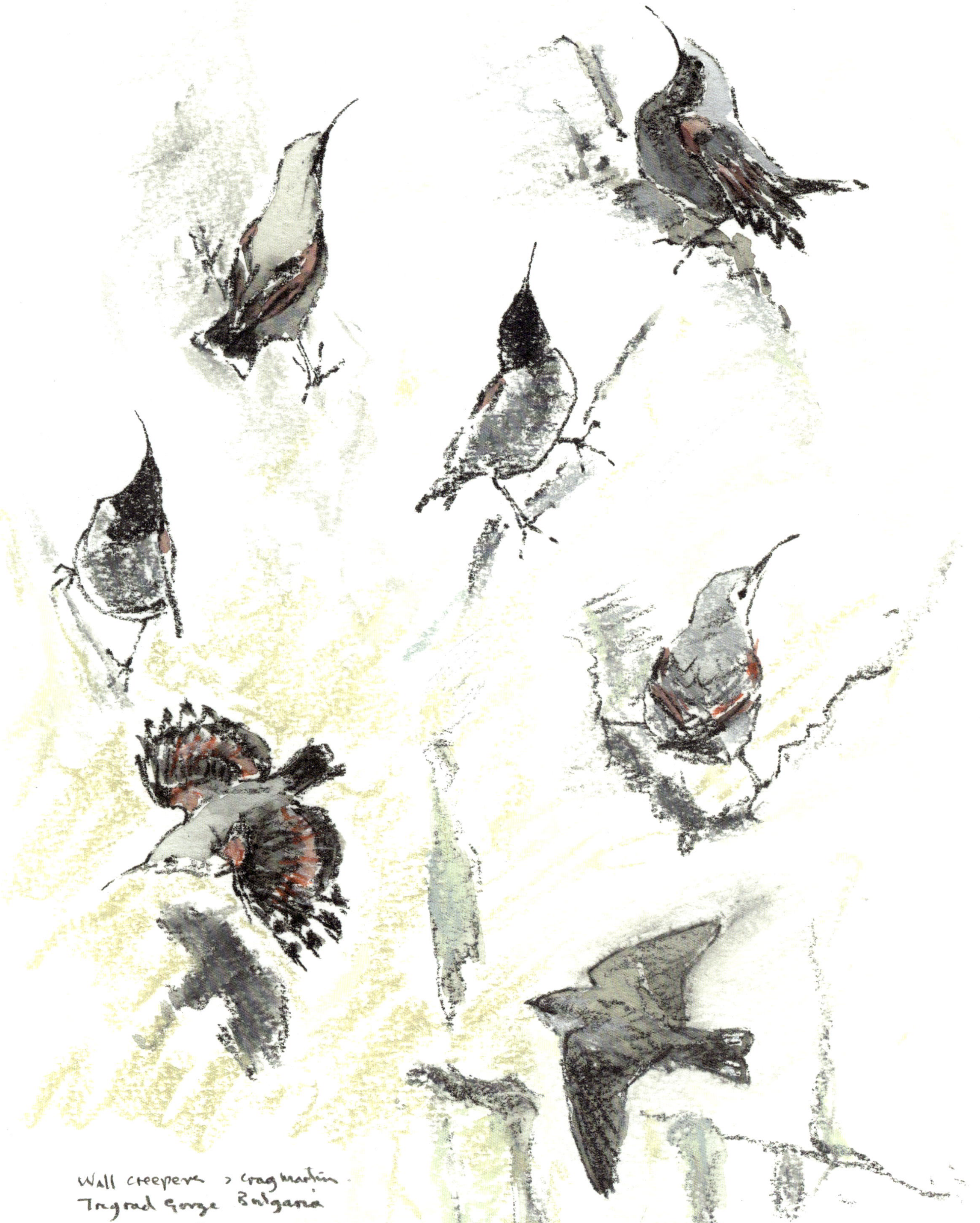

Wallcreepers and crag martin, Trigrad Gorge, Bulgaria

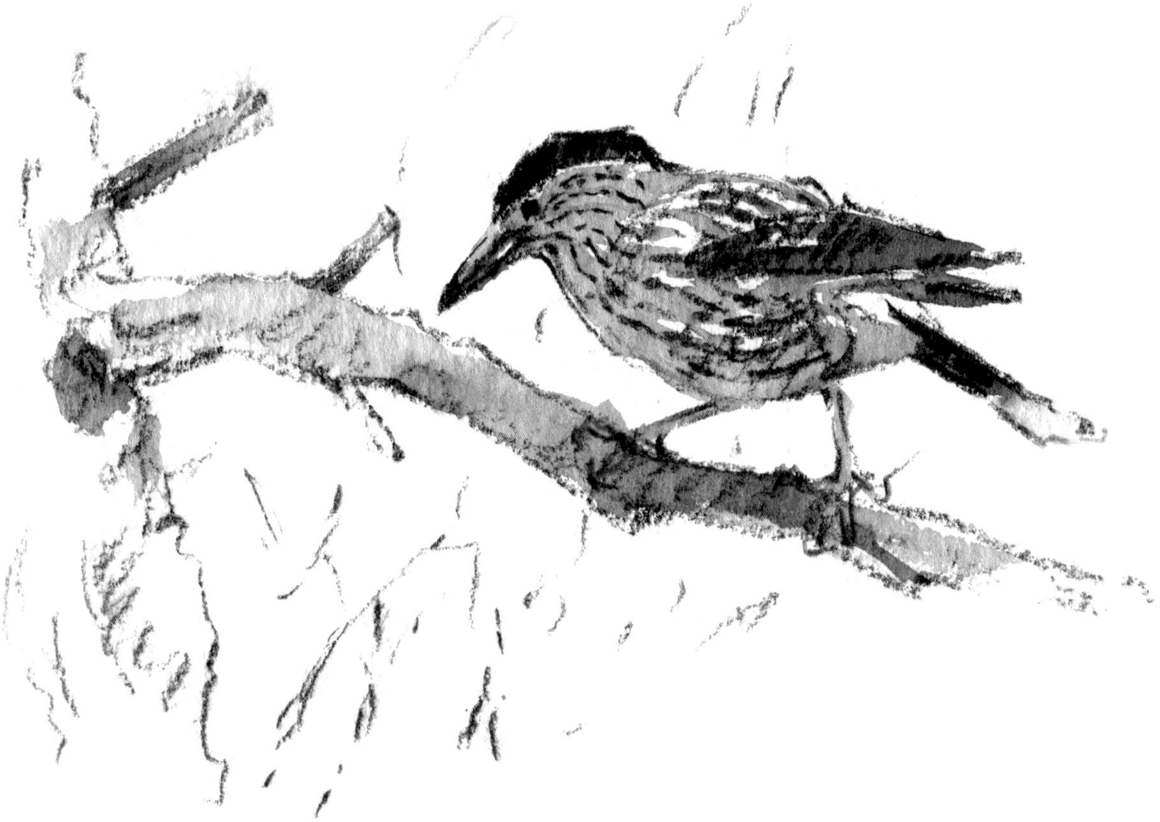

Nutcracker

On a visit to Bulgaria I saw my first nutcrackers among the pine trees of Mt Vitosha. It was a delight to be shown wallcreepers in the narrow limestone Trigrad gorge in the south, and a rock nuthatch building a nest under an overhanging rock in another part of the country.

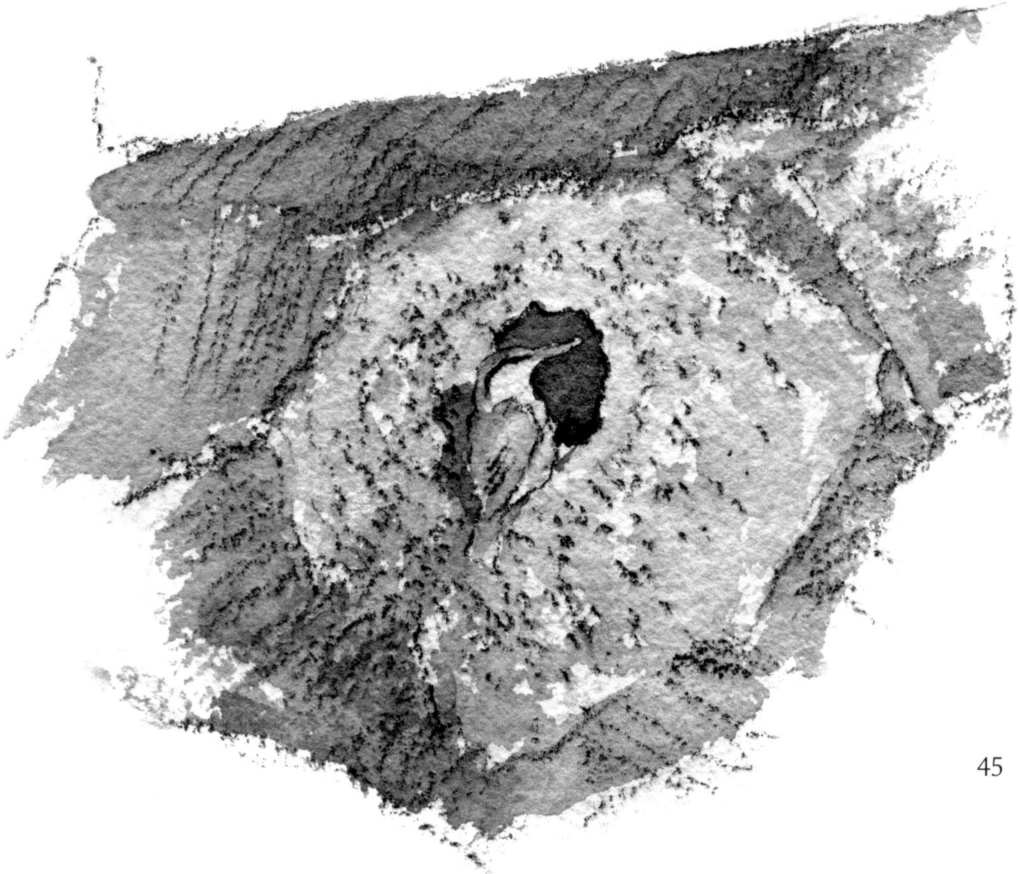

Rock nuthatch

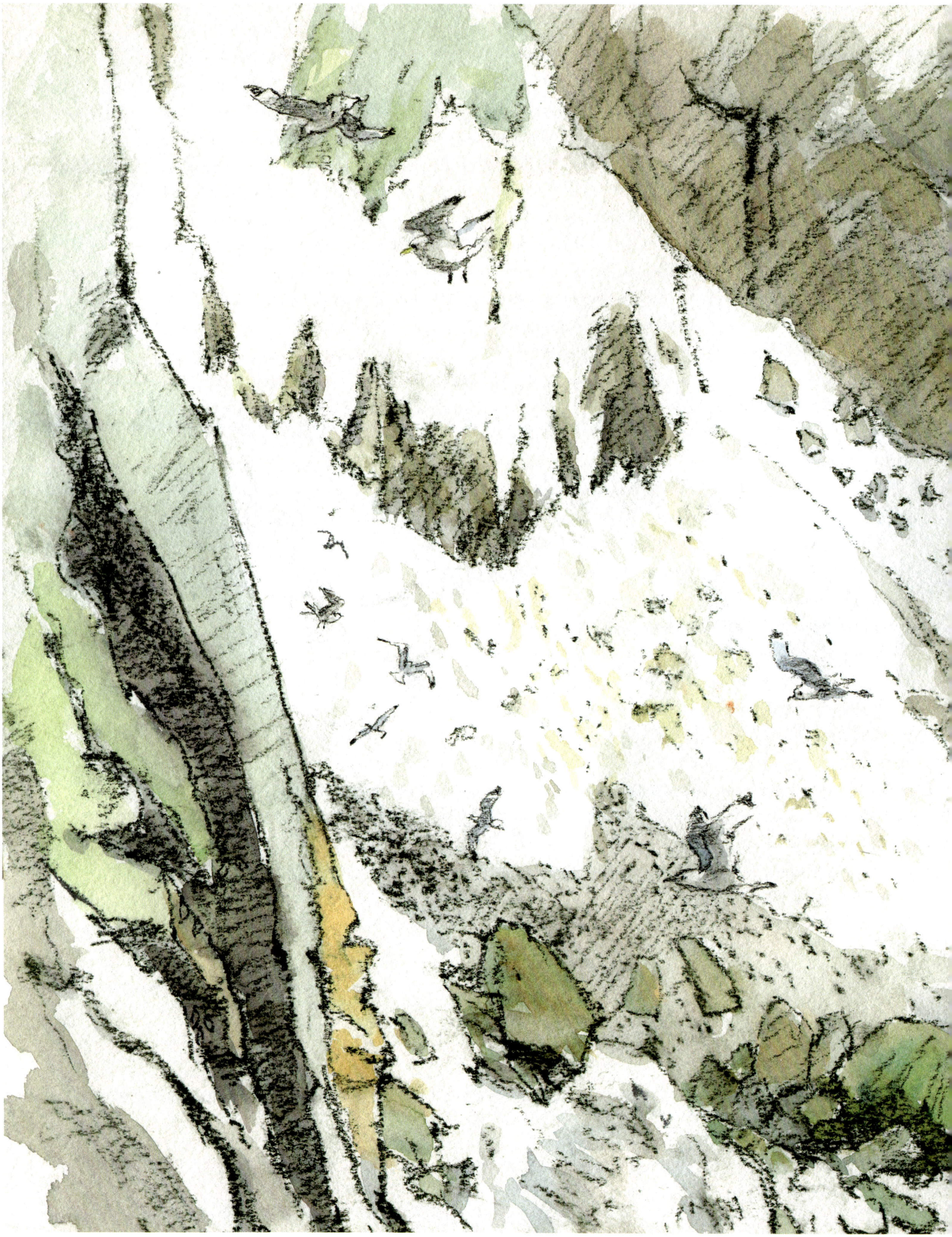

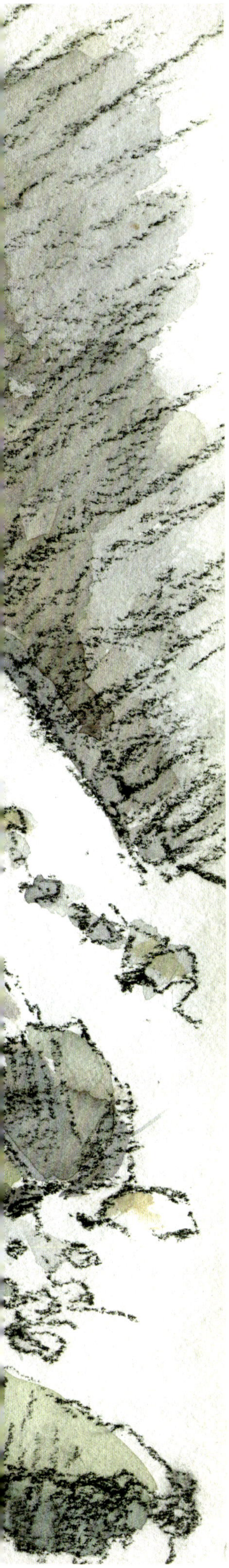

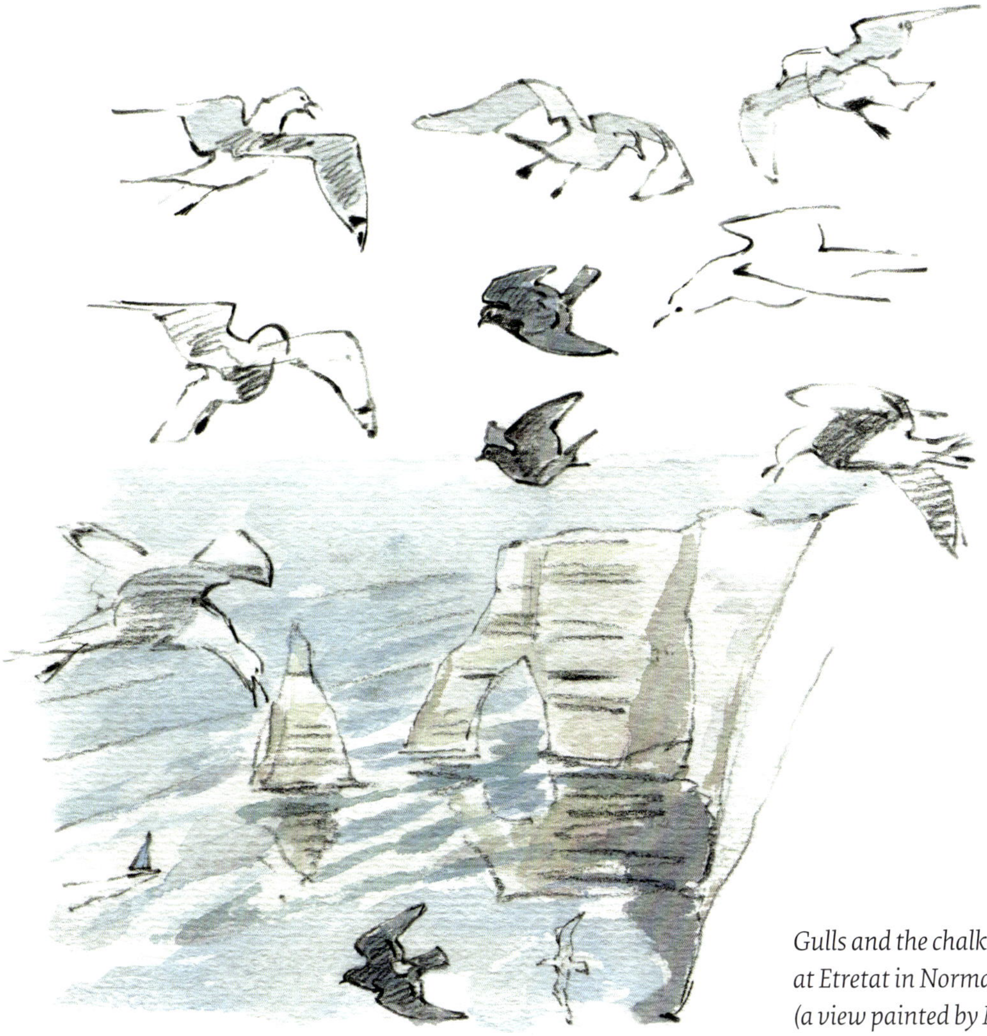

Gulls and the chalk cliffs at Etretat in Normandy (a view painted by Monet)

Sea cliffs and shorelines

When painting seabirds nesting on islands and sea cliffs in Scotland, I seldom take binoculars. I concentrate more on birds nesting close at hand, and on the interplay of the light, and the forms and patterns of the cliffs and the sea.

The cliffs of St Abb's Head in Berwickshire give stunning views of the red sandstone crags that bring the rolling landscape to an end. They provide the breeding ledges for auks and kittiwakes, with fulmars, rock doves, pipits and peregrines thrown in, but no nesting gannets. 'The Cleaver' is one well-named pinnacle near the mainland lighthouse.

Kittiwake cliffs at St Abbs Head, Berwickshire

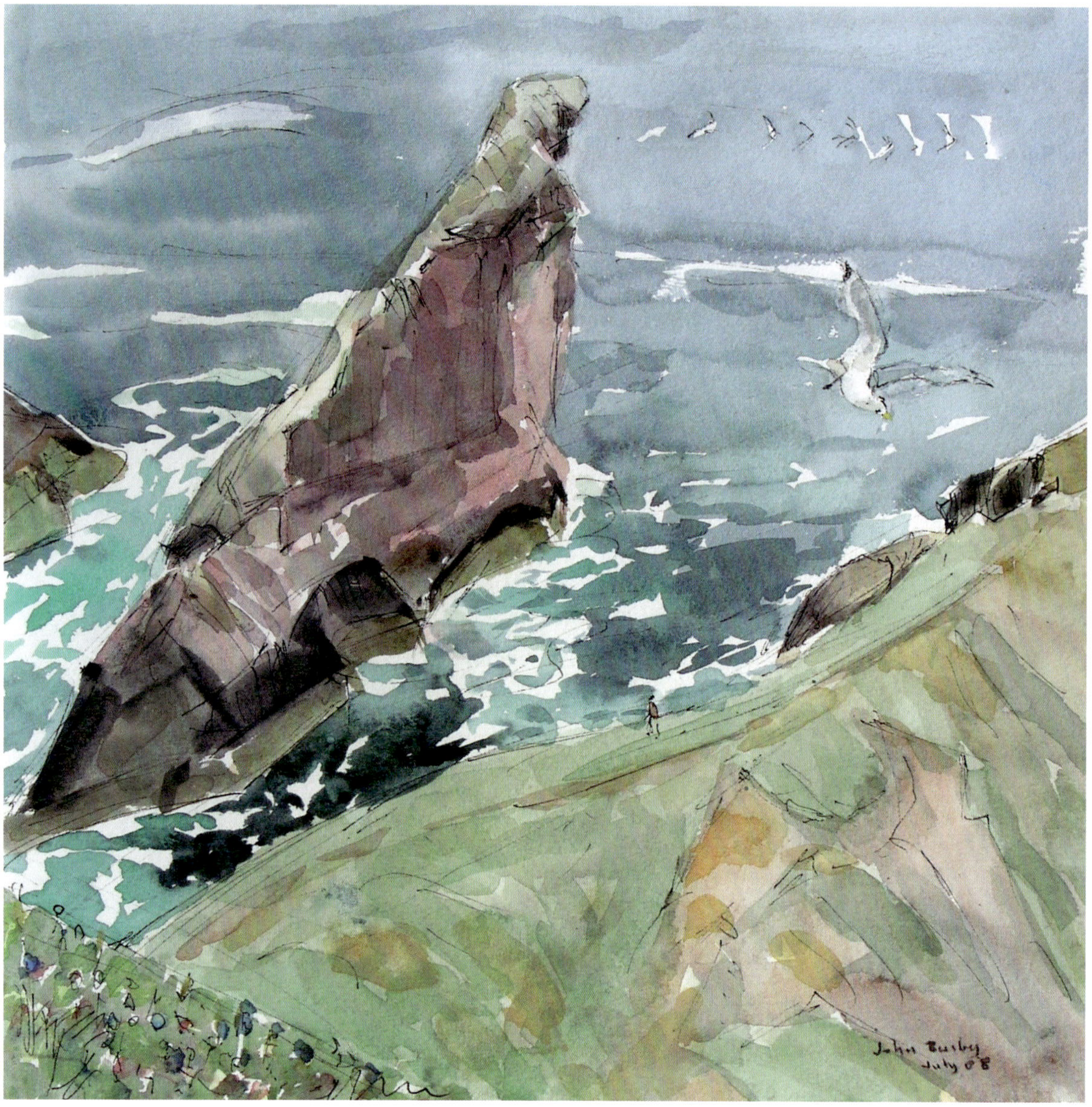

The Cleaver, St Abbs Head

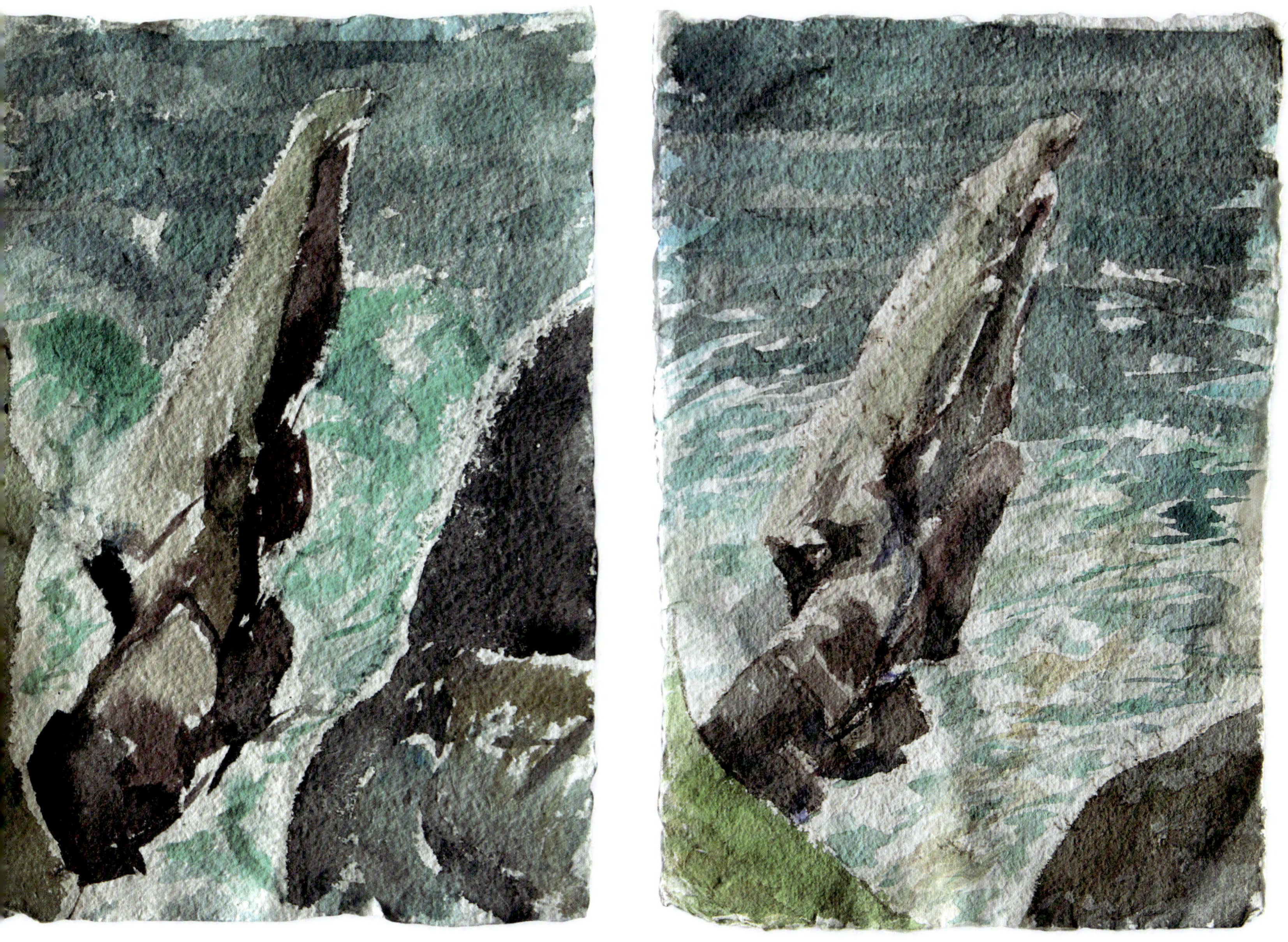

The Cleaver, St Abbs Head

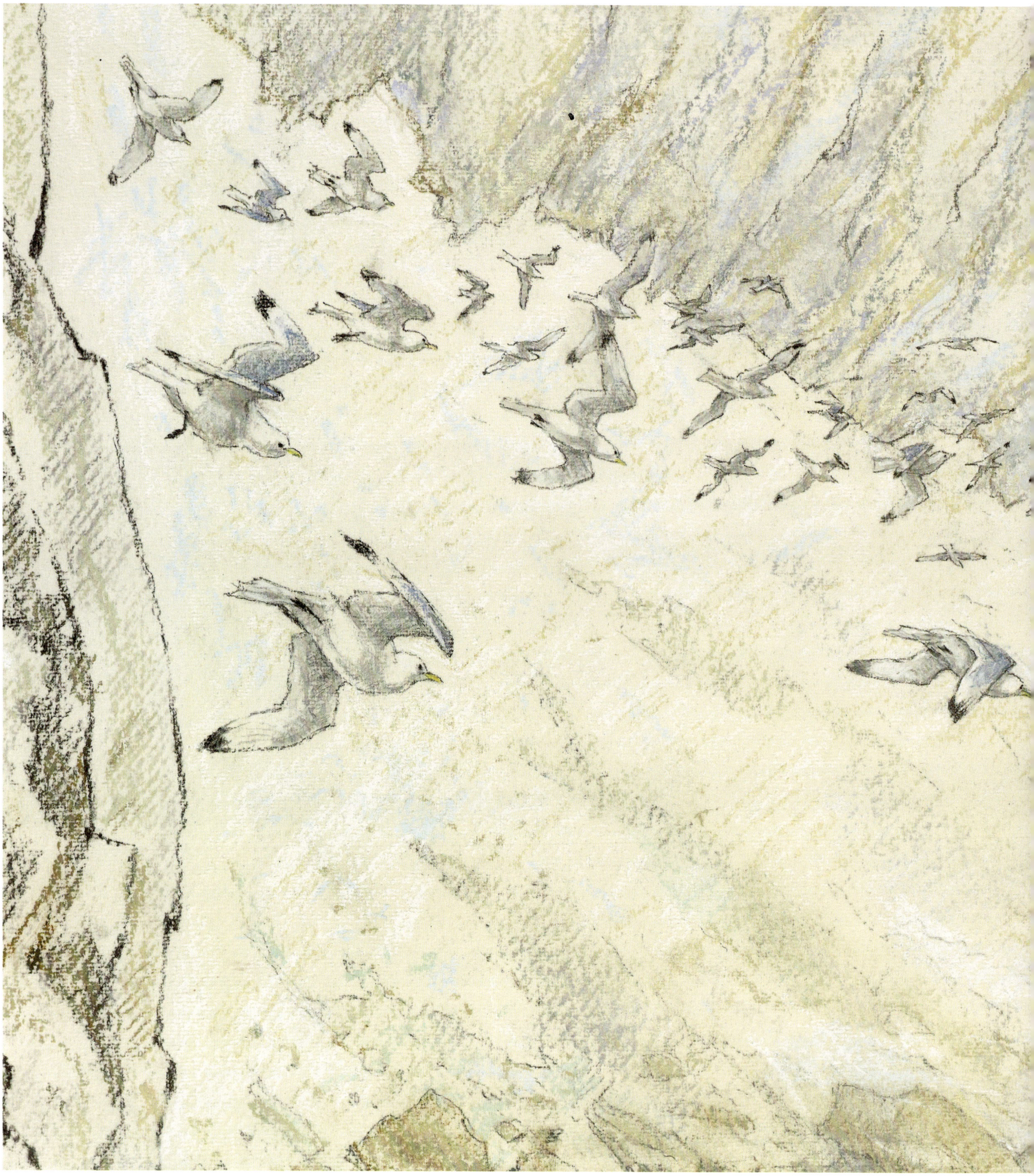

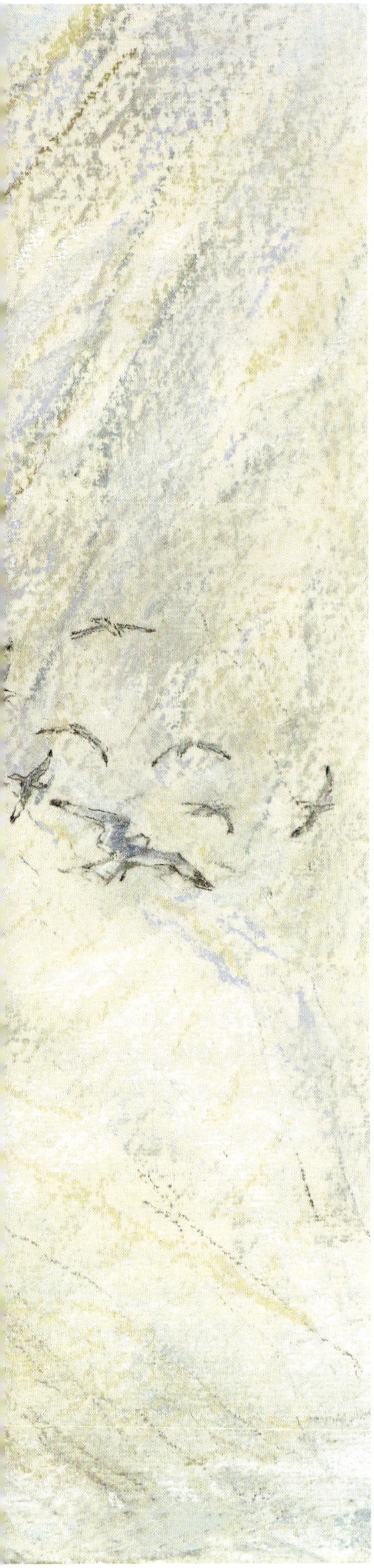

St Abbs is a good place to observe a kittiwake 'dread': a strange moment when the noisy colony suddenly goes quiet. Those gulls not sitting on eggs fly out to sea as a group in complete silence, circle round and return to the cliffs, and their noisy calling resumes! The whole event lasts only a few minutes.

The harbour at Dunbar is another great place to watch kittiwakes nesting at close quarters on the old castle wall.

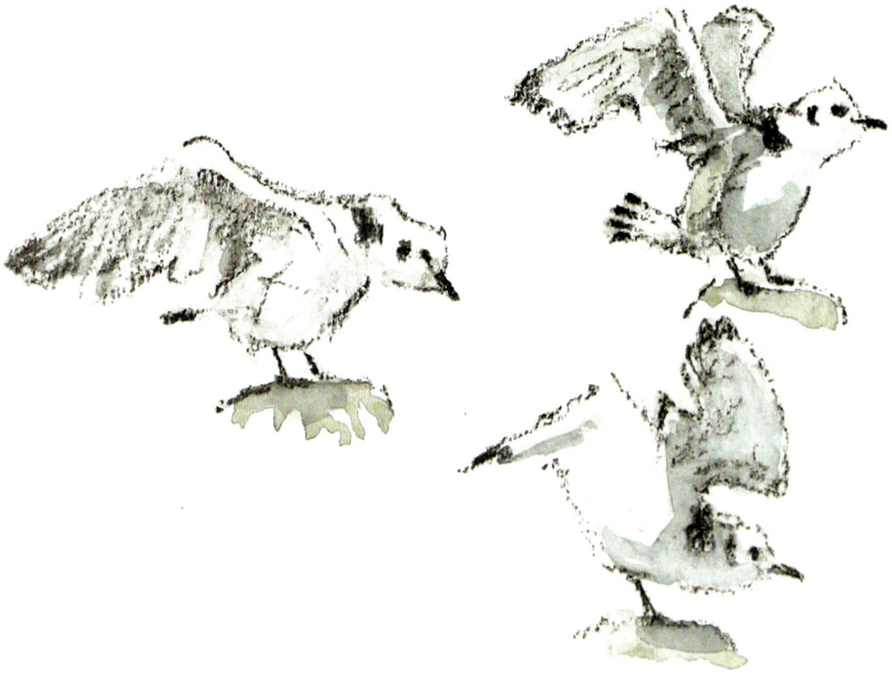

A kittiwake dread, St Abbs

Young kittiwakes wing-stretching

Shags and razorbills, Craigleith Island, Firth of Forth

The Bass Rock has been a focal point for years of drawing and painting. Illustrating Bryan Nelson's *The Gannet* gave me his insights into their behaviour, and to illustrate his seabird books that followed took me to other parts of the world to draw boobies and species not found on our local seas. See Bryan Nelson's *On the Rocks* (Langford Press).

The Bass today is so crowded with gannets that there is hardly space to sit down. Without wishing to deplore the gannets' breeding success, I fondly remember the grass-covered top of the island in the sixties and the clear pathway from the lighthouse to the foghorn. A gannet paradise has become a stinking mess for humans, but bursting with inter-colonial bird action.

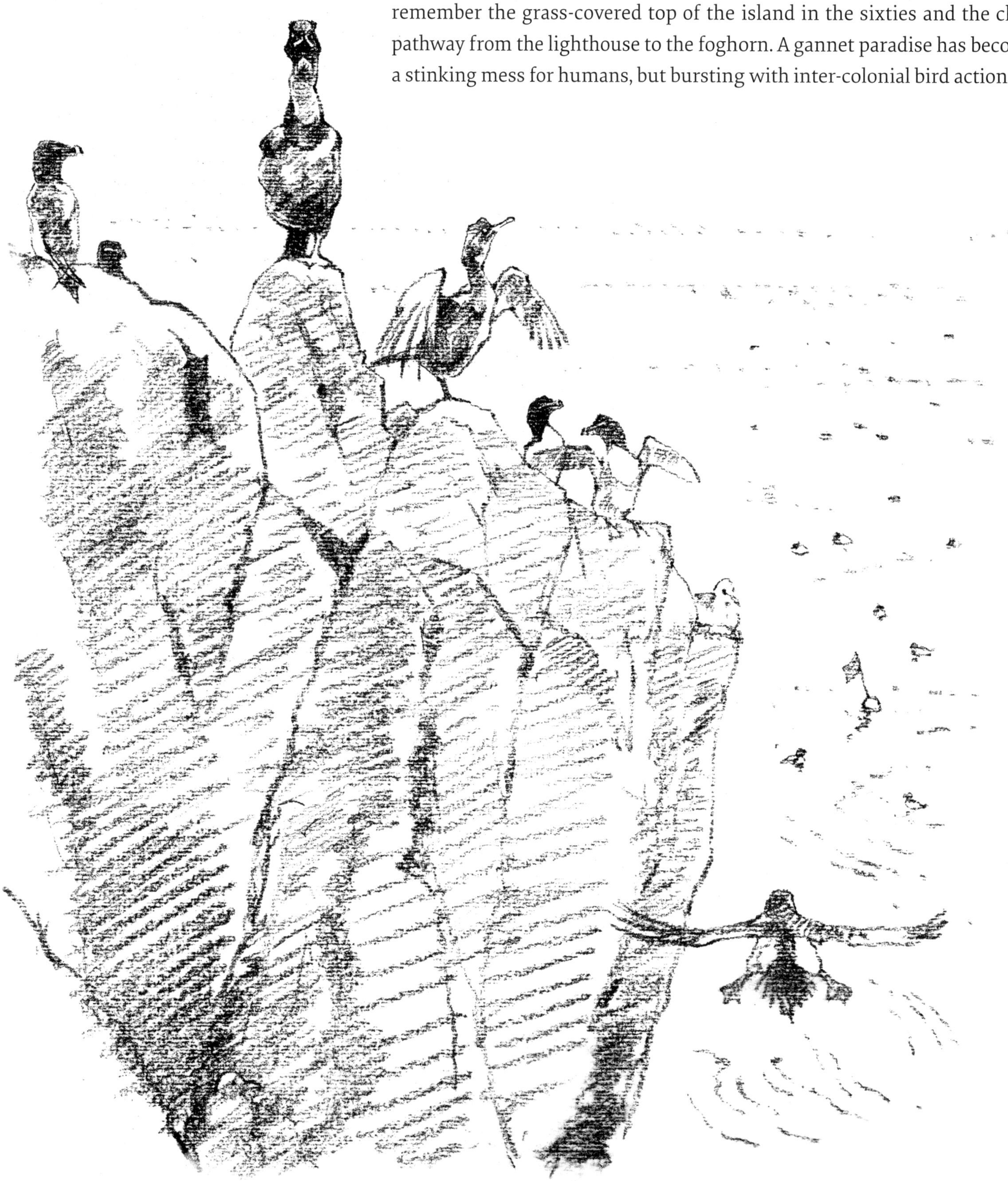

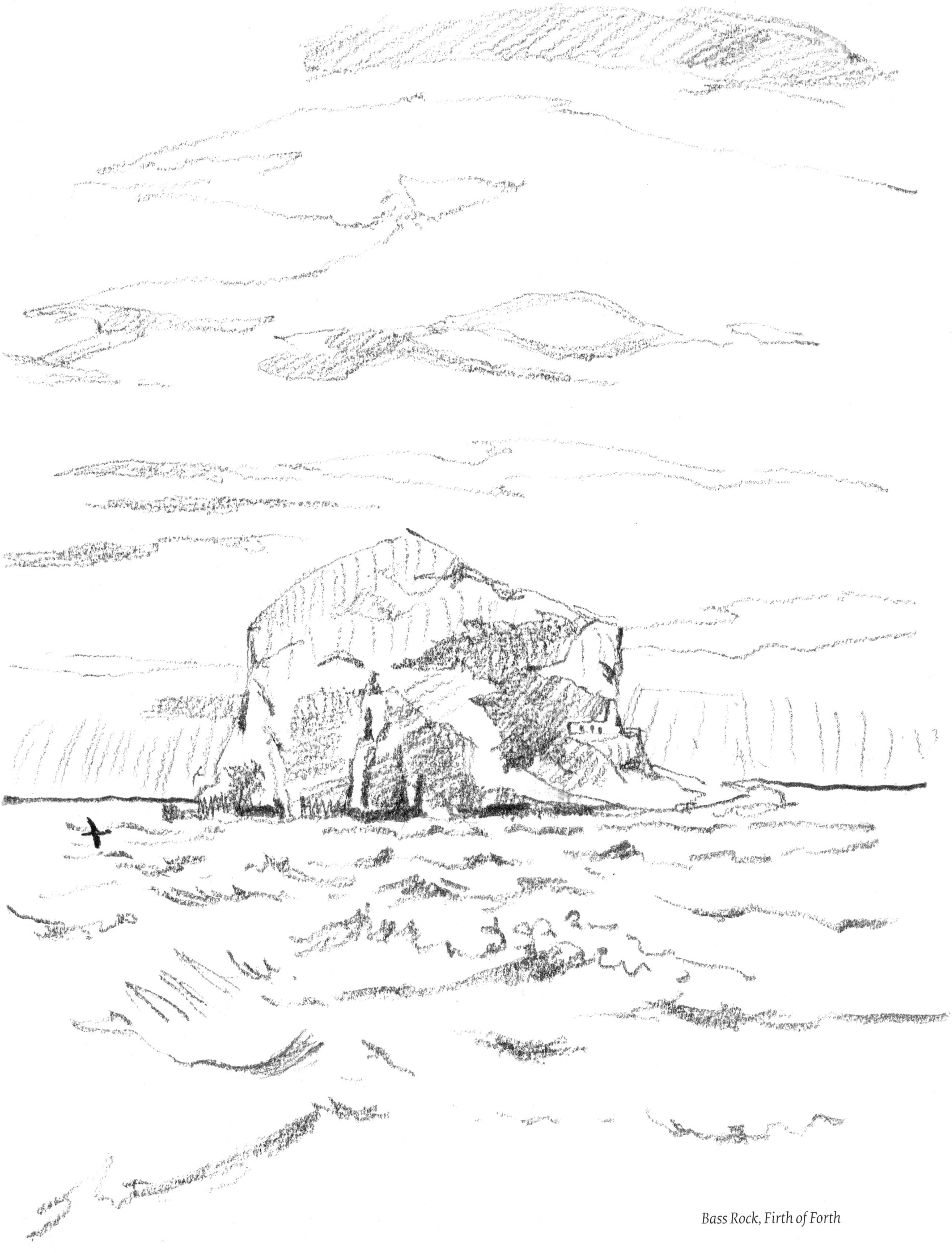

Bass Rock, Firth of Forth

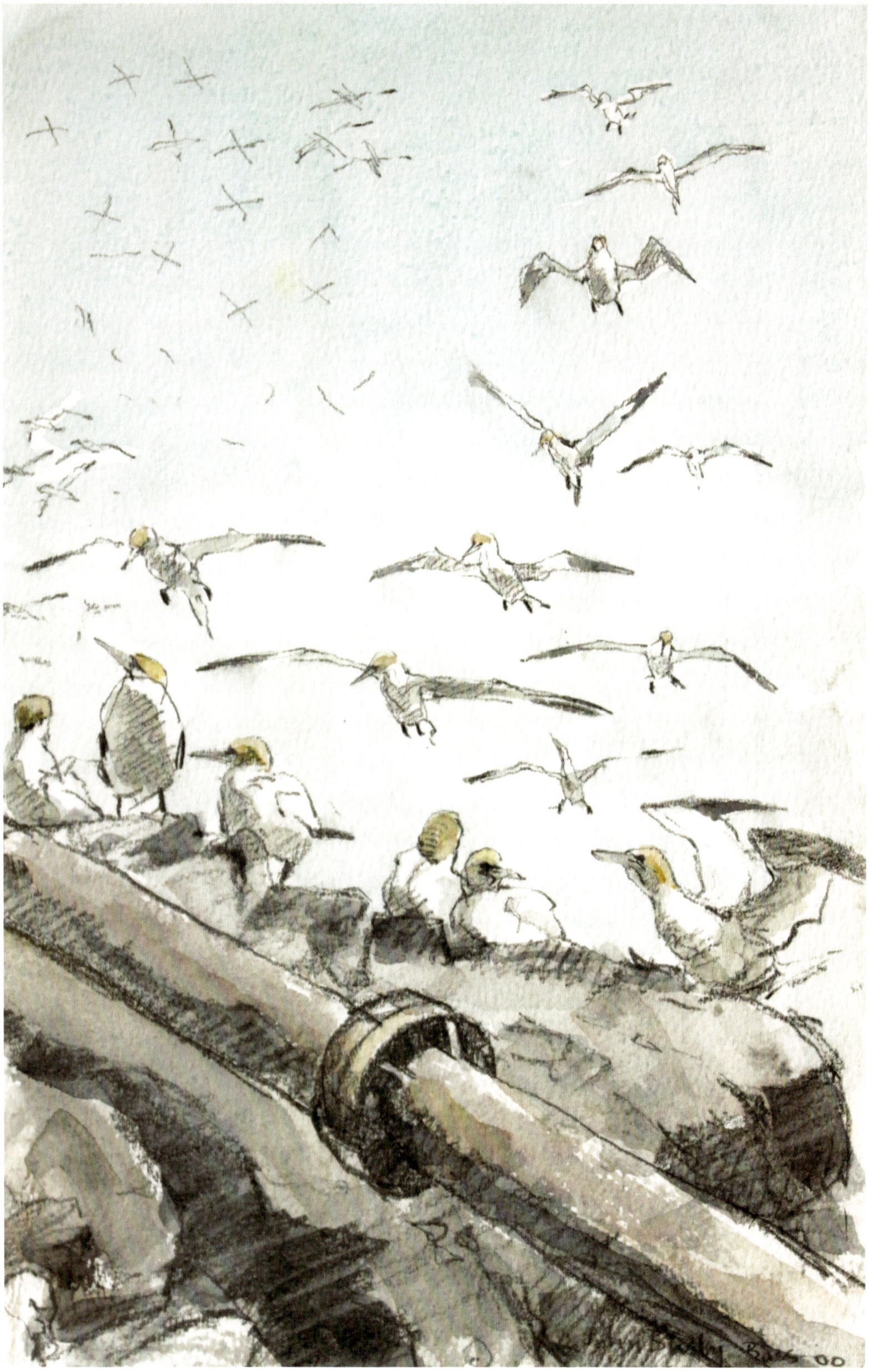

Gannets hanging in the wind over the west gully. If the wind is strong enough, even a razorbill with its short wings can hold stationary >

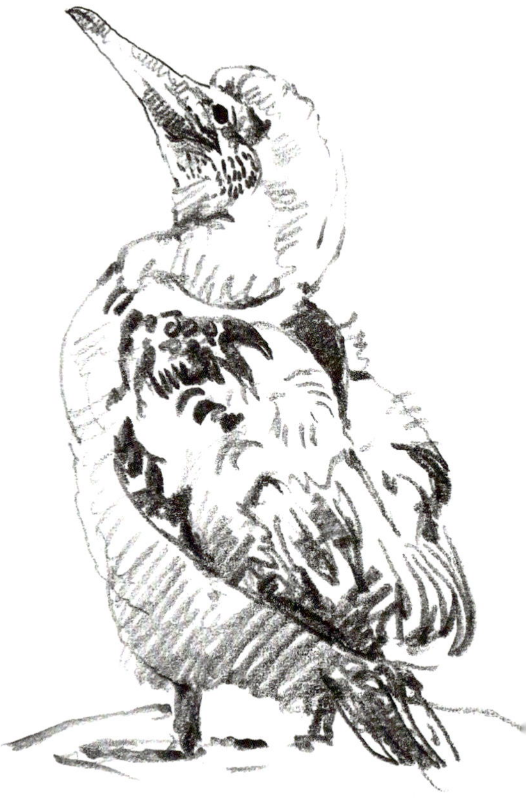

Gannets on the Bass Rock

Young gannet, feathers beginning to replace down

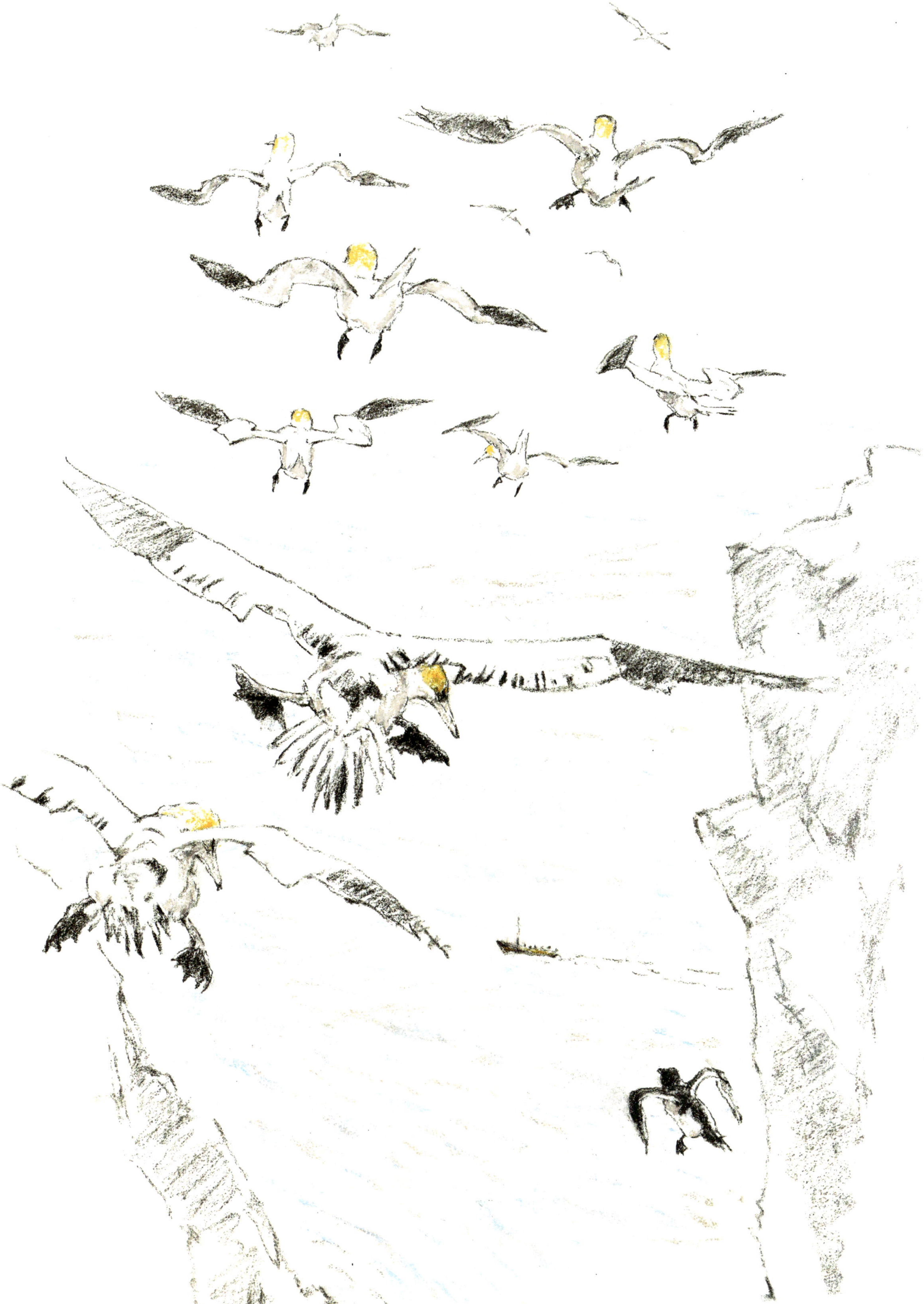

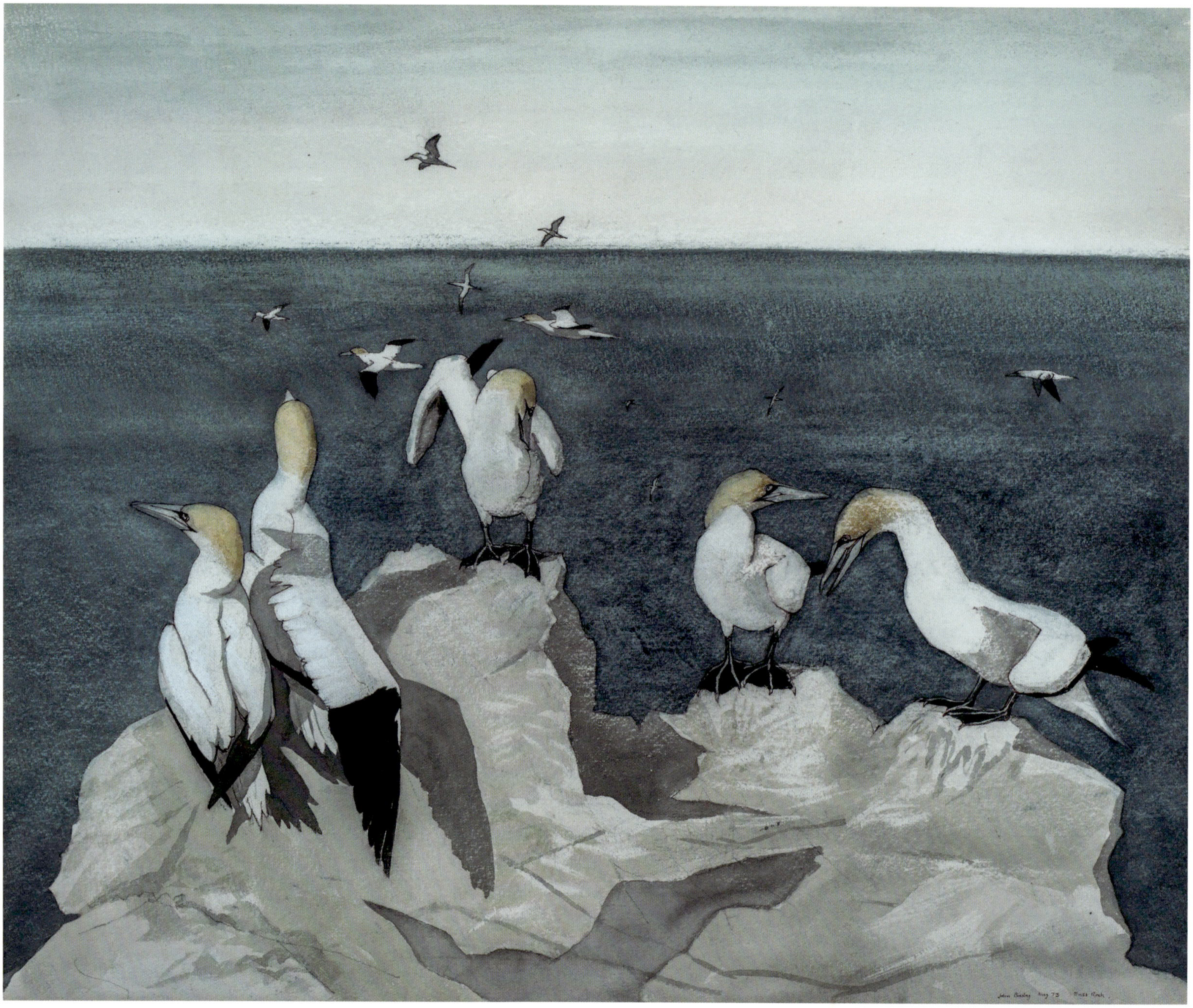

Bass Rock, 1973

Nesting gannets above the Bass lighthouse; a view no longer accessible through the nesting gannets >

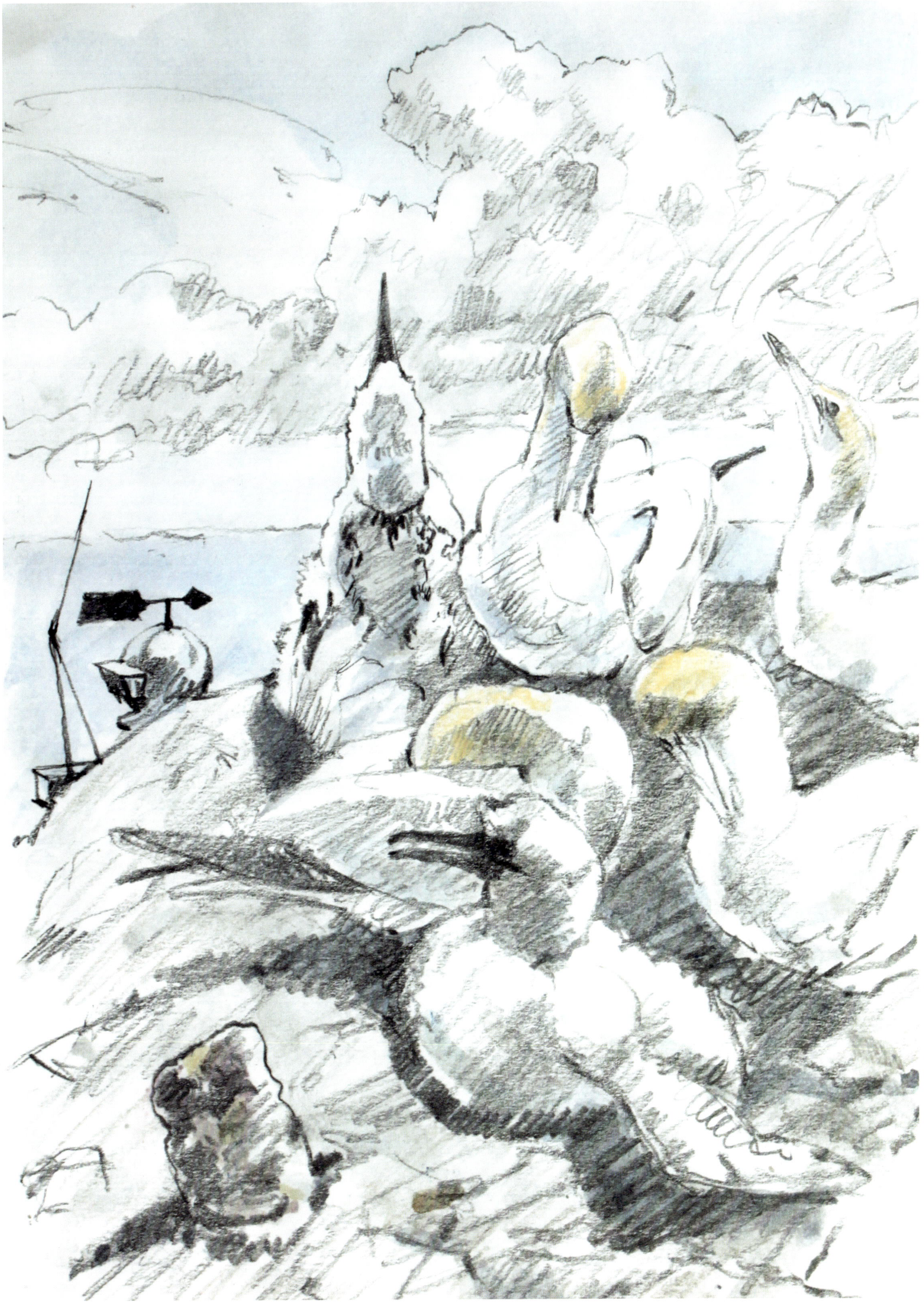

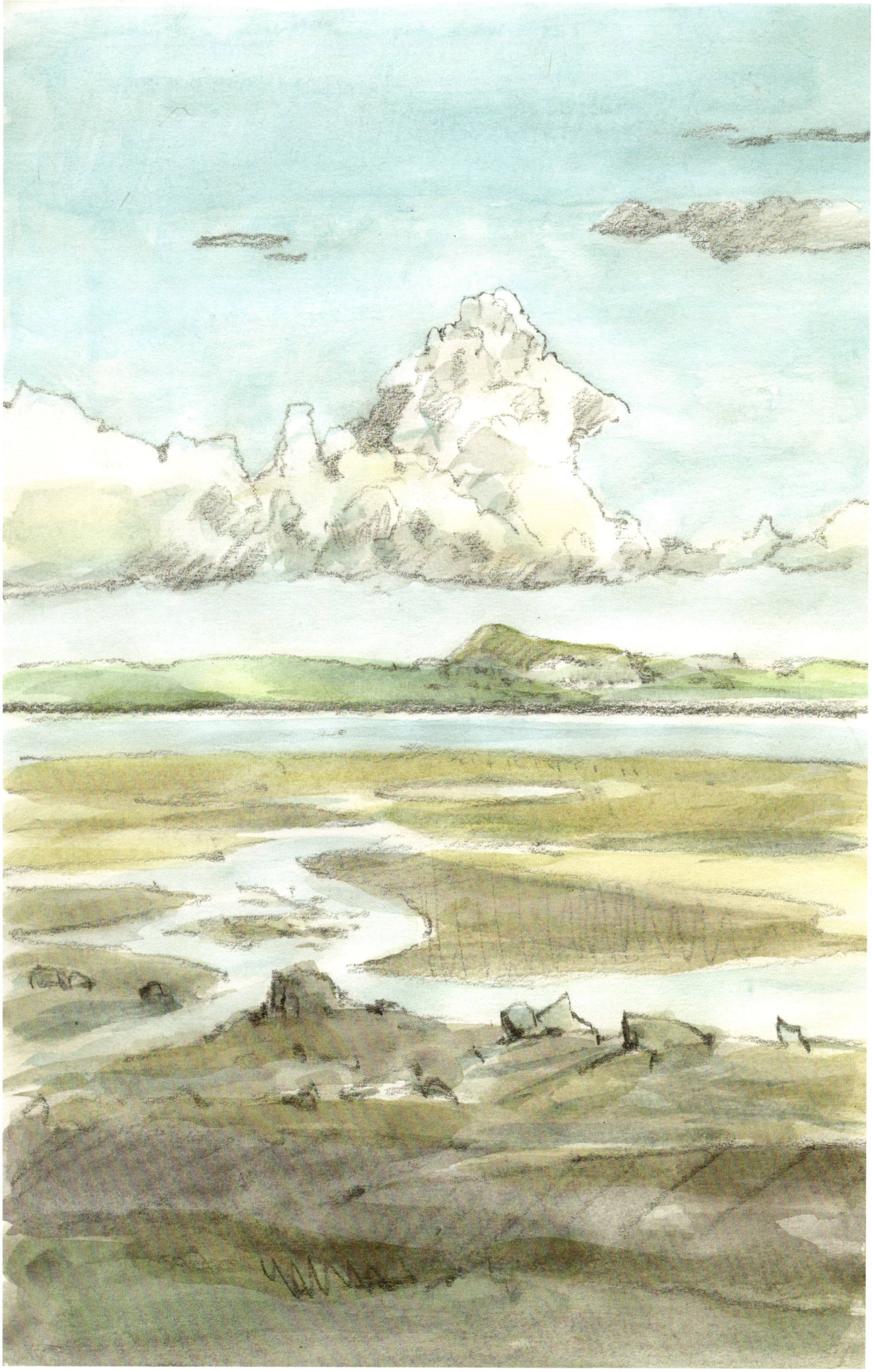

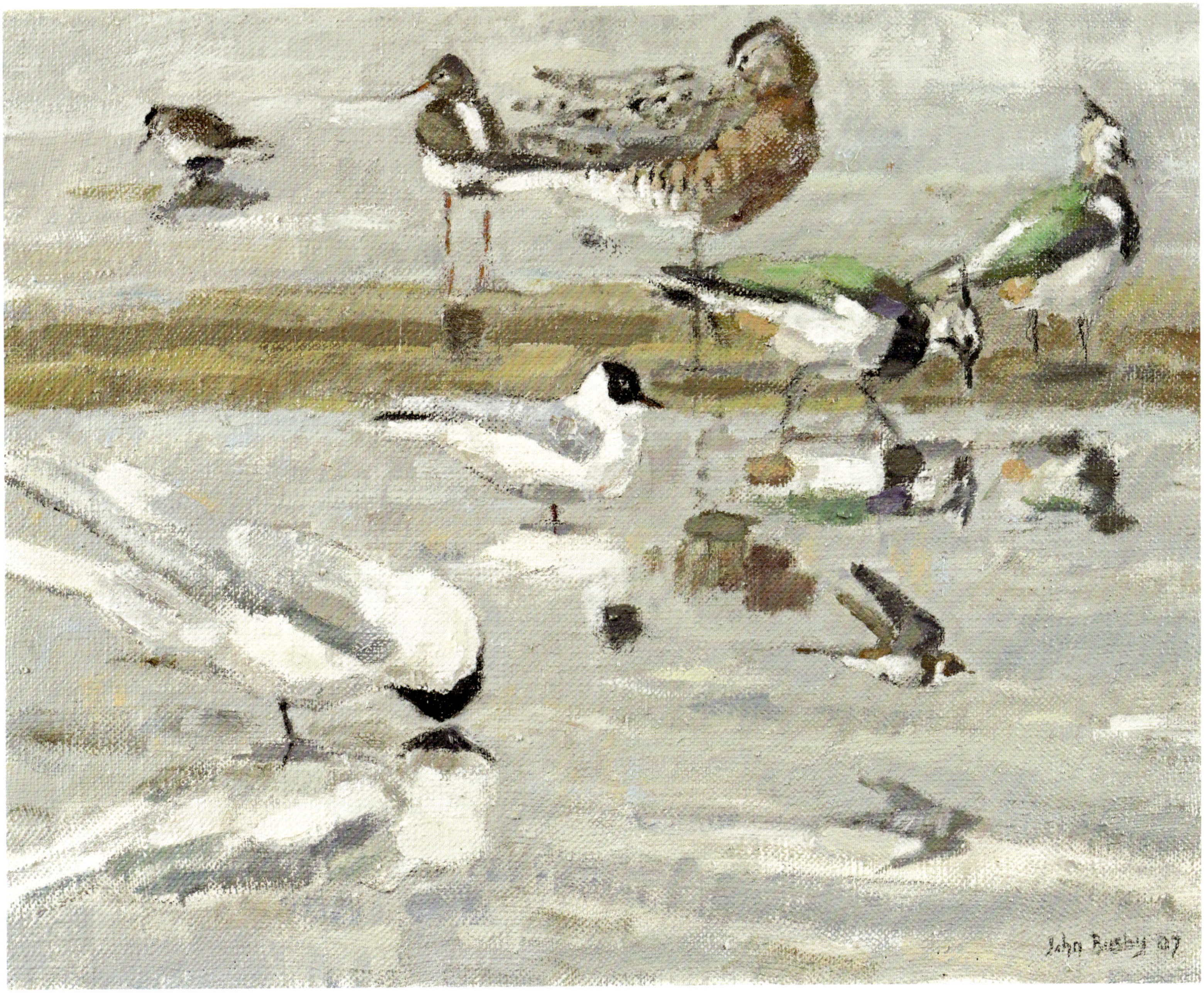

An autumn mixture – Sandwich tern, little gull, lapwings, black-tailed godwit, redshanks, dunlin and sand martin, Musselburgh Lagoon

< Low tide, Gosford Bay, East Lothian

Our local estuaries are full of interest; most of all in the winter months when waders and ducks and geese arrive on migration in large numbers, and a flock of waders can behave as one organic unit. I like the between-times especially, when summer and winter visitors overlap and one can see the about-to-leave sand martins and terns flying among newly-arrived godwits and dunlins. Contrasts of shape, behaviour and movement, among species in a mixed flock, give plenty of material for the sketch book.

Here are some images from the local estuaries of Musselburgh, Aberlady and Tyninghame.

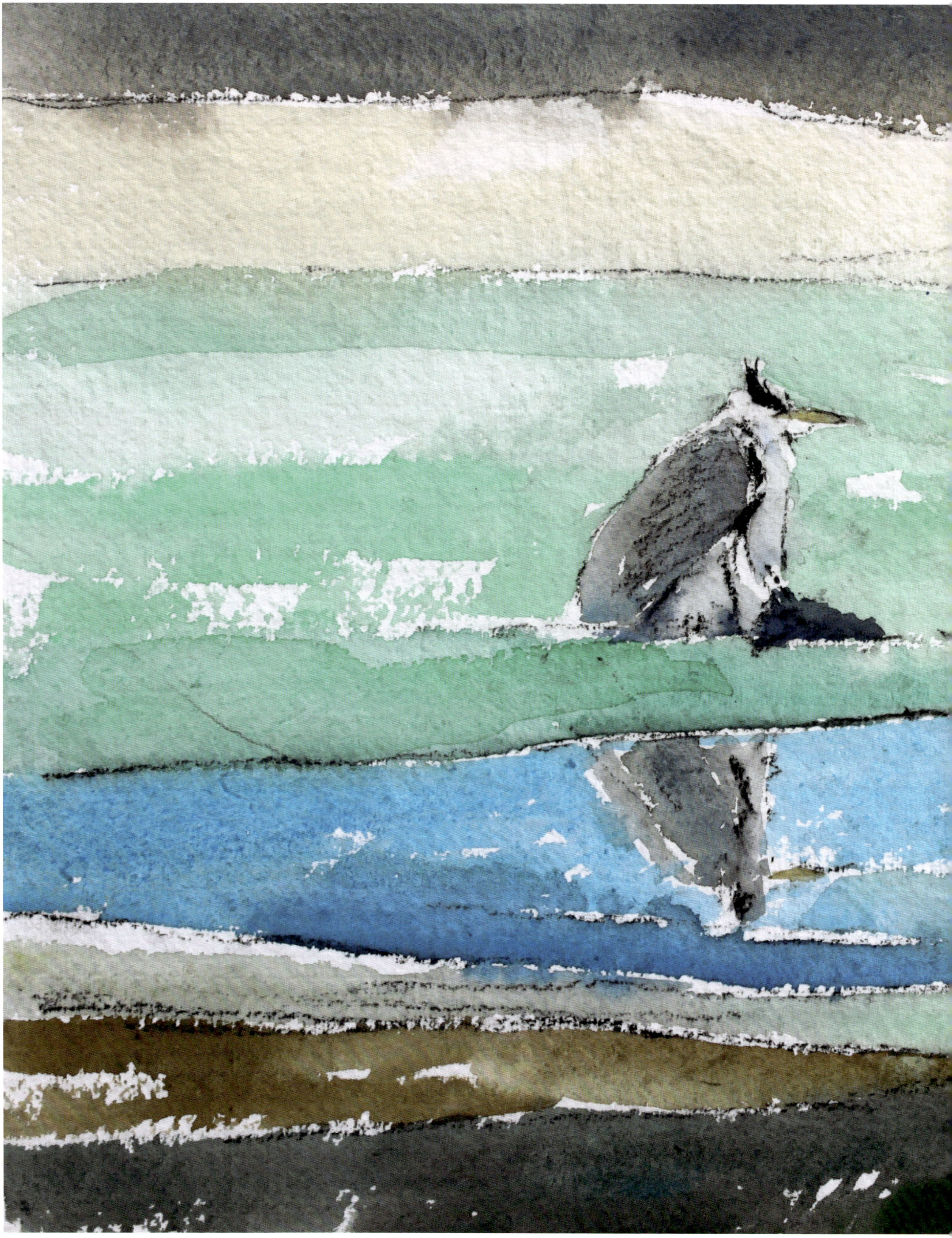

Heron by the blue estuary river at Aberlady

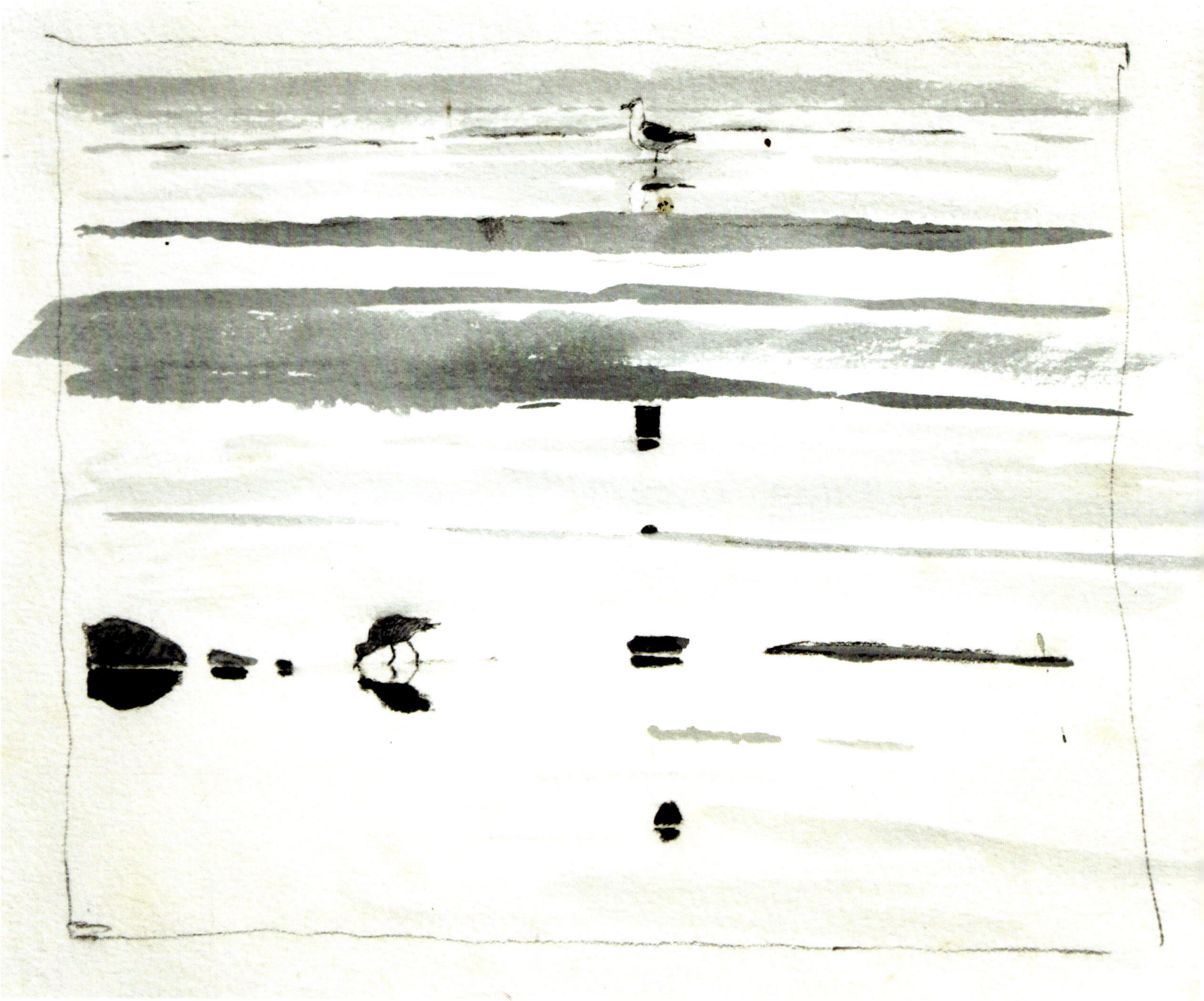

Estuary scene, Aberlady

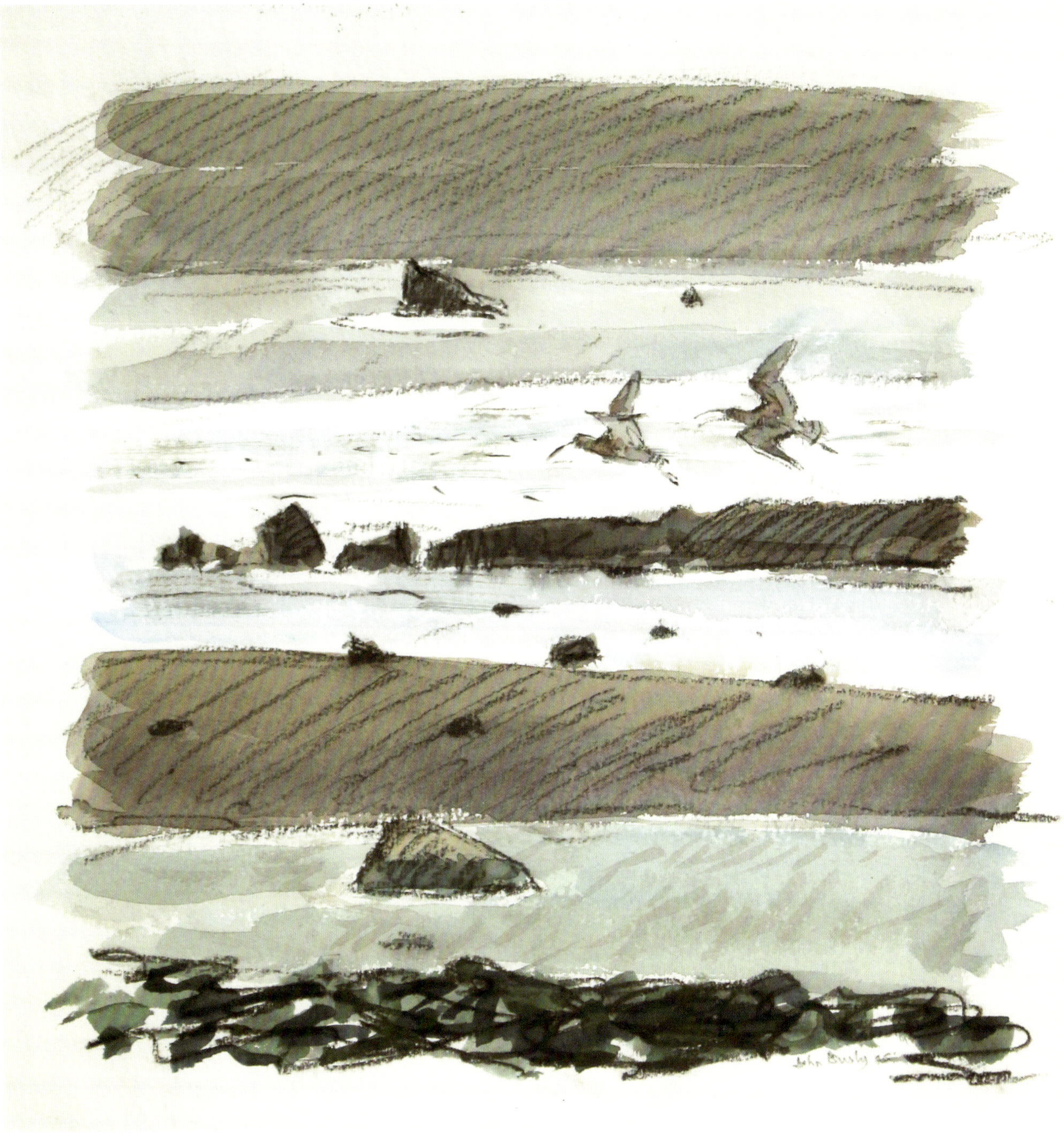

Estuary scene, Aberlady

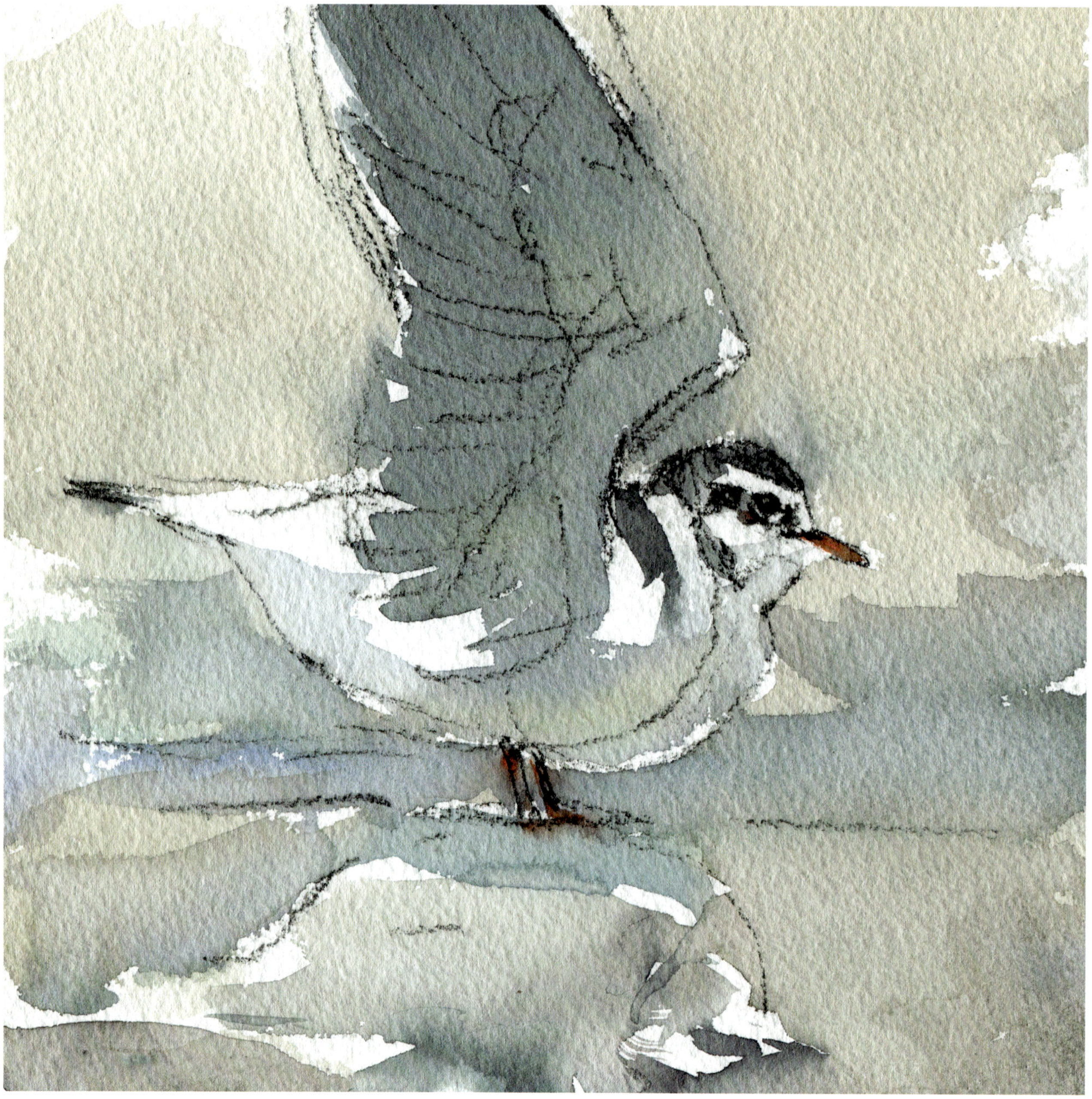

An autumn little gull at Musselburgh lagoons

Lapwing, little gulls and dunlin

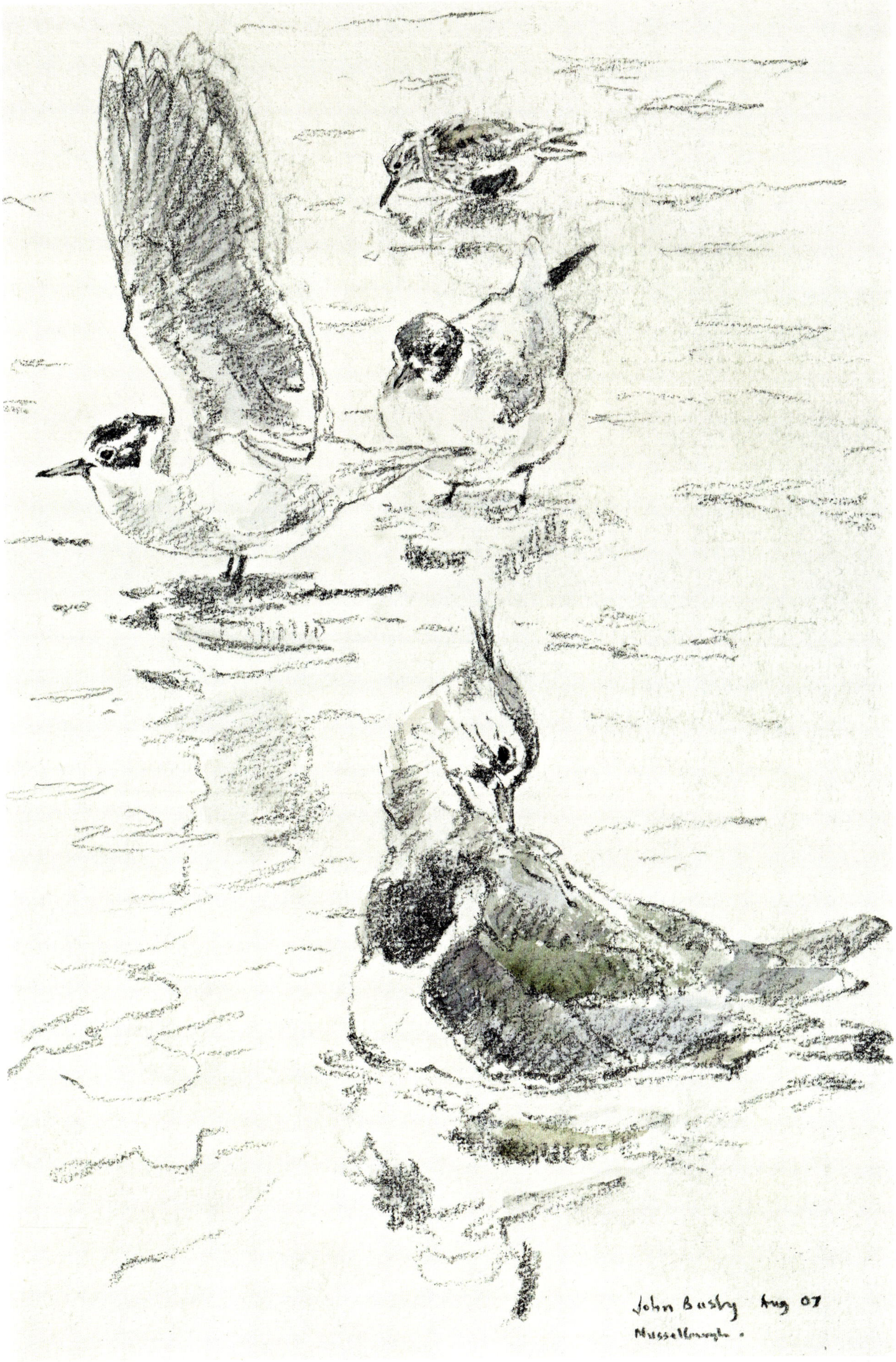
John Busby Aug 07
Musselburgh.

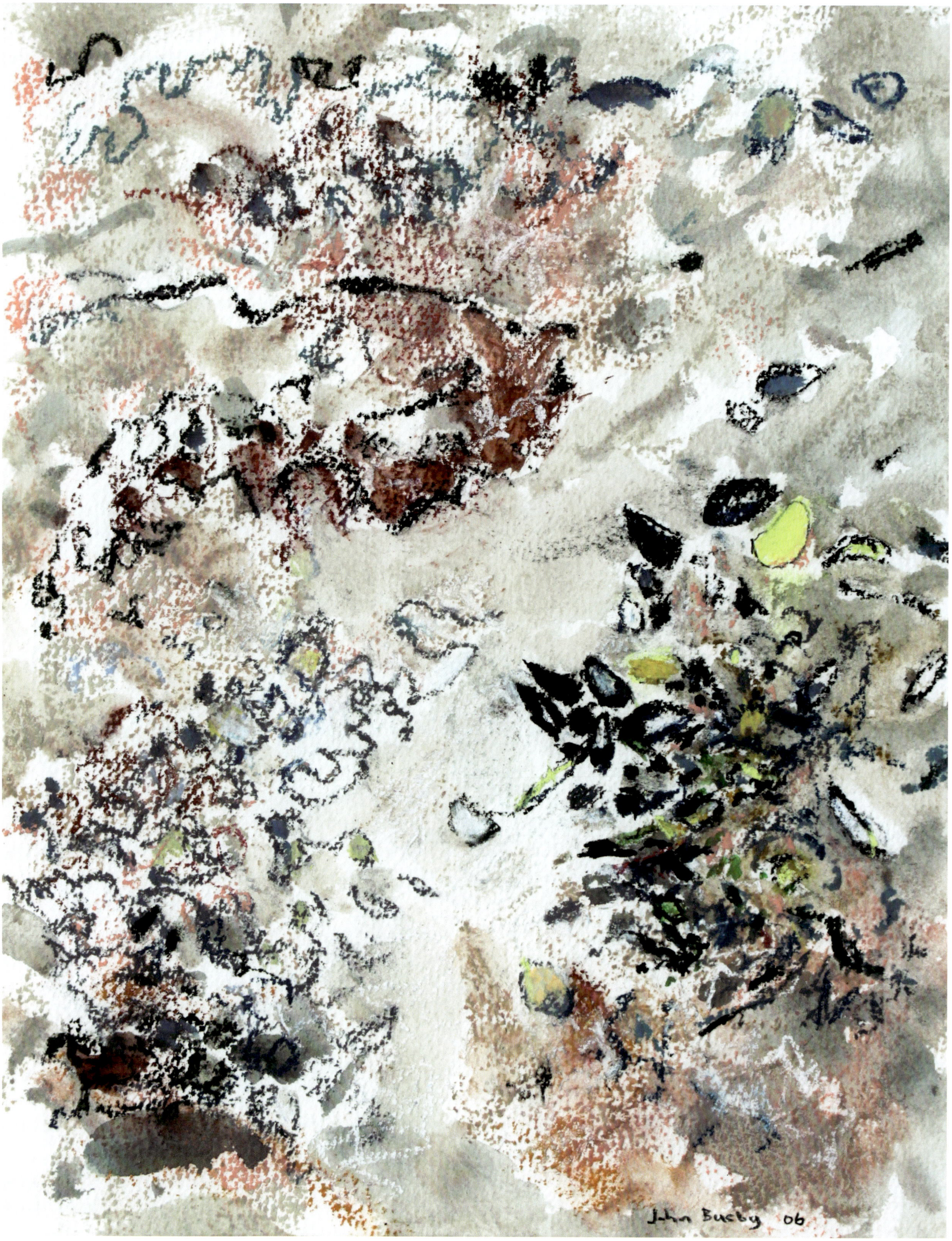
John Busby 06

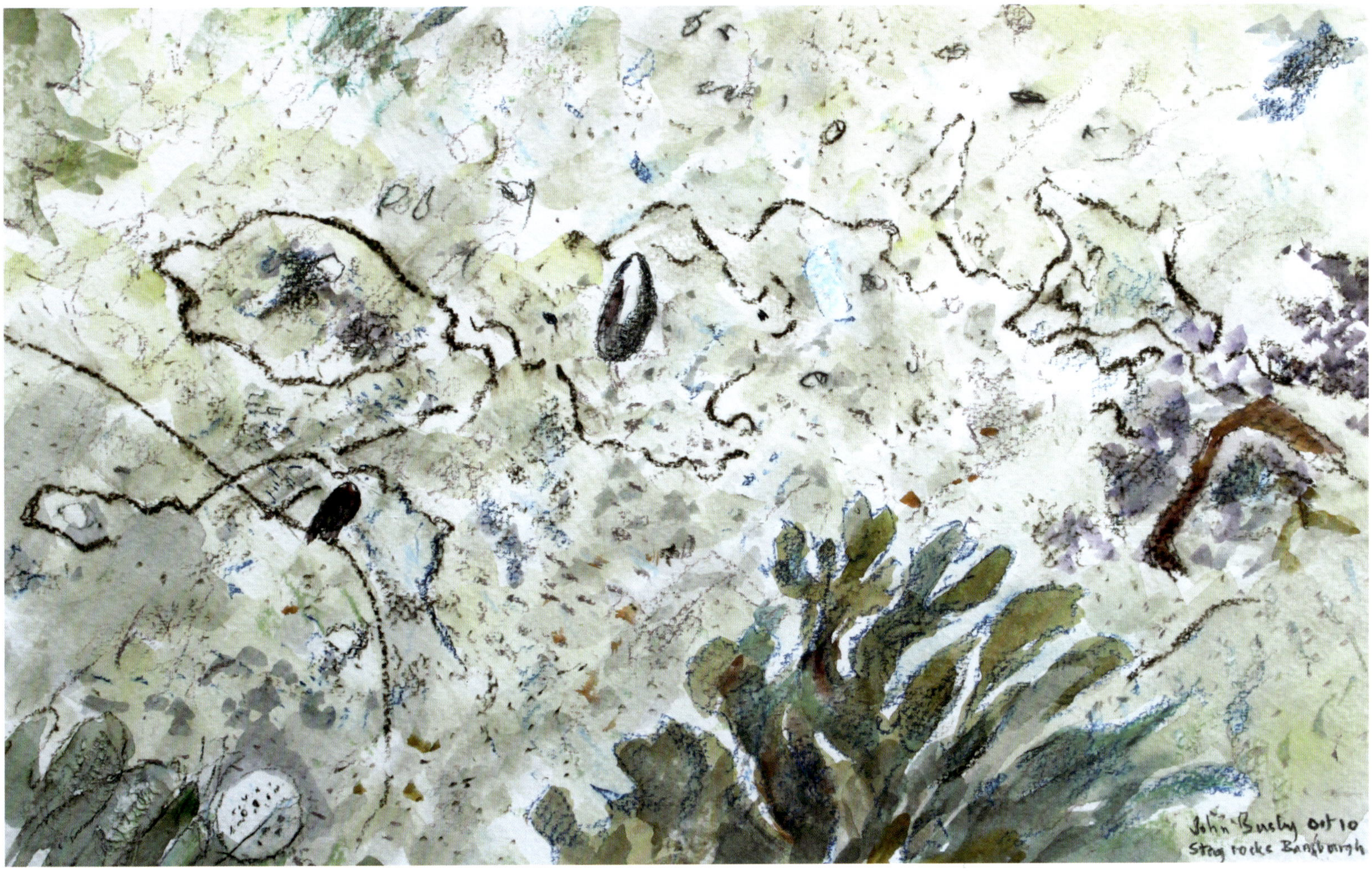

The magic of rock pools

An estuary is rich in other sea life. The ground at one's feet contains shapes and colours to delight any artist, especially one young at heart. As a child I would imagine myself as the pilot of a toy Spitfire held at arm's length above my head. Looking down at the seashore from this imagined height, all the drama of a full scale landscape was there – great mountain ranges, deep canyons, lakes and ocean depths, as exciting as a primeval world at the beginning of time. That fascination has never left me.

The sea shapes the rocks and constantly re-arranges patterns on the shore, shifting collections of shells and shards of seaweed with each tide.

Periwinkles make trails on the floor of the pools, leaving their own drawings in the sand.

Shells, tracks and Seaweed

< Patterns in a sea pool

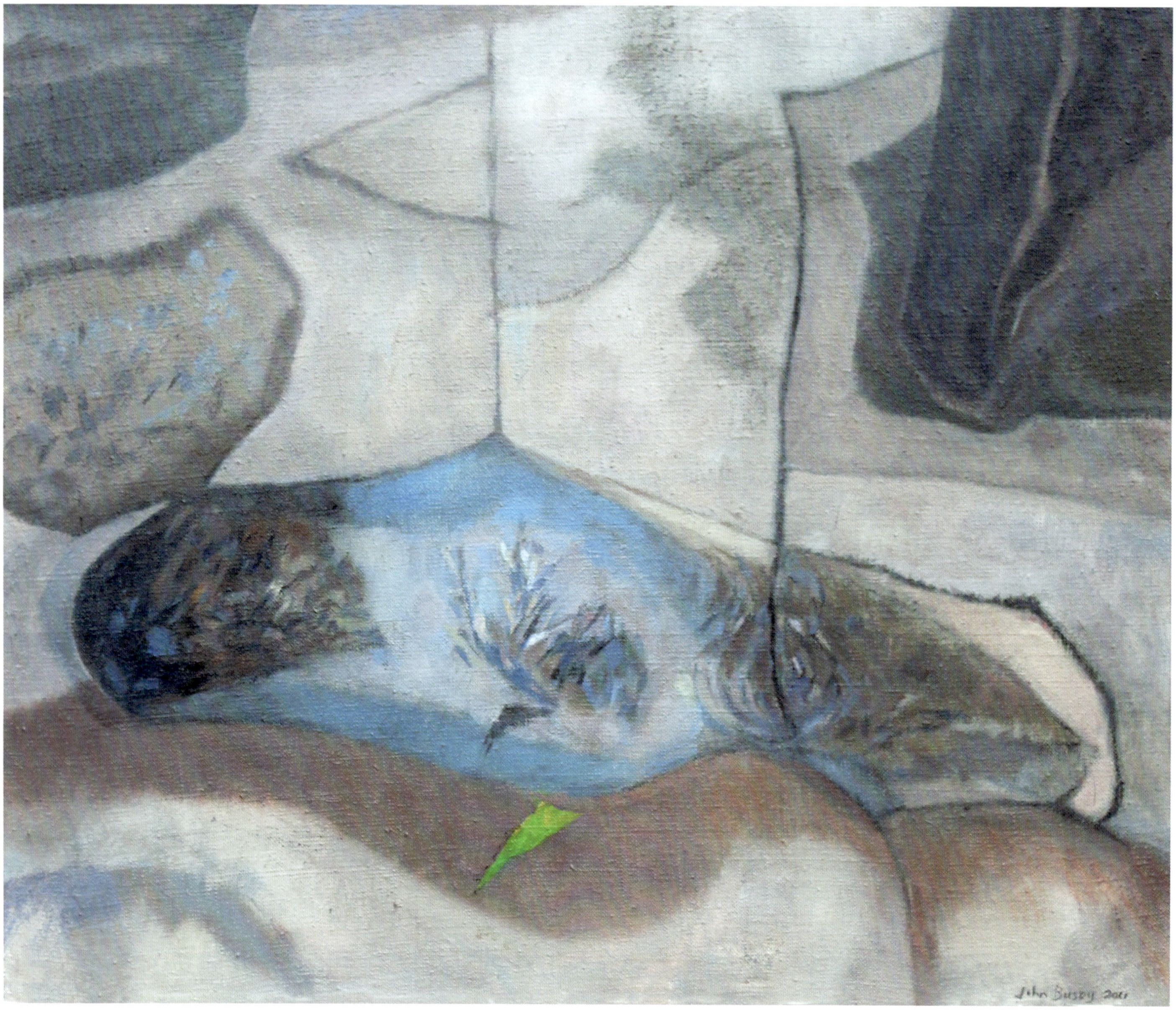

Tide pool, Tyninghame

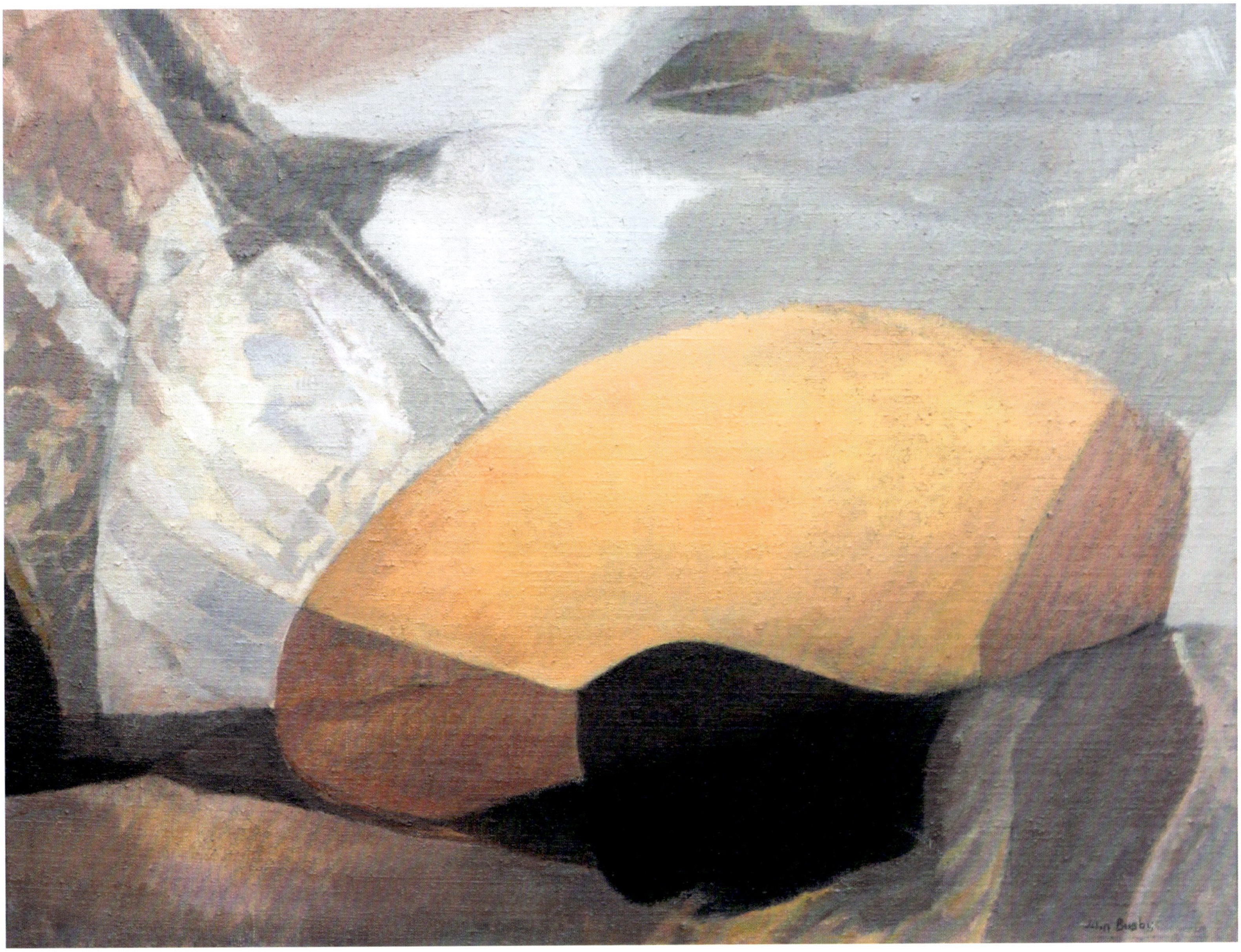

Still Yellow Pool

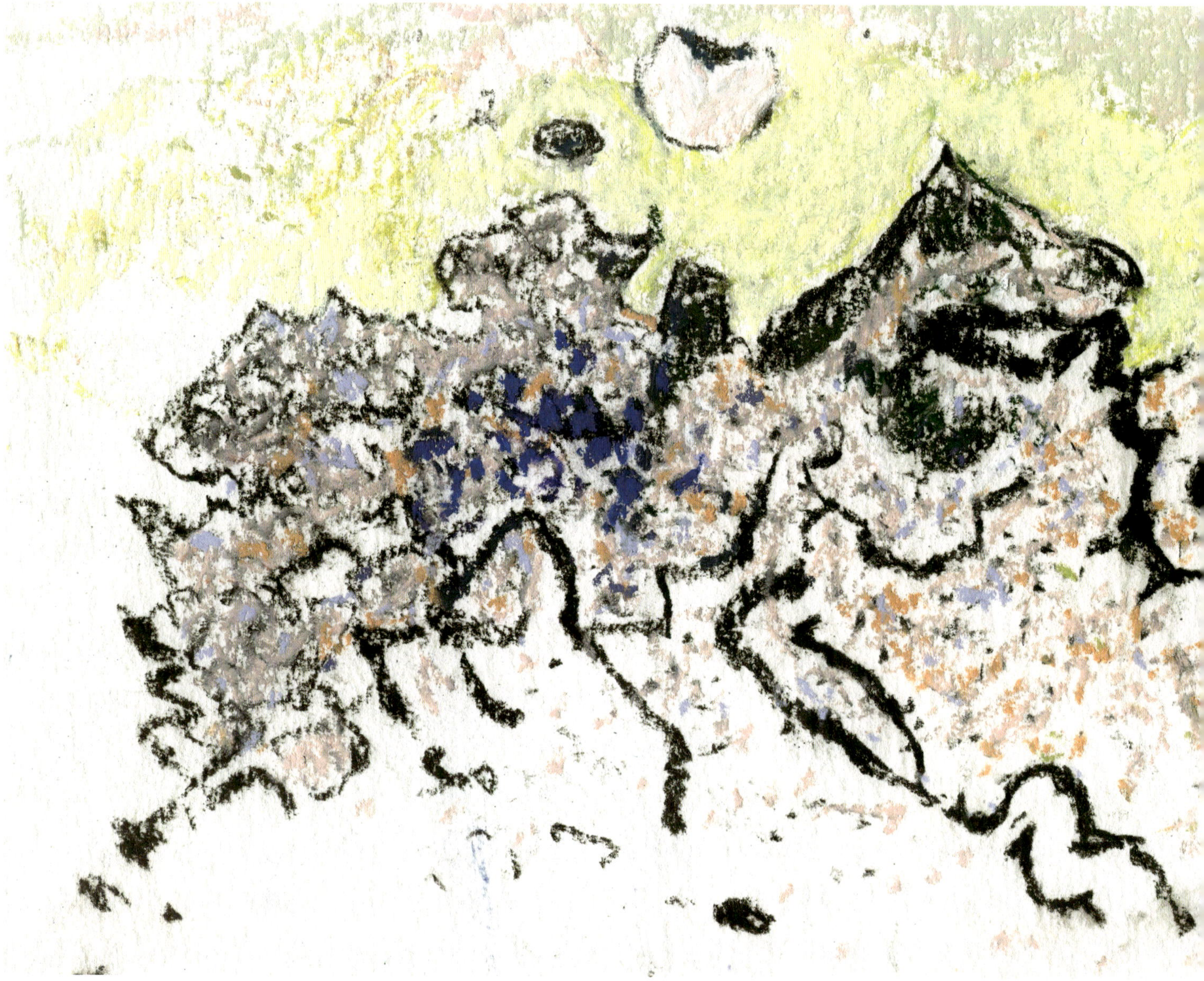

At low tide the pools are still – a contained world, casting colours into a strange unity: a transitory part of the amazing beauty of the natural world uncovered for a few hours. As we grow older and more sophisticated, perhaps this magic fades and the shore is left marooned between the wordless wonder of a child and the specialised language of a marine biologist. The creatures and plants living there all have scientific names, but when it comes to describing the beauty of water-shaped rocks, floating seaweeds, the magnifying density of water reflecting clouds in the sky, or the first ripple of a returning tide – we are lost for words!

My response has to be visual – images that dance to their own counterpoint of time, and to the artist's personal choreography.

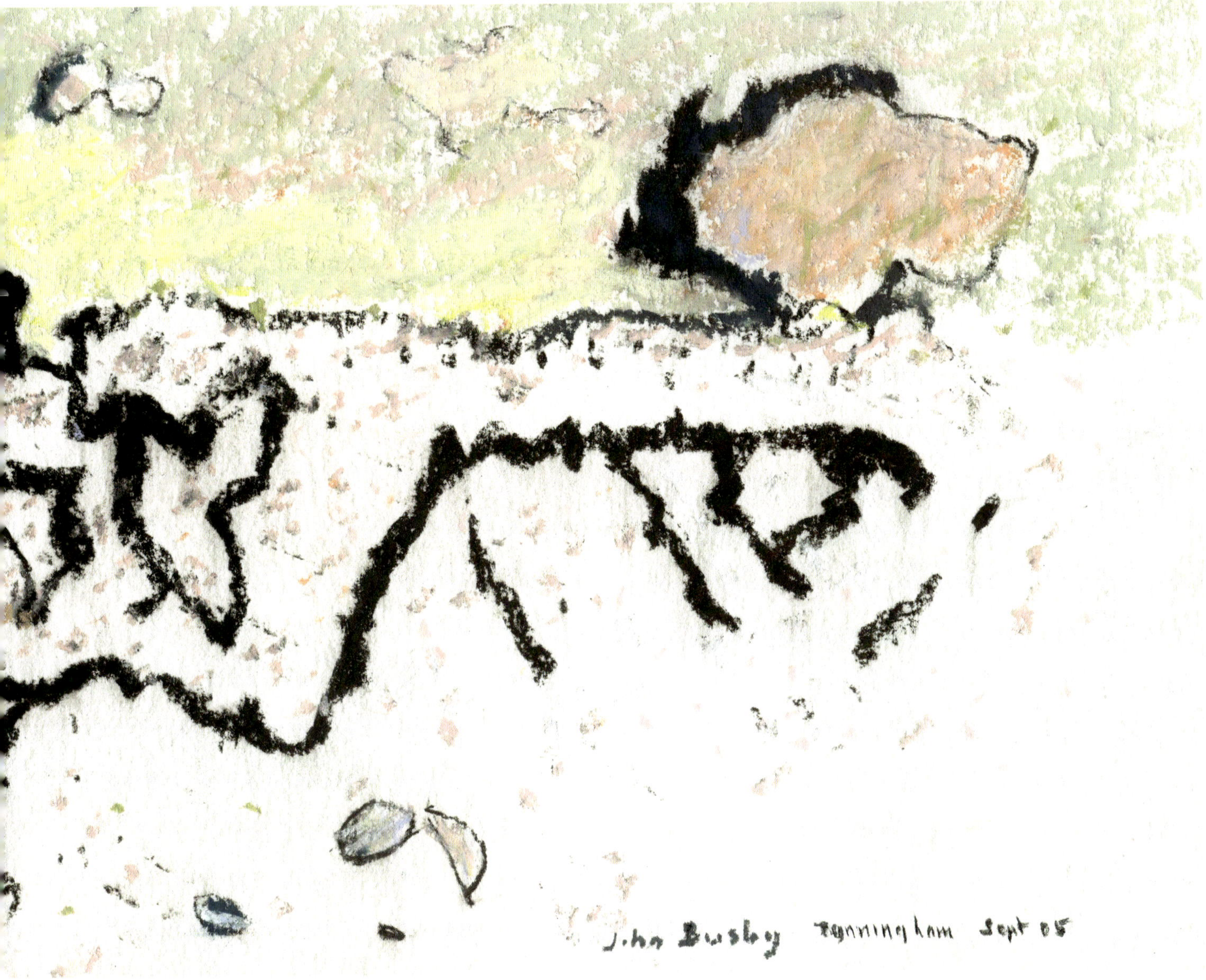

Periwinkle tracks. The lines made in the sand by the shellfish resemble a prehistoric artist's cave drawing

These paintings grew mostly from pools seen on the shore of the estuary at Tyninghame near Dunbar. The bay has many layers of coloured sandstones – red, yellow, black and green – as well as limestone outcrops. It is a coastline, not of crashing waves, but of the slow ebb and flow of tides and the ringing calls of waders.

There is one particular pool I always visit, which is quite small and close to the high-water line. On each visit it is different; sometimes it is empty, at other times full of seaweed or clusters of shells. Shadows from surrounding rocks create new patterns as the day progresses. It has proved a 'theme' with many 'variations' in my paintings.

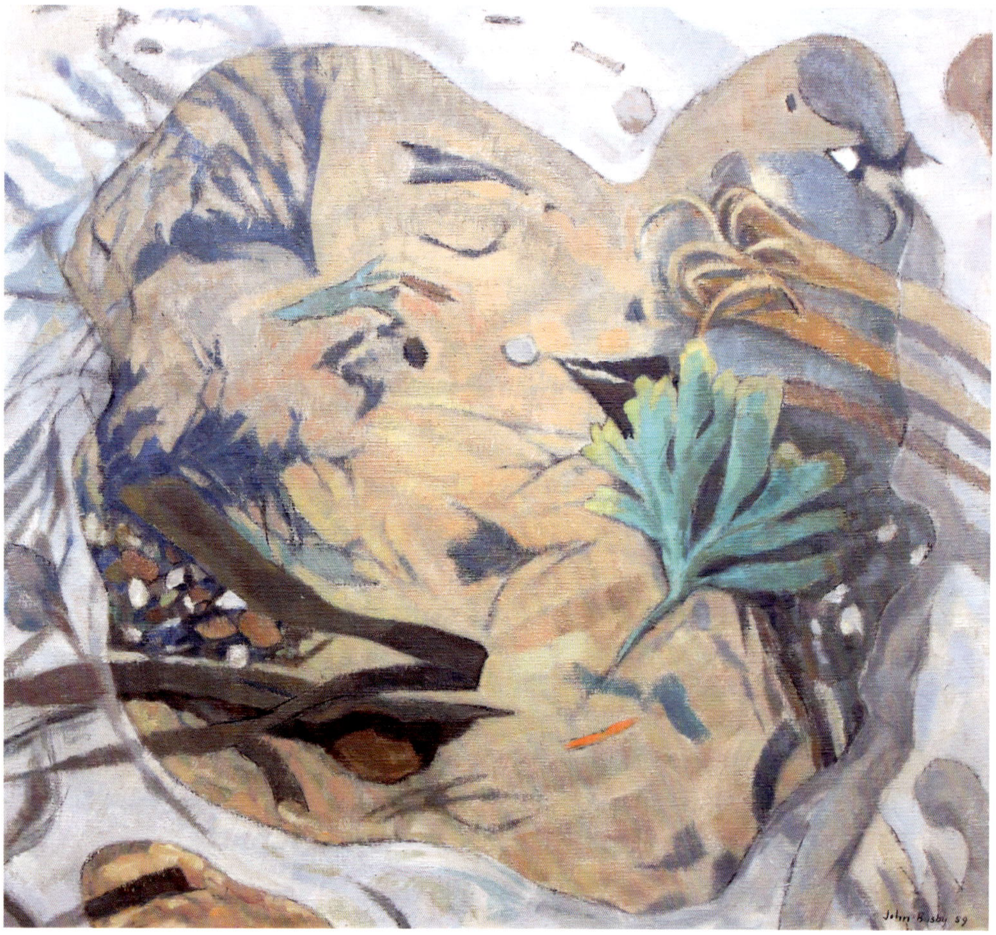

Seaweed pool

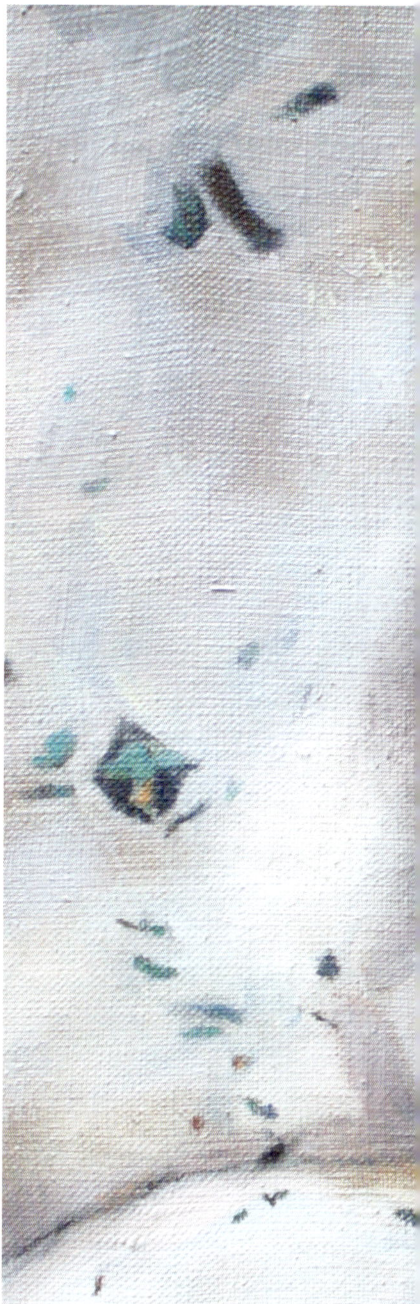

Even a small pool can hold the sky

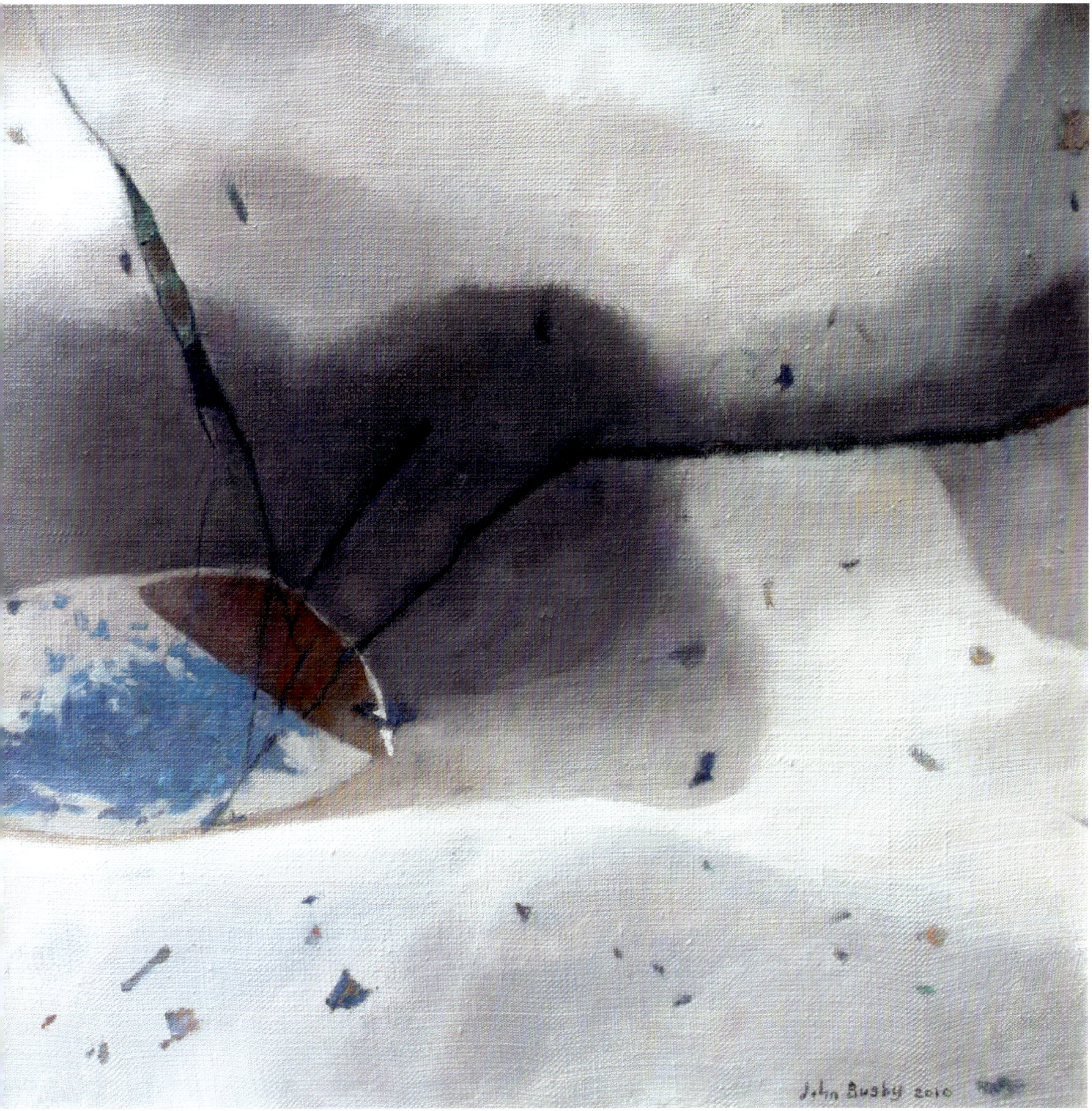
John Busby 2010

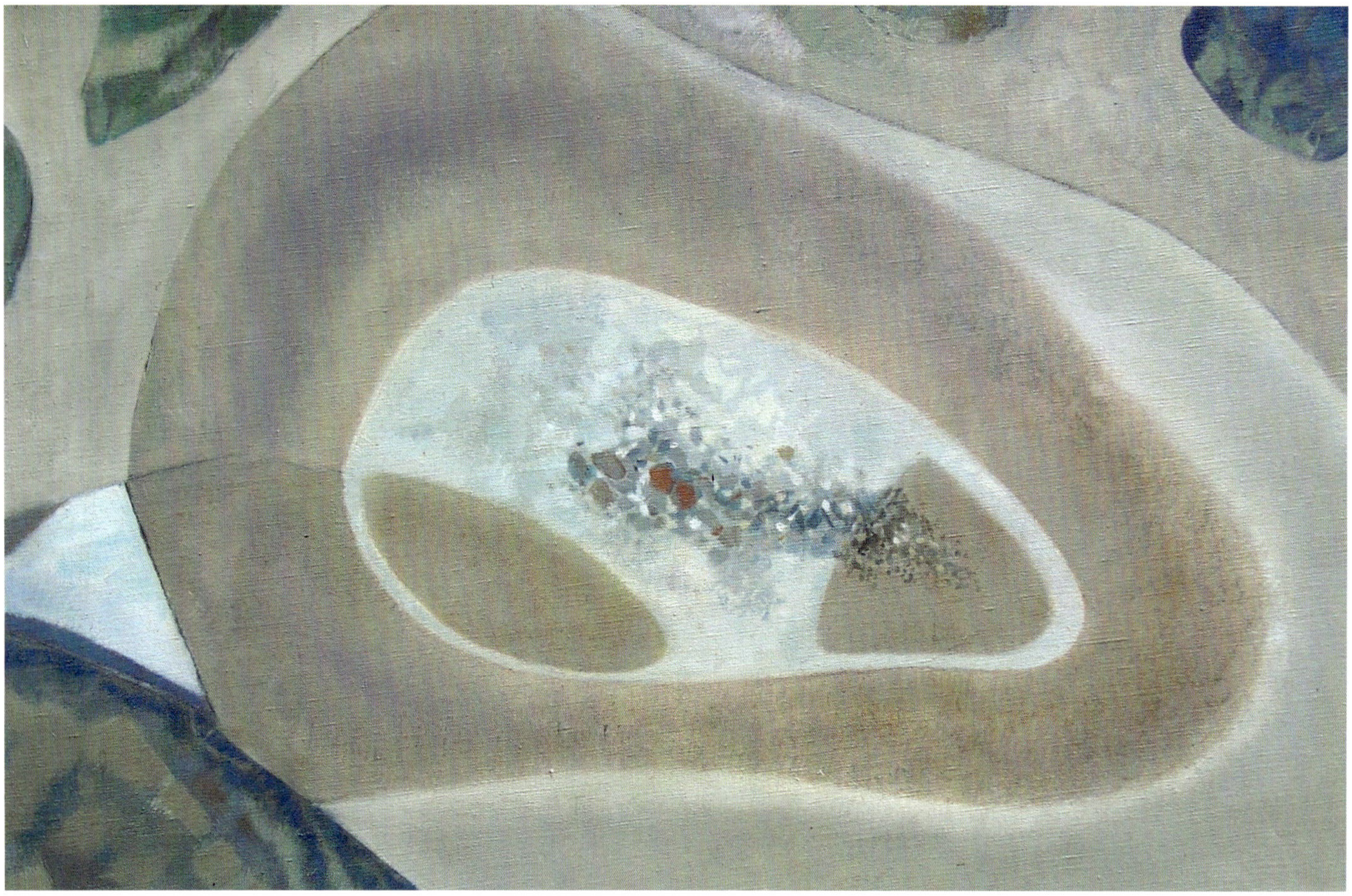

Silent pool

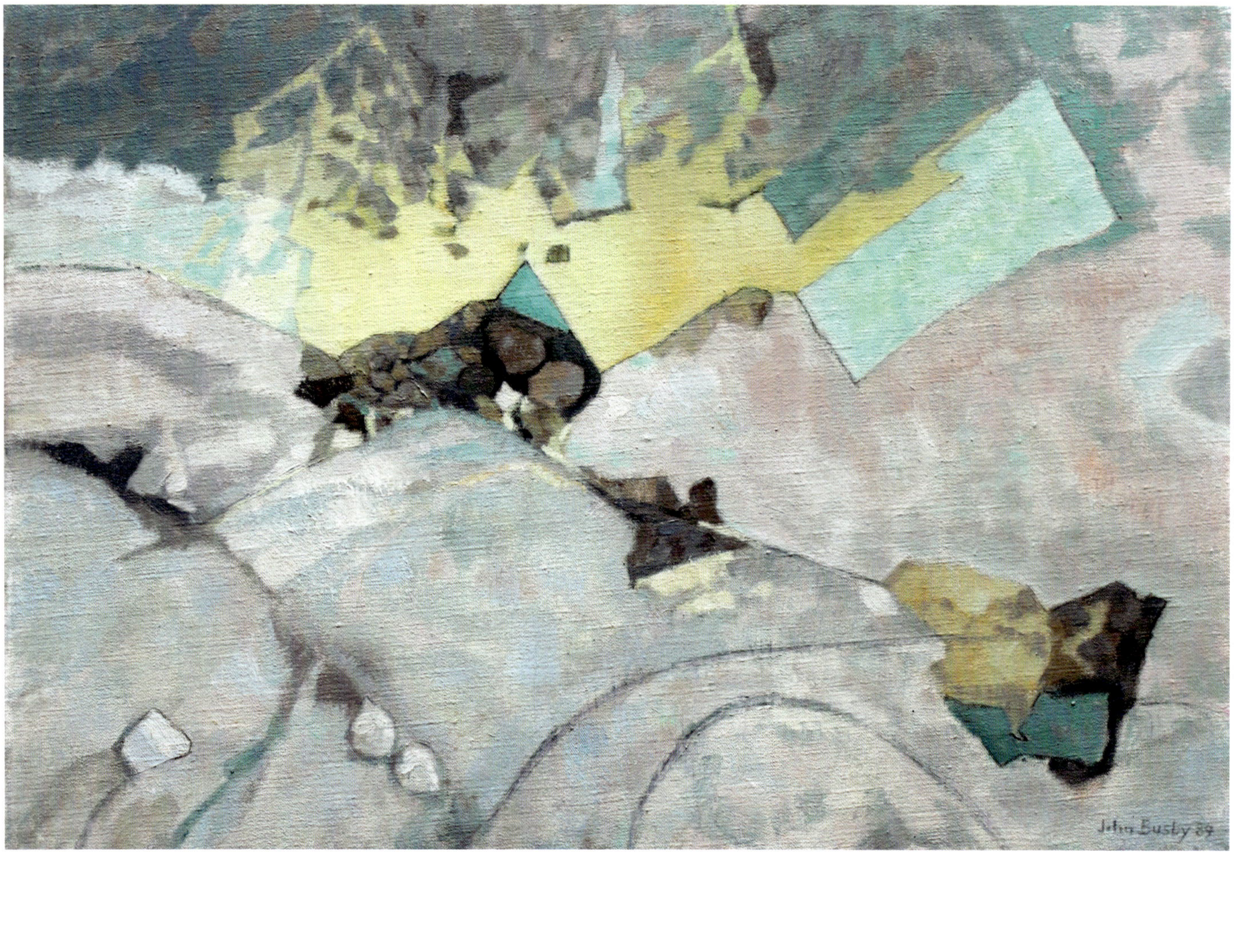

Small rock pool

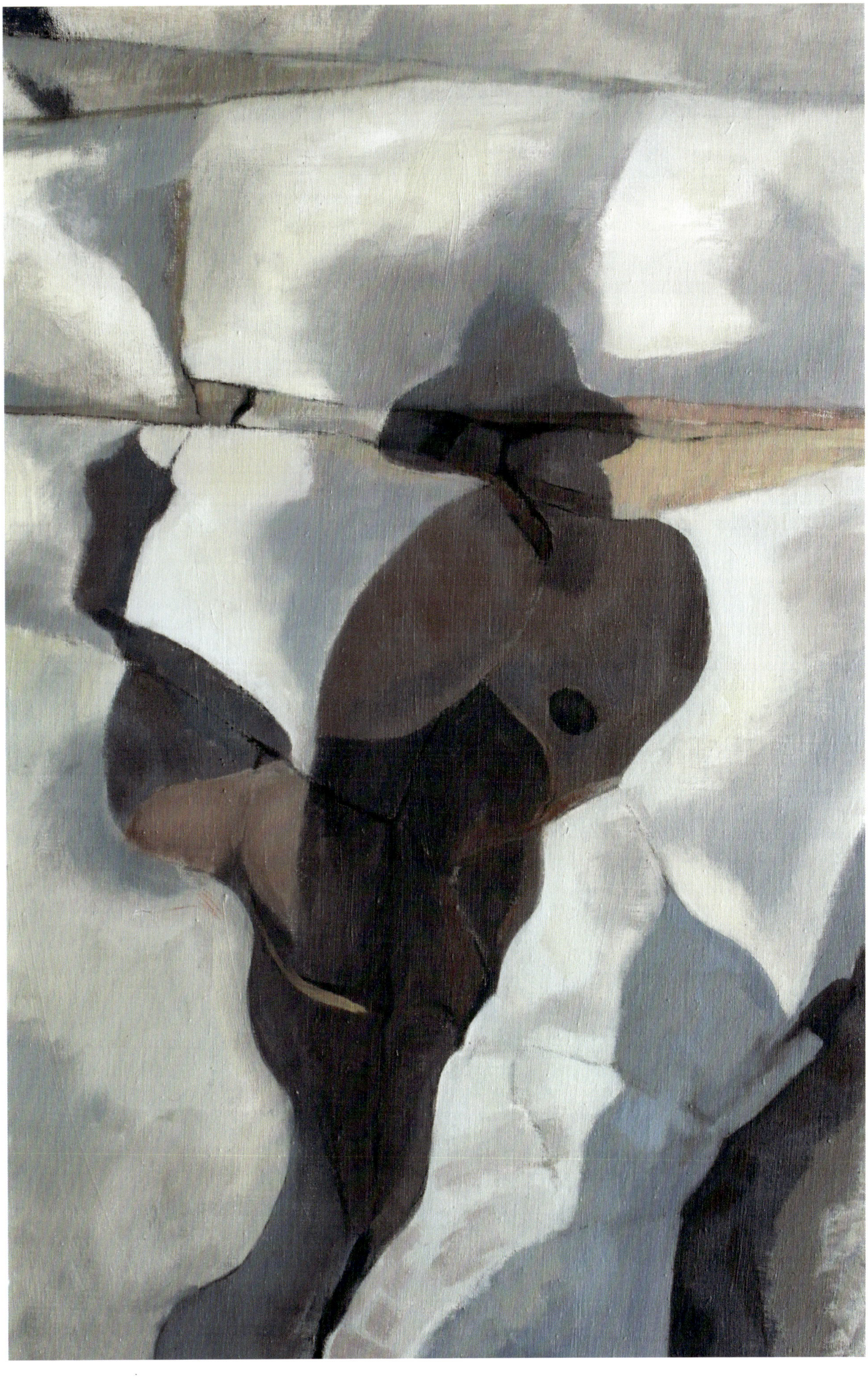

Variations on a rock pool, number 5

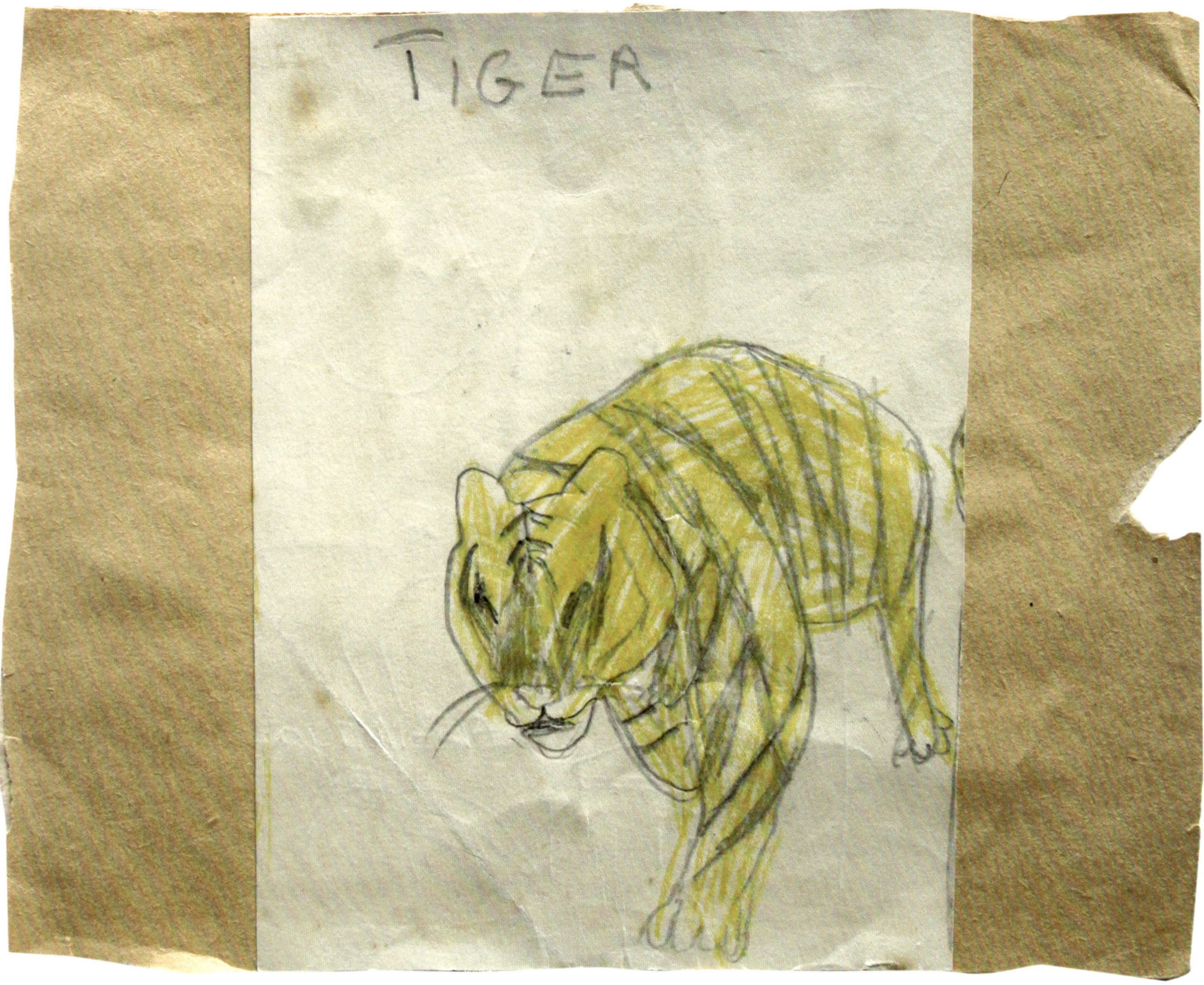
TIGER

Tigers in India

'India' – the name itself conjures up many images. To my generation in the West these inevitably include tourist pictures of the Taj Mahal, exotic temples, elephants, sari-clad women, turbaned men, the Jungle Book, Ghandi, Mother Theresa, and news footage of poverty and natural disasters.

I have only seen a small part of Madhya Pradesh, but I suspect that for all who have been to India, the reality leaves a confused impression – the pressures of a teeming population; dust, noise, colour, smells, golden light and star-filled nights – life close to the earth and the gods of nature, a resilient, but fatalistic spirit in the struggle for existence.

The seeming chaos of human life contrasts with the calm of wild India. Jungles which once dominated large areas are now preserved as diminishing islands in the sea of humanity. Here, the animals can live their own lives, if humans allow, and among them the tiger is still 'Lord of the Jungle': but for how long?

Whether or not many Indians have actually seen a tiger, the big cat plays an important part in the culture, folklore, and psyche of the people, rather as the wolf did in mediaeval Europe – a fearsome presence lurking out there. It also represents a fierce independent spirit and a symbol of national pride – a force to be reckoned with!

A real tiger, hanging on in the remaining jungles, has to carry a lot of human conceptual baggage around with it; not least a belief that its bones have magic healing properties. A dead tiger represents a fortune to the hunter.

Perhaps wildlife filmmakers come closest to showing the real life of a tiger: the objective eye of a camera recording moments unaffected by human emotions; something that is almost impossible for artists to do. Art has to have feelings!

When I was a young child I wanted to be a tiger. Tigers burned bright in my imagination and I could imitate their actions long before I had heard of William Blake or Henry V. I am not sure why; perhaps because progressing

< A childhood tiger from imagination (aged 6)

(This text is based on a talk to the ANF Tiger exhibition at the Burrell in April 2000)

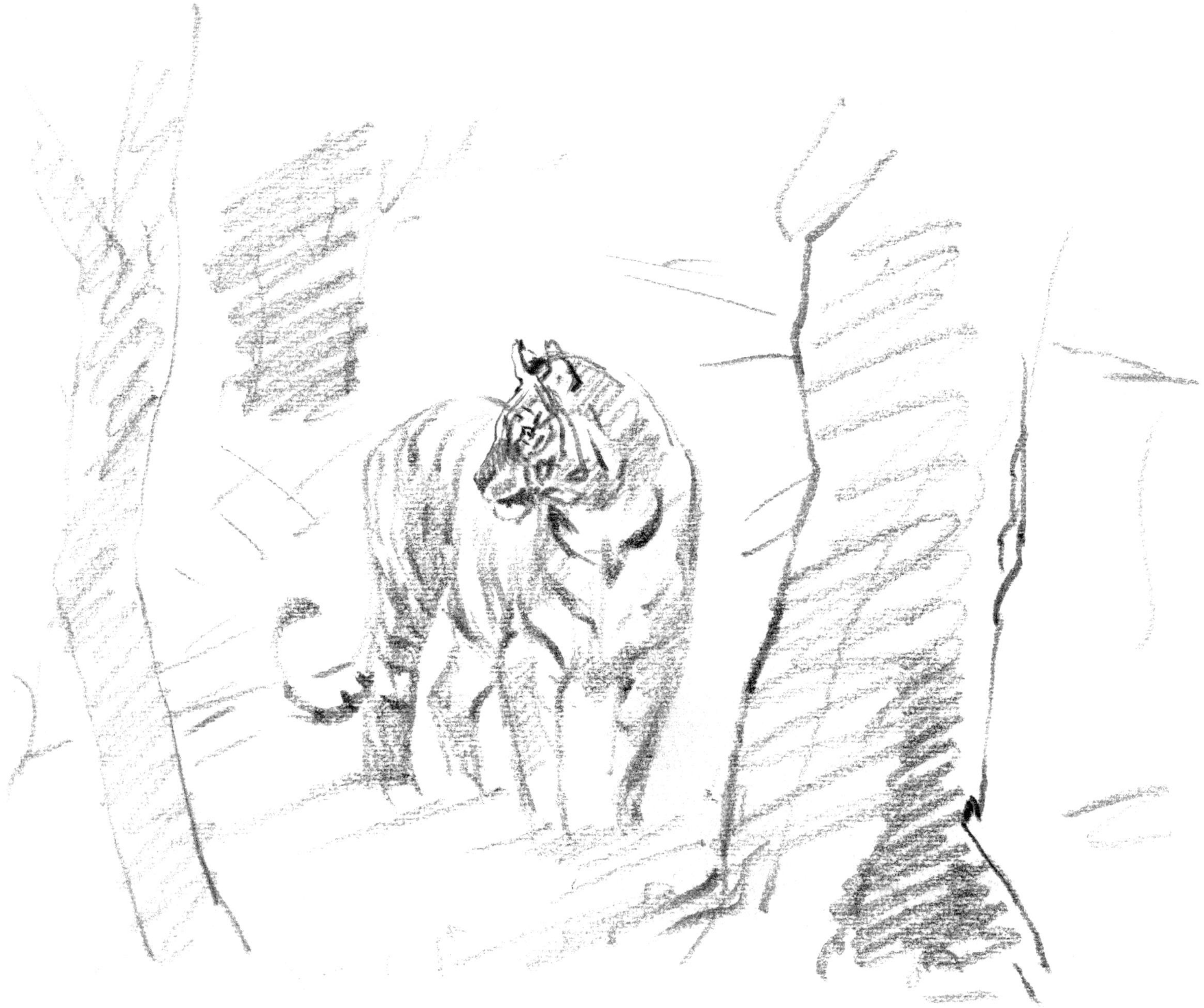

Sita, a female tiger at Bandhavgarh

on all fours was not long past. I could prowl round the house ready to pounce on my younger sister, my treble growls transposed into deep reverberating roars in my mind's ear.

At that age I could fully identify with the little boy whose adventures with tigers also filled my imagination. I mean of course, that classic of children's literature; *Little Black Sambo* by Helen Bannerman – a story I knew by heart long before I could read.

So, Little Black Sambo put on all his fine clothes and went for a walk in the jungle. And bye and bye he met a tiger who said to him, 'Little Black Sambo, I'm going to eat you up'. And Little Black Sambo said, 'Oh please mister tiger, don't eat me up and I will give you my beautiful little red coat'. 'Very well', said the tiger, 'I won't eat you this time, but you must give me your beautiful little red coat'. So the tiger put on the beautiful little red coat and went away saying, 'Now I'm the grandest tiger in the jungle'.

You will have to read the rest to find out what happened to our hero later – that is if you can find a copy not banned by those who see only colour prejudice in the title.

Bye and bye I found myself in an Indian jungle facing a tiger, but safe on the back of an elephant, not having to exchange clothes for my life.

At first, it all seemed unreal; the mechanics of getting there; air flight; crowded Delhi, an horrendous six hour taxi drive, and finally queuing for an elephant and a guided search for a tiger – a tiger with a name even!

My natural inclination in the wild is to be still and to watch: to understand and experience the animal's world. Sharing time with an otter and her cubs on the shore of a Shetland loch after a long dawn wait was a time of magic. In India, the stage is set for you and your entry and exit are managed. Tigers are powerful. One is grateful for the size and strength of an elephant and accepts the limitations. With time rationed to 10 minutes, does one draw or just watch? Instinctively I react as an artist; I make marks.

My elephant-back sketches were rather less tiger-like than those I drew when I was six years old, before I had seen one. Perhaps the tiger of our imagination is imbued with more 'tigerishness' than the real thing.

Sita, a female tiger at Bandhavgarh

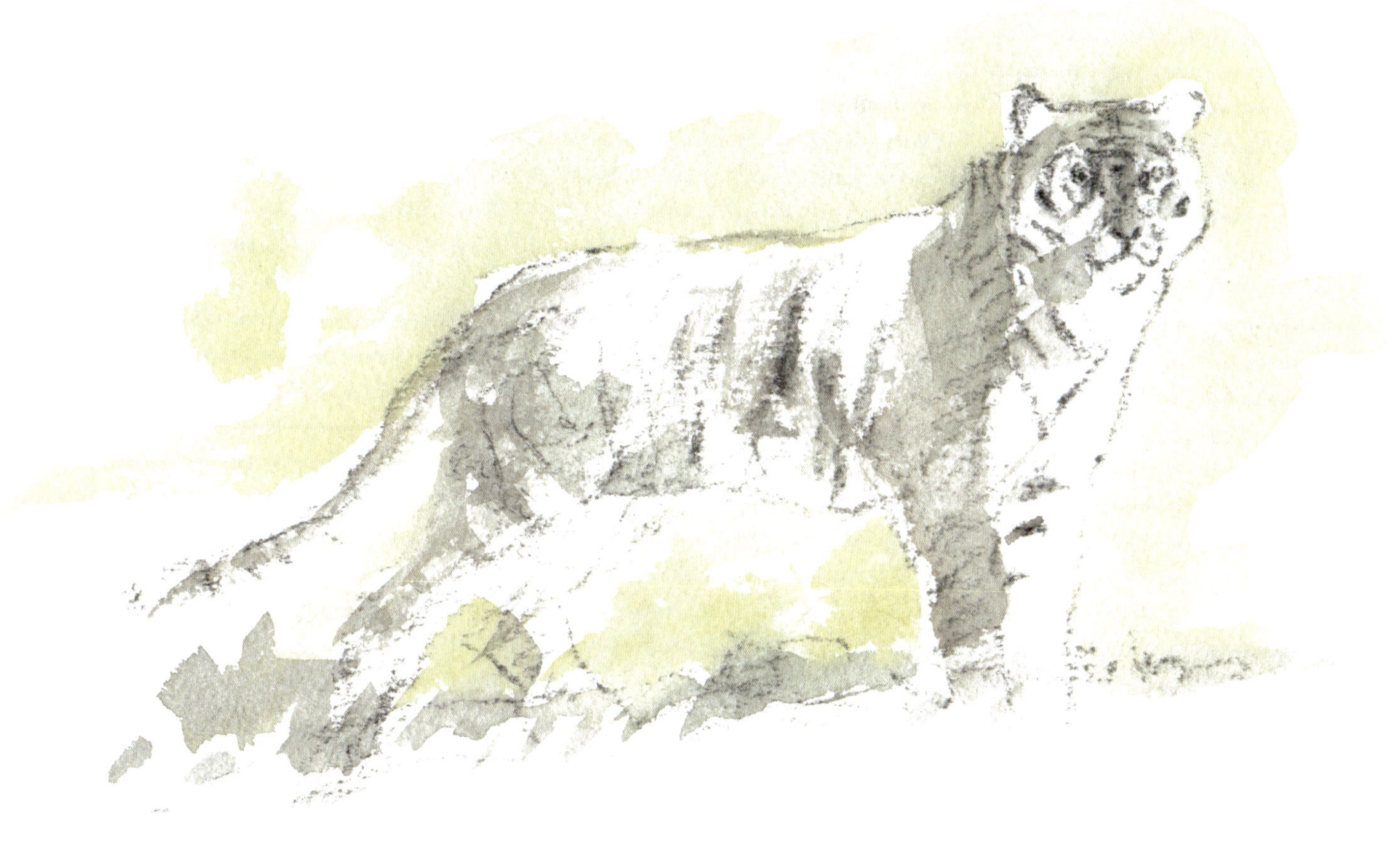

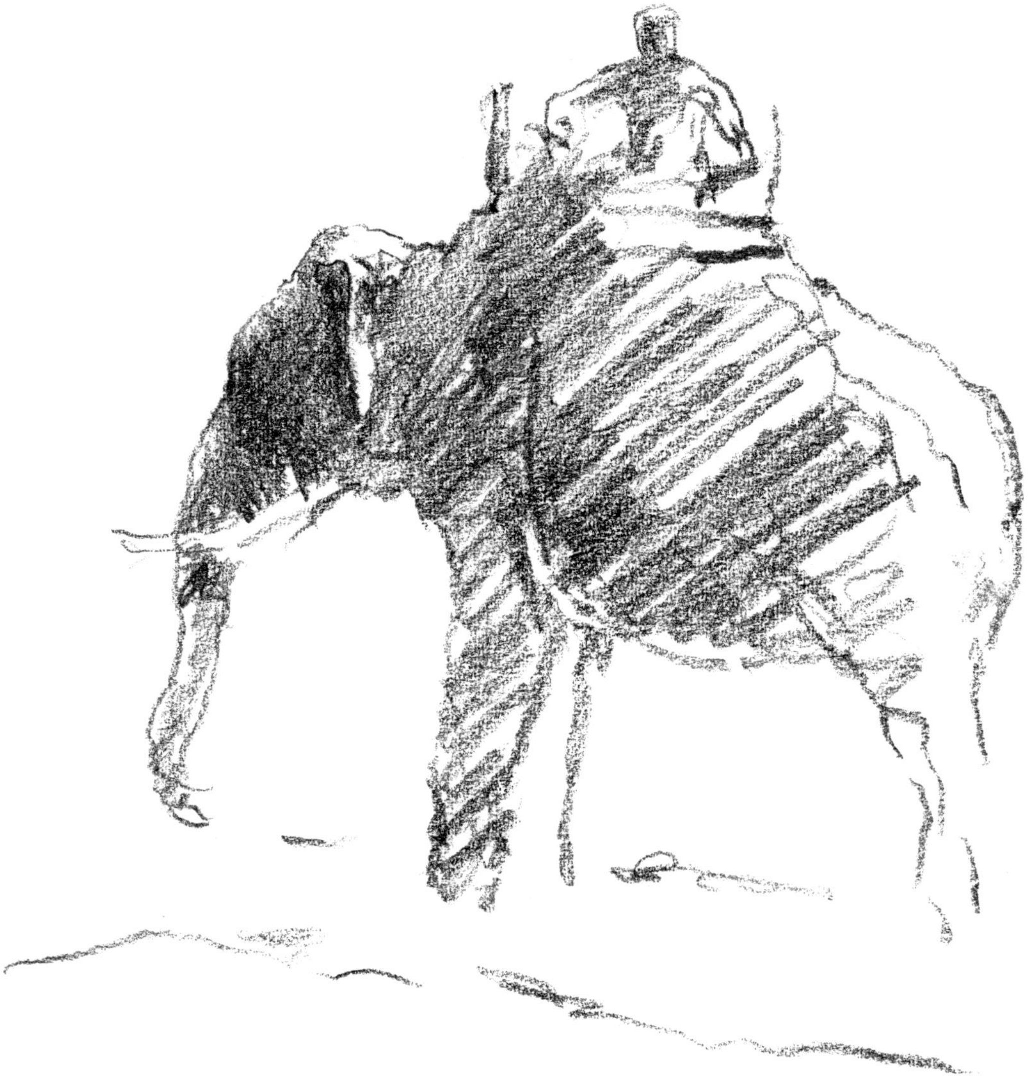

An off-duty elephant

Sitting on the back of an elephant looking at a tiger a few yards away – what is important? The setting; the tiger lying in dappled sunlight; drawing the right number of stripes; the crows and parrots overhead; jungle noises; the anxious shifting of the elephant from one leg to another?

Perhaps even those things one could not see – the tiger's night of hunting before this rest; the secret burning of its life out of human sight?

This first tiger, a female called 'Sita', was resting with a half-eaten carcass of a chital deer. After a few minutes of being peered at, she rose and walked away. As she did so she disturbed another deer, and more as an instinctive reaction than in earnest she rushed in pursuit. The deer escaped and the action only lasted a few seconds.

Later we saw the male tiger, 'Charger', walking along a jungle track with his tail held aloft, and the guide pointed out another tiger which was invisible to us until an ear twitched, and the pattern of leaves and shadows resolved into fragments of tiger stripes and a watching yellow eye.

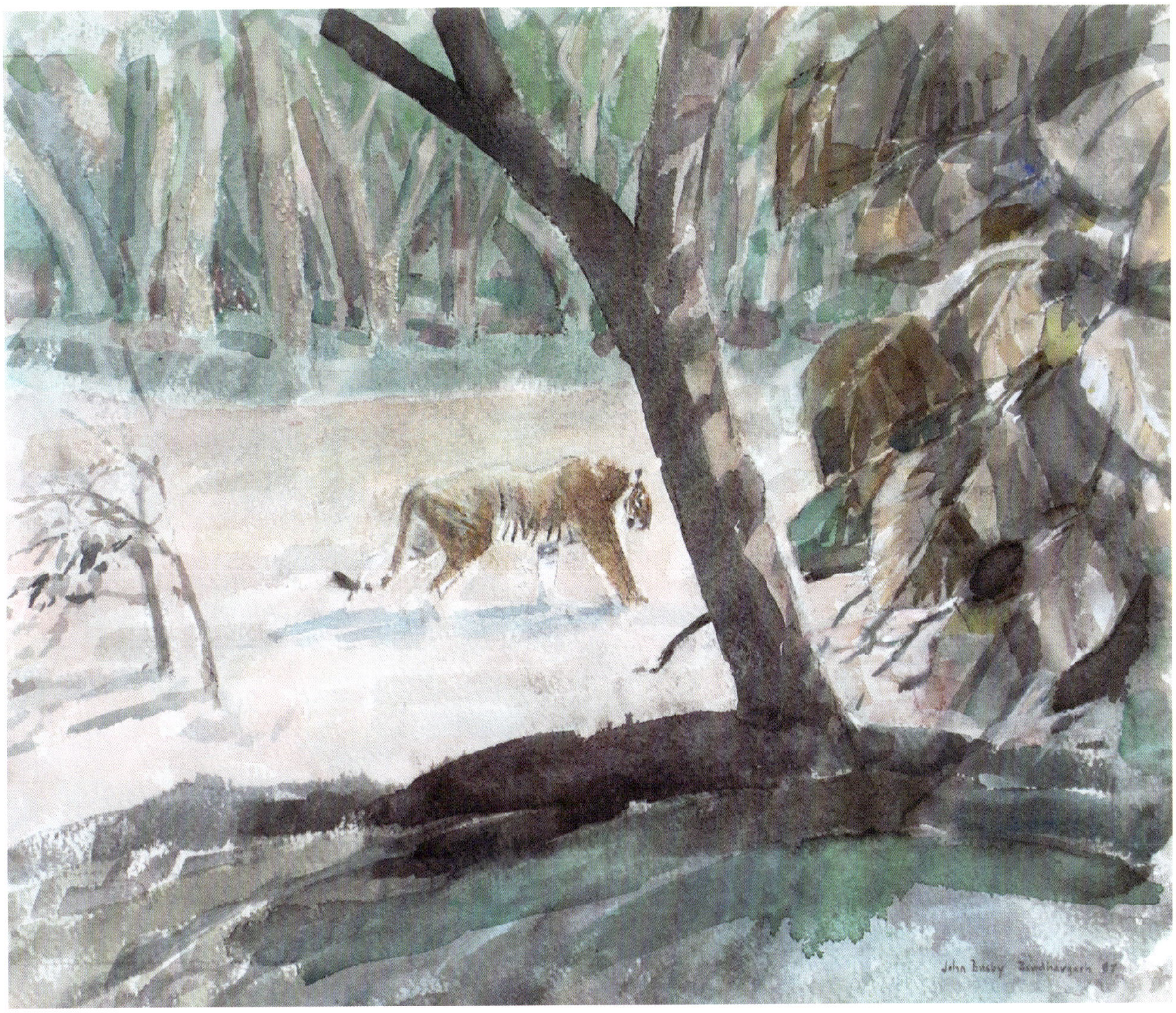

The male tiger 'Charger'

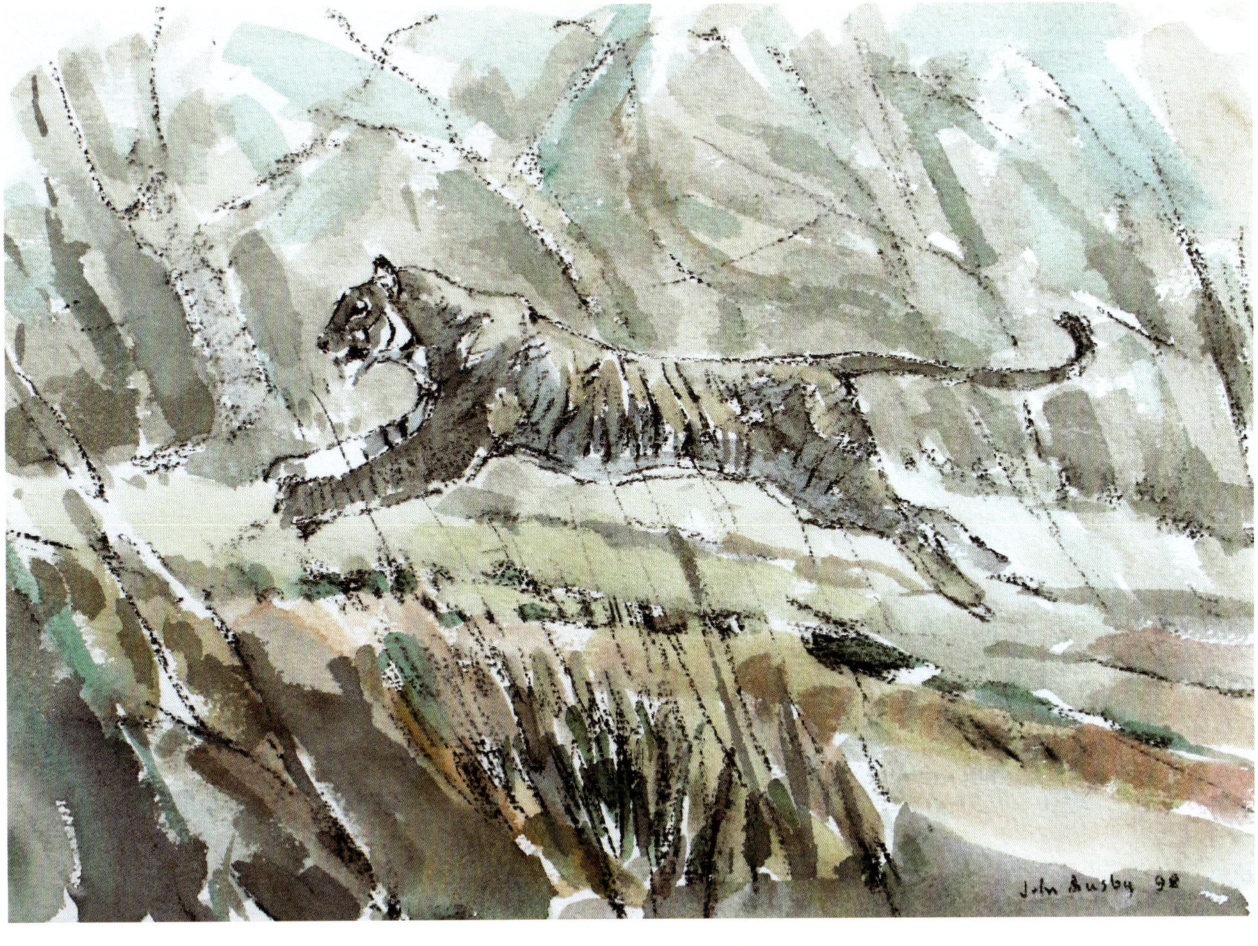

The female tiger 'Sita'

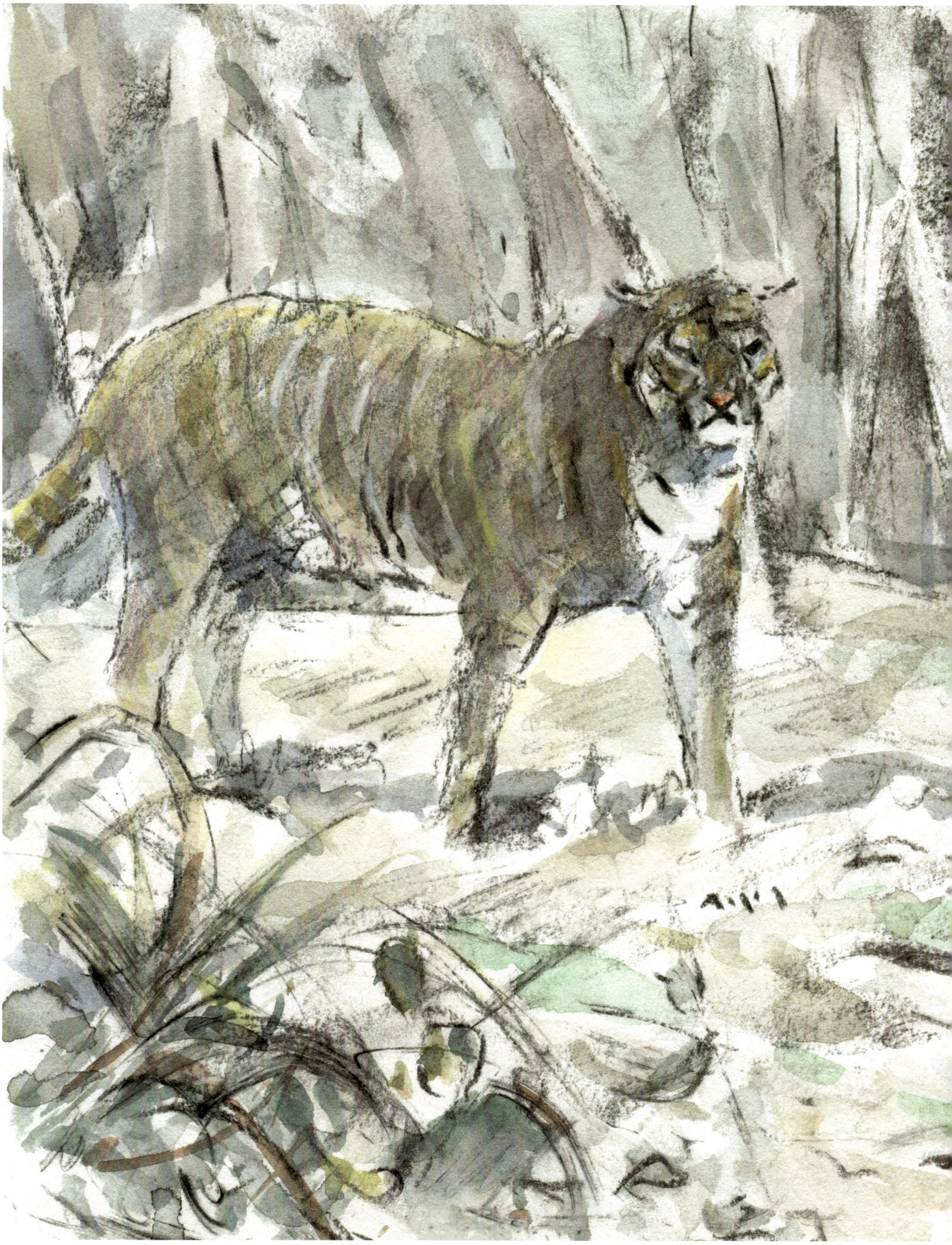

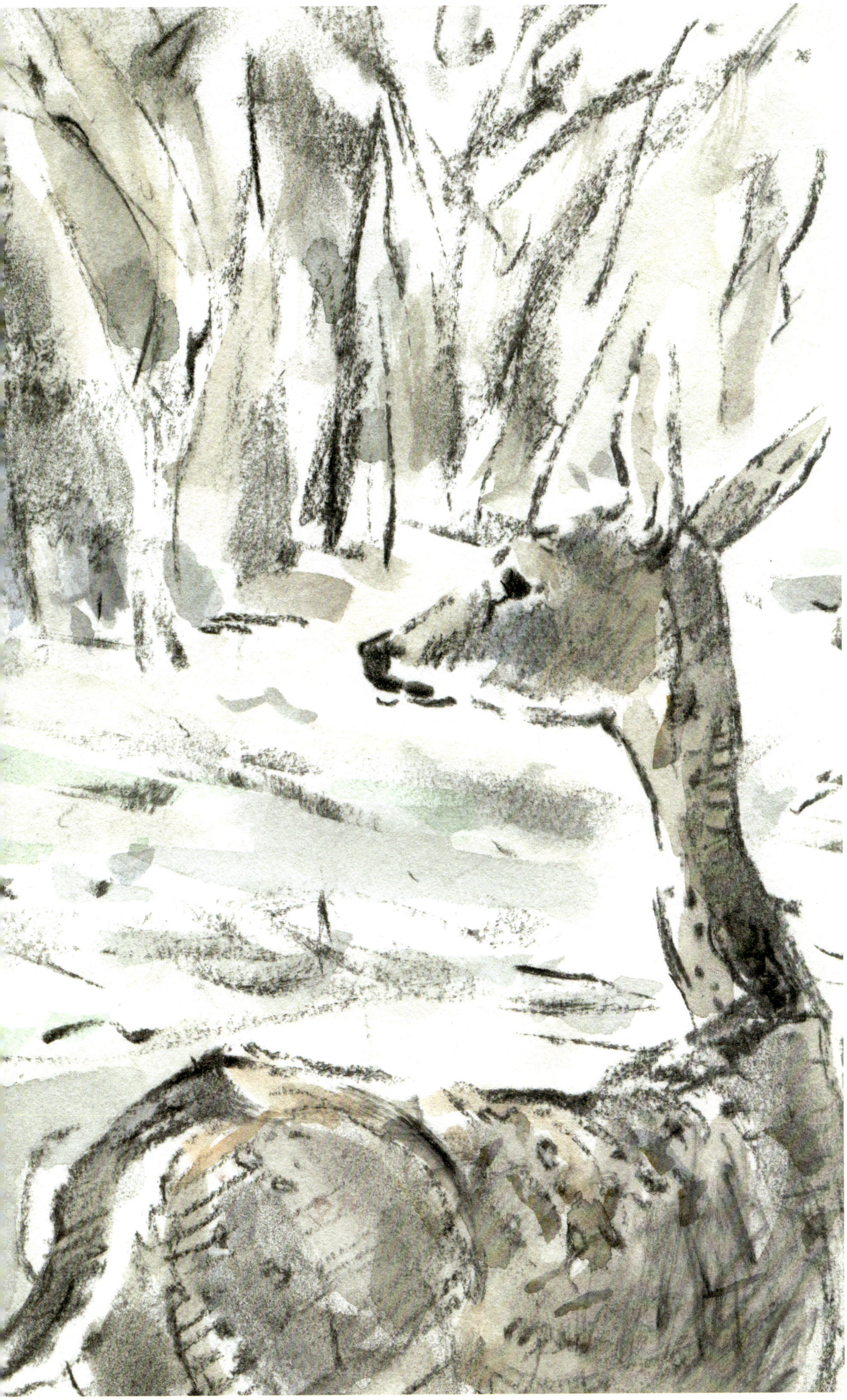

Sita is woken by a spotted deer: tension before the chase begins

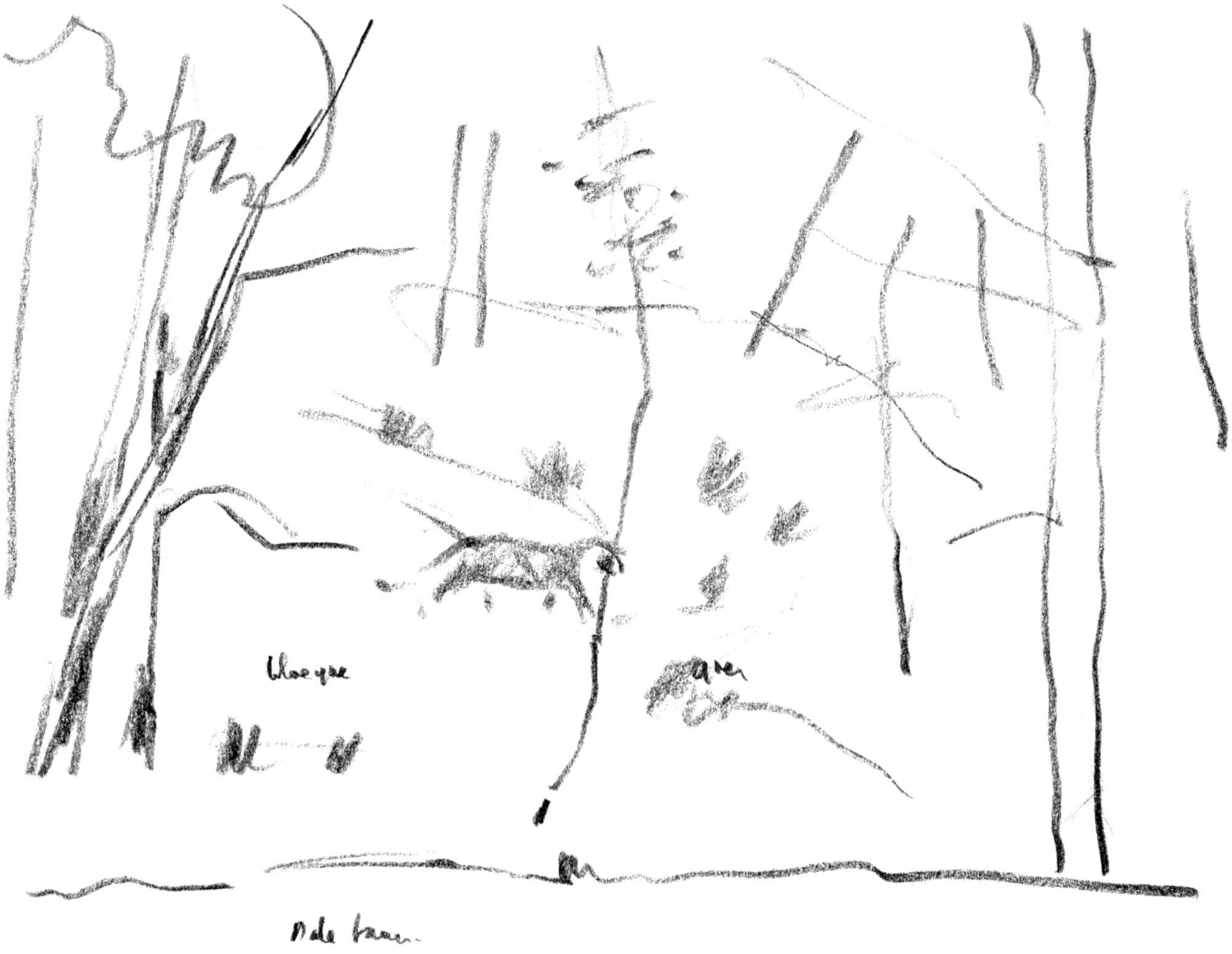

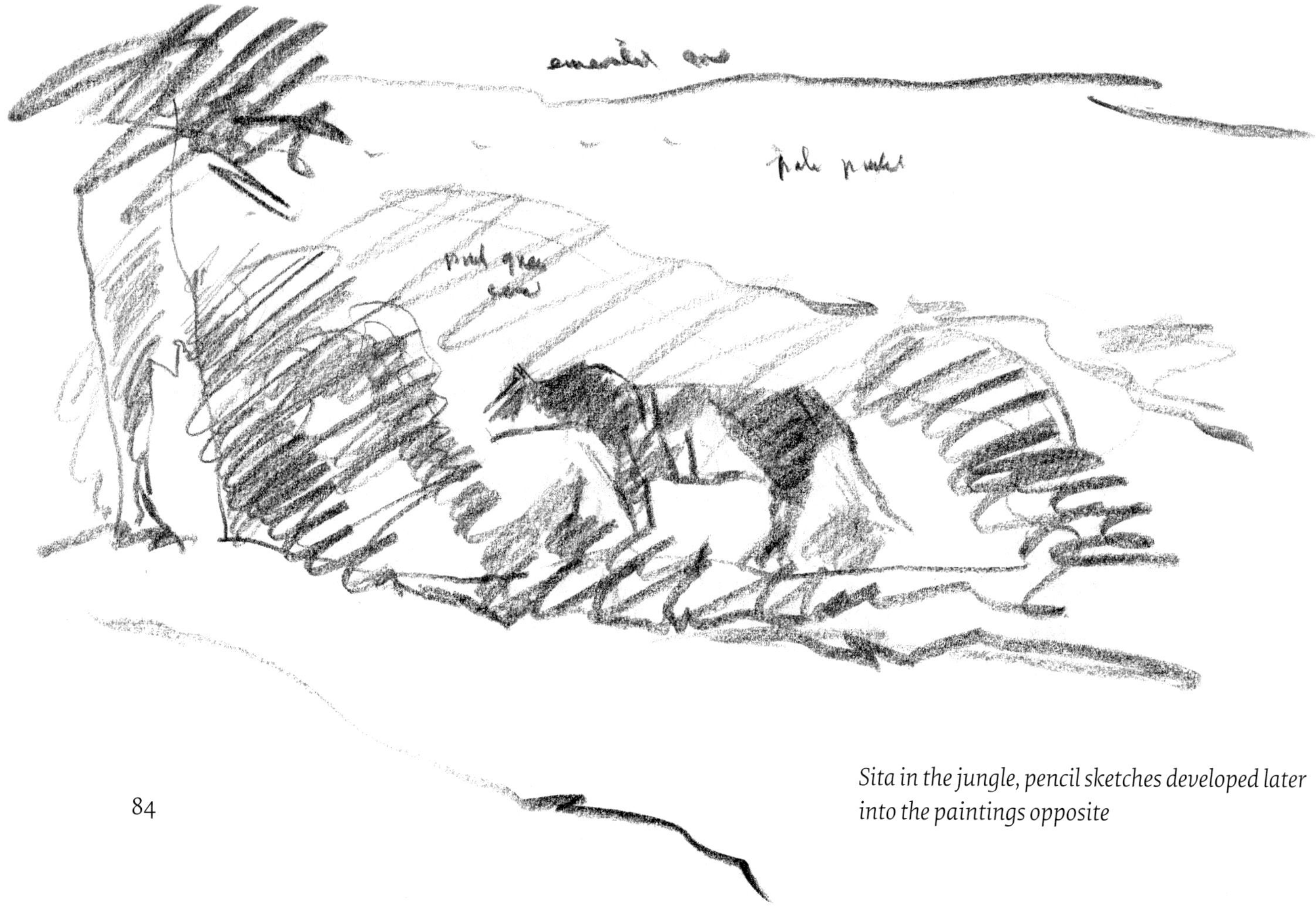

Sita in the jungle, pencil sketches developed later into the paintings opposite

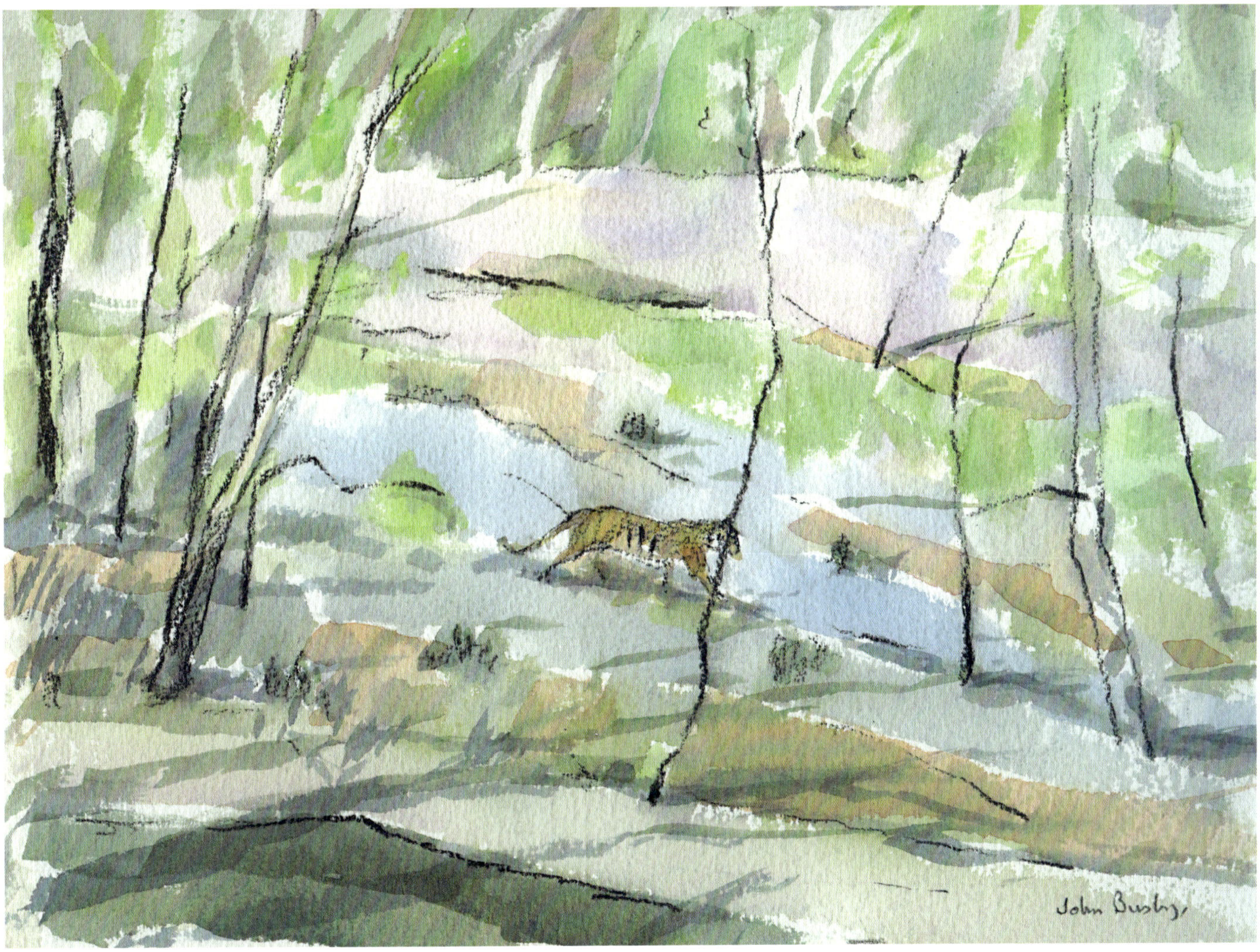

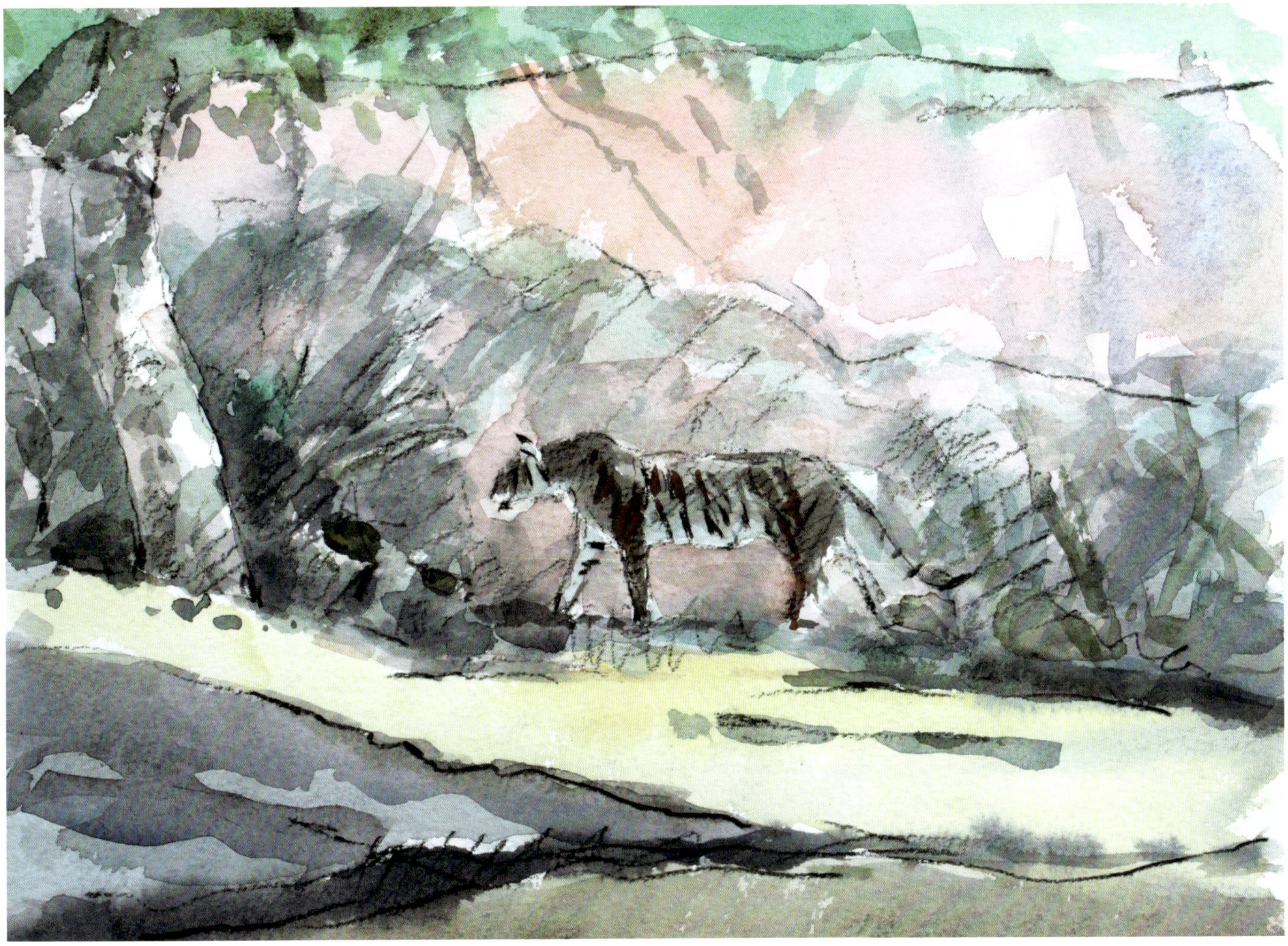

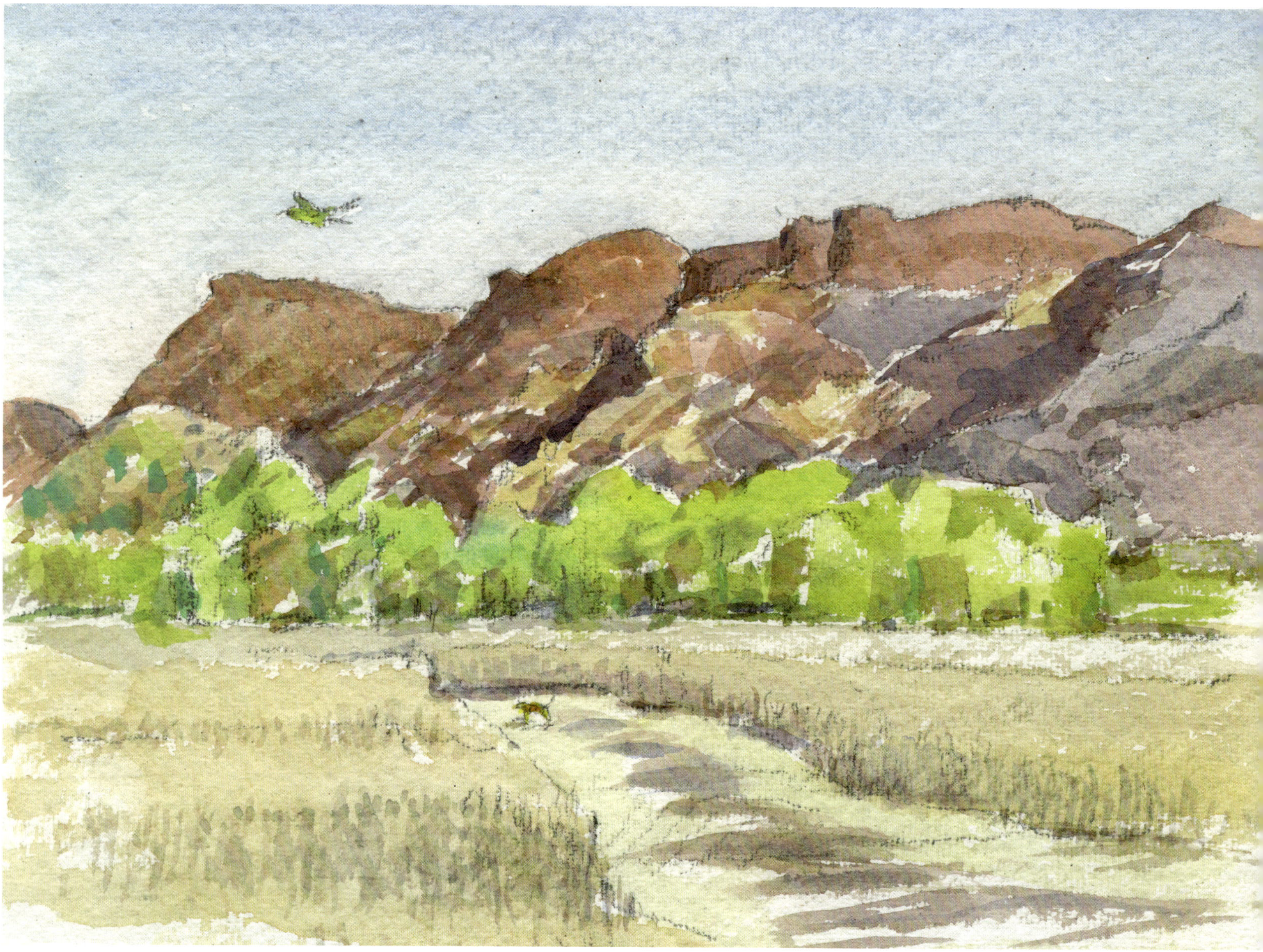

Red sandstone cliffs and tiger

I found the jungle more beautiful than I expected. The terrain of red sandstone crags with grassland valleys in between was as open as a European forest. The trees, some still to come into leaf, were tall and elegant, sometimes draped with sinister creepers. Bomb-burst clumps of bamboo and the carpeting of fallen leaves criss-crossed by shadows, gave ideal cover for predators and prey alike. We had views of many animals – monkeys, deer, boar, mongoose and jackal, and more than 80 species of bird including noisy barbets and parakeets, brilliant blue rollers and kingfishers, emerald green bee-eaters, a sleepy fish owl, storks, eagles and hornbills.

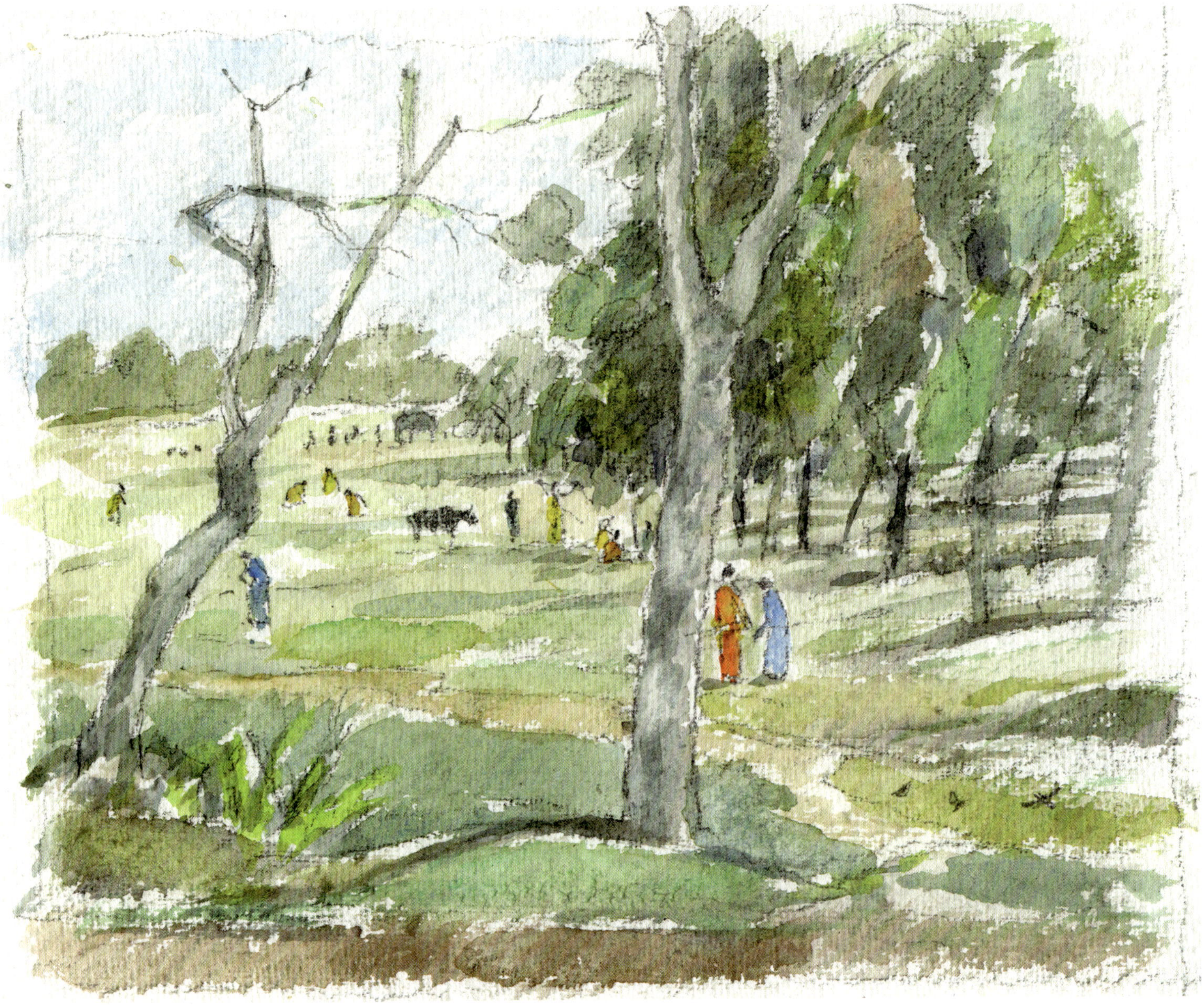

Villagers and elephant

The little river was a focal point for village life. Water for washing – everything from clothes to children, cars to elephants – a colourful scene of women in bright saris, cattle and egrets, reminiscent of Gauguin's Tahiti.

The village itself was a street of open stalls for trade, simple houses and small-holdings, barefoot children, craftsmen skilled enough to mend our taxi's split engine casing in a few hours; much poverty even by Indian standards, but also laughter and curiosity without hostility.

Some children wanted to see what I was drawing and they recognised the animals. A young girl drew a peacock for me. Others treated the paper I

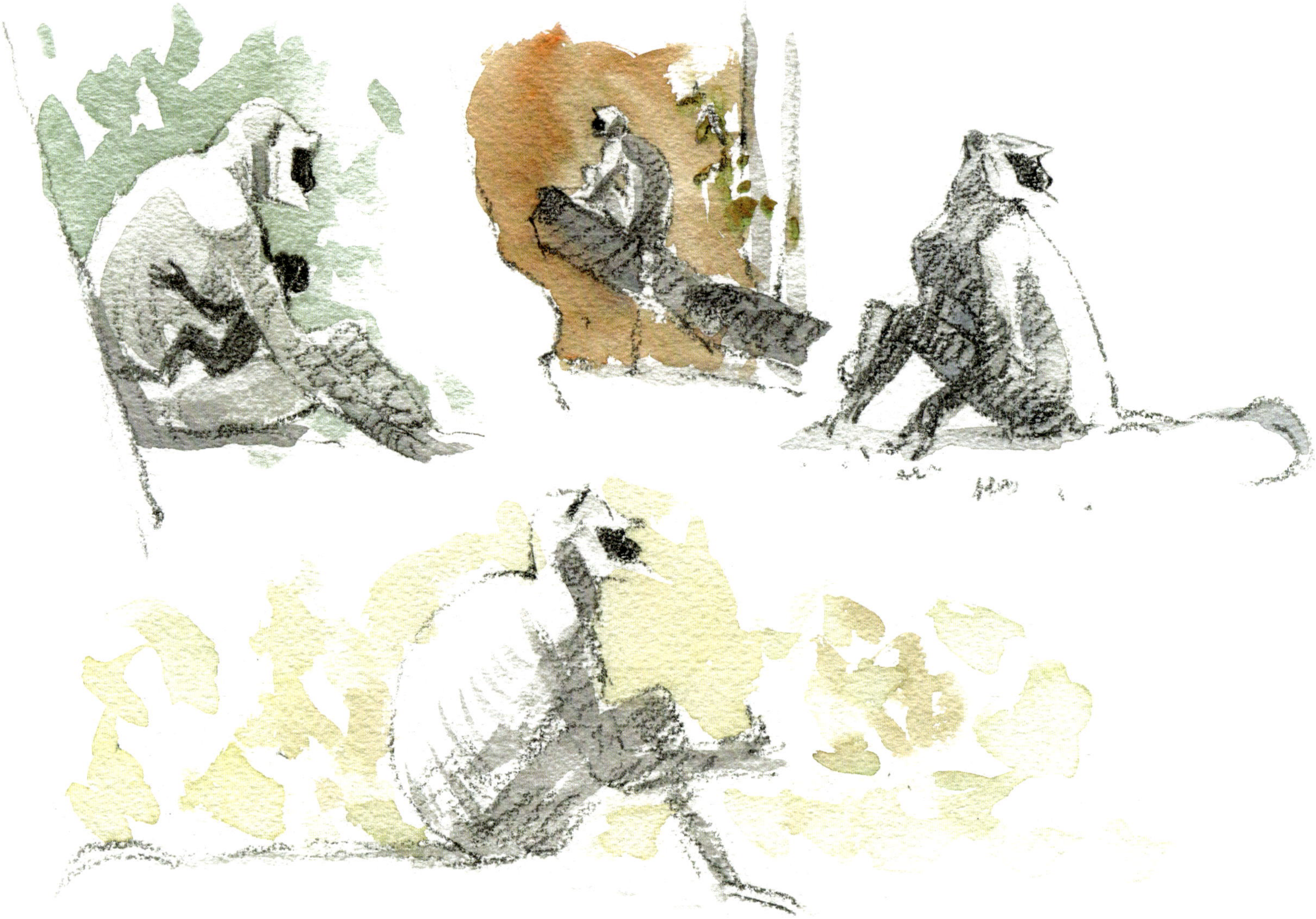

Langur monkeys with baby

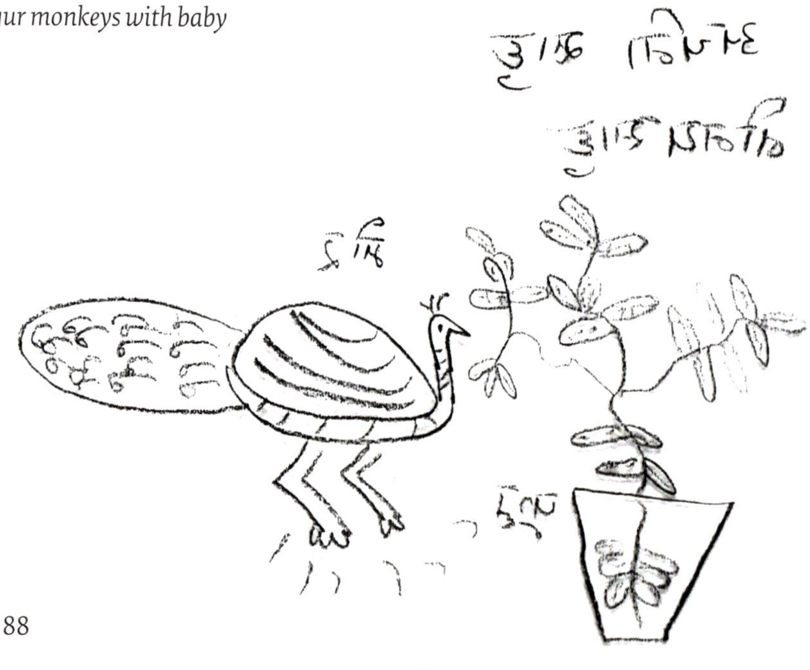

Peacock by young Indian child

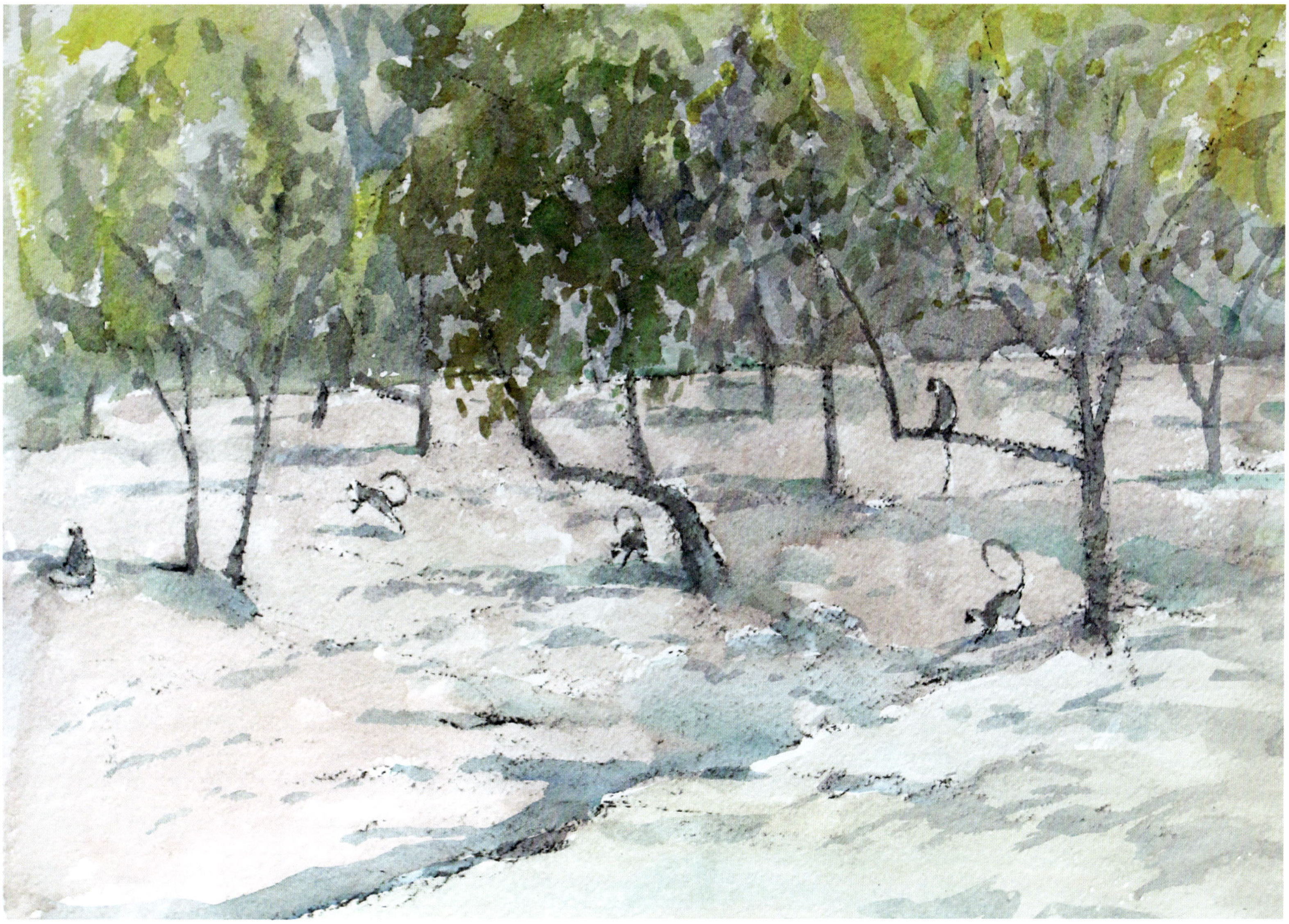

Langur monkeys

gave them as a rare substance, not to be marked in any way: they worked on slates at school.

Later with encouragement from other ANF artists they painted jungle animals on large sheets of paper with great gusto.

Whether my work gets close to a true image of India I don't know. Like my childhood miming of the action of animals and birds, I feel that my drawing has to prowl, spring and fly; launching into the empty whiteness of a page with marks that may grow – sometimes becoming clear and meaningful in the process; sometimes disappearing behind a confused undergrowth of thoughts. Not all our experiences can be resolved in art, yet many remain, like tigers, to haunt us all our lives.

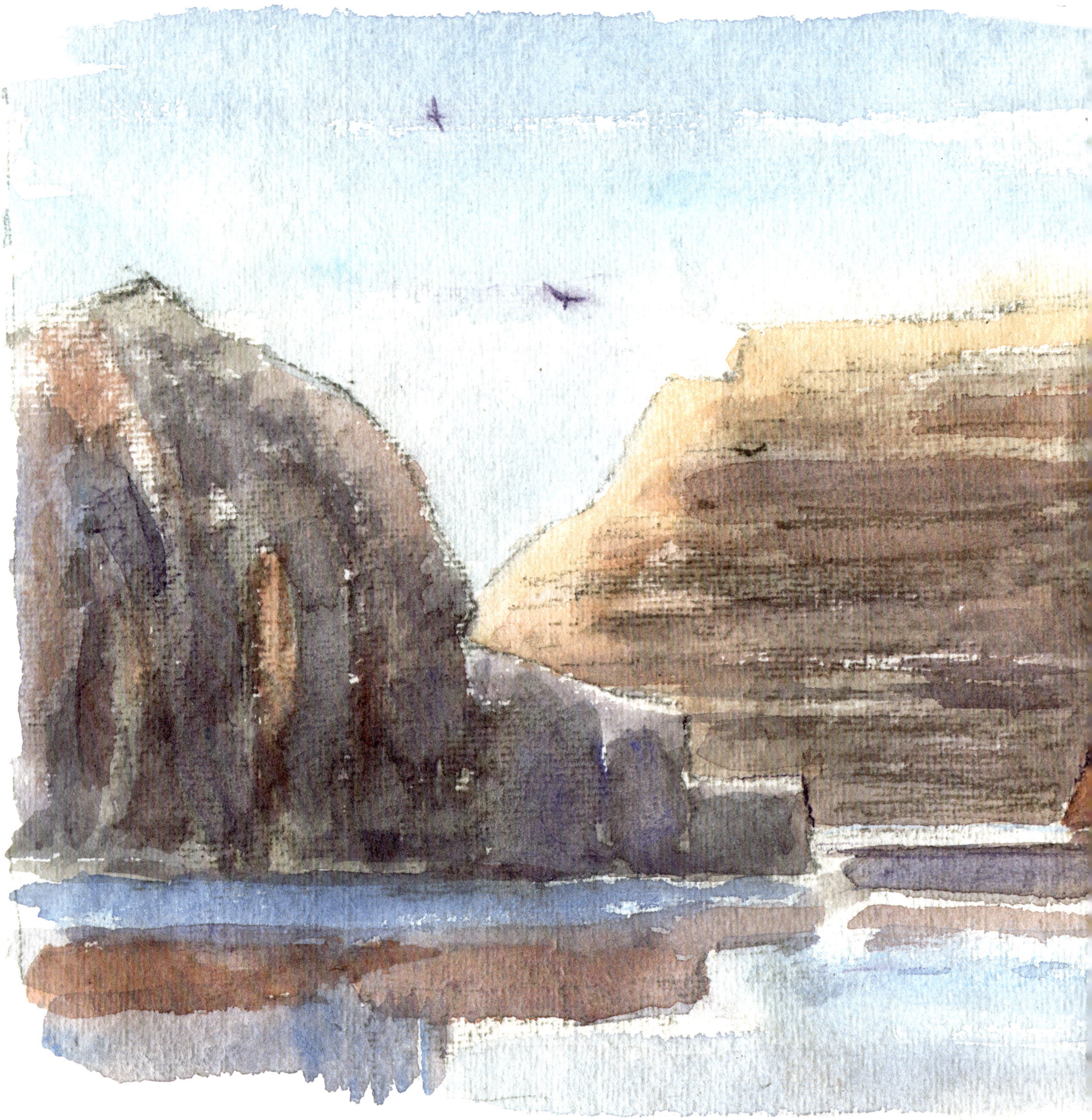

Kimberley Coast

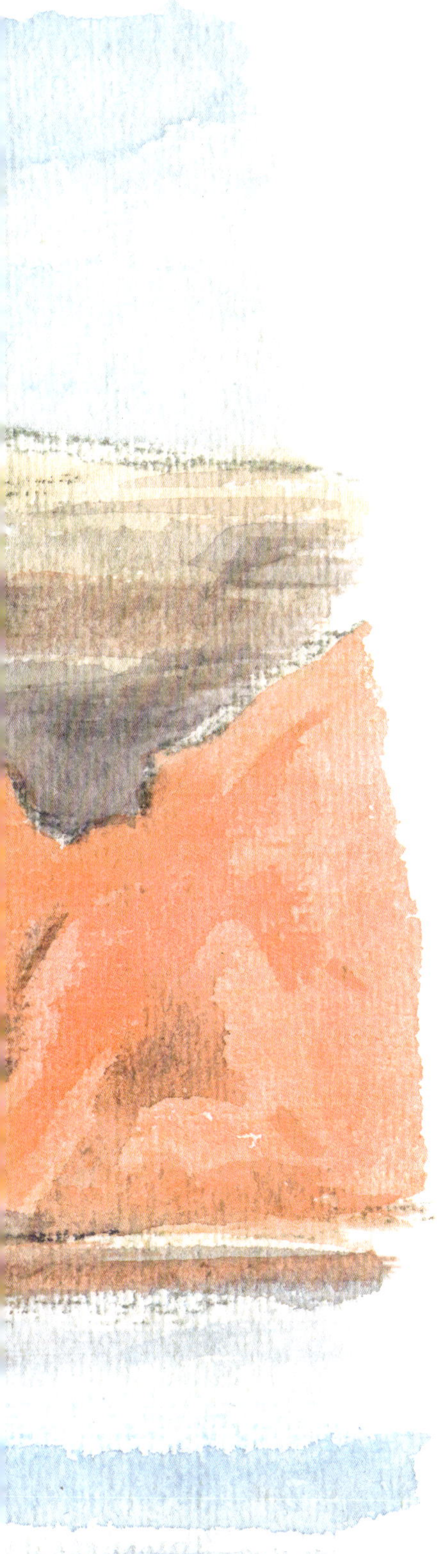

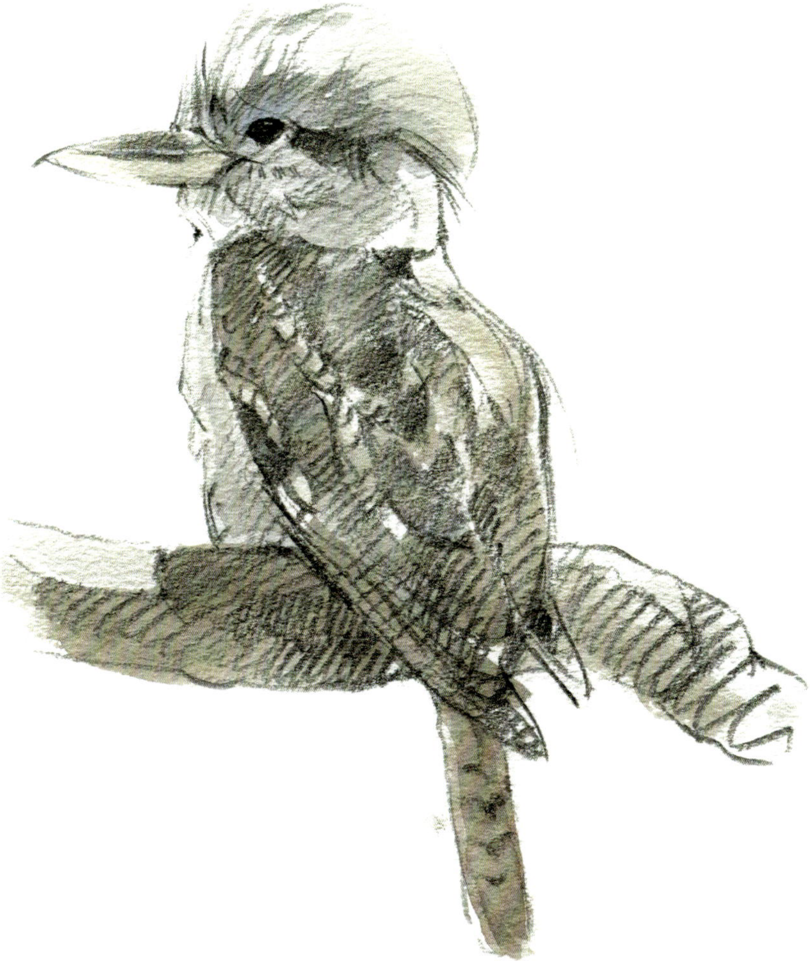

Kimberley coast

Kookaburra

The kookaburra is a bird synonymous with Australia. It is a handsome kingfisher renowned for its striking appearance and loud laughing call. But even after two visits to Australia, which included Sydney, its parks, islands and the eucalyptus forests and ravines of the Blue Mountains, Uluru, (Ayres Rock), and the Northern coastline – I never saw one.

This bird was drawn at Harewood Park aviary in Yorkshire!

In 2006 my wife and I journeyed along the north coast of Australia from Broome to Darwin in a small cruise boat. It was a coastline of cliffs, reefs, mangrove fringed lagoons, islands and river creeks, little changed since the days when first discovered by European explorers.

We covered hundreds of miles without seeing any habitations – no houses, towns or villages. The boat was small enough to venture into the river gorges that cut through high red sandstone cliffs. Early explorers thought these waterways would provide a way into the interior, only to find, as we did, that the navigable river ended abruptly; blocked by a sheer rock face with a waterfall. On the Berkley and King George rivers, these waterfalls had carved channels back from the coast for some 40 miles over millions of years!

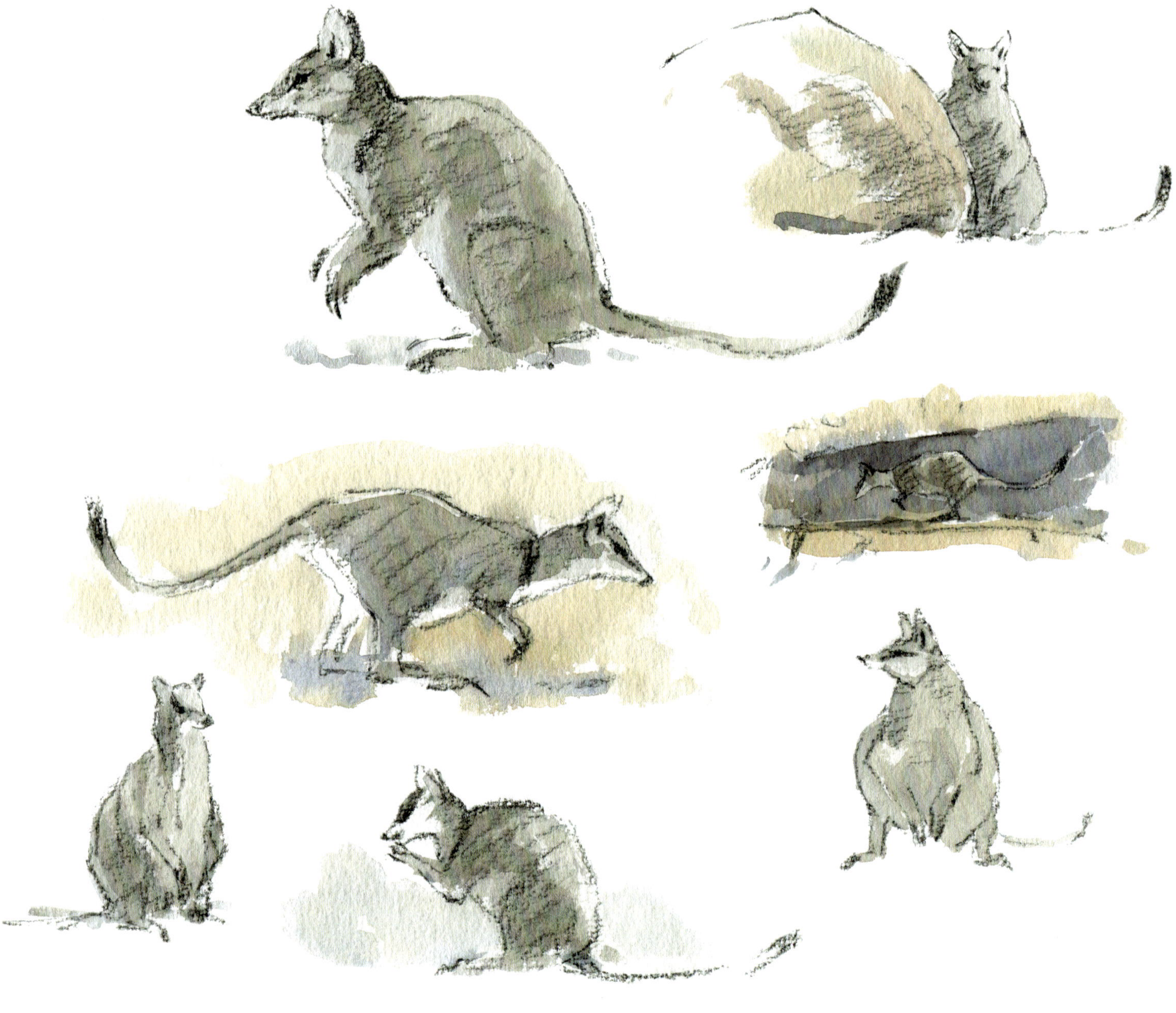

Rock wallabies

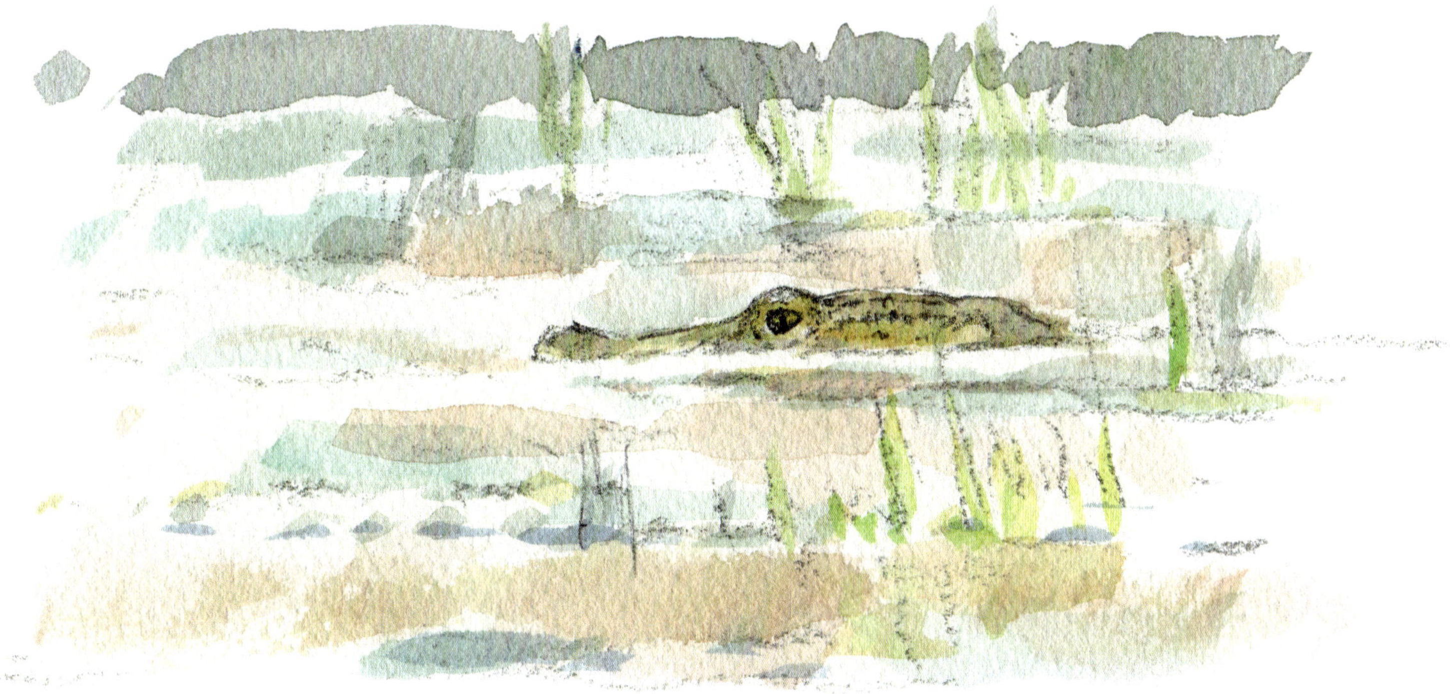

Young 'Saltie'

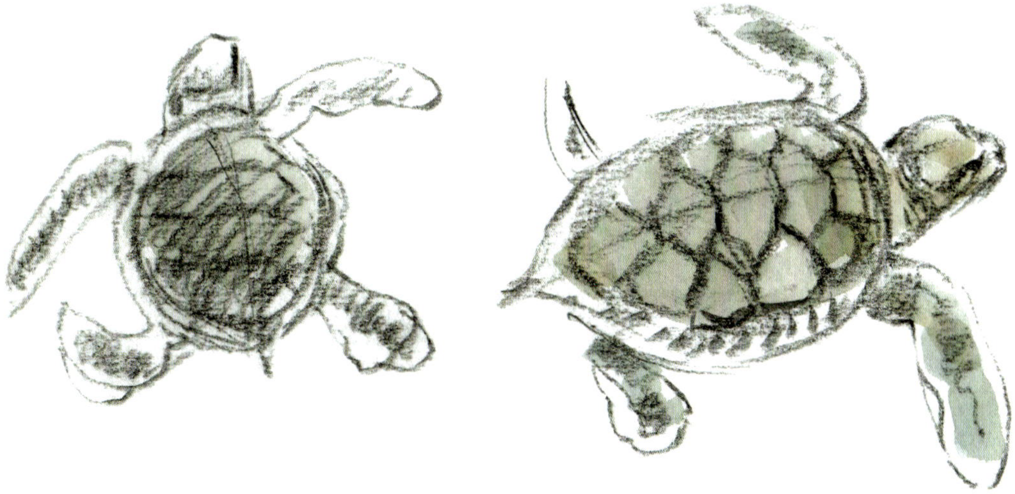

Flat-backed turtle hatchlings

From the boat we saw rock wallabies on the cliff ledges of the Berkley River gorge. They are smaller than kangaroos, standing about two feet tall. On this terrain there was not much space for jumping.

Other fauna included humpback whales on the open sea, dugongs (manatees), in the estuaries, and salt-water crocodiles up the creeks (which made any thought of bathing too dangerous to contemplate). We watched flat-backed turtle hatchlings making their way from sand to water on Bare Sand Island.

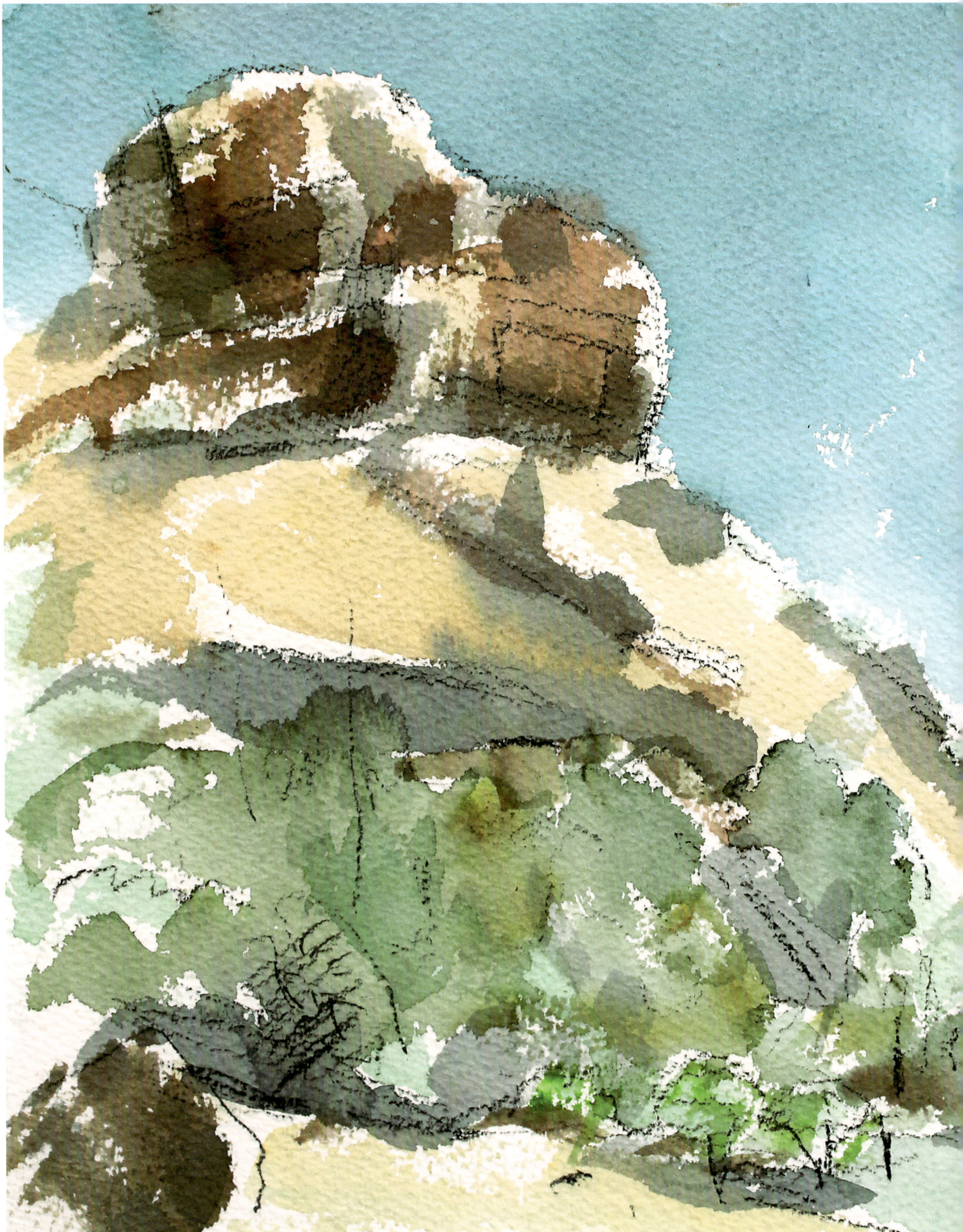

Colourful landscape by the Prince Regent river

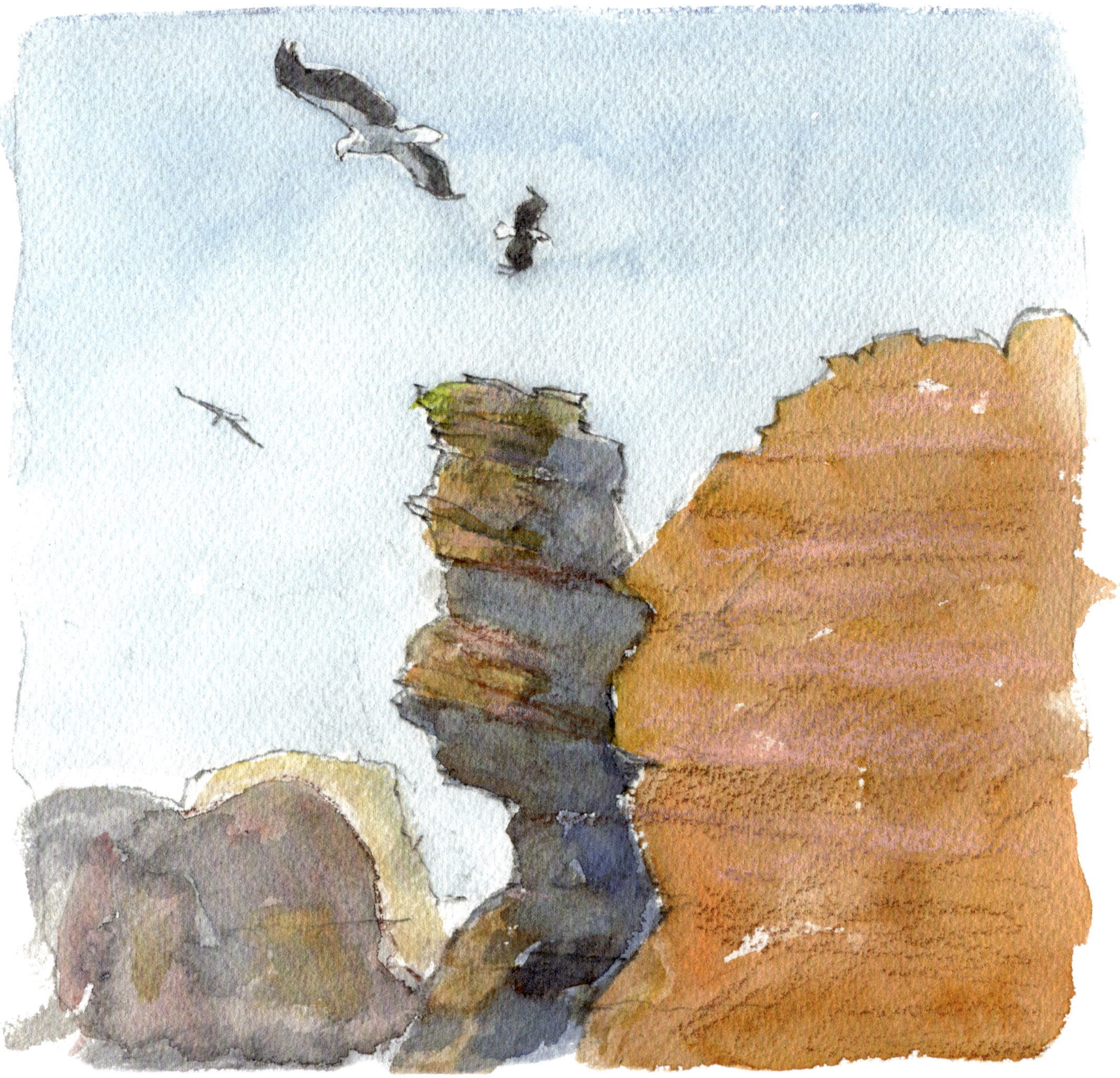

One of the most spectacular birds was the large jabiru (black-necked stork), seen near the mouth of the King George River, together with beach stone curlews. Ospreys and white-bellied sea eagles and various kingfishers fished the rivers. It was a rich area for birds of many species, all new to me; and as remote a wilderness as one could hope to find.

White-bellied sea eagles

As far back as 15,000 years ago the area had been inhabited by Wandjina people, who lived in the north on land now under the sea. At Raft Point we saw paintings on the walls and overhanging roofs of shallow rock caves showing many images of human, fish and animal-like figures. The Aboriginals say that they did not create these paintings, but inherited them from the Wandjina

Jabirus, (black-necked storks), and beach stone curlews >

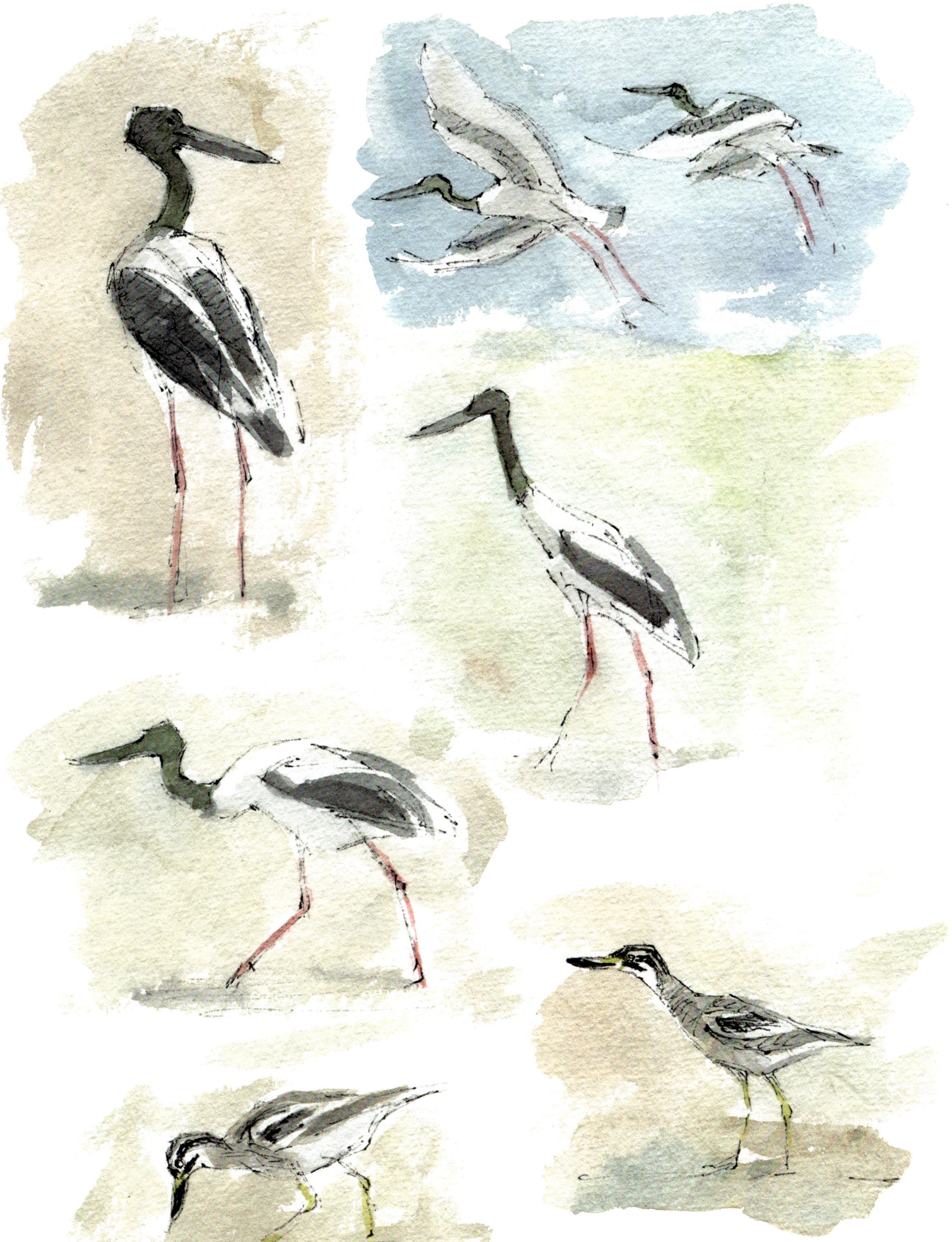

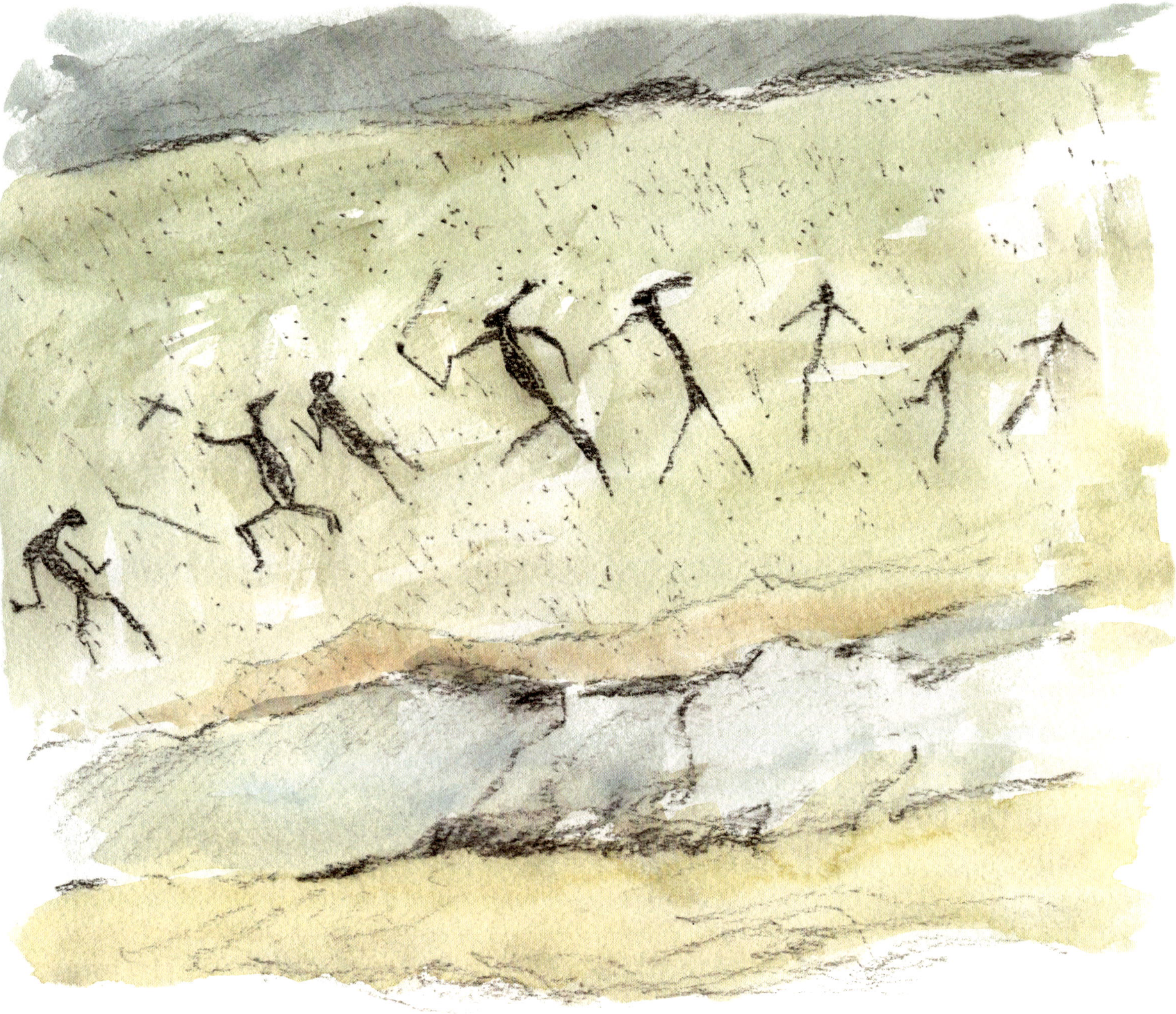

spirits. They have dual meanings as both human and cloud forms. Halo like head surrounds are also lightning in the clouds.

I tried to replicate them as accurately as possible in these drawings.

Another cave showed Gwion Aborigine paintings of hunters; one with a weapon that looked like a boomerang.

Aborigine painting adds another dimension to what we think of as 'art'.

It is good to see that it still thrives in modern Australia.

Gwion figures painted on a cave wall

Wandjina overhanging cave ceiling paintings at Raft Point >

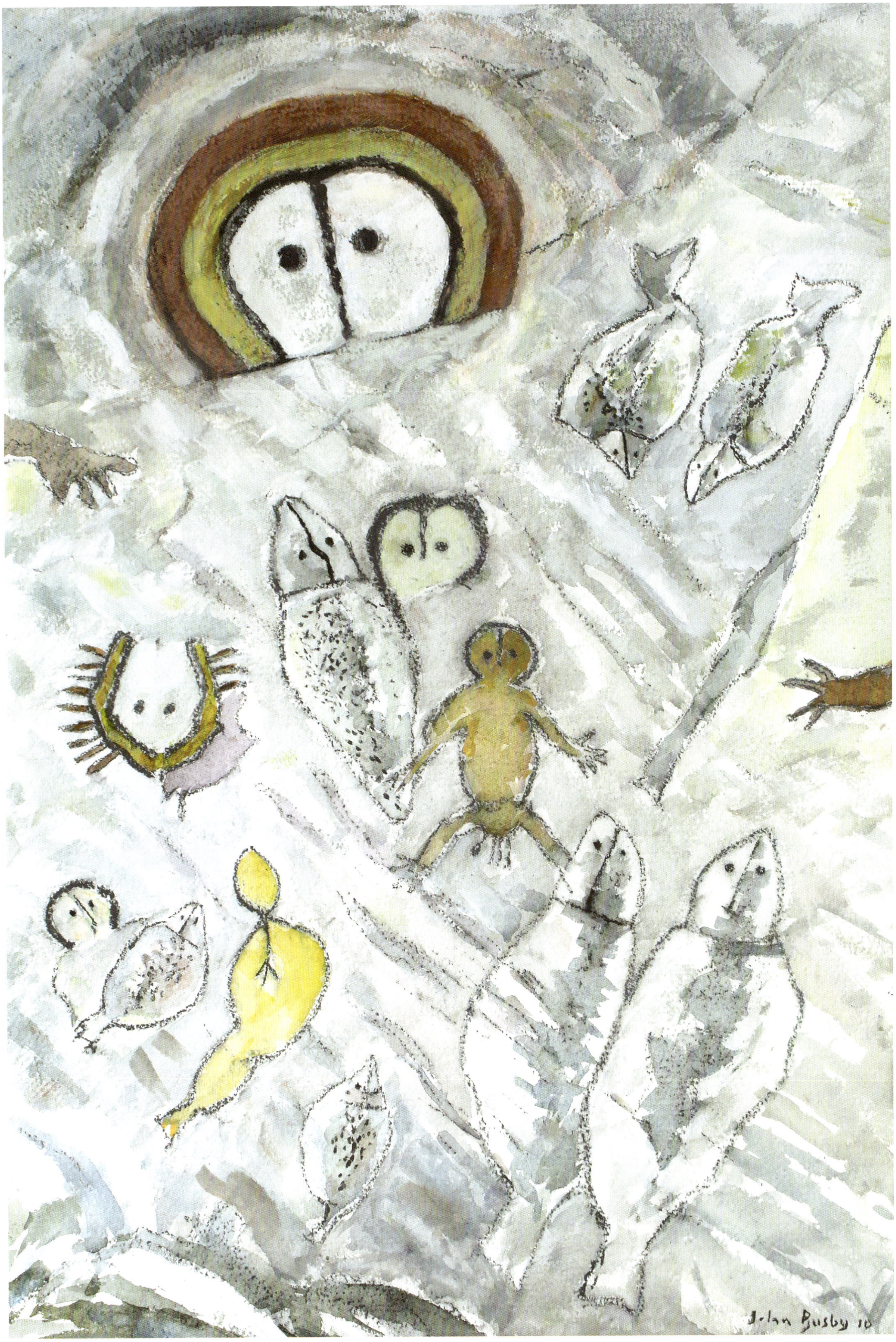
John Busby 10

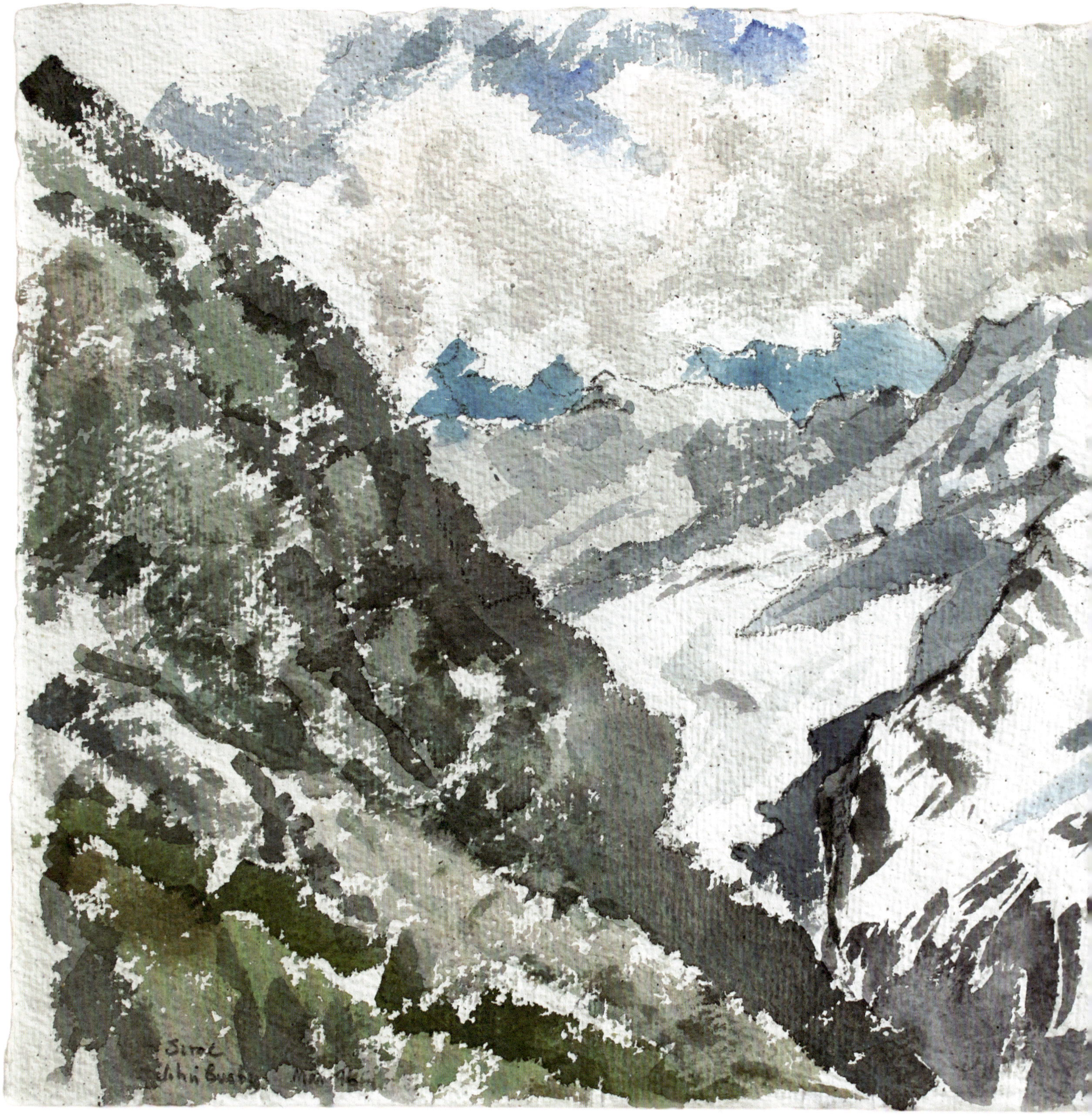

An Alpine scene – Les Escrins – chamois, choughs and marmots

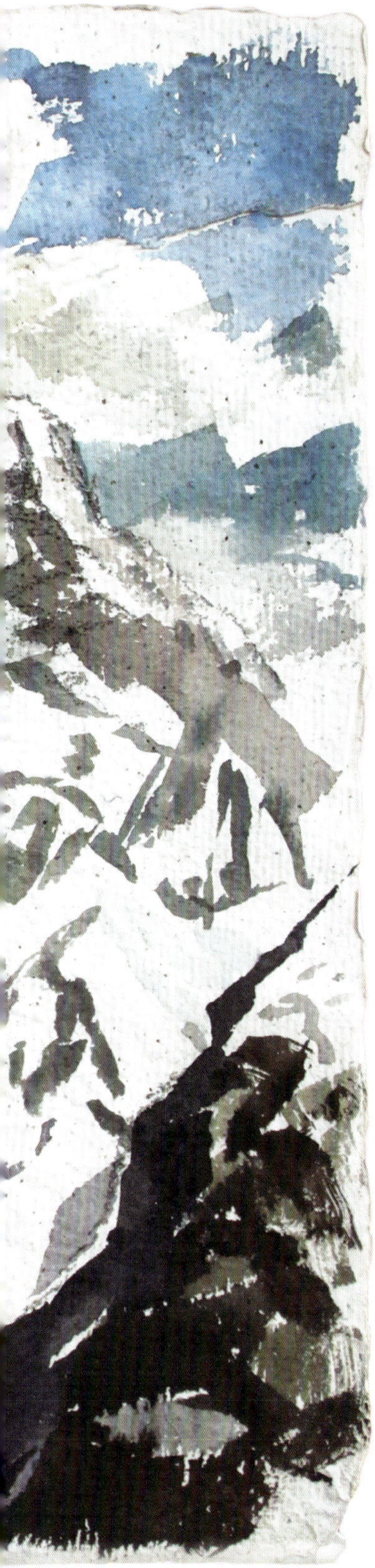

When clouds envelope the entire mountain, one can only imagine where the immediate slopes, which disappear into hidden heights and depths, might lead.

Sounds of cascades and torrents of water near and far give clues. Gradually, the sun and the high peaks become visible. The sunlight releases the aroma of wild thyme, and the freshly leafed beech woods shine against the dark shaded valley. Swallow-tailed and orange-tip butterflies appear. Sounds of goat bells combine with the constant noise of rushing water. Three buzzards spiral up from the lower slopes to the snow line. A Bonelli's warbler trills within the nearby bushes.

I can only look at these awesome mountain-sides at a climber's pace, inching my eyes upwards, and this is exhausting. How to see with the sweeping vision of an eagle and paint with broad confident strokes?

One longs to be as free in the mountain air as are the choughs, not earthbound by the pull of gravity on one's unsteady legs.

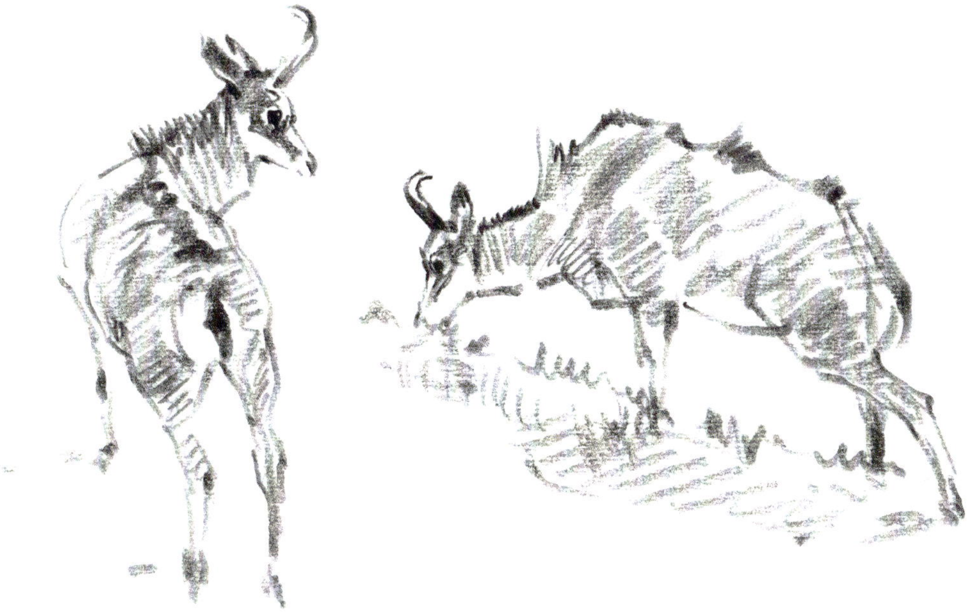

Les Escrins in the French Alps

Chamois

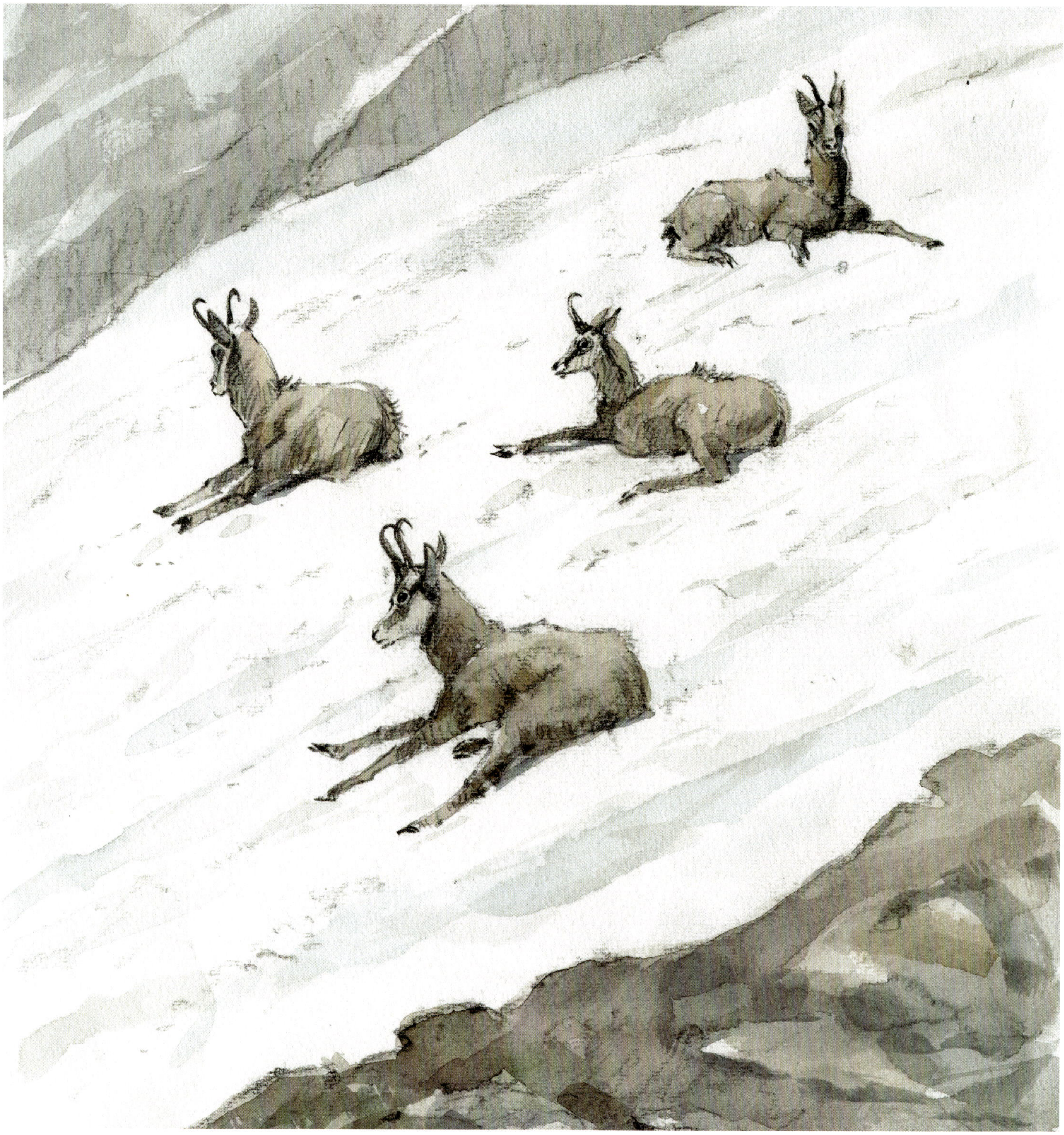

Snow fragments make precise shapes against the darker colours and textures of the screes, yet they seem to float free. They are like pegged-out pelts of winter, slowly shrinking to nothing. A group of chamois rest on the snow rather than on the rocks, bracing themselves against the slope with spread legs.

Chamois resting on the snow. They seem to prefer to rest on snow rather than on uncovered ground where they would be less visible

Snow shapes on the hill slope with resting chamois *>*

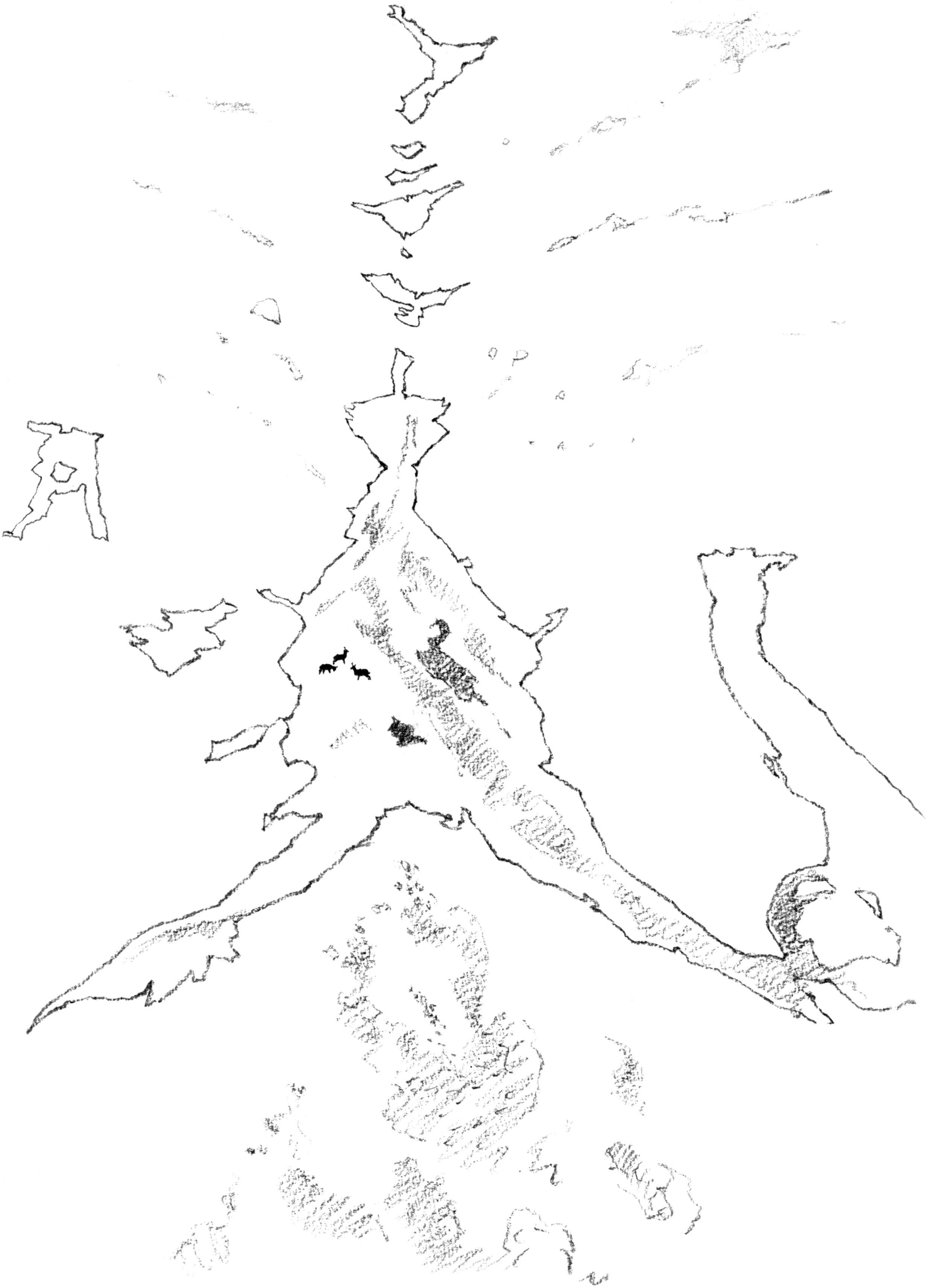

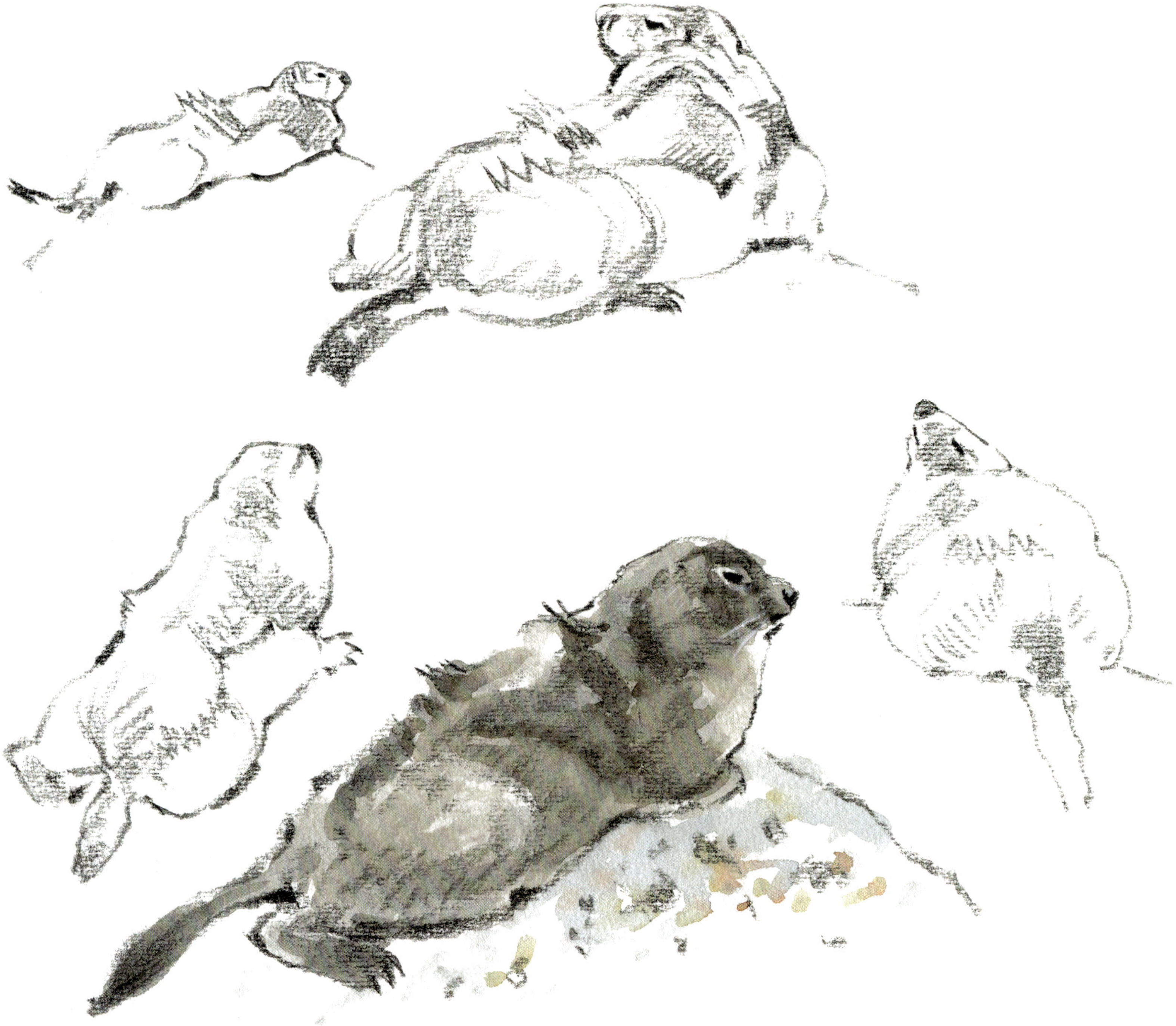

Marmot colonies always have a dominant male sitting on a boulder as a look-out, giving shrill warning if an eagle appears. Alpine choughs land to torment one sentinel I am watching. Like their red-billed cousins of the sea cliffs, the Alpines are great flyers contending with the cross winds and up-currents of these high craggy slopes.

Marmot on his look-out rock

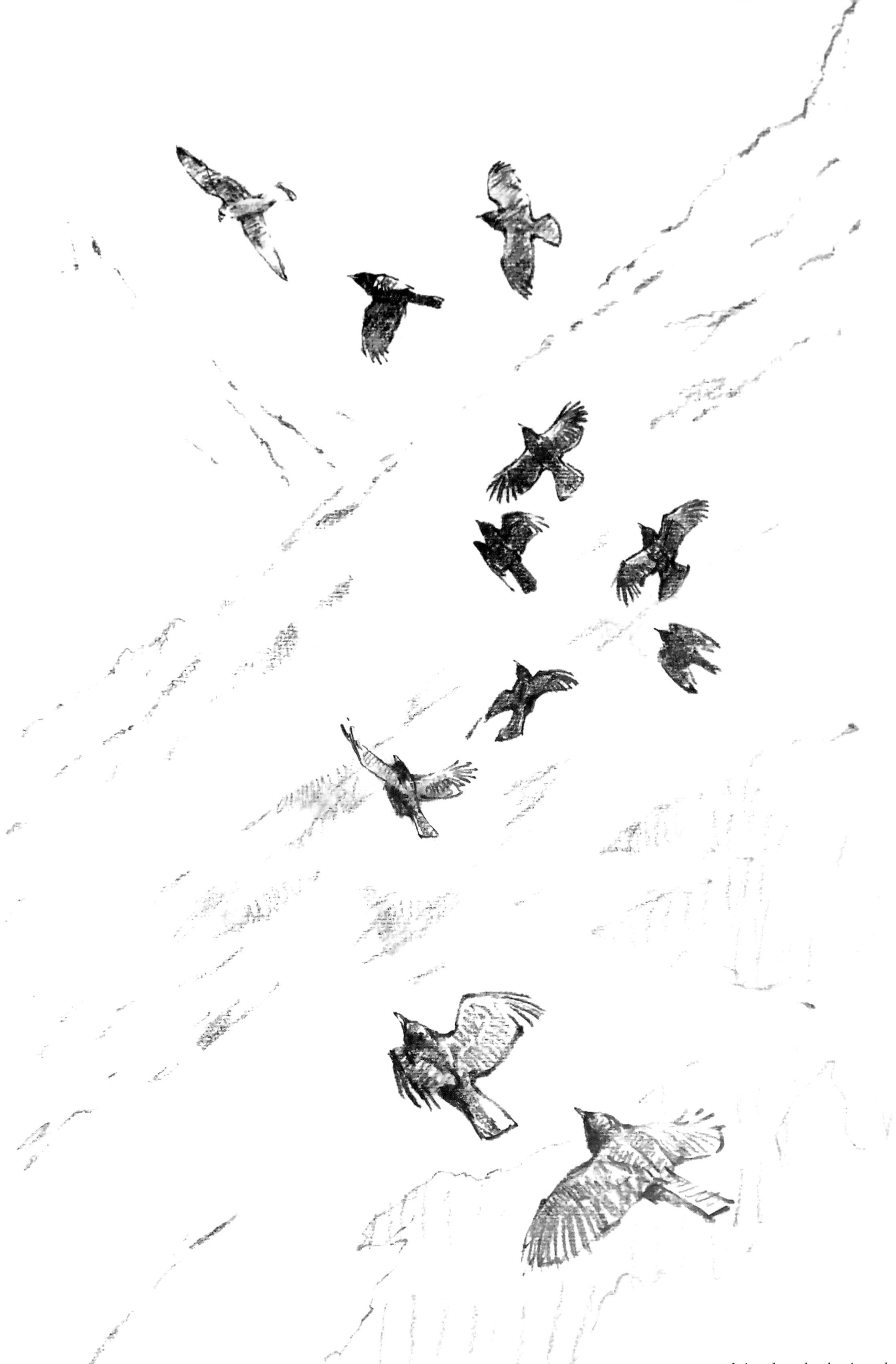

Alpine choughs chasing a kestrel

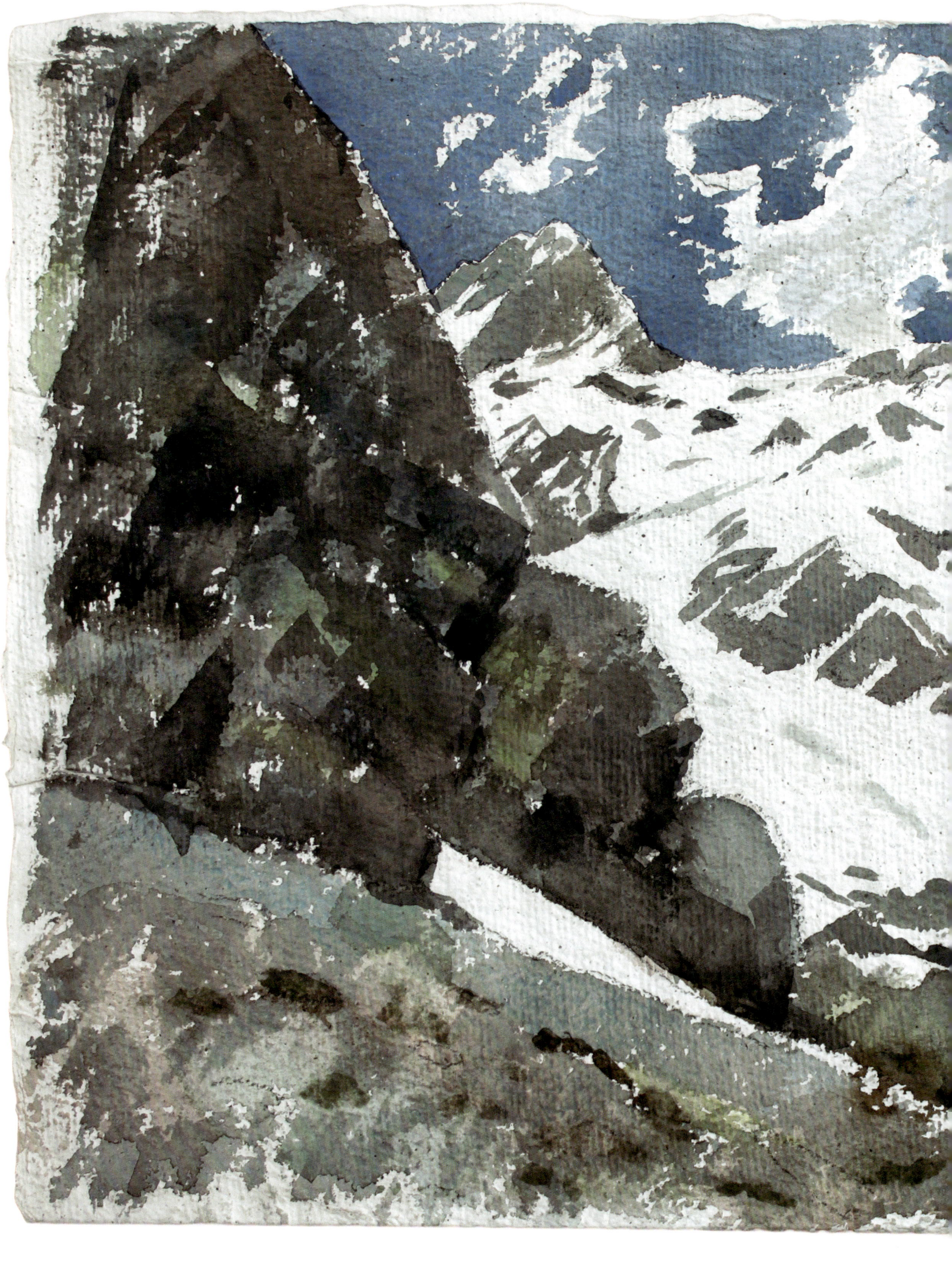

Mount Sirac in April

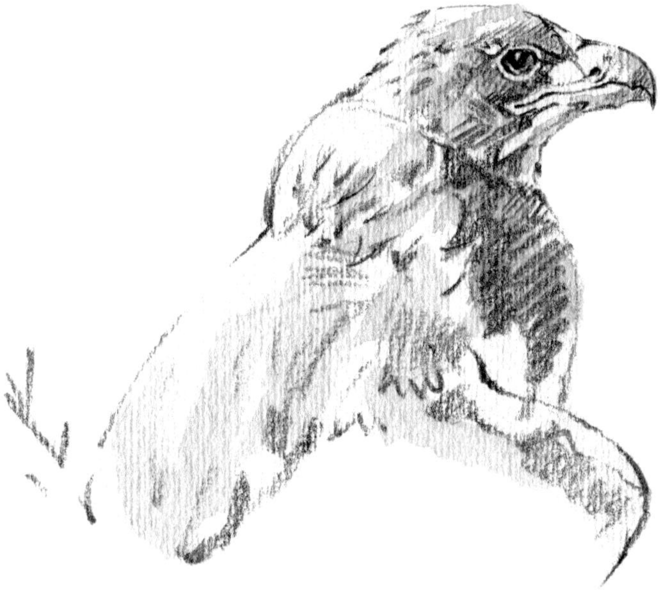

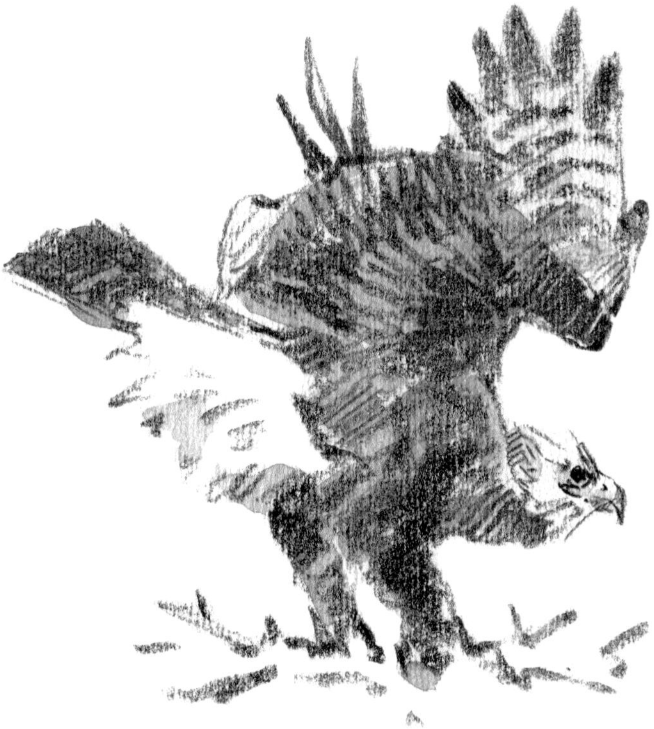

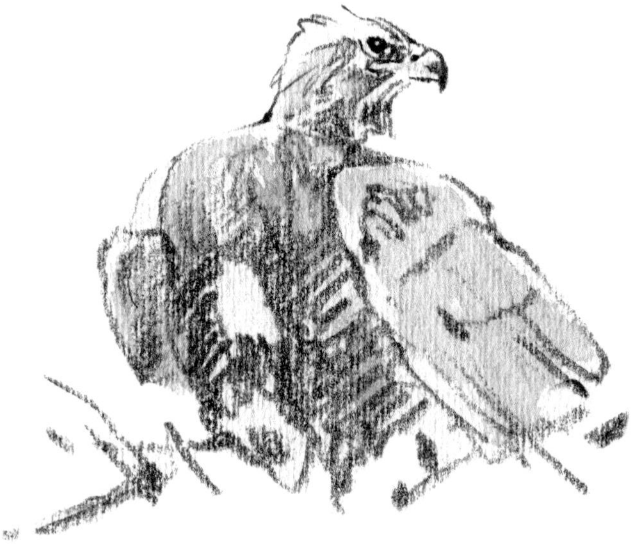

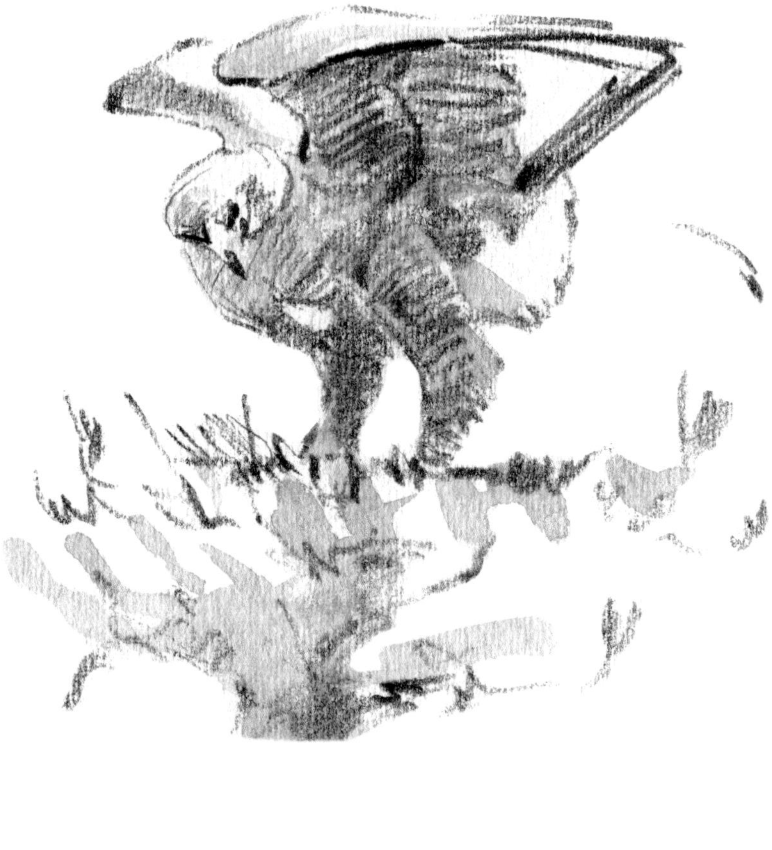

Young golden eagle from a hide at a nest in Speyside

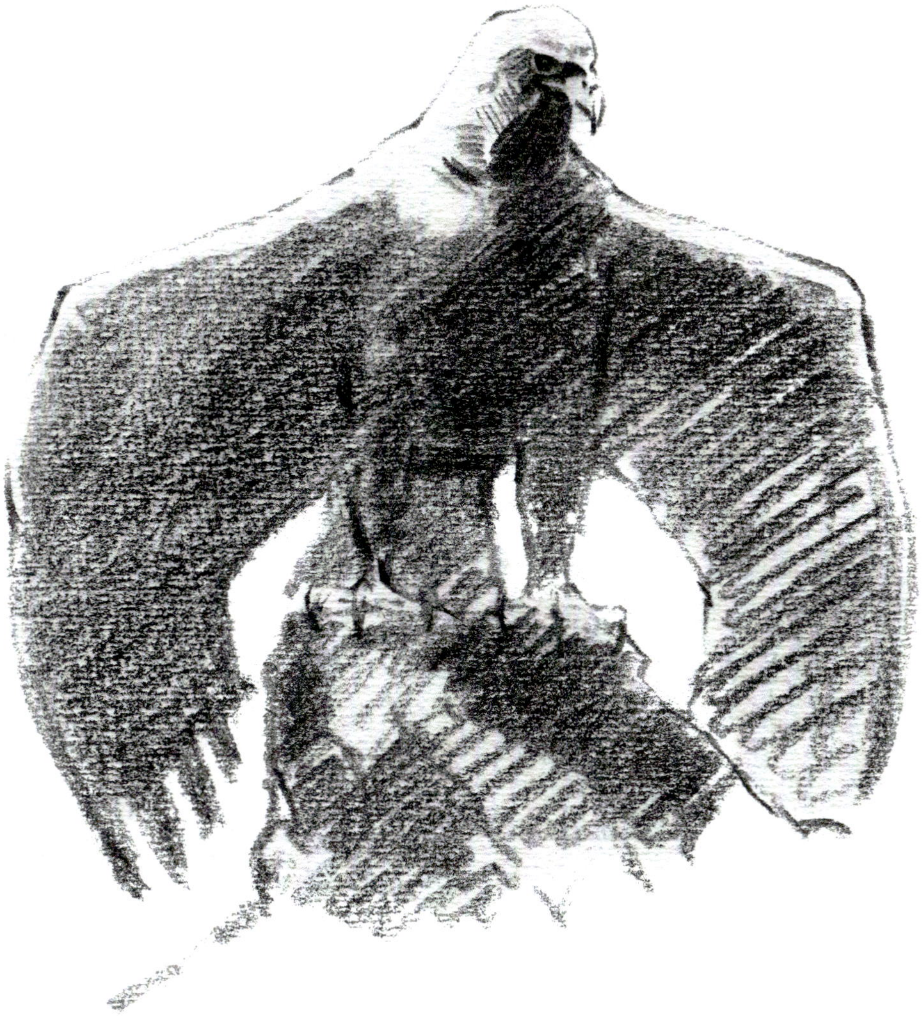

Golden eagle, study from a falconer's bird

Eagles, hawks, and falcons

The sight of a bird of prey always seems to set the pulse racing. A soaring eagle, a fishing osprey, a dashing sparrowhawk, or a hovering kestrel, give a focus to the day and open up exciting possibilities. A single hawk or falcon appearing over an estuary can set it alight, with waders and ducks taking to the air in defensive response. What does this confusion look like to the hawk? What would a mountain landscape look like if one could see with the intensity of an eagle?

Like the tiger, the peregrine falcon caught my imagination as a child and I longed to see one stoop on its prey. I read *The Peregrine's Saga* by Henry Williamson avidly; but these falcons were rarely seen in my part of Yorkshire and I had to wait many years to match my dream to reality.

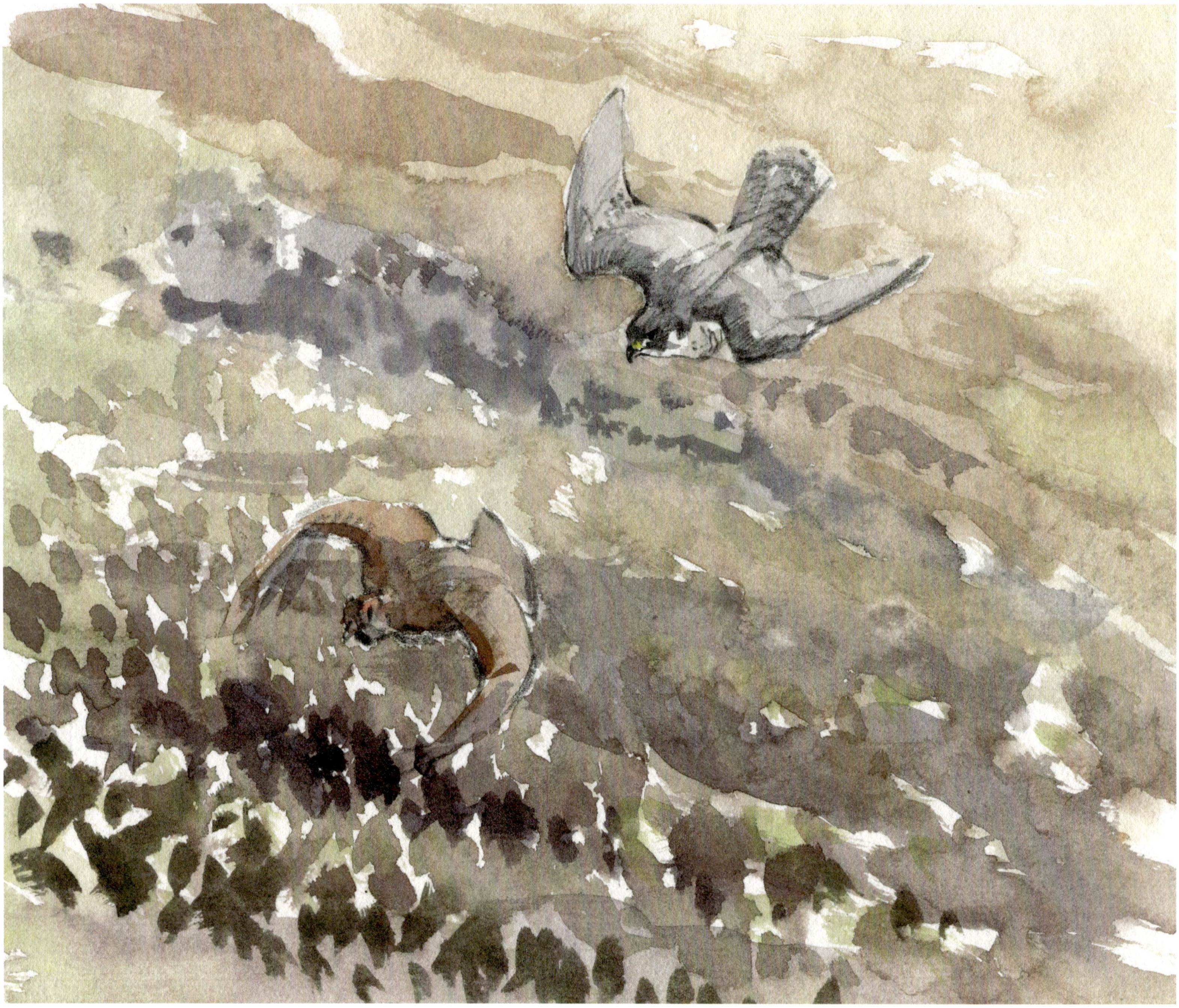

The finest written portrayal of peregrines comes in J.A Baker's book *The Peregrine*. He conjured up such vivid word pictures from his years of close association with the wild birds. My sightings of all the British falcons have been intermittent and far less intimate, but still memorable to me: peregrines nesting at Malham Cove in Yorkshire, in a local quarry and on islands in the Forth. It is great to encounter merlins nesting in Orkney, as it is to watch kestrels hovering over local fields, and a brief visiting red-footed falcon near Edinburgh one autumn. The hobby rarely comes as far north as Scotland, and my sightings have all been in southern woodlands of England.

Peregrine chasing a red grouse

Peregrine stooping on a red grouse. On this occasion the red grouse escaped the peregrine by landing and running into a narrow stream gully

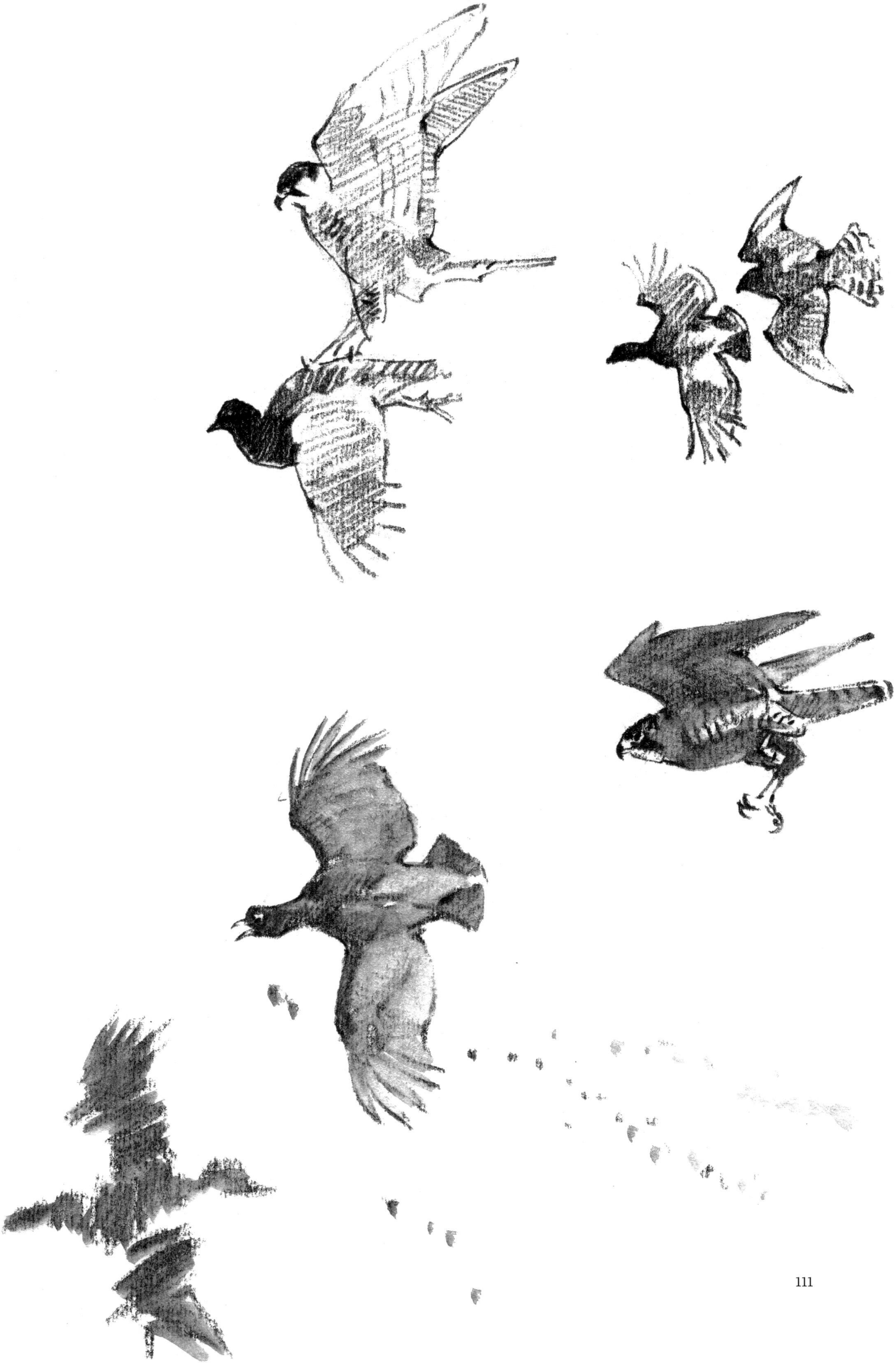

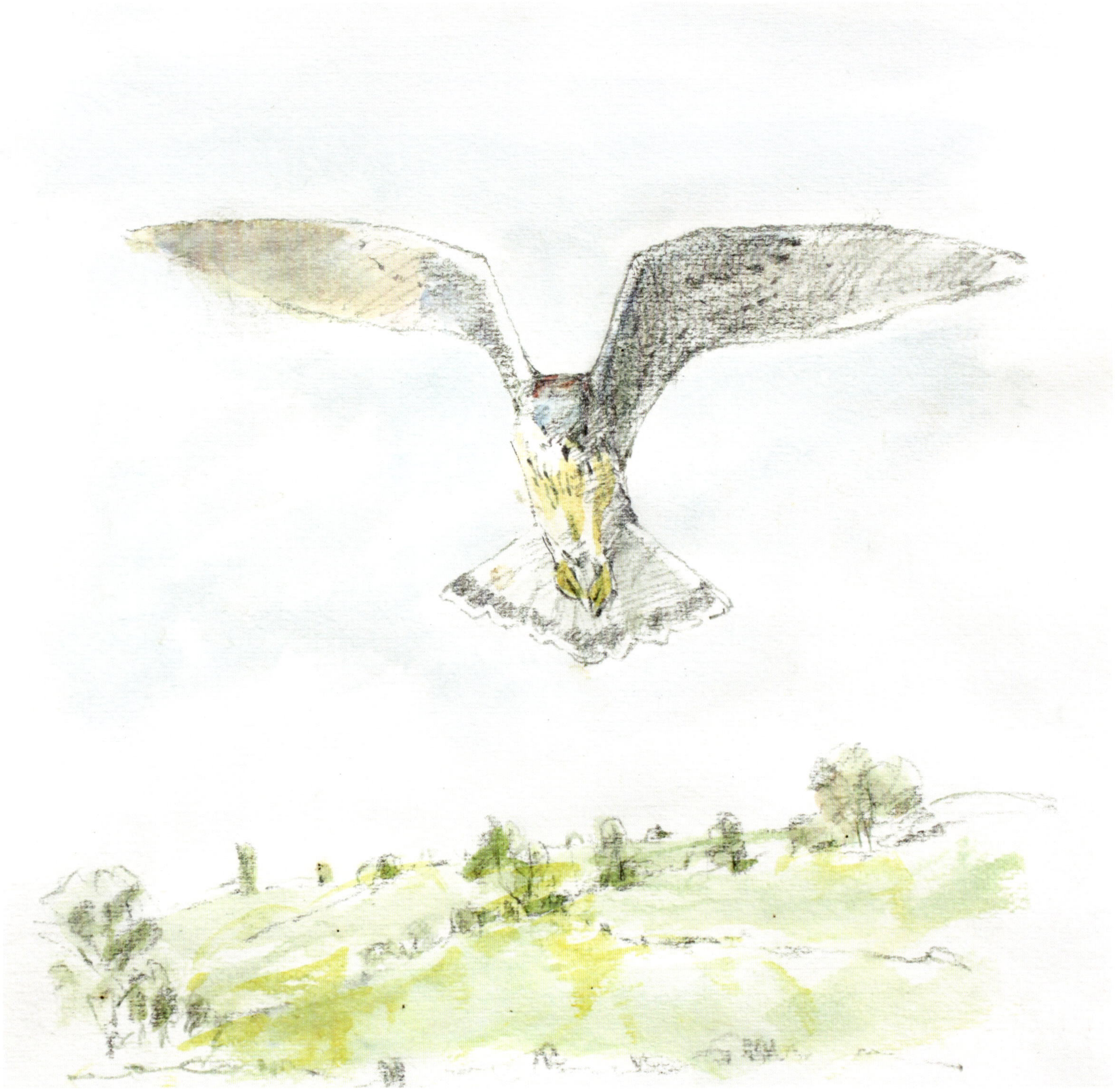

Hovering kestrel

In recent years the numbers of some birds of prey in Britain have increased thanks to protection laws and reintroduction, so one can be fairly confident of seeing a golden eagle on a good day in the Highlands, ospreys nesting on some lochs and lakes. Sea eagles and red kites are spreading in places where they have been re-introduced, and buzzards have increased in my part of Lothian, but kestrels and merlins have declined.

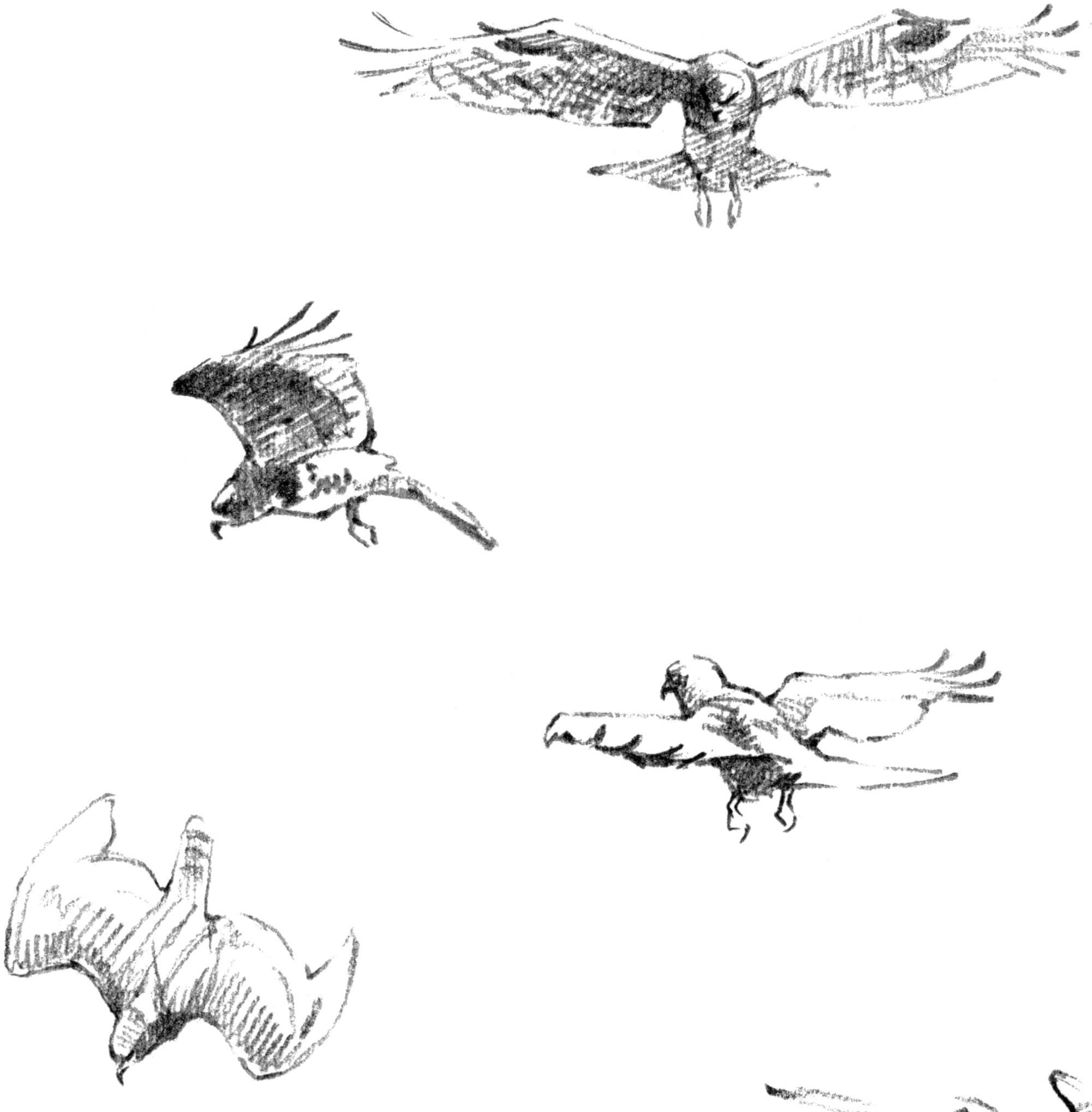

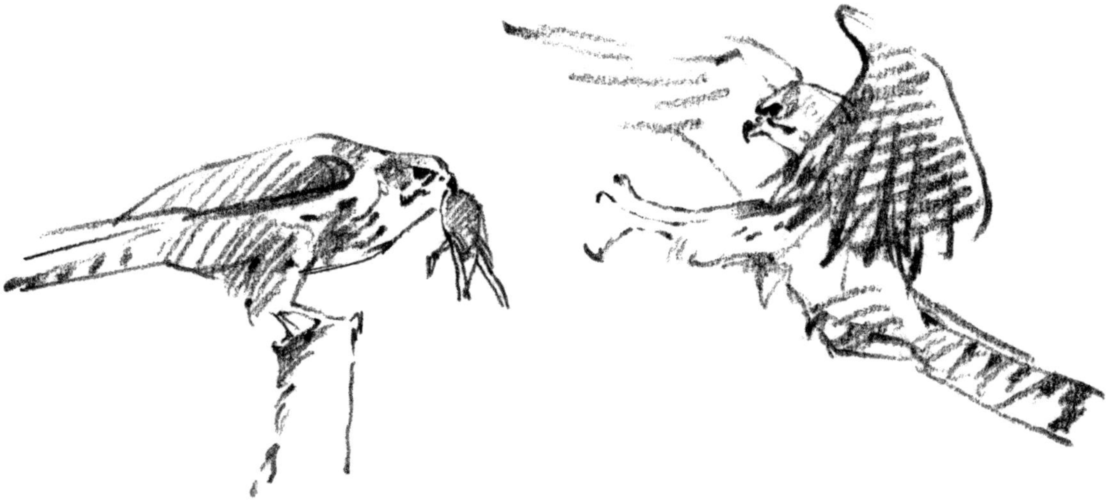

Hovering common buzzards

Merlins – a male holding food for female to collect to take to the young

I have watched ospreys closely from a photographer's hide at a nest by a Scottish loch and others fishing on occasions or on migration; even seeing one in New Zealand which looked no different from our native birds.

The moment of impact with water on a dive for a fish always intrigues me and I like the variety of splash shapes and sizes.

Osprey with two young, Loch of the Lowes

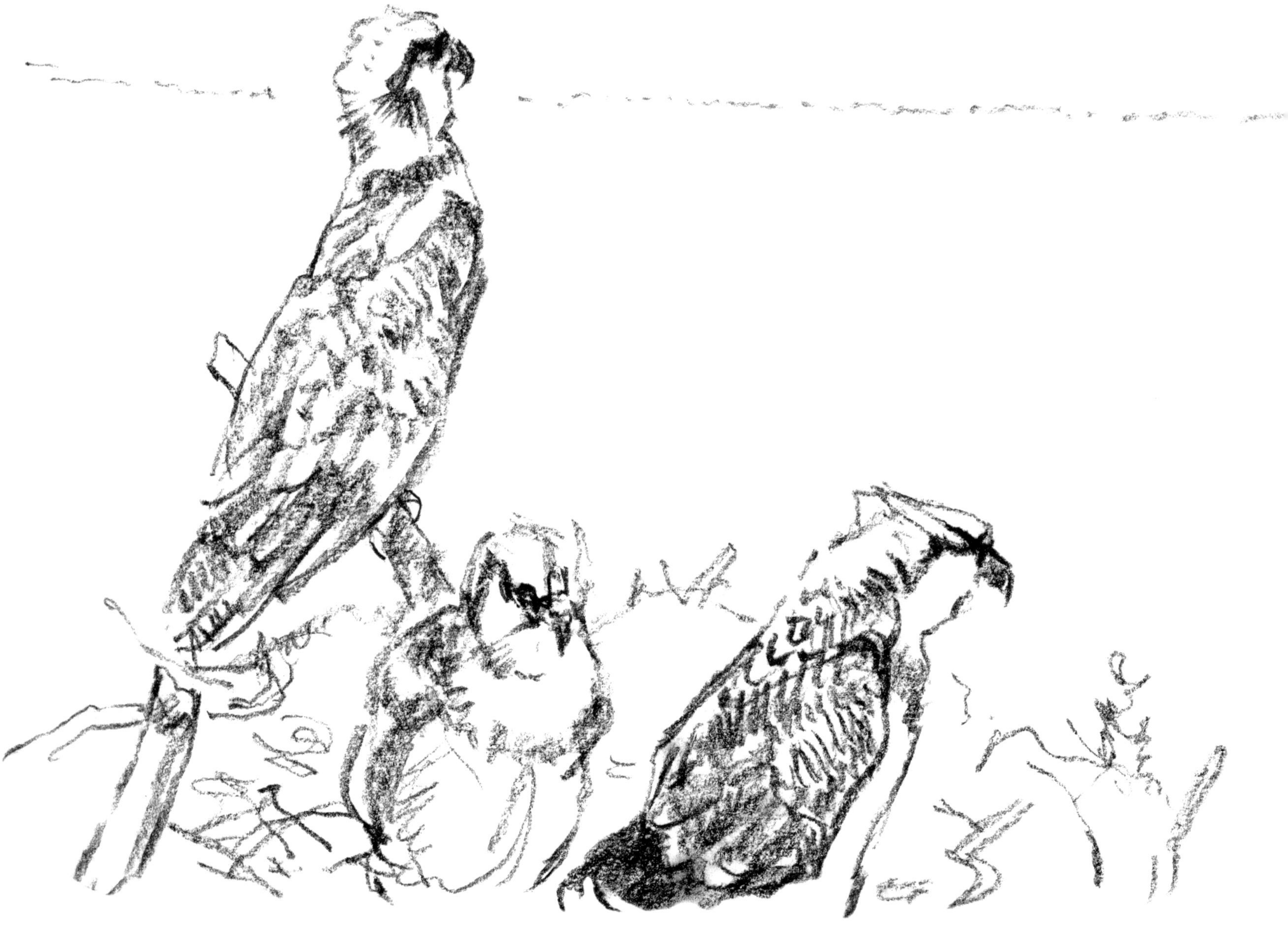

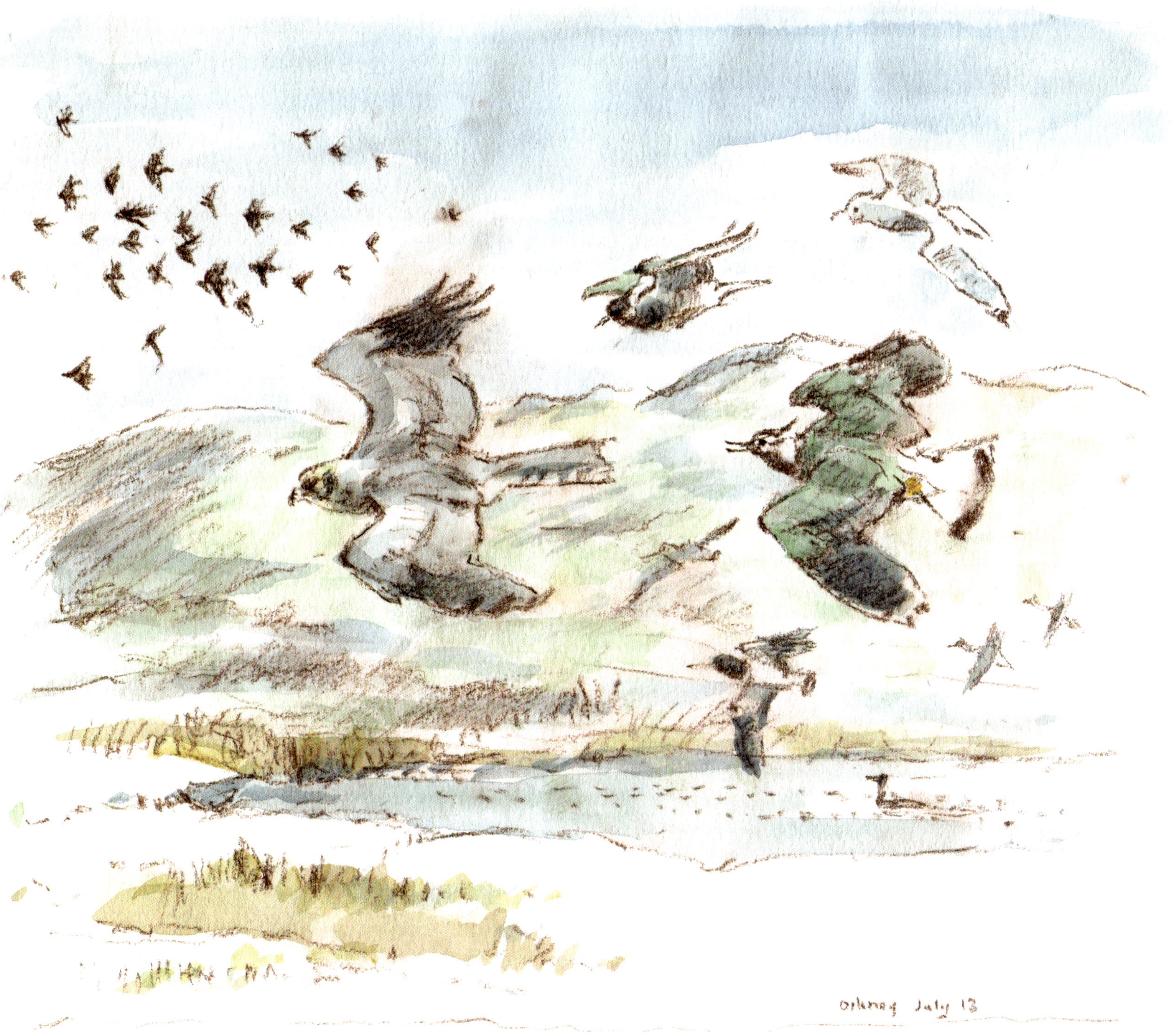

Hen harrier, harried by other birds over an Orkney loch

It is good to see hen harriers still present in the Orkney Islands, thanks perhaps to the vole population. The harrier drawn here was seen in Orkney recently. It was pursued by lapwings, curlews, common gulls, oystercatchers, snipe and starlings when it ventured over their moorland nesting area.

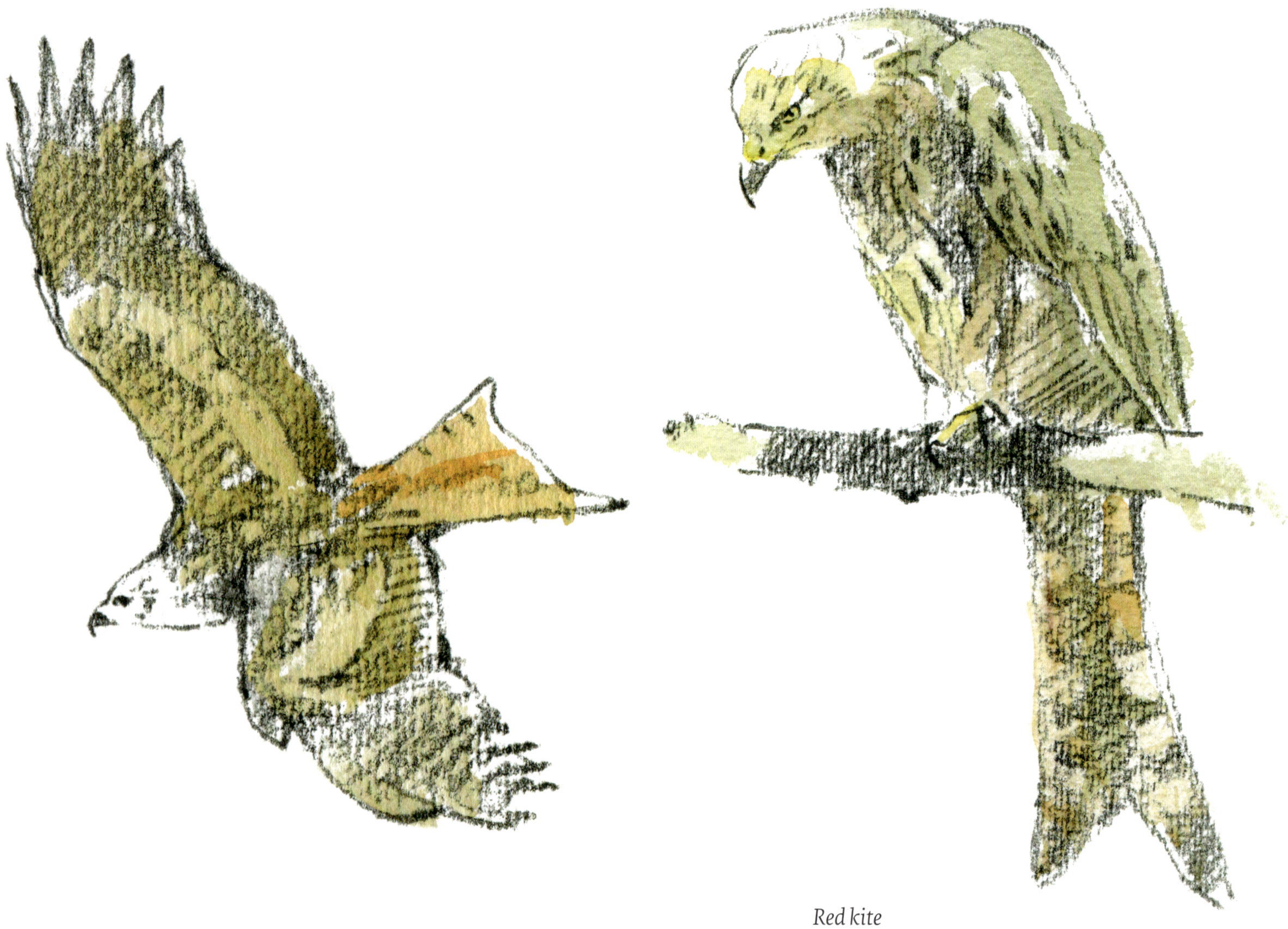

Red kite

Red kites are now familiar in areas where they have been reintroduced, and it is lovely to see their buoyant flight and forked tail tilting in response to currents of air. These studies of rescued young kites, being reared by a falconer, were in made in Wales.

Gladstone's Land in Edinburgh is said to take its name from the 'Gled' – the name given to the kite which once nested in the heart of the city in earlier times.

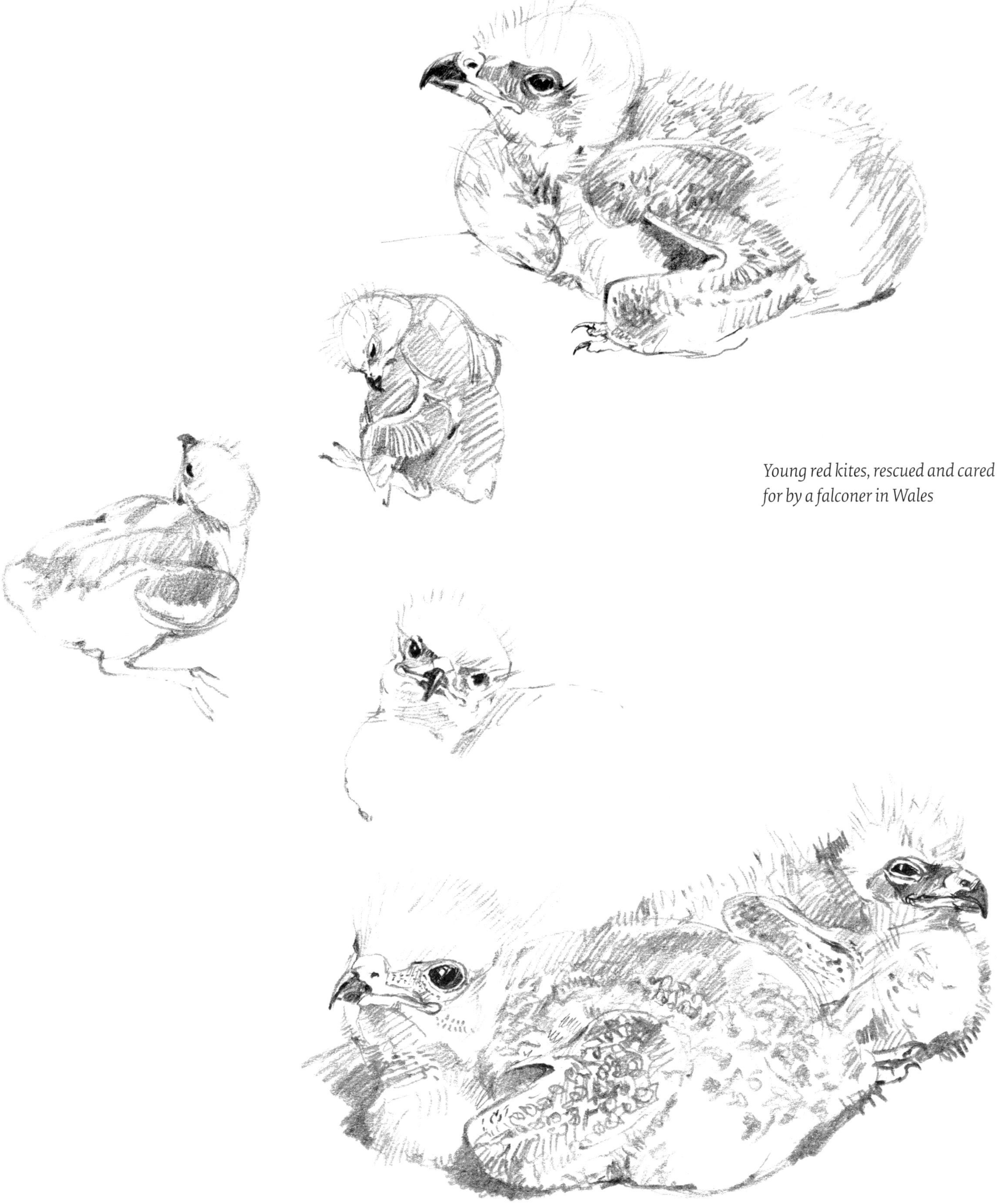

Young red kites, rescued and cared for by a falconer in Wales

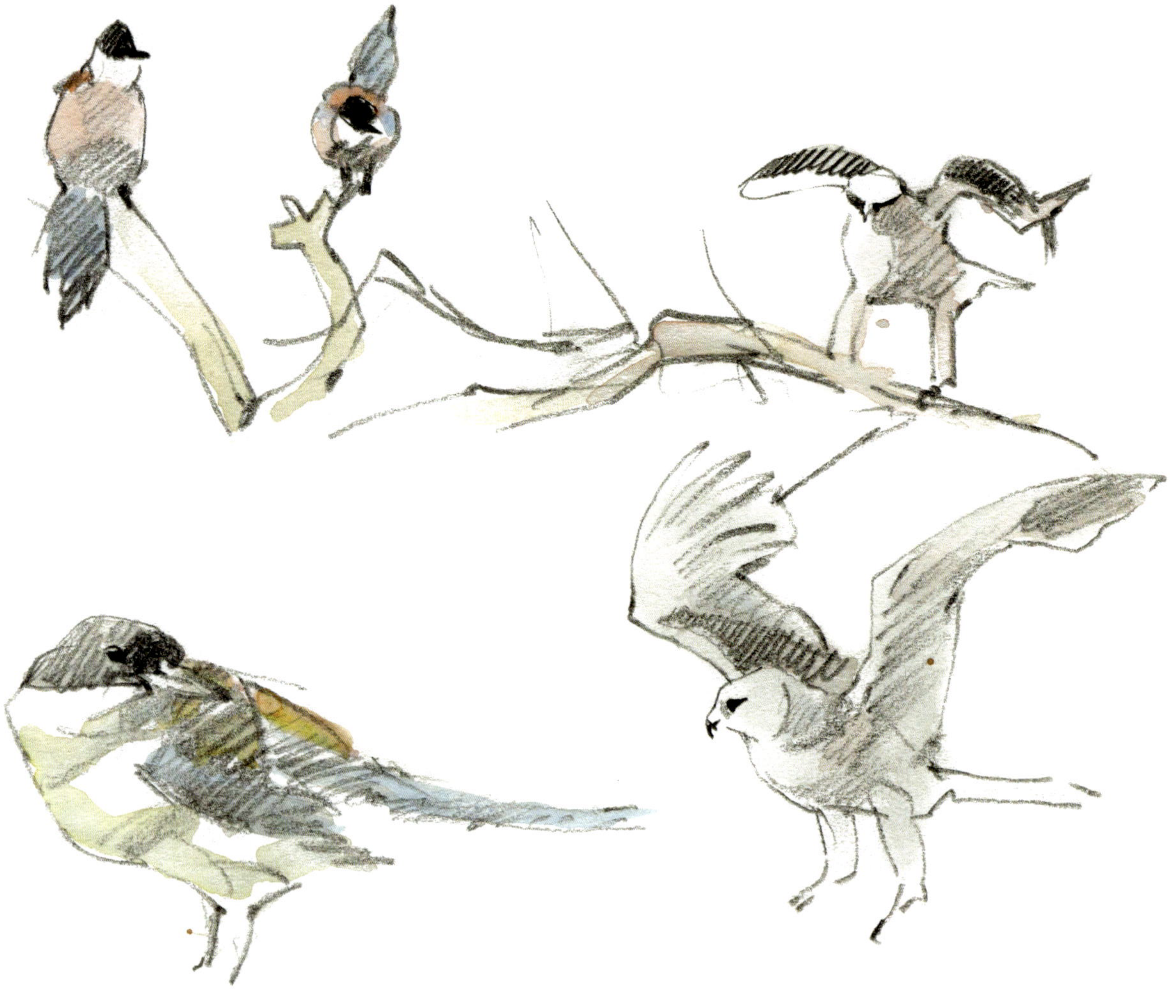

Azure-winged magpies mobbing a black-winged kite; Extremadura, Spain

I have been lucky to see some rare birds of prey – the Aldabra kestrel, native to that Indian Ocean atoll; the striated caracara of the Falklands and the Galapagos hawk – a bonus for visiting such places; and a few of the many eagles and hawks of North America and Africa.

When I was young I wanted to be a falconer, and even tried to join the RAF falconry unit during my two years National Service. To train for that would have meant signing on full time, so drawing is the closest I have come to owning a bird of prey.

In wild parts of Europe the excitement grows with new possibilities – booted and short-toed eagles, griffon and black vultures, lesser kestrels and red-footed falcons, and a favourite of mine – Eleonora's falcon.

It is slightly smaller than a peregrine and is named after Queen Eleonora of Spain. Perhaps she had one as her falcon, rather than the lady's more usual merlin. It is an autumn nester in coastal areas of the Mediterranean, rarely seen in Britain, although one of these falcons turned up over Aberlady Bay, right on my doorstep in 2012, but I missed it.

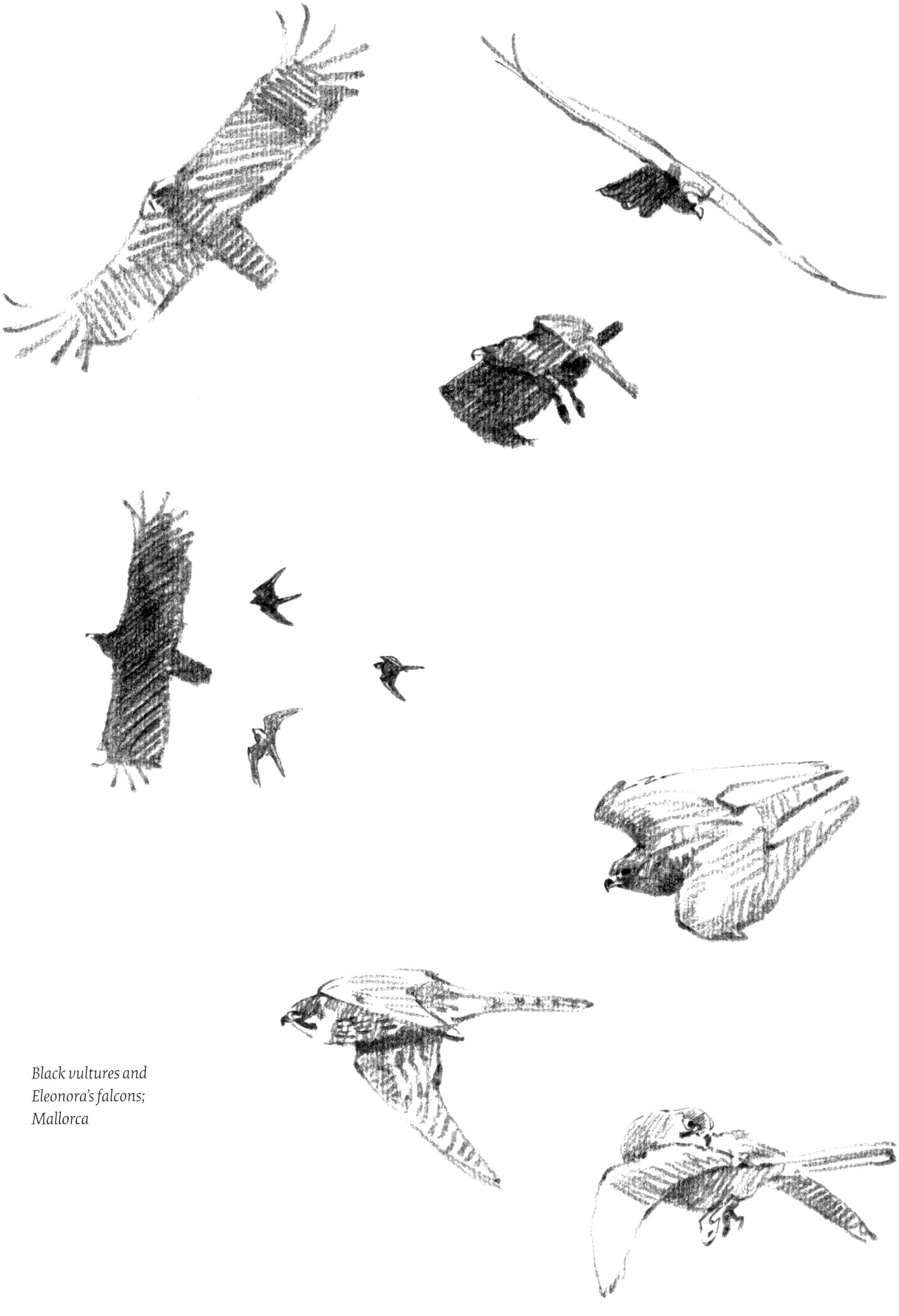

Black vultures and Eleonora's falcons; Mallorca

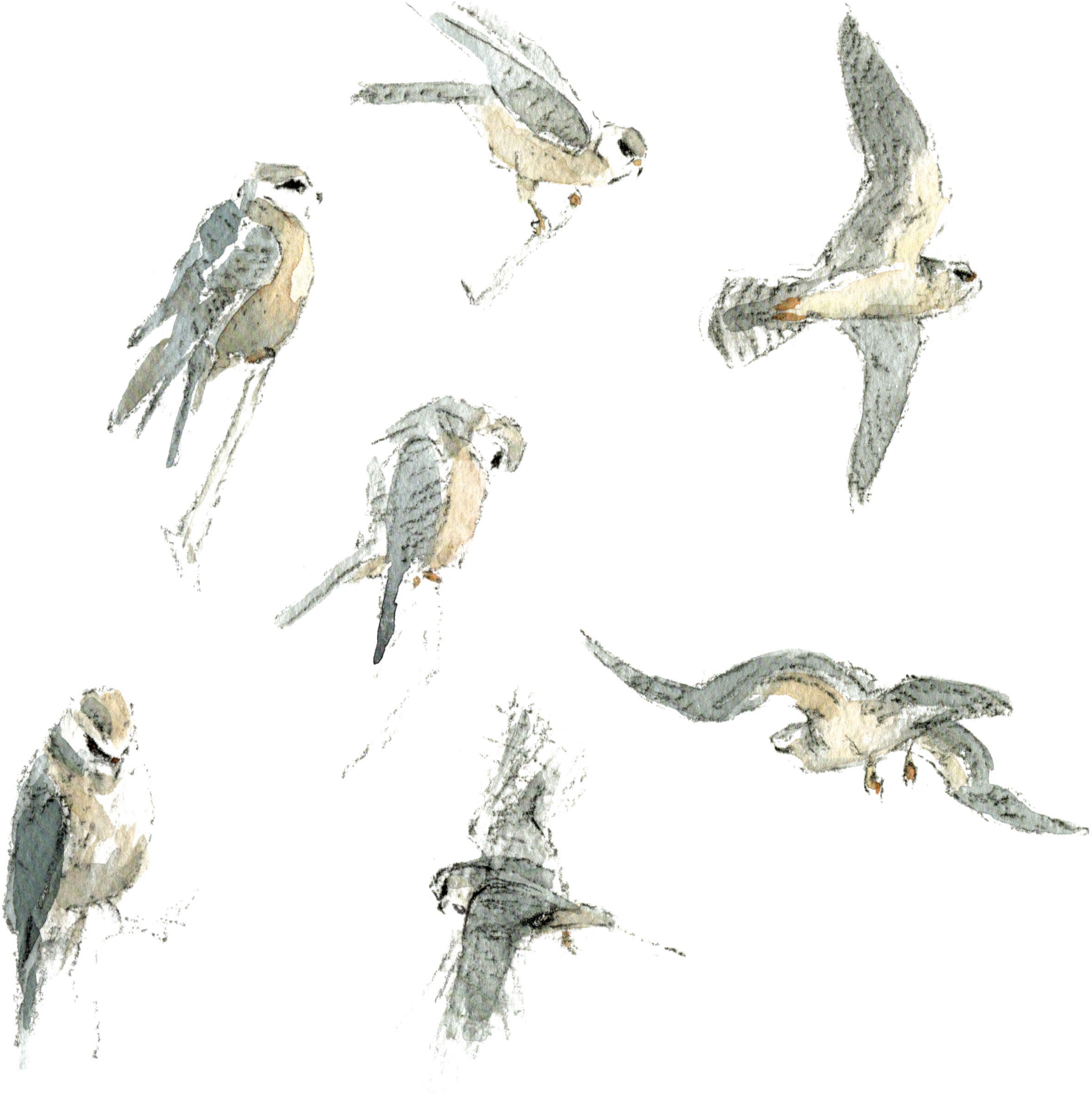

Another falcon way out of its normal range that I saw near Edinburgh, was a red-footed falcon. It stayed for a few days by a viaduct over the river Almond. This delightful immature bird flew close by people on the bridge, in pursuit of dragonflies and was itself chased by local jackdaws.

Immature red-footed falcon

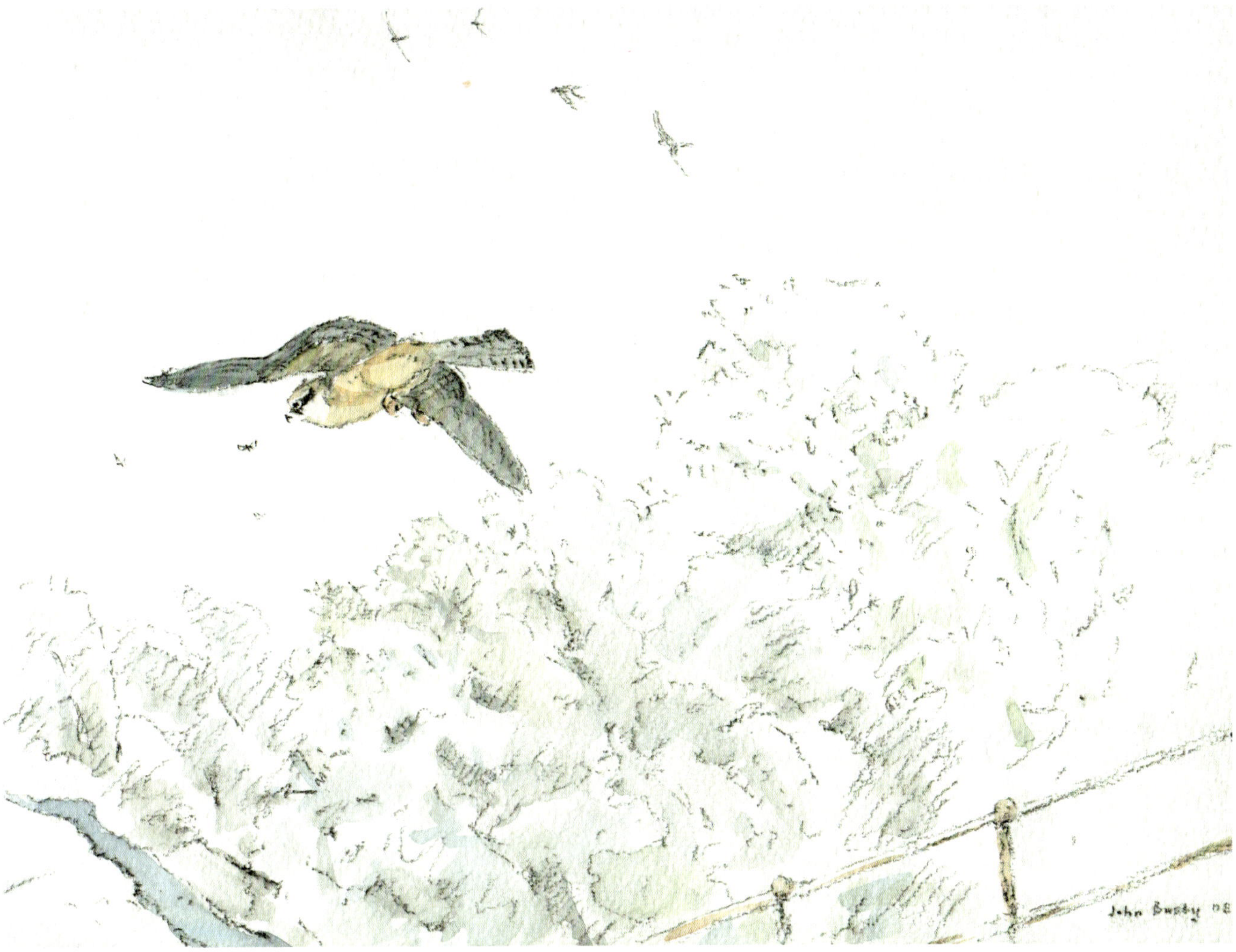
John Busby 08

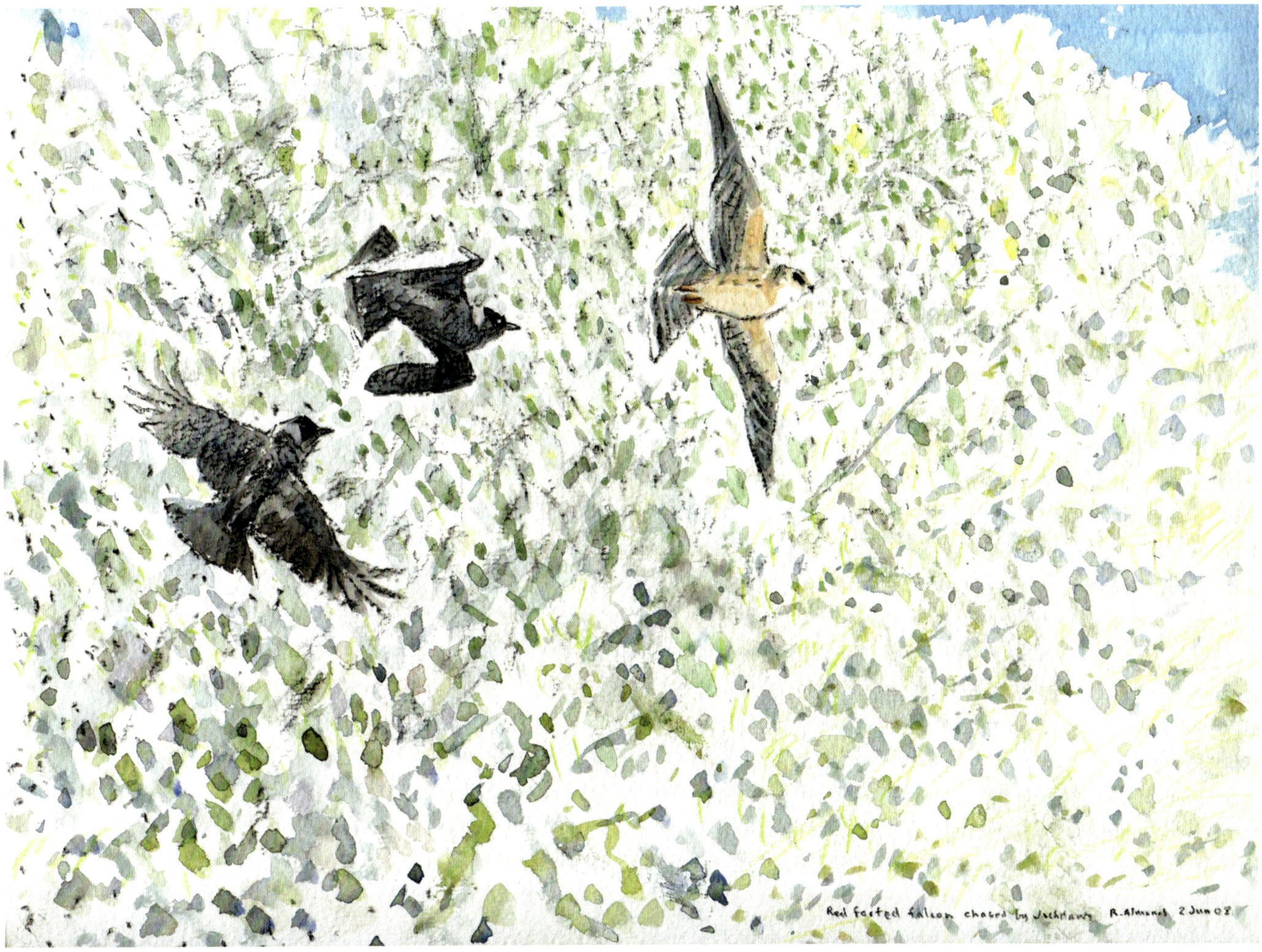
Red footed falcon chased by Jackdaws R. Almond 2 Jun 08

The mountains and valleys of Bulgaria are rich in bird life. I spent a week there with a group from A Rocha in 2003. Mt Vitosha rises to 6,000ft near to the capital Sophia. In the pine forests on the slopes were nutcrackers, and crossbills. A ski lift took us above the tree line to the top of the mountain where distant sightings of golden, booted and lesser spotted eagles added to the feeling of being on top of the world. Another walk among lower hills in the SE of the country brought us within telescope range of a nesting imperial eagle, and I watched an adult arrive and begin to feed a single white eaglet.

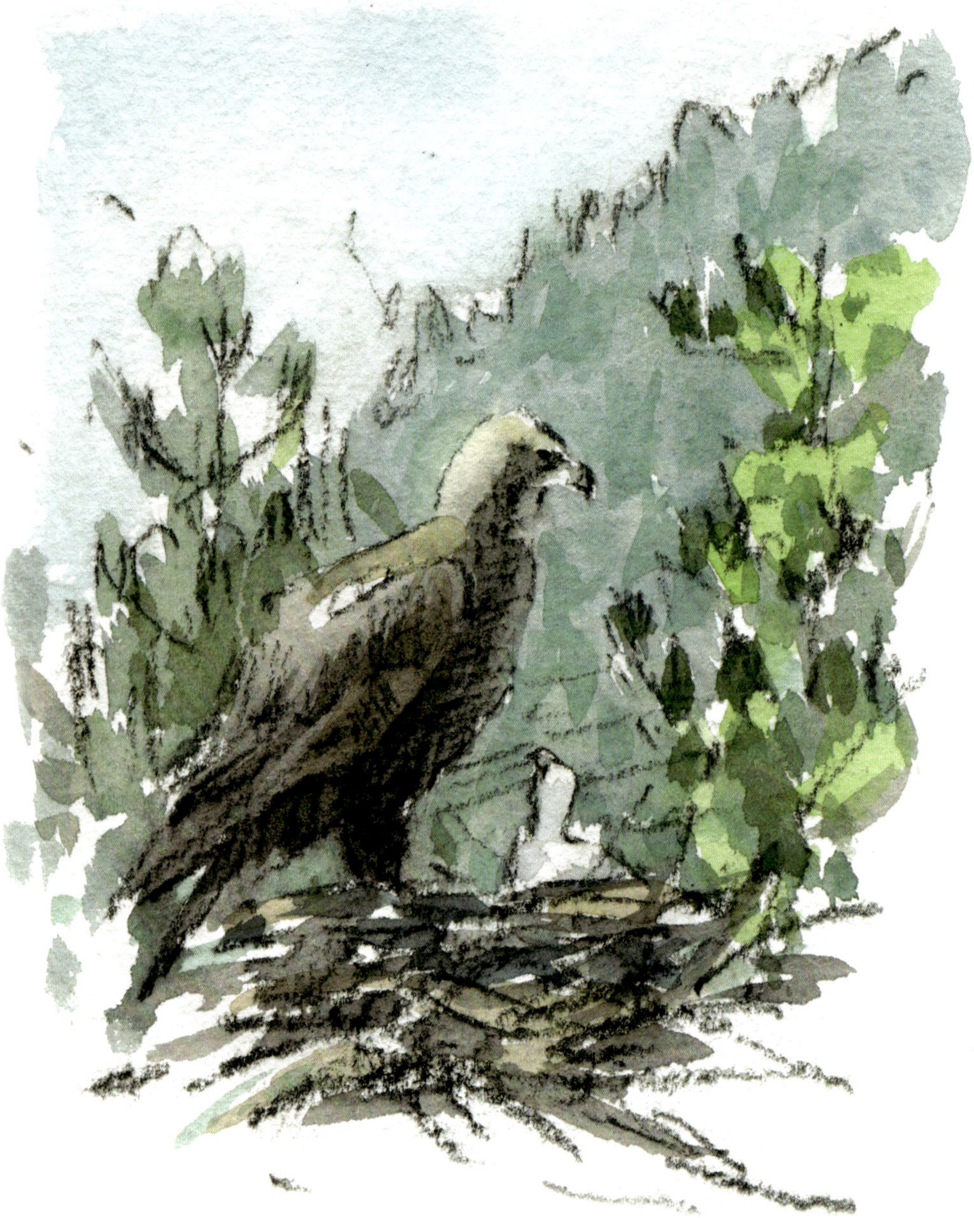

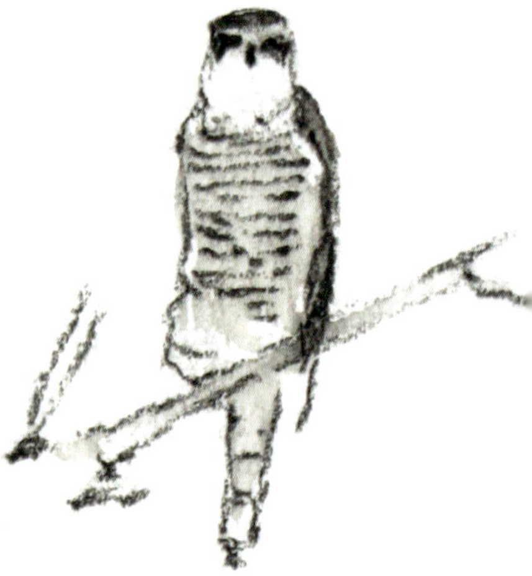

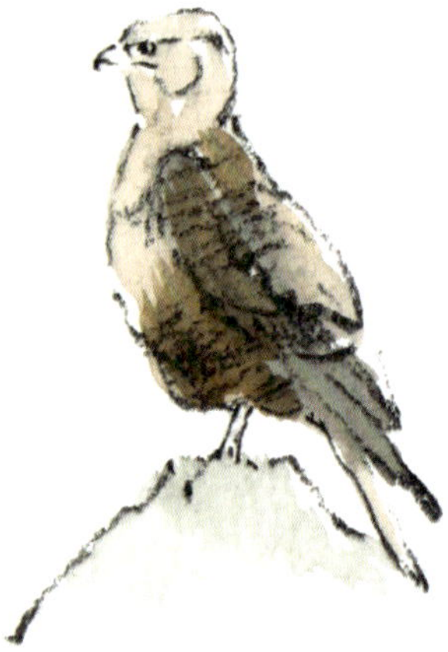

Goshawk and long-legged buzzard

< Imperial eagle with a single chick; telescope range, Bulgaria

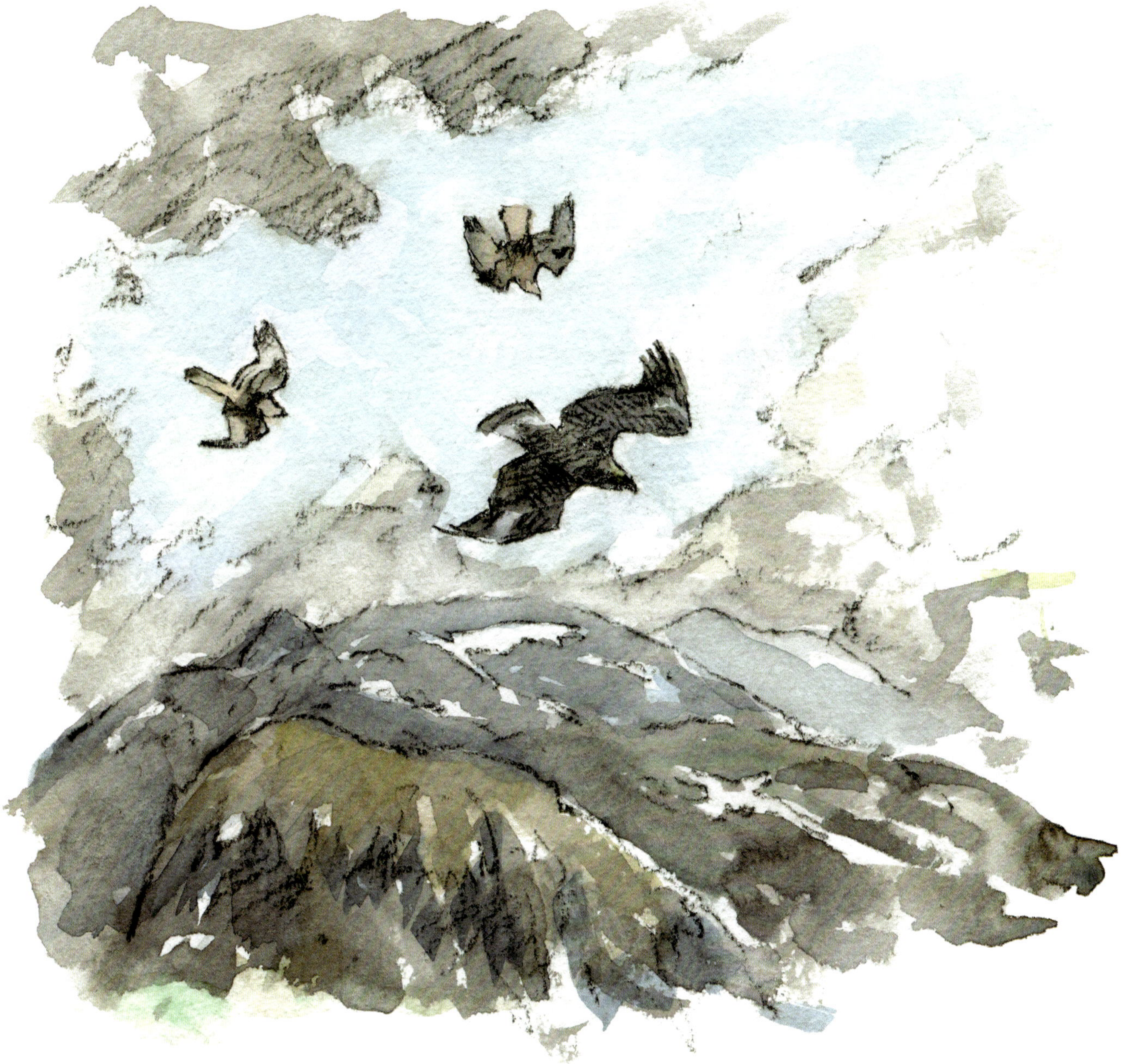

Golden eagle mobbed by long-legged buzzards; Bulgaria

Raptors were never far away in the central Balkan National Park, and we had excellent views of golden eagles, sometimes mobbed by long-legged buzzards, peregrines and ravens. Goshawks were regularly seen, and a single Levant sparrowhawk. Several species of woodpeckers were found in the older woods including black, grey-headed and middle spotted, as well as the familiar ones from Britain. The area by the river Kroumovitsa was rich in birds including rollers, bee-eaters, hoopoes, buntings, warblers and a black stork. On a nearby outcrop was the nest of a rock nuthatch.

Another highlight for me was to watch Isabelline wheatears displaying: the male hovering with head up and tail down in front of a mate. They live in the river meadows and use the burrows of guinea-pig like rodents called susliks to nest in.

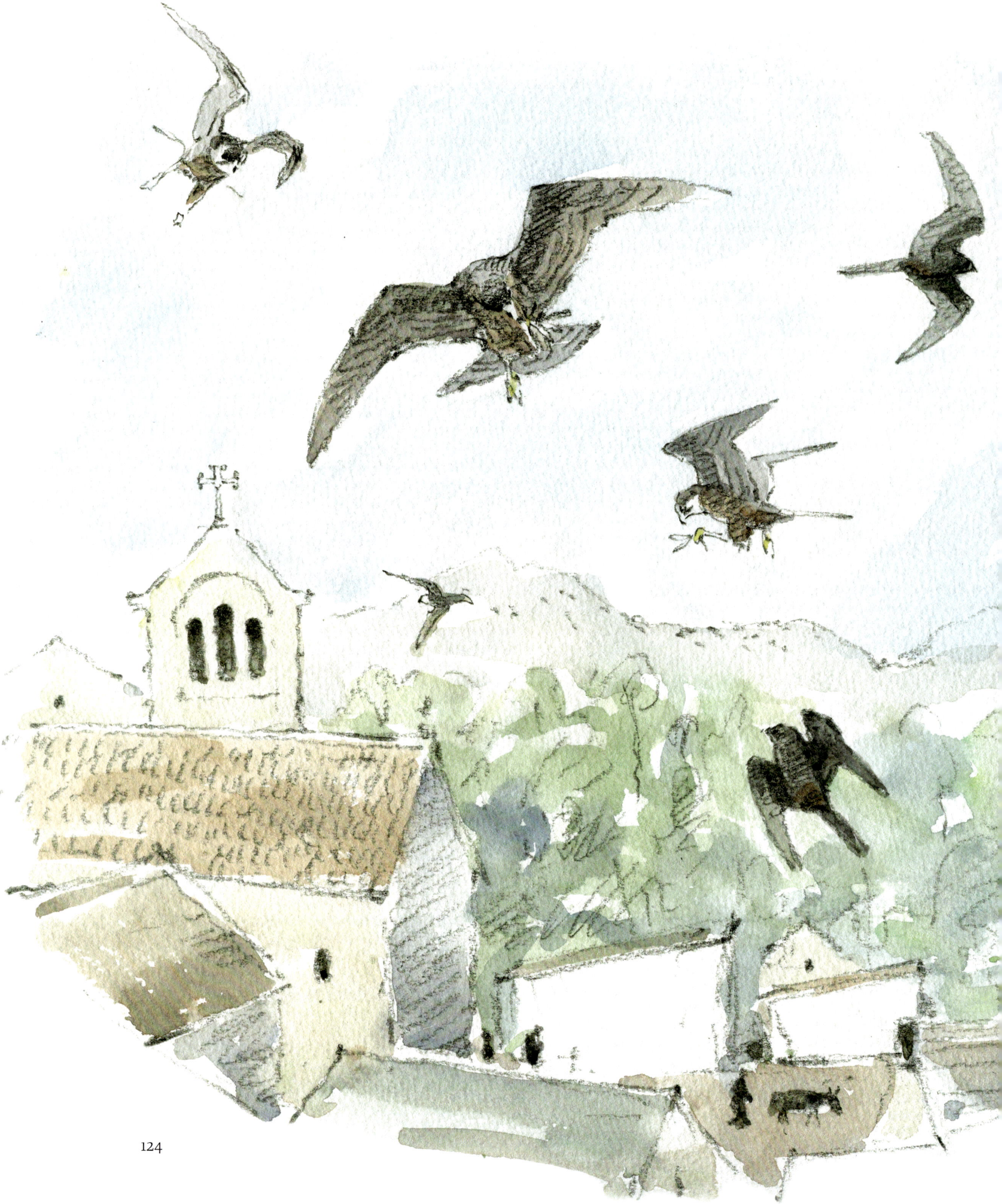

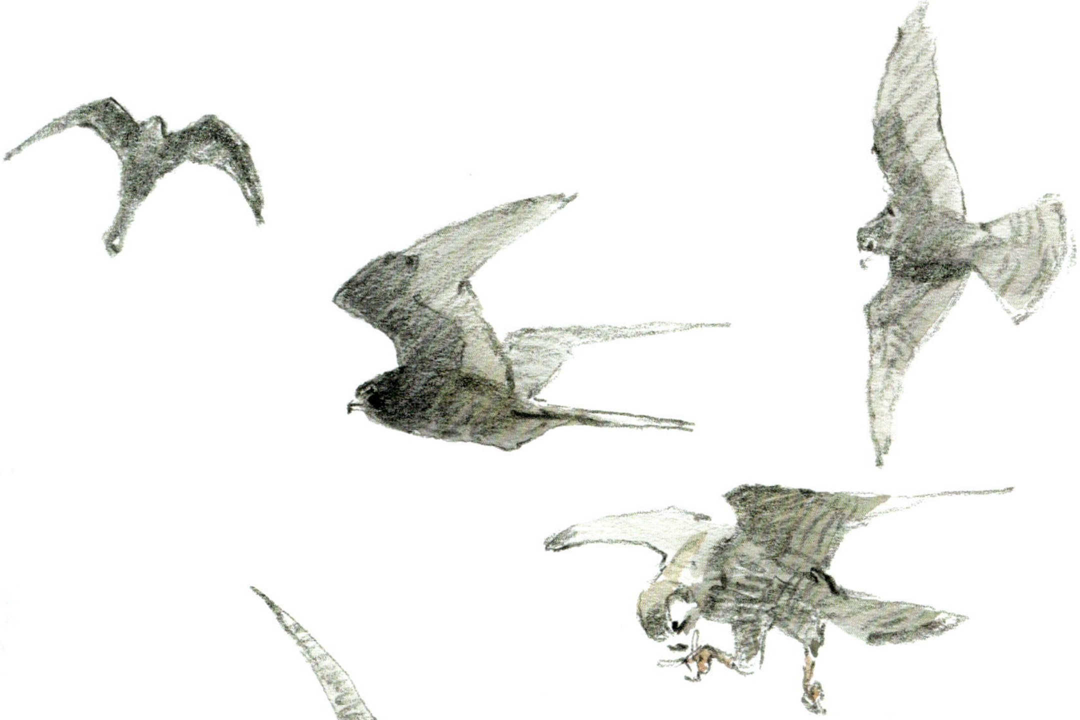

Eleonora's over a village in Crete, catching dragonflies one evening

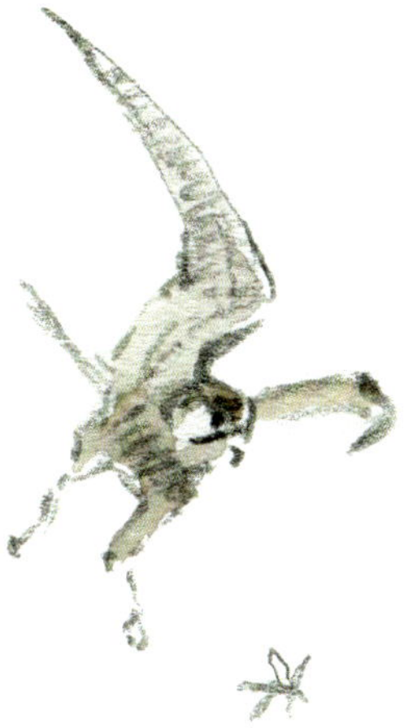

If you visit Mallorca you are sure to see Eleonora's over the marshes or the sea-cliffs. On one visit to Mallorca, I wrote this in my sketch book:

'It is around 7 pm on the cliffs at Formentera; all is quiet. Three falcons fly slowly past me, effortless in their gliding; quartering the cliff tops; sparring in dives and evasions with each other. Two are the light form and one dark. In the evening light against the gentle blue of the sea they glow like agates. At eye level with the sun at such a low angle their undersides are lighter than their backs. They put me in mind of a 'perfect' flying machine I often tried to make. Their proportions are ideal for soaring and for gliding only feet above the waves – then, with a quick flick backwards of primaries, their geometry is set for speed and they drop through the air like darts.

A pair of ravens cross into this 'no go' area and the scene is suddenly alive with Eleonora's, calling and harassing the crows from all directions: later, a bird-watching 'high' – falcons driving off a lone Audouin's gull.

The falcons resume their circling, some preening on the wing with frequent body shakes, done with closed wings. I watch them for two hours and fill my mind with their movements, so that I have only to close my eyes to recall this most lasting ending to a Mallorcan day.'

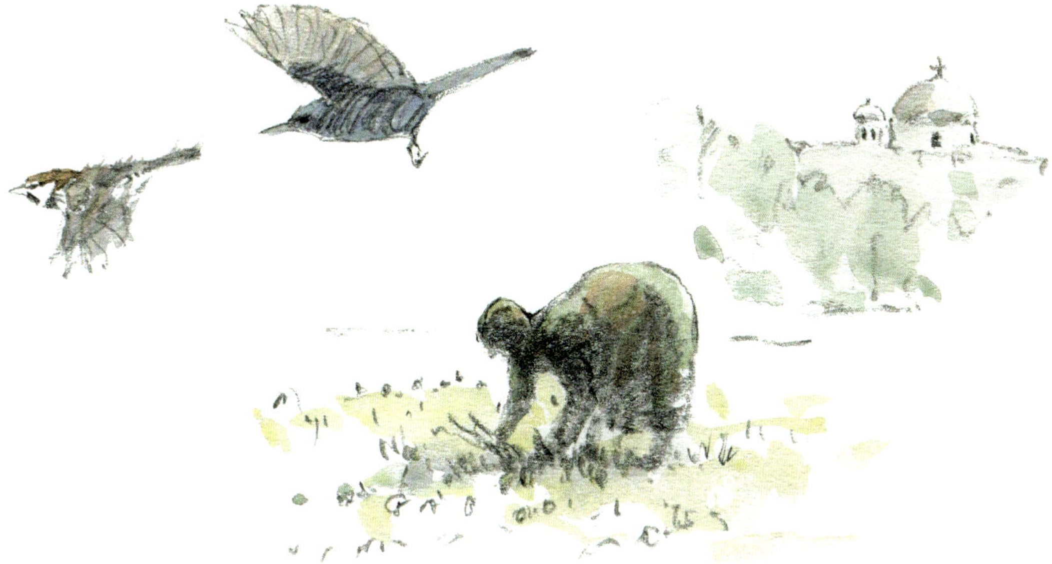

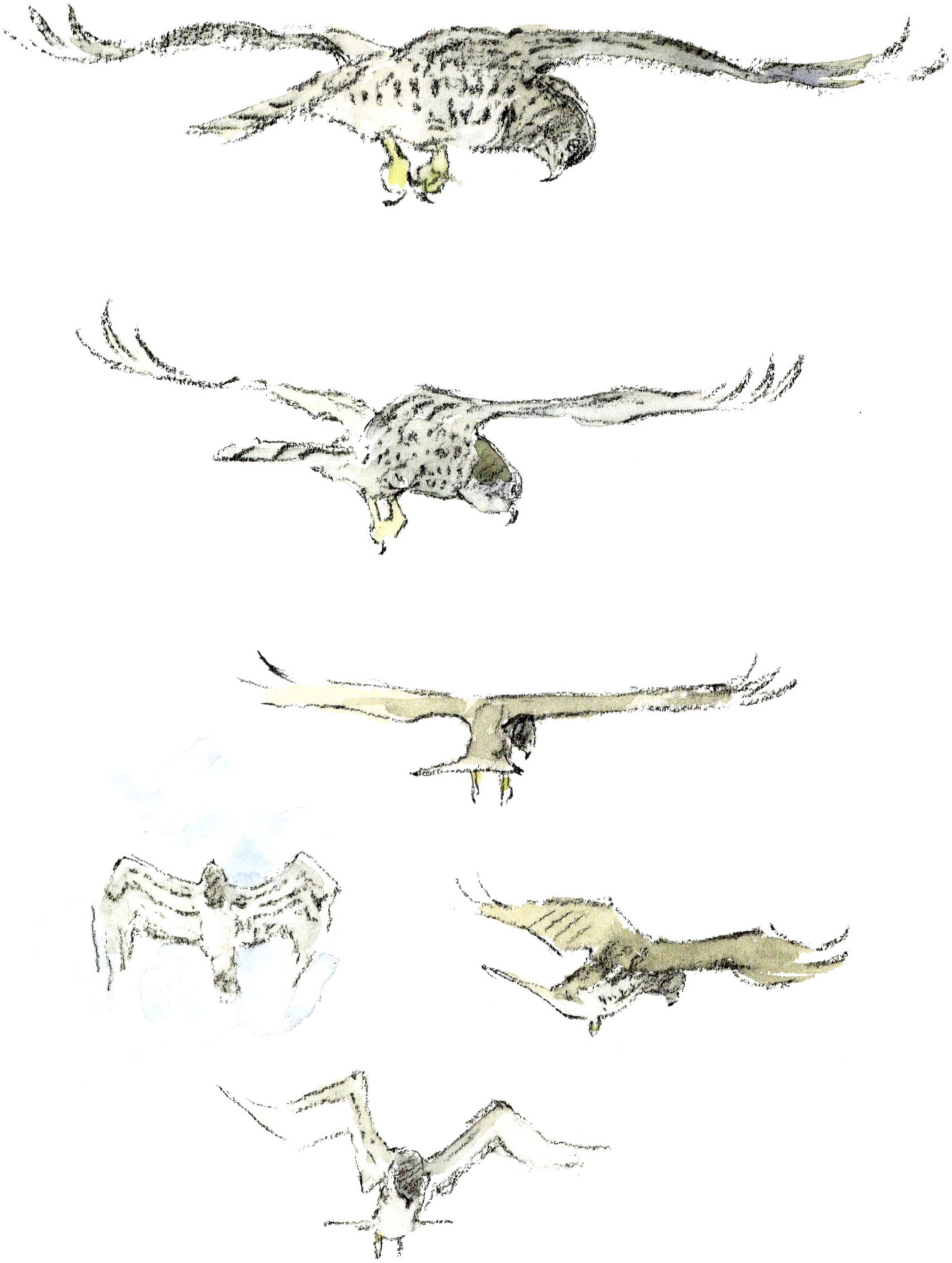

Short-toed eagle hunting snakes; Golan Heights, Israel

The short-toed eagle is a similar size to Bonelli's eagle. It is a hoverer, and it seemed to like roadside verges in Provence where my wife and I had cycling holidays some years ago. This one was drawn more recently in Israel on the slopes of Golan, where it found a snake to catch.

Bonelli's eagle was my quest bird for many years whenever I visited southern Europe. It is a rather secretive bird, but I eventually tracked it down

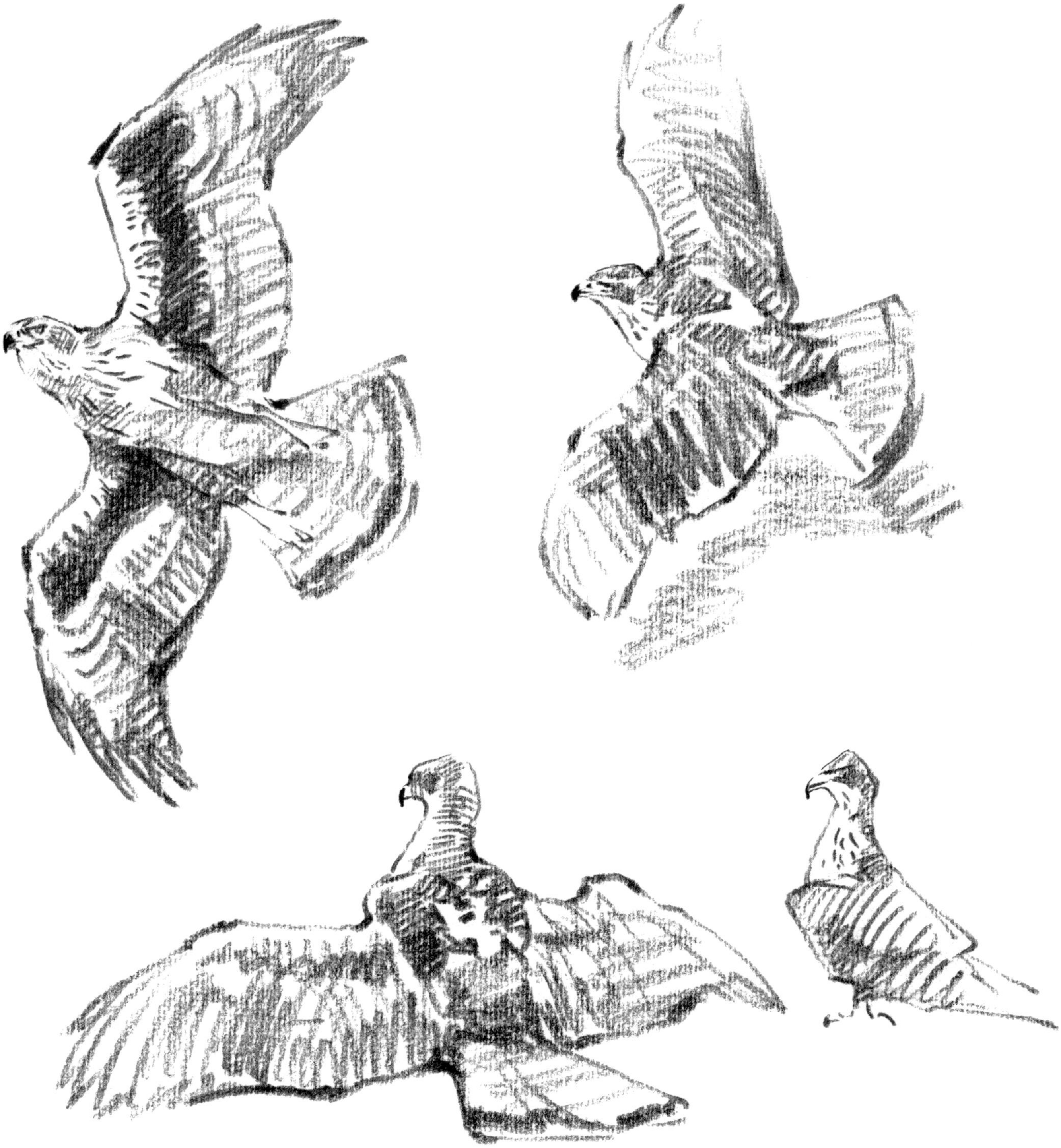

Bonelli's eagle, from a falconer's bird

in the Extremadura of Spain. Even distant views were exciting as it mostly catches prey – partridges and pigeons – by an aerial chase.

I had the opportunity to draw a Bonelli's, kept and flown by a falconer in Scotland. It had a fierce hawk-like expression and huge talons, as big as those of a golden eagle, but when this bird was flown it lacked the energy of a wild eagle on the hunt.

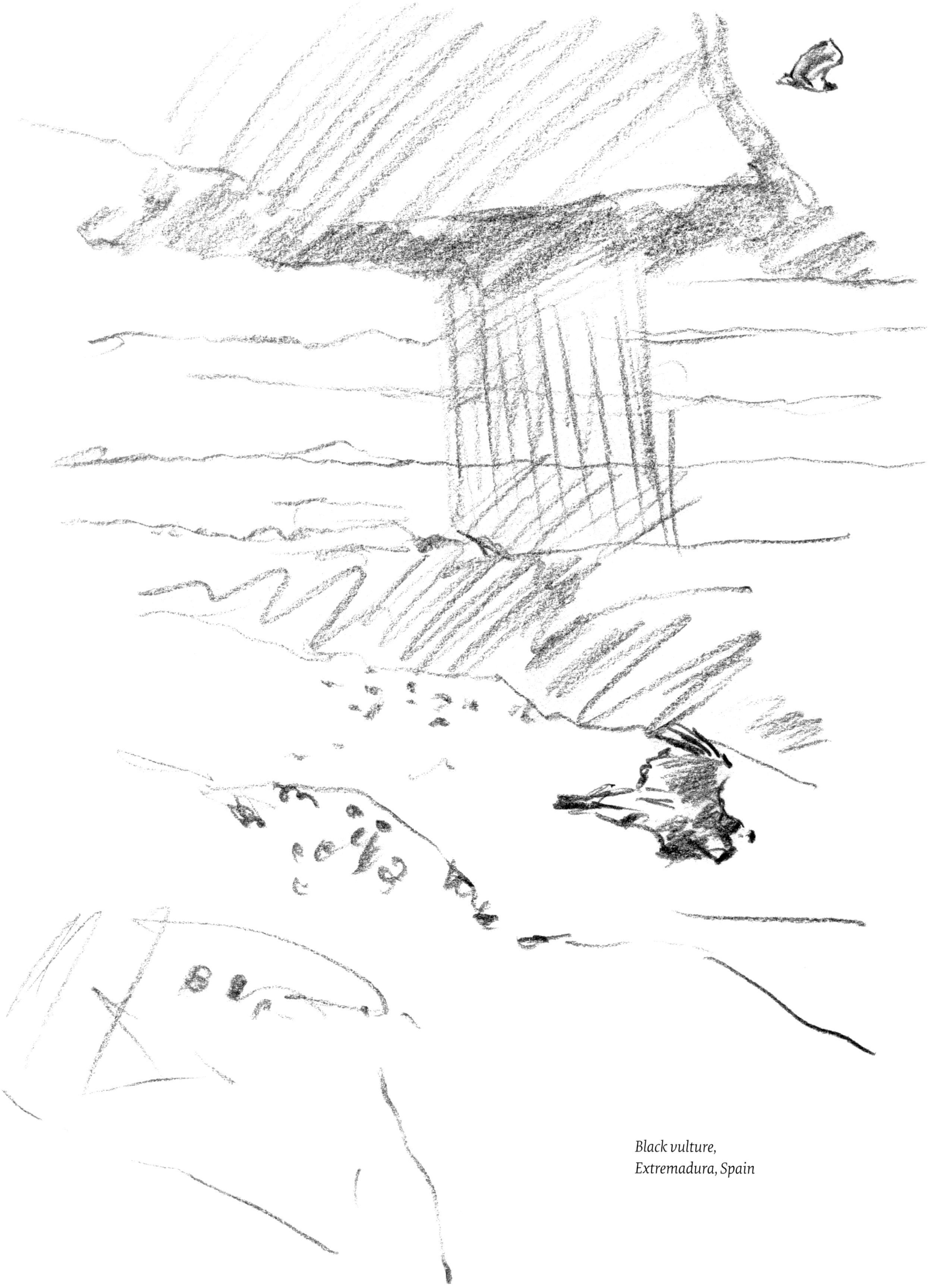

Black vulture,
Extremadura, Spain

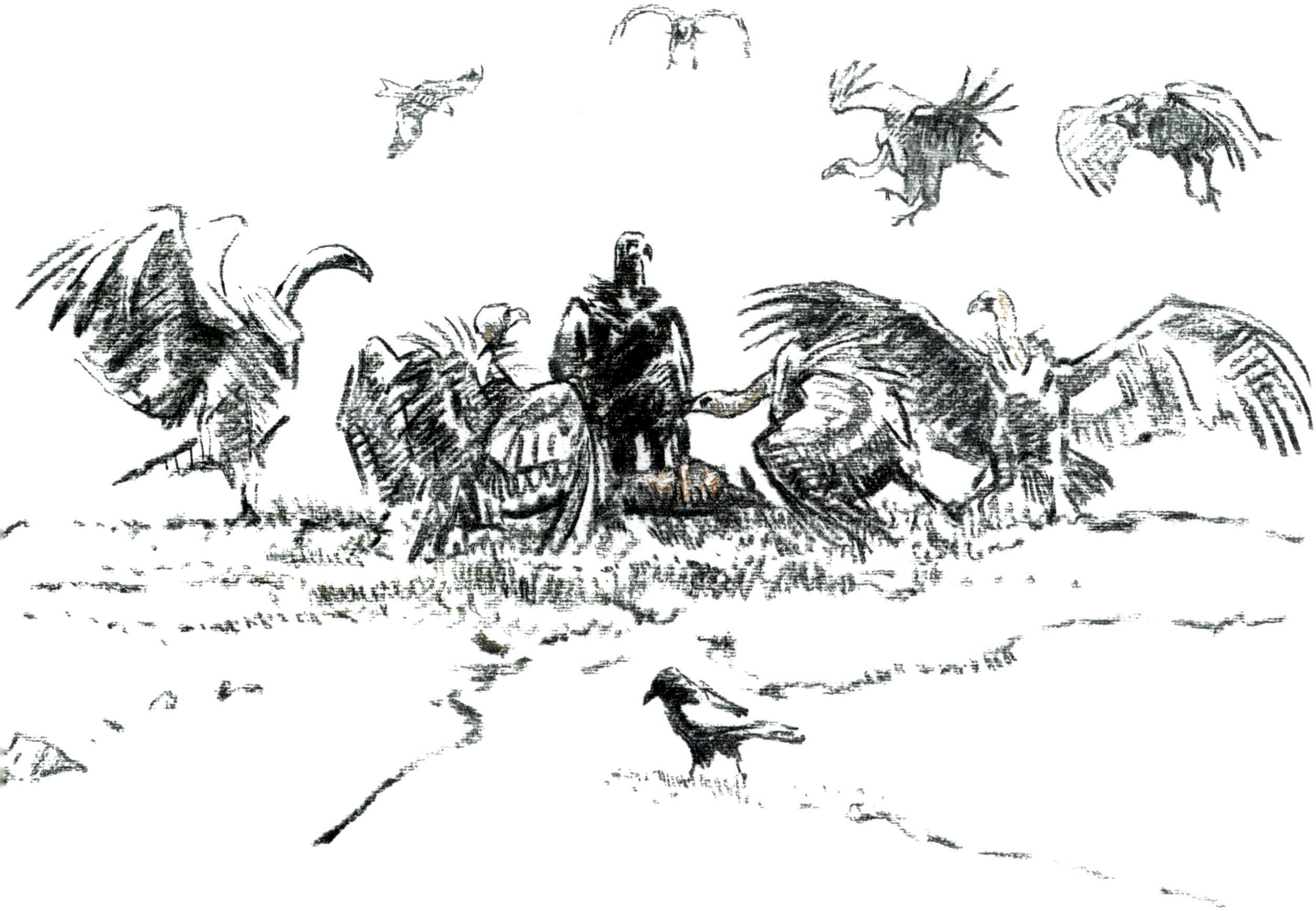

Vultures

I rather like vultures, especially in flight. Feeding on the ground they are grotesque and graceless, but airborne they have such a mastery of lift, and defy gravity with ease. Close to the castle of Monfrague in Spain, black and griffon vultures fly past at eye level. In the Vercours in France one sees griffons planing down to roost in the evenings making wonderful shapes in the sky.

John Paige and I watched from a car, vultures gathering on a carcass in a field by a roadside in Spain. The scene became more frenetic as griffons and a few black vultures arrived from all directions out of a clear sky to join the feast.

Griffon and black vultures, Extremadura

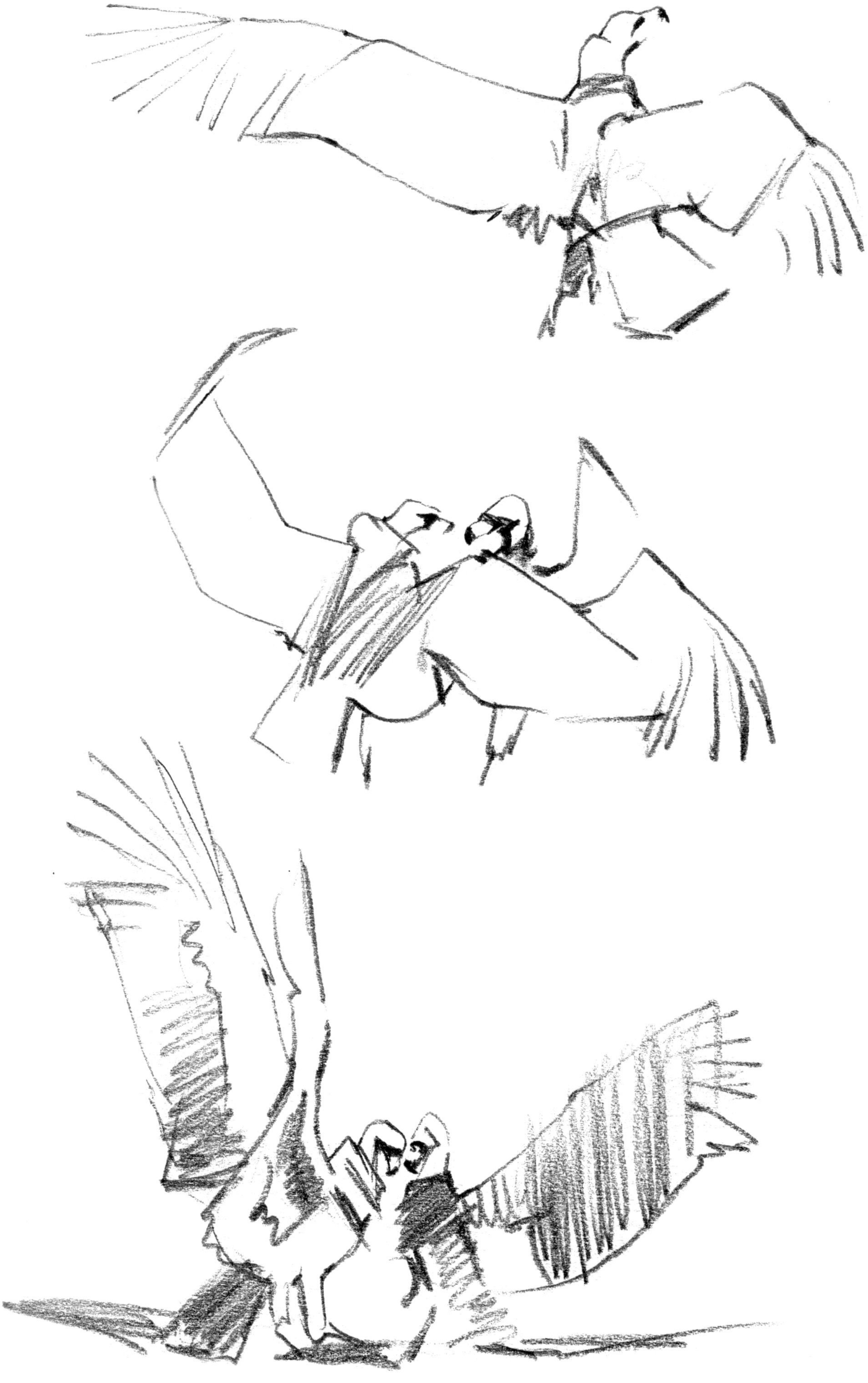

Black vultures

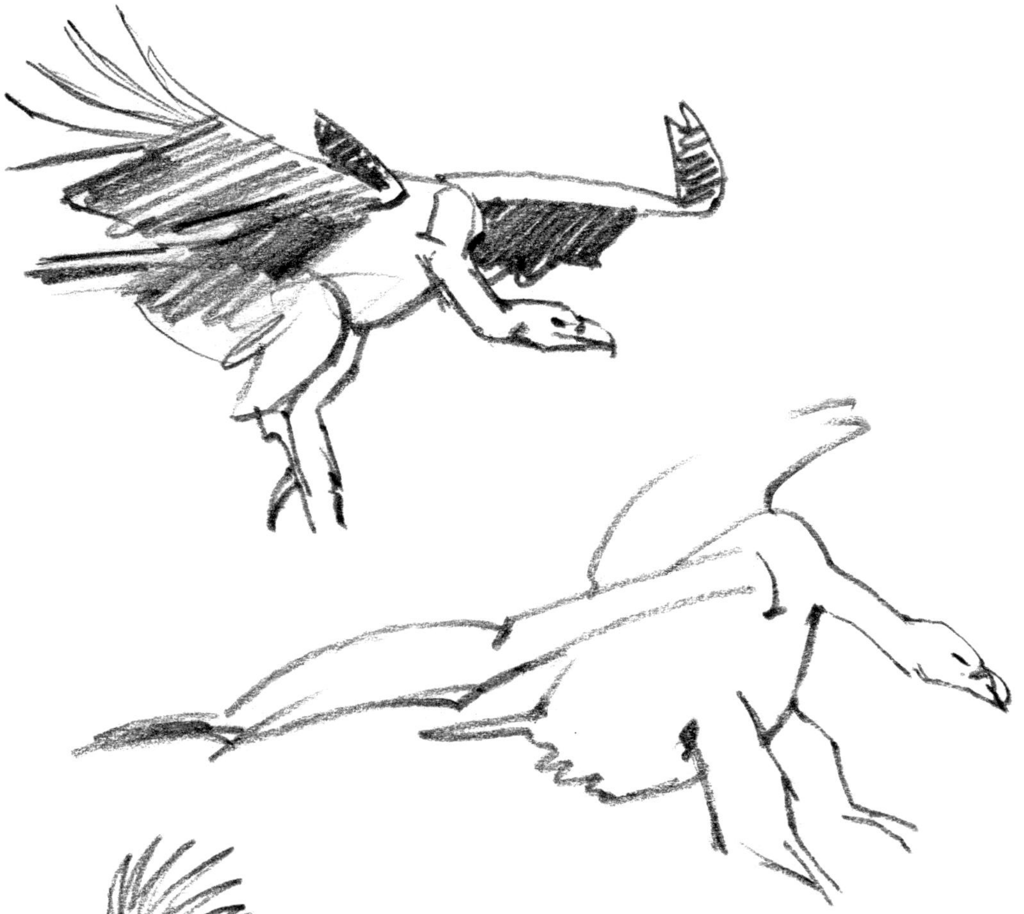

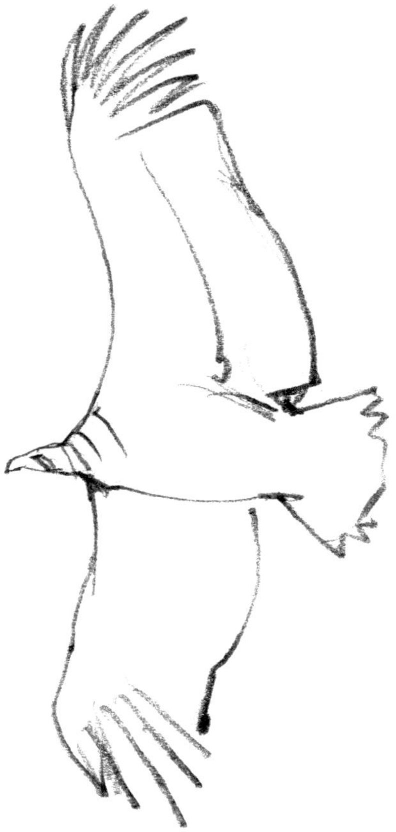

In India vultures sit around by busy roads. I wonder why? They are also becoming much fewer in number in all parts of the country.

Again in Mallorca I recalled a red-letter day for raptors at the Cuber reservoir:

'Seven Eleonora's are hawking over the mud fringe of the reservoir and landing at the water's edge. Their presence will be a good indicator of any other raptors in the area as they are sure to react. They rise to harry a red kite, which follows the ridge on the south side. A black vulture, with another very much higher, descends from Puig Mayor heading west. More follow and settle on the rocks below. One of the vultures is paler with a light head: it is a griffon. Its flight angle is more dihedral than the black vulture and its wings have a more rounded trailing edge with more splayed wing 'fingers'.

A peregrine, two kites and a raven fly over, and as I walk over towards L'Ofrir, a gentle kestrel hovers in the sky'

Griffon vultures about to land

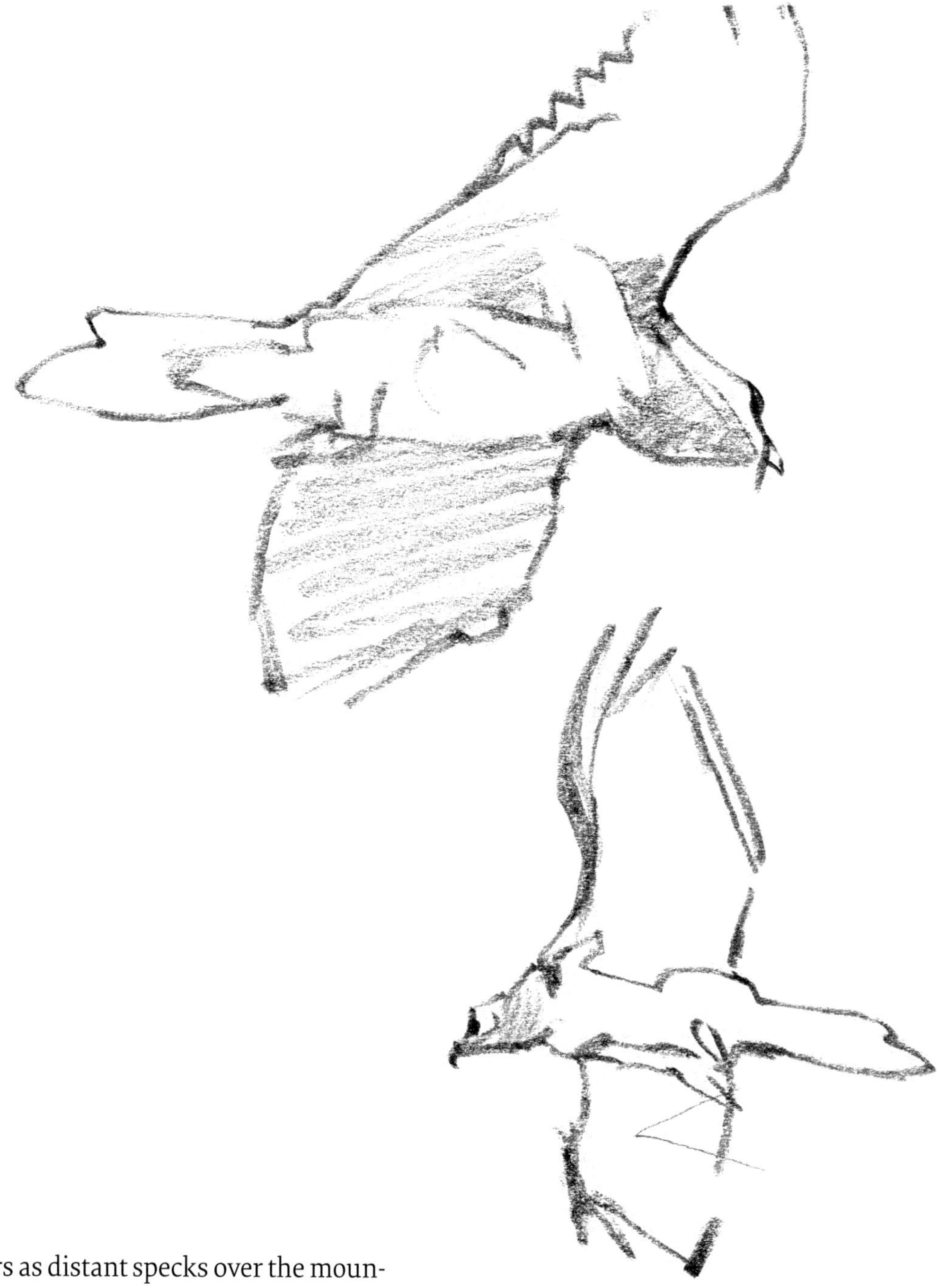

I have only seen lammergeyers as distant specks over the mountains of Jordan. These were drawn while watching the BBC documentary film, *The Bone Breaker*. Drawing from someone's film does not have the same adrenalin rush of excitement as an experience of one's own, but these images were still inspiring enough to draw from, though you never knew when the camera shot would change and leave you floundering. I could imagine myself back in Wadi Rum.

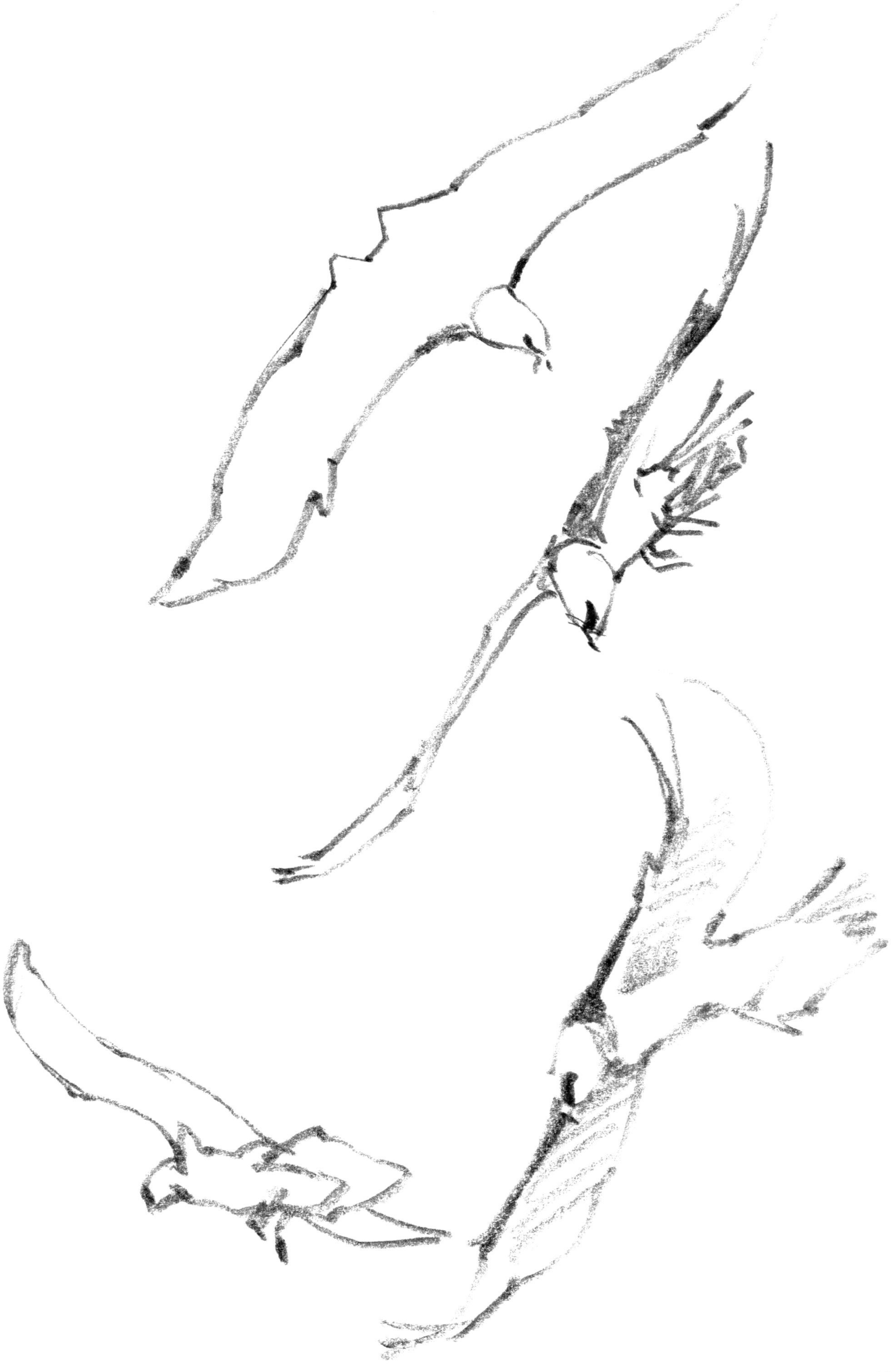

Lammergeyers drawn from film

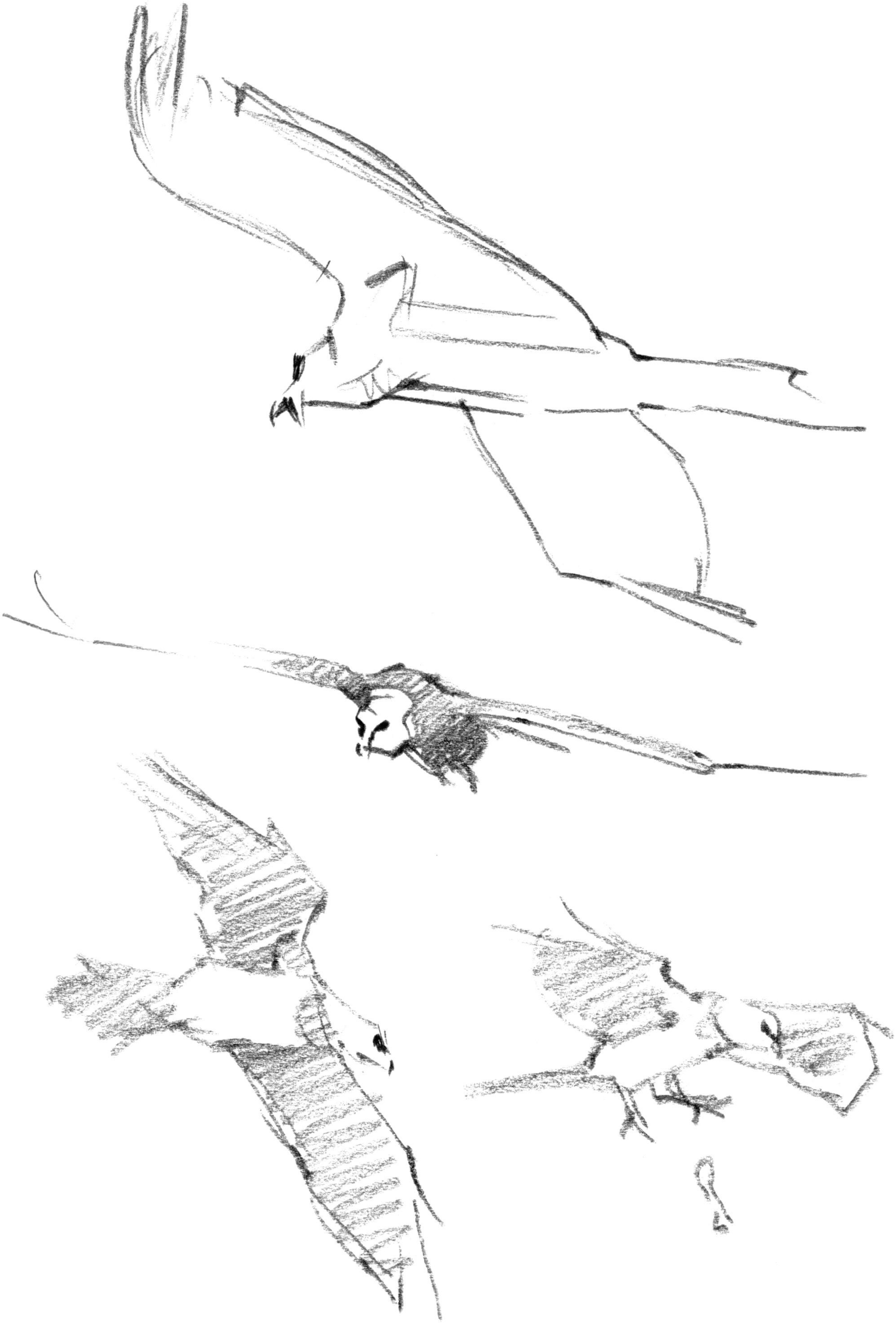

Lammergyers, the bone breakers

I have not seen a wild condor, only this one in Chester zoo, which allowed time for a detailed study. I was surprised by its fowl-like feet and smallish eyes compared to other vultures. Chester zoo also had a nesting pair of black vultures.

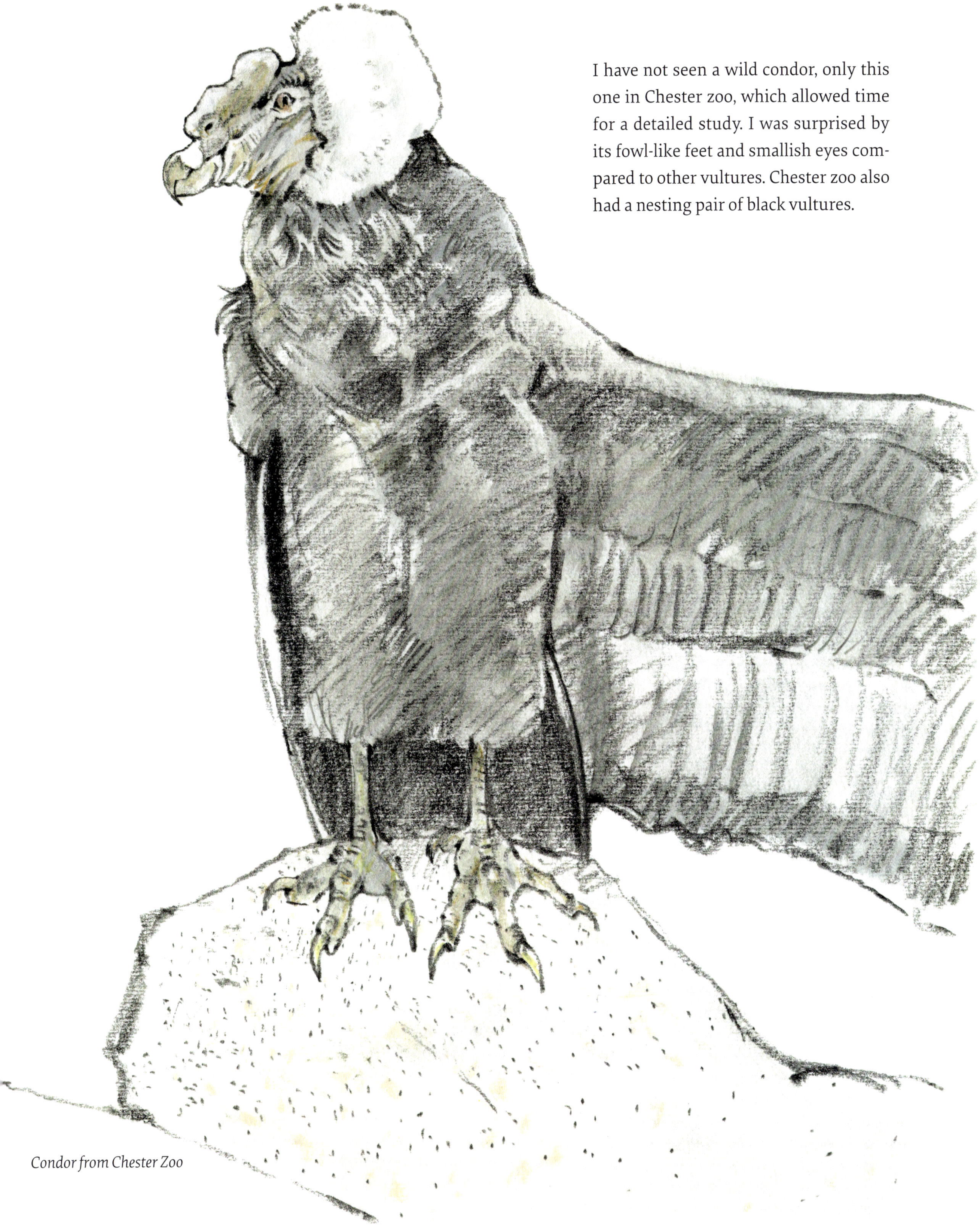

Condor from Chester Zoo

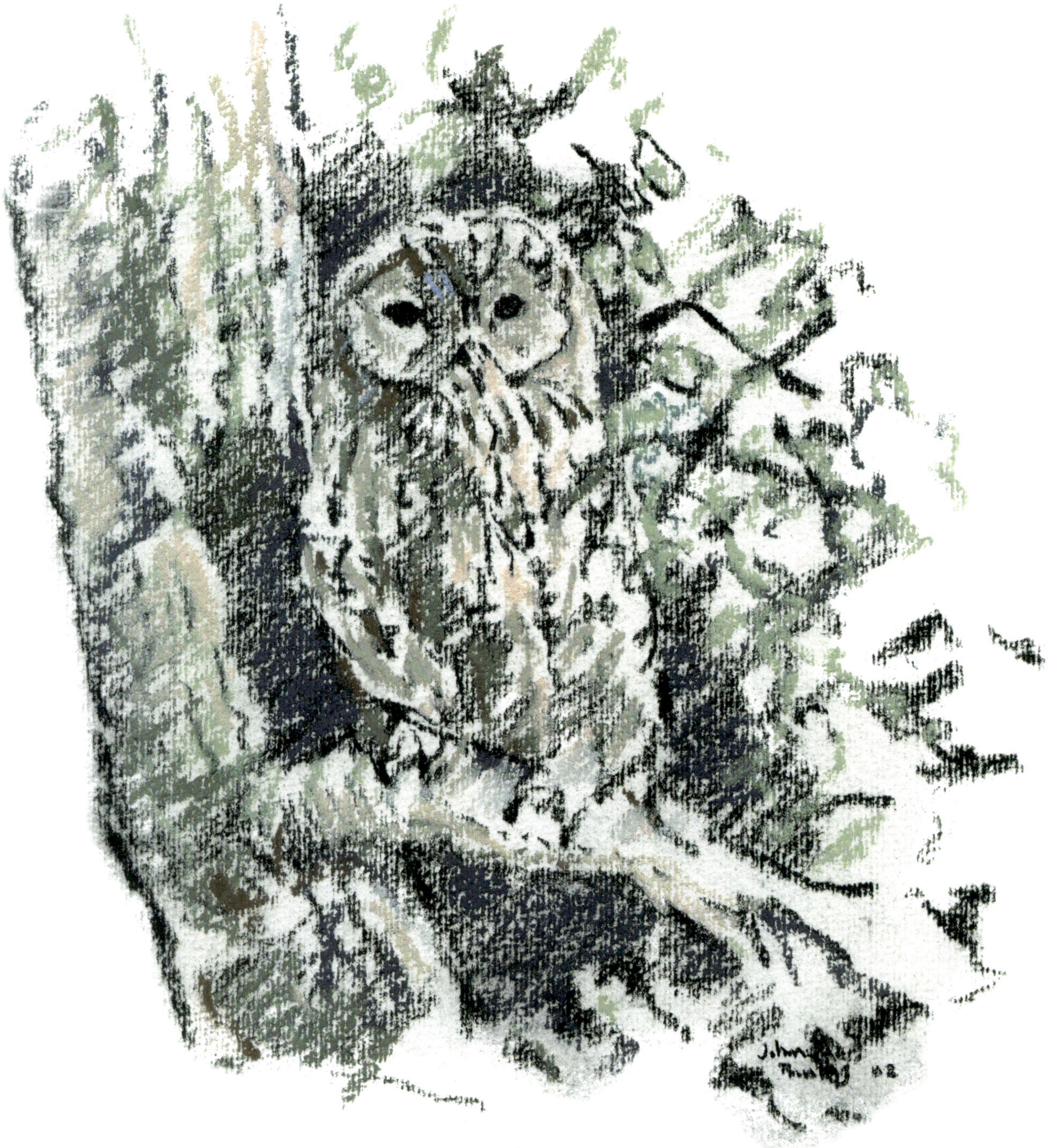

Owls

Owls have strong associations in human thought and art: symbols both of wisdom and of dark forces. Seen face to face their direct stare gives them an arresting presence.

Being mostly creatures of the dark, they are not easy to find and to draw. Our most common owl, the tawny, is more often heard than seen. The male's "to-wit-to-woo" echoes through the woodlands especially when the bird is setting up territory in the autumn, or an owl is revealed by the alarm cries of mobbing birds if it is discovered hiding during daylight.

Tawny owl

My sightings of long-eared owls have been few, but I remember a young family perched out along a fence in Northumberland: tallest and eldest on the left; youngest on the right!

Little owls are great characters to draw; seen mostly in northern and southern counties of England, rarely coming as far north as Scotland.

I saw my only wild snowy owl in Shetland many years ago sitting and preening itself. (I still have its cast off tail feather).

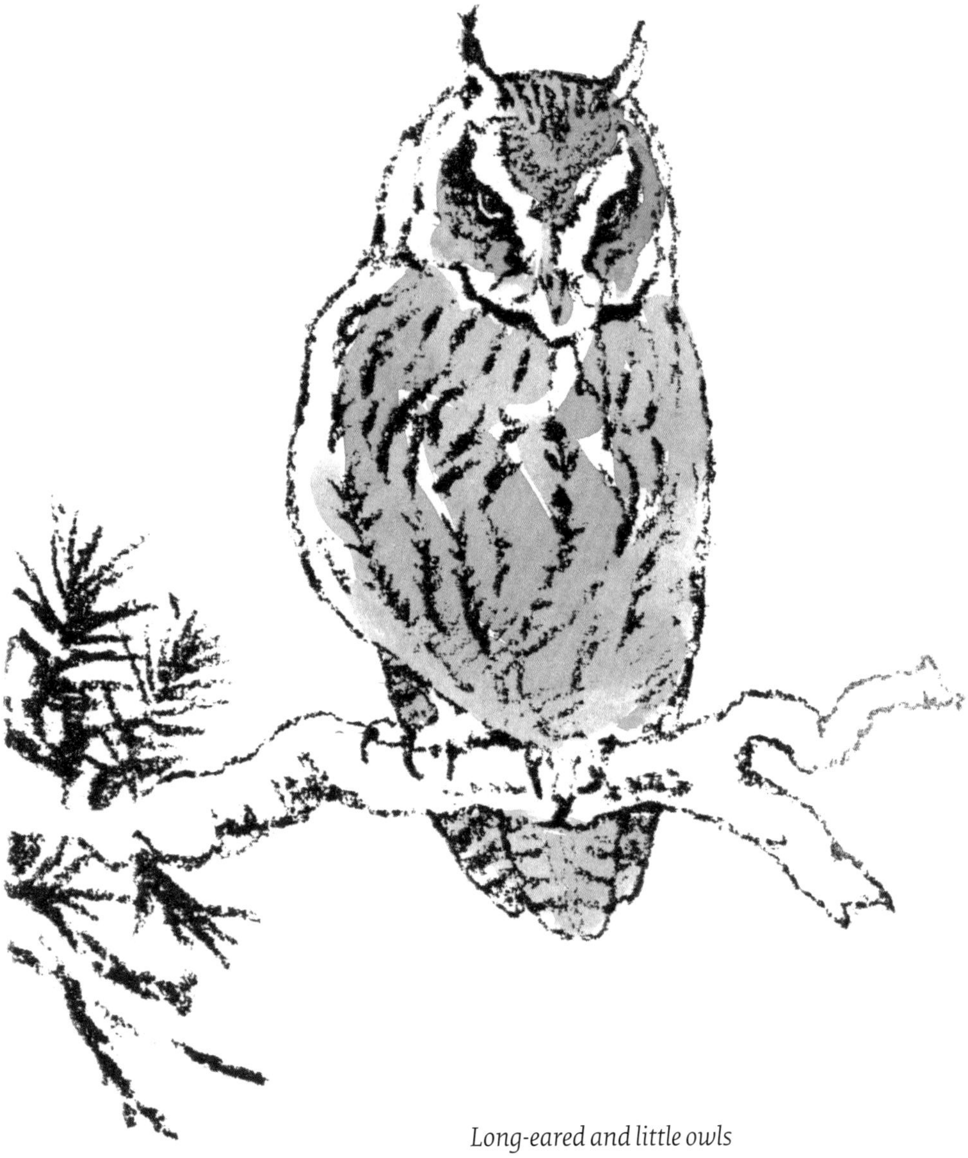

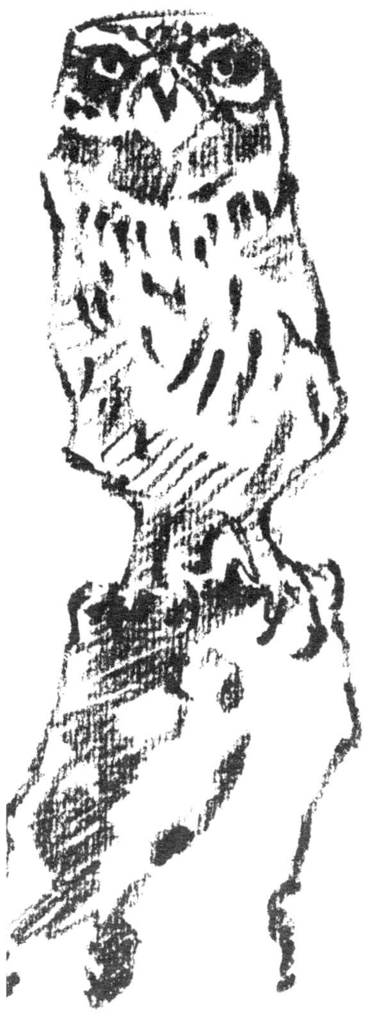

Long-eared and little owls

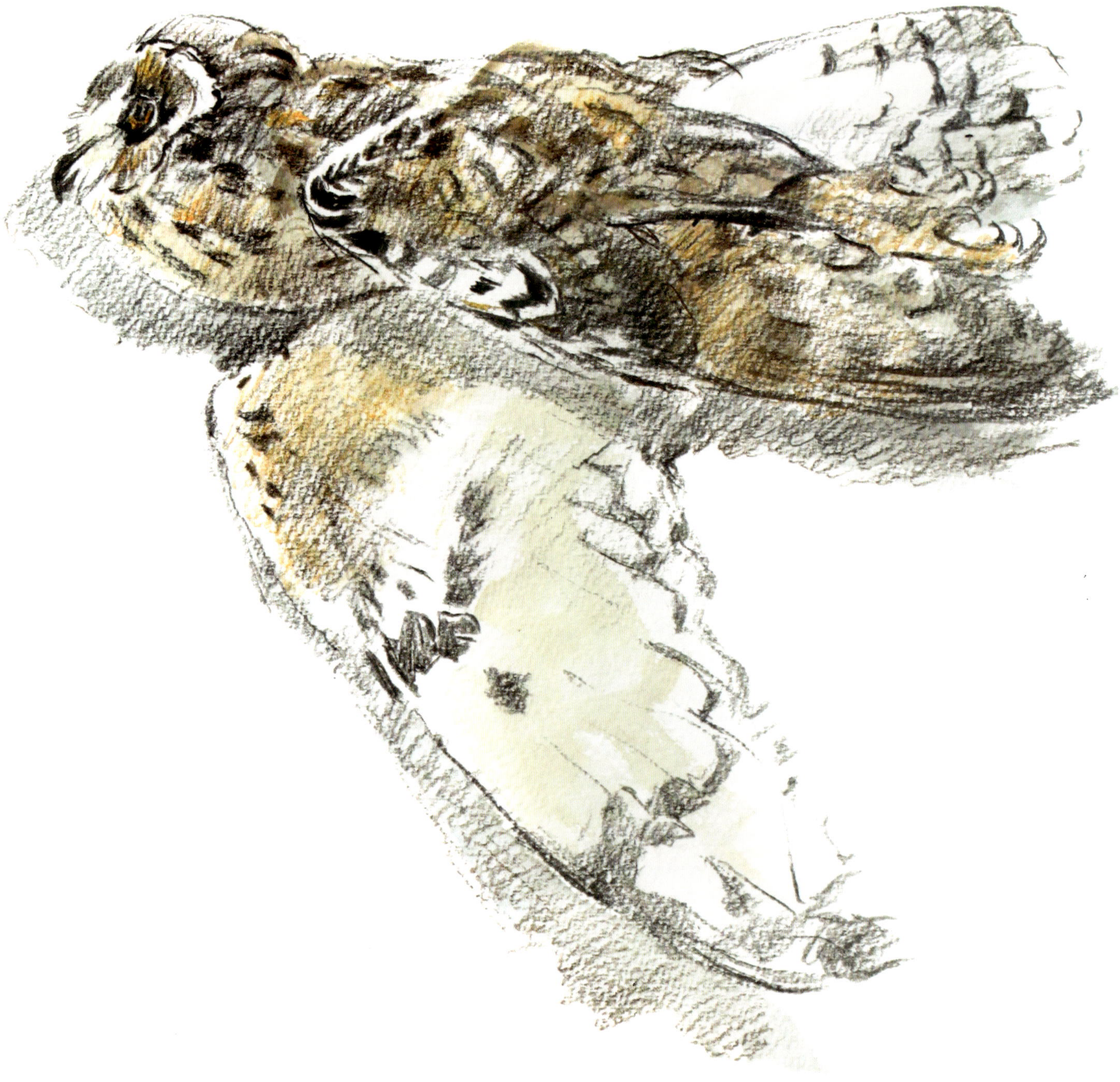

Short-eared owl, study from a dead bird

Best of all to draw, perhaps because they are active in daylight, are the barn owl and the short-eared. In places where voles are plentiful short-eareds can be seen perched on fence posts or quartering the fields with slow measured wing beats. I was fortunate to spend time drawing from in a photographer's hide at a short-eared owl's nest in Speyside. This bird is sheltering its young from the sun.

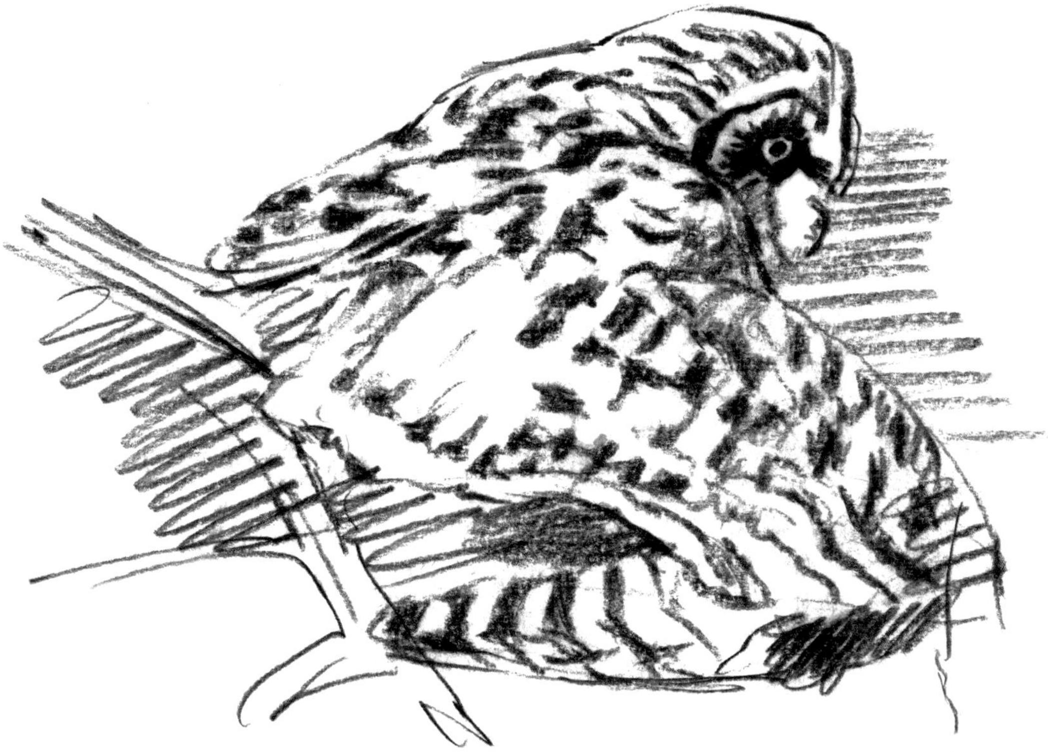

Short-eared owl, drawn from a photographer's hide at the nest

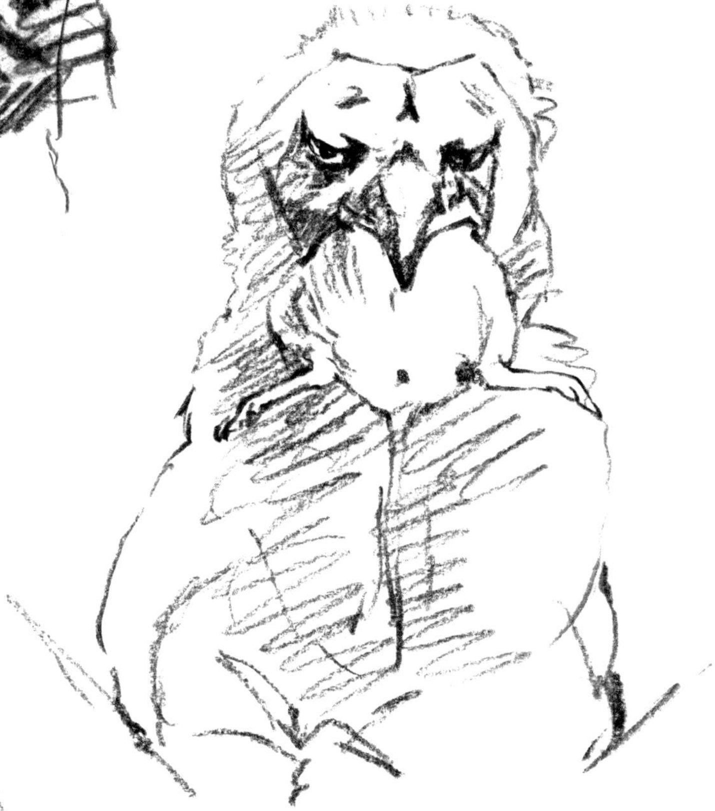

Short-eared owlet, eating a rat.

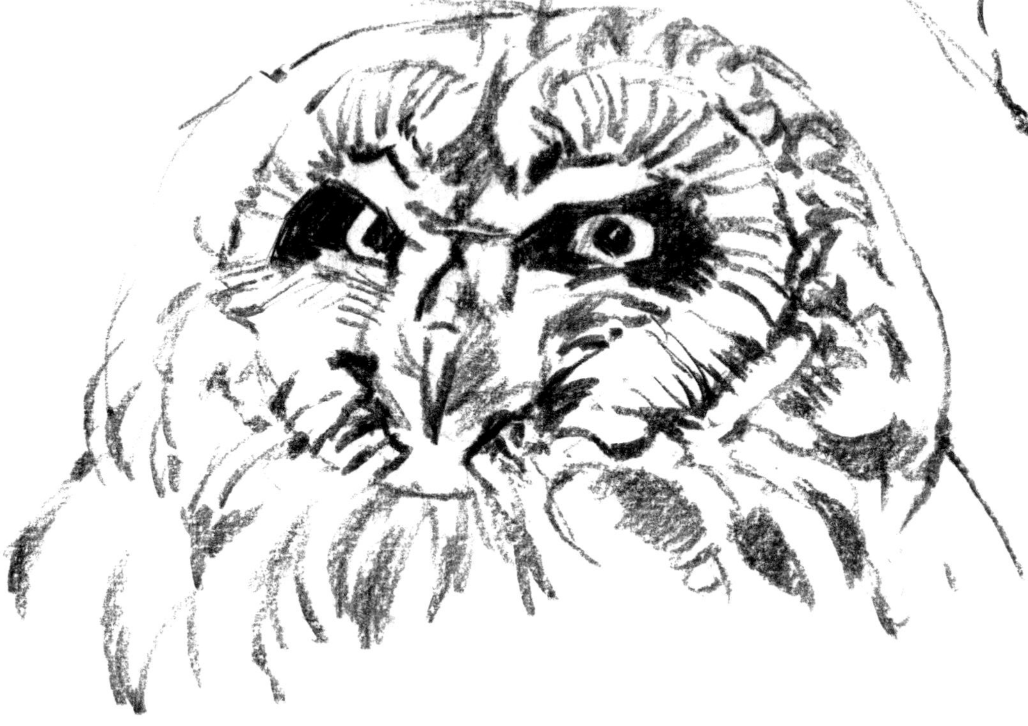

Head of a female short-eared owl

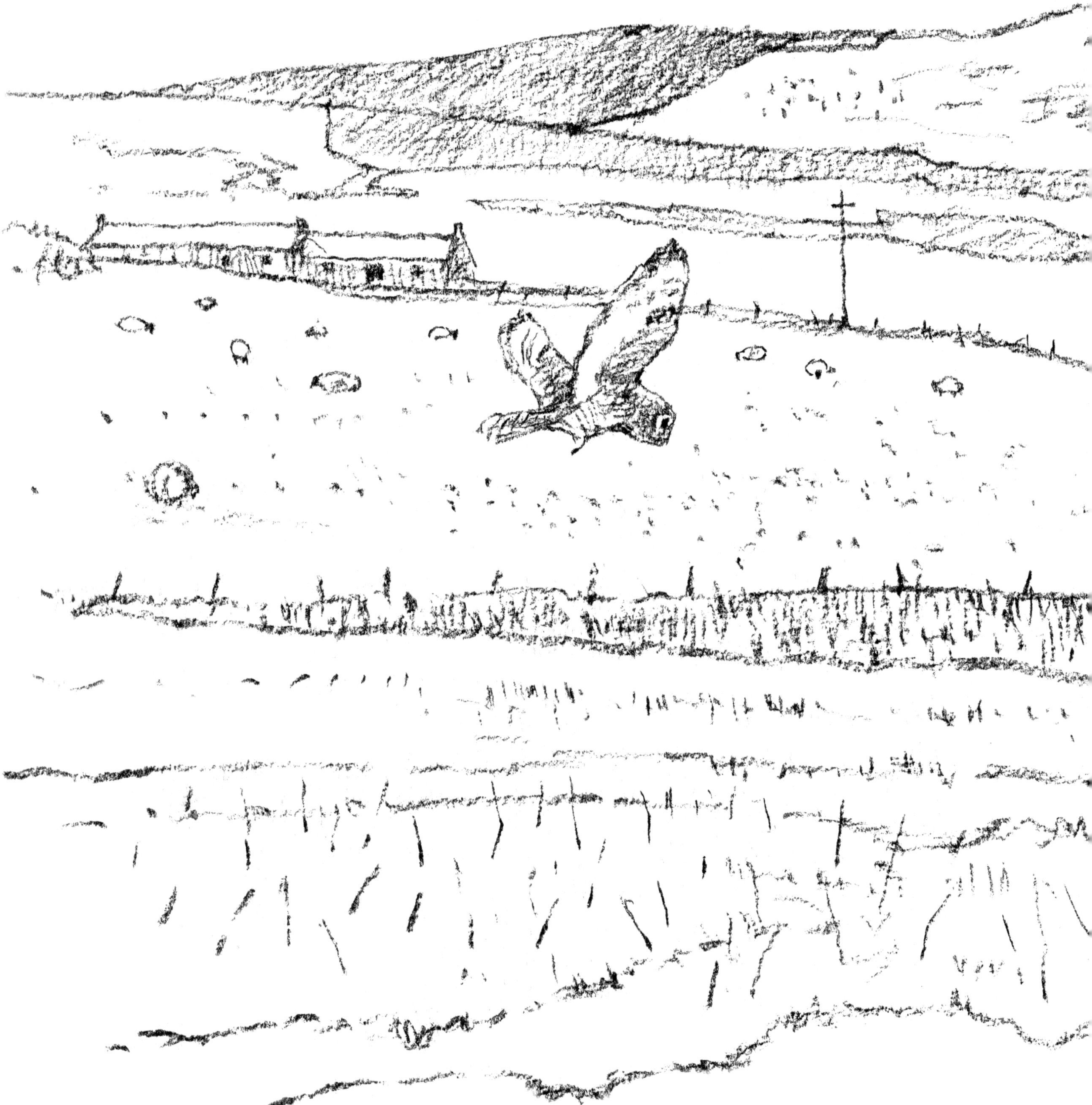

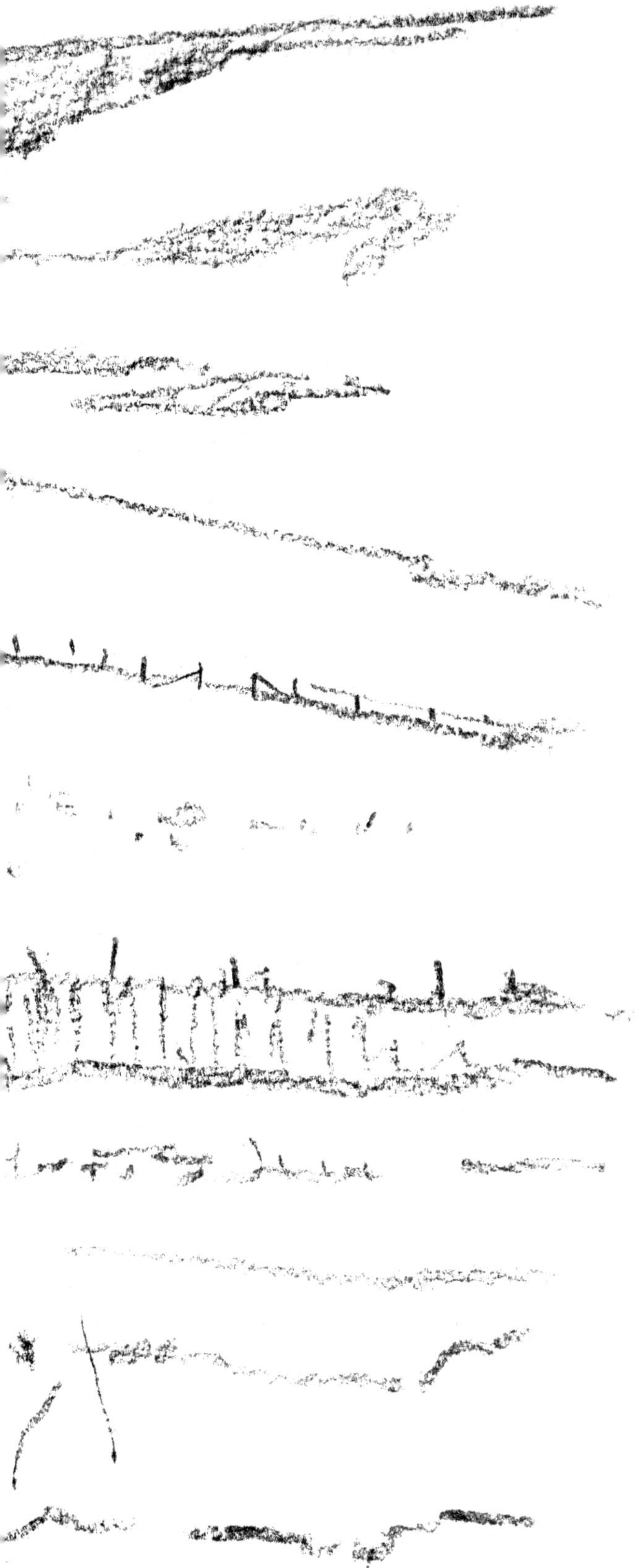

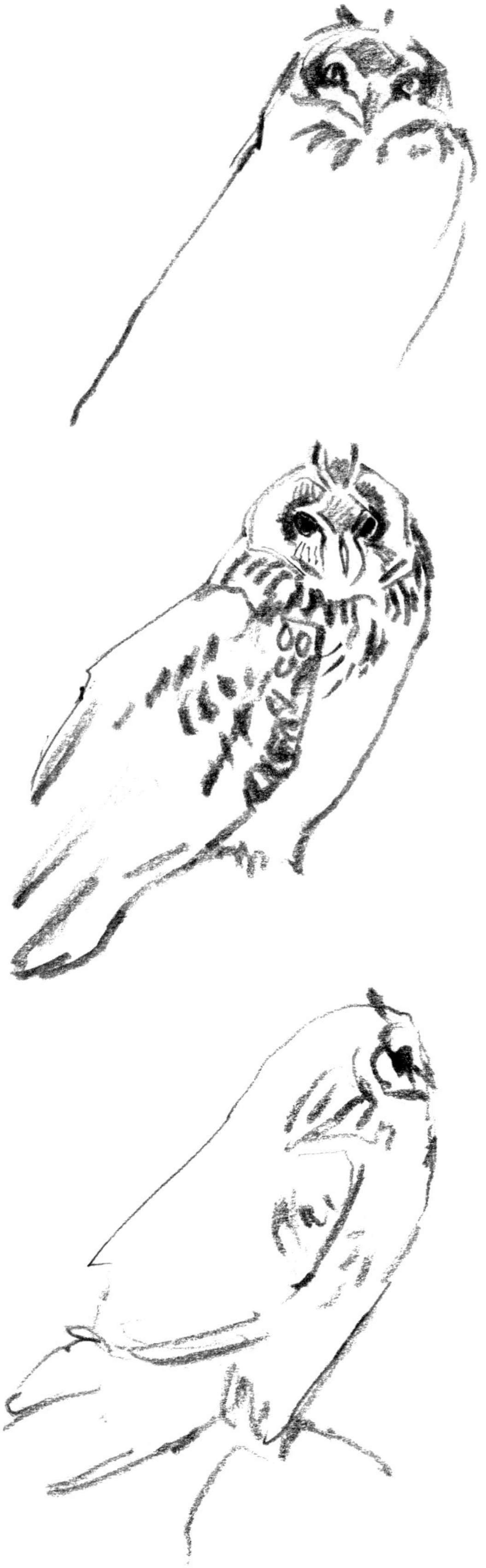

Short-eared hunting over fields near Evie in Orkney

Short-eared owls

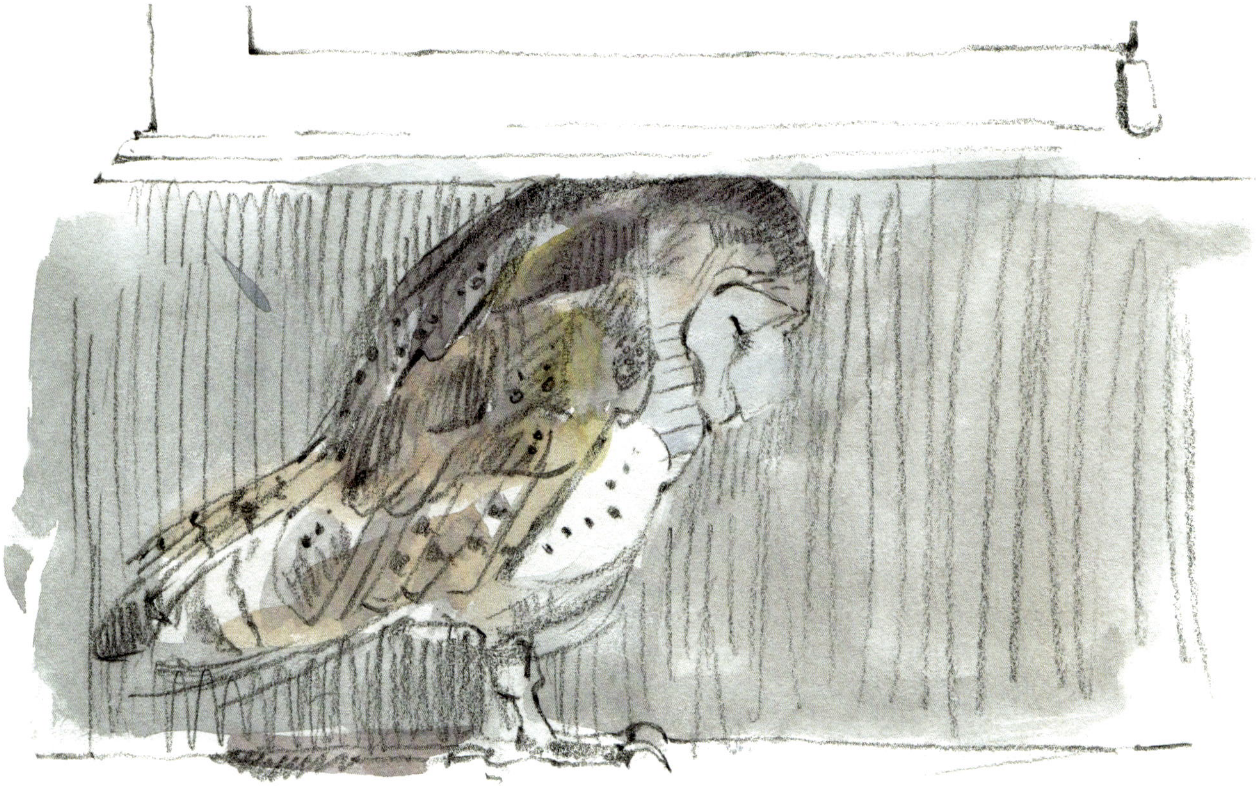

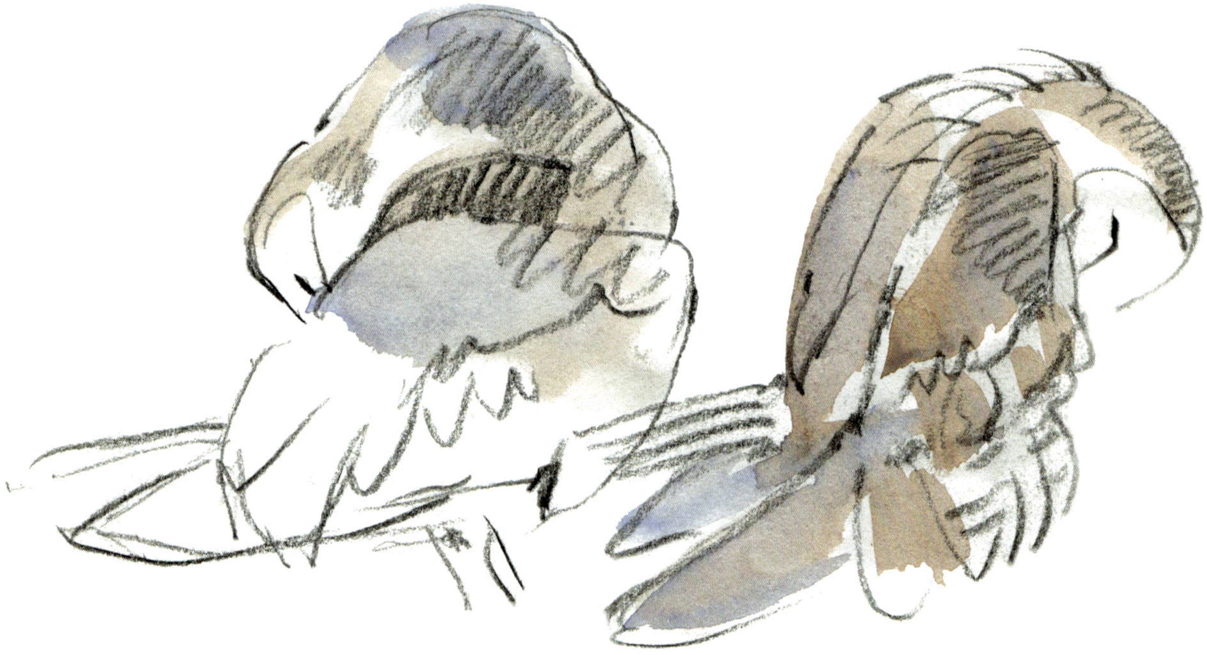

My friend David Measures had a tame barn owl, rescued when a chick, which would take a bath in a washing-up bowl, and retire to sleep on top of the fridge. It would sit on Christine Measures' shoulder and nibble her ears.

Wild barn owls are lovely to see in flight, floating over the fields at dusk. They make the ending of any day memorable.

'Penelope': a tame barn owl, resting on top of the fridge

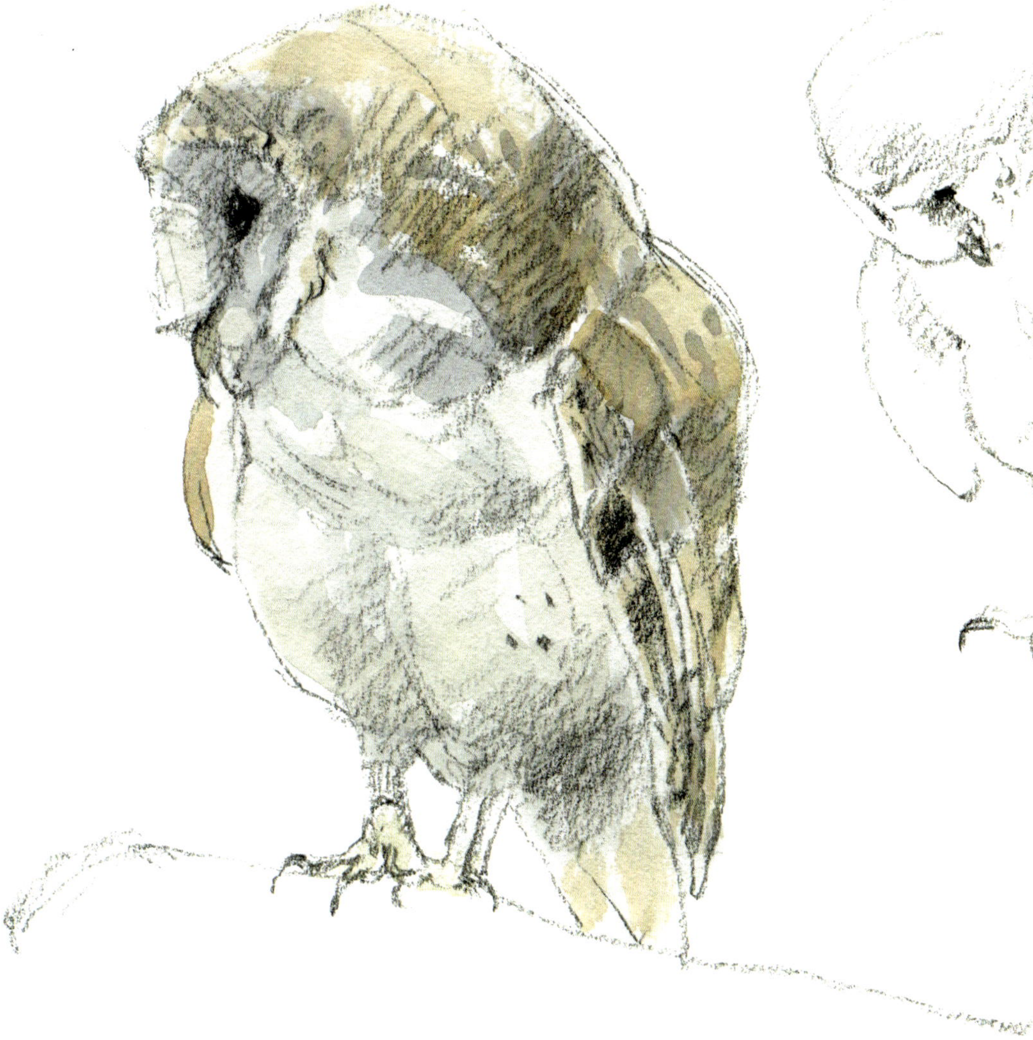

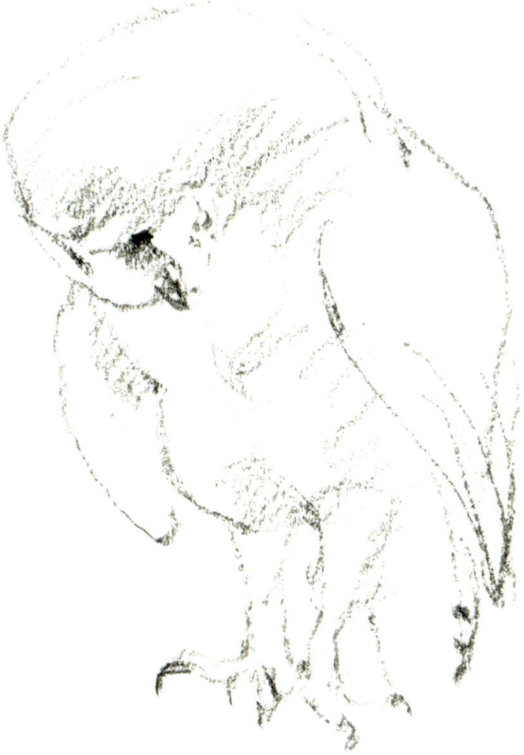

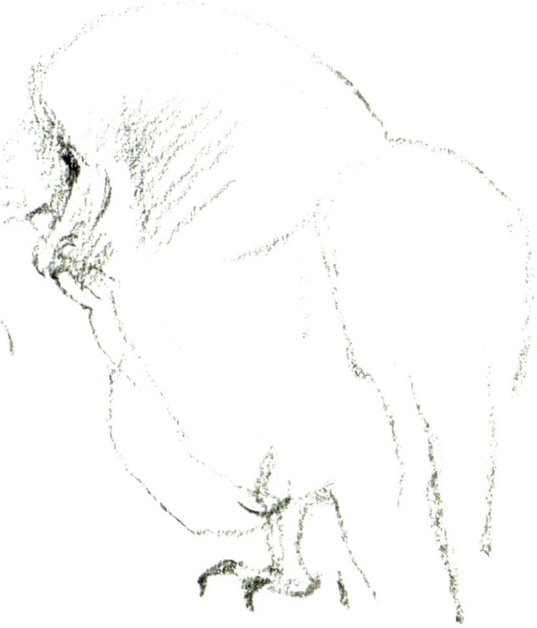

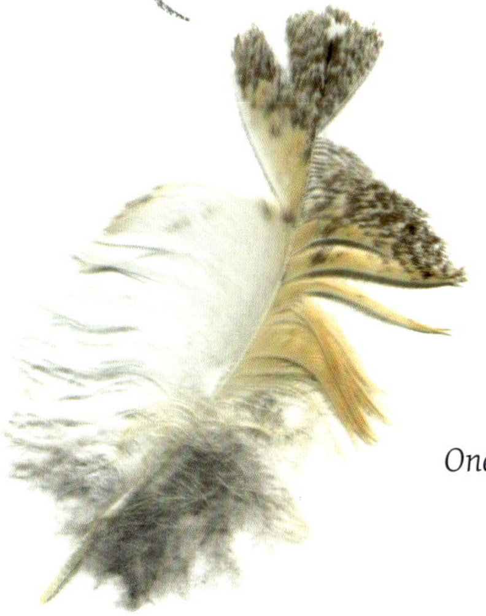

One of Penelope's feathers

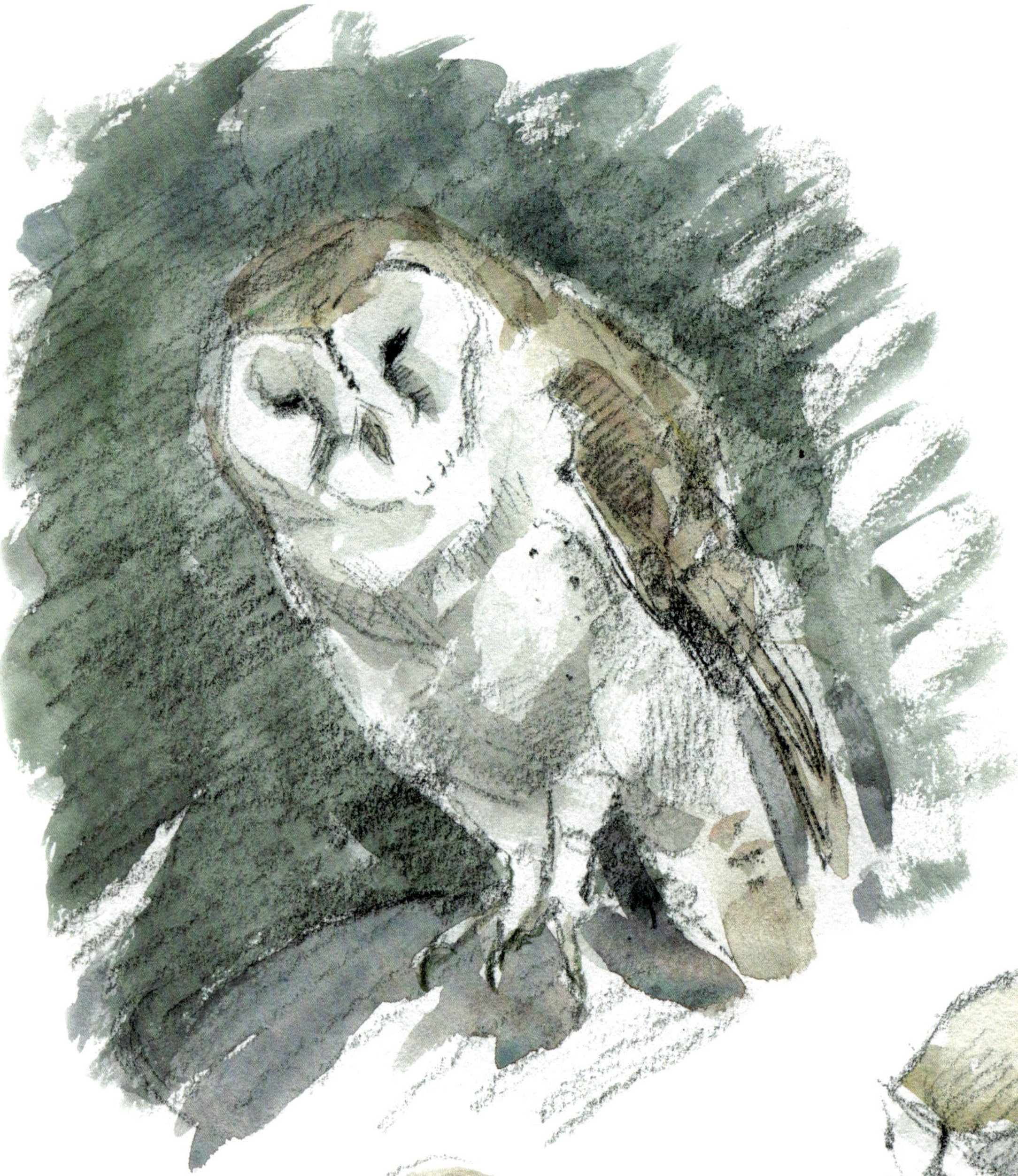

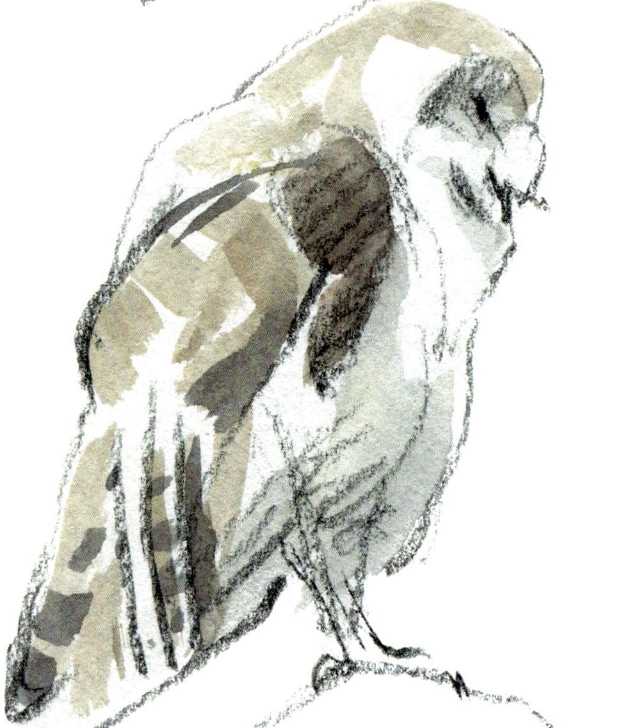

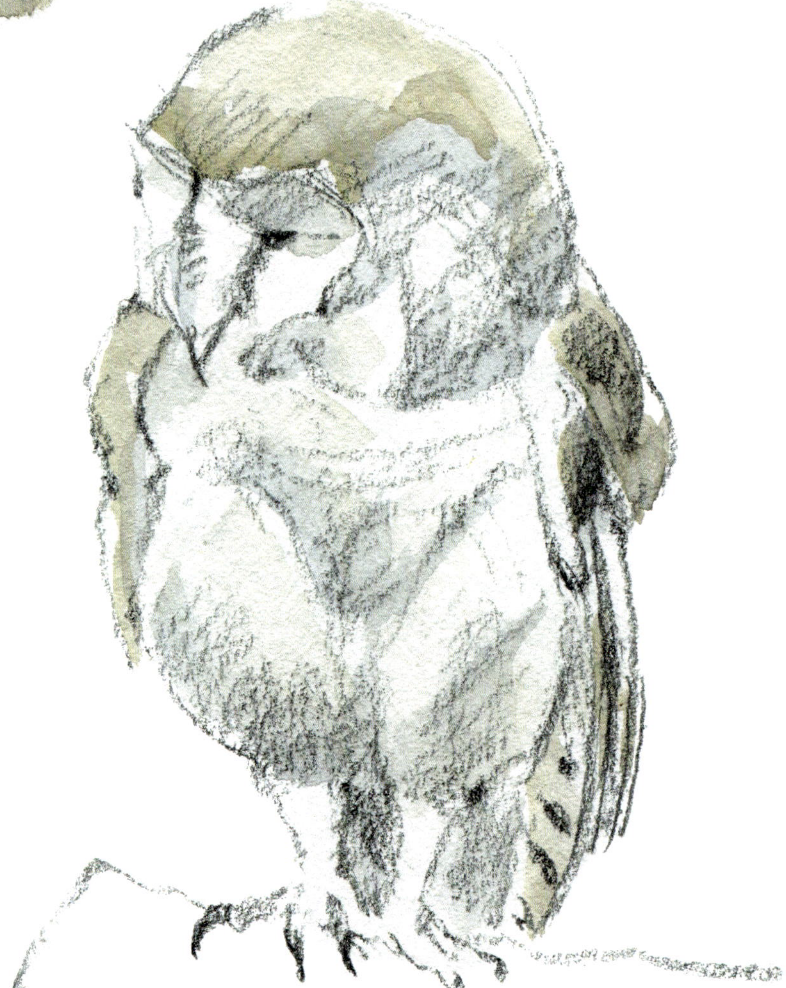

'Penelope'

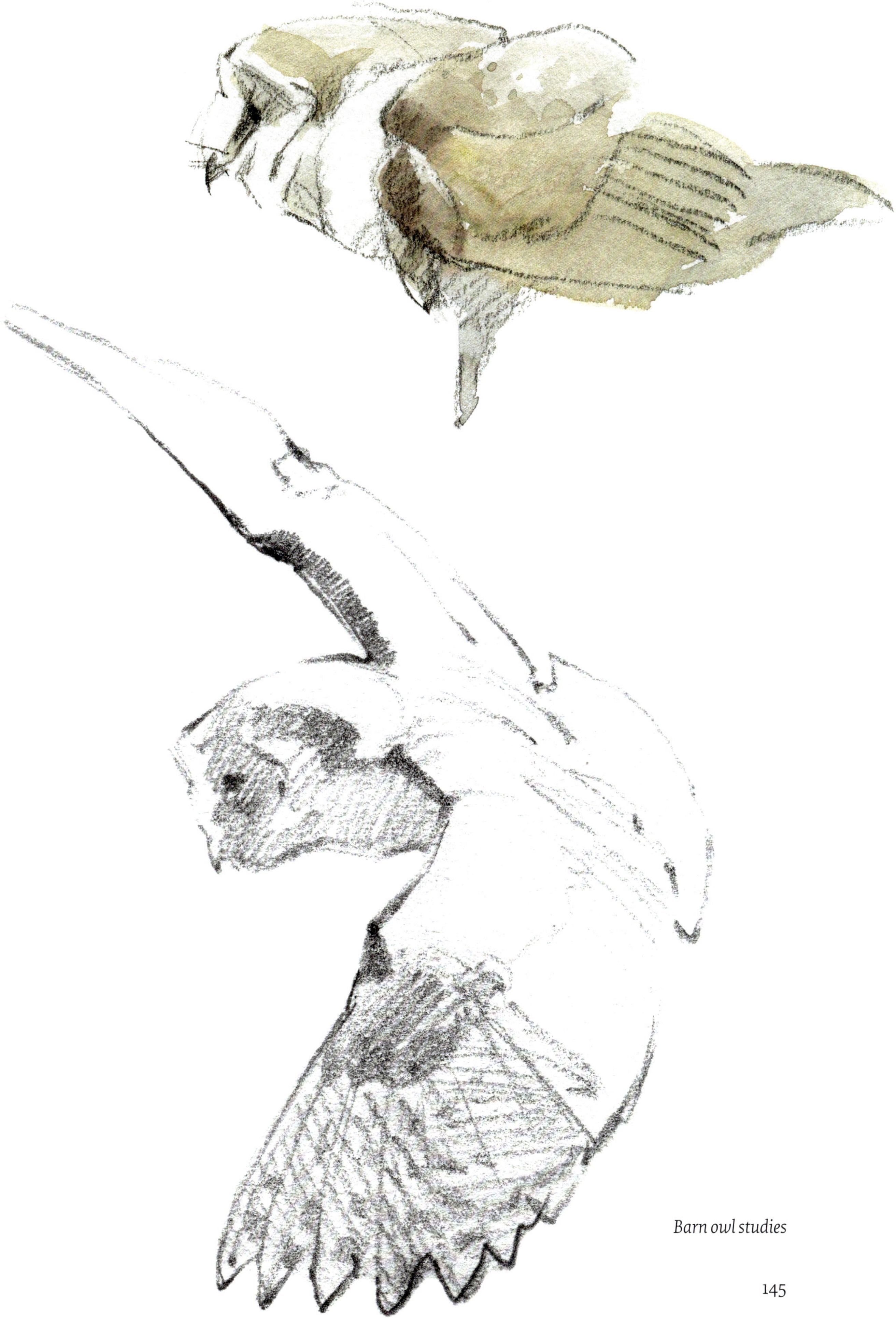

Barn owl studies

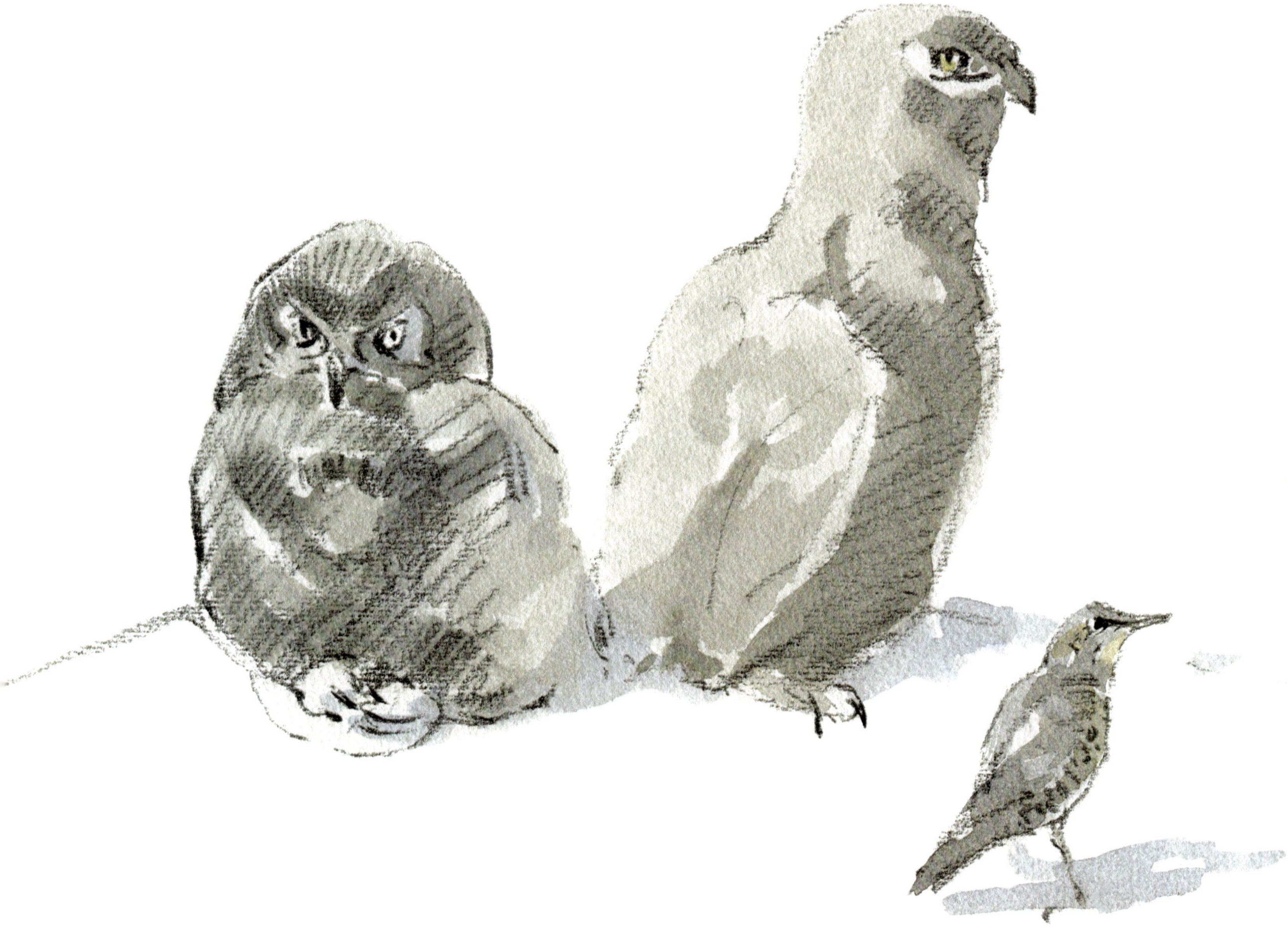

Young snowy owls and starling,
Edinburgh Zoo

I am grateful to zoos for the chance to draw owls from many parts of the world. Of all birds owls carry with them the air of mystery and unfathomable knowing!

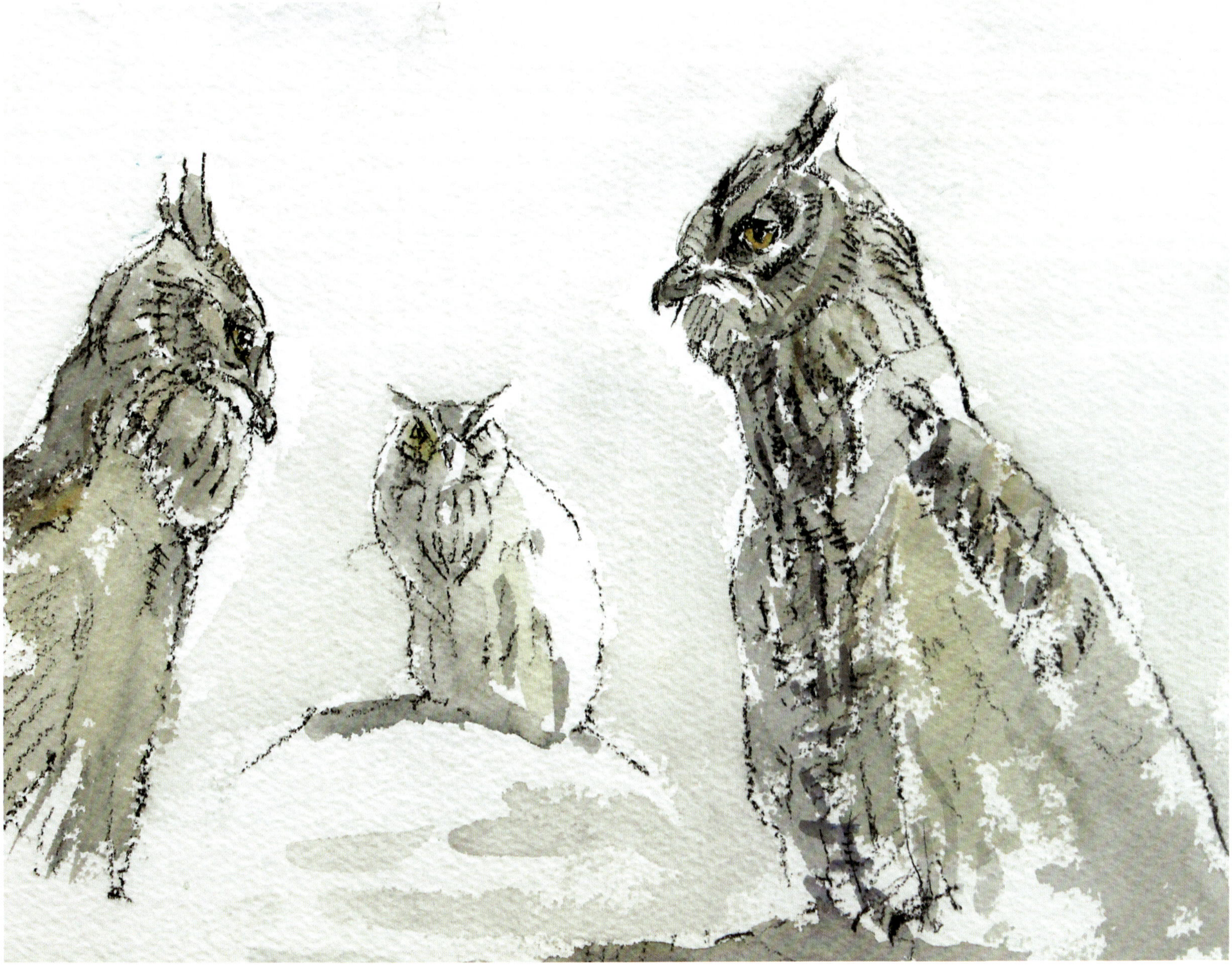

Eagle owls from a falconer's bird

Mammals

In Britain our native wild animals are mostly wary of humans and scarper or stay under cover if they catch sight or smell of one. Most of my encounters with our rabbits, hares, deer, foxes, badgers and so on, have been at a distance, or if I had managed to remain still and hidden for long enough to become part of the landscape. Earlier I mentioned one such occasion in Shetland while working with Hugh Miles on his book *Track of the Wild Otter*. Thanks to Hugh's skill in field craft we managed to keep close to a female otter and her two kittens for several days, and they were great to watch and draw as they learnt first to depend on the mother for food and protection, be taught to fish through the year and gradually reach maturity and independence.

Otter in Shetland >

Young otters eating fish

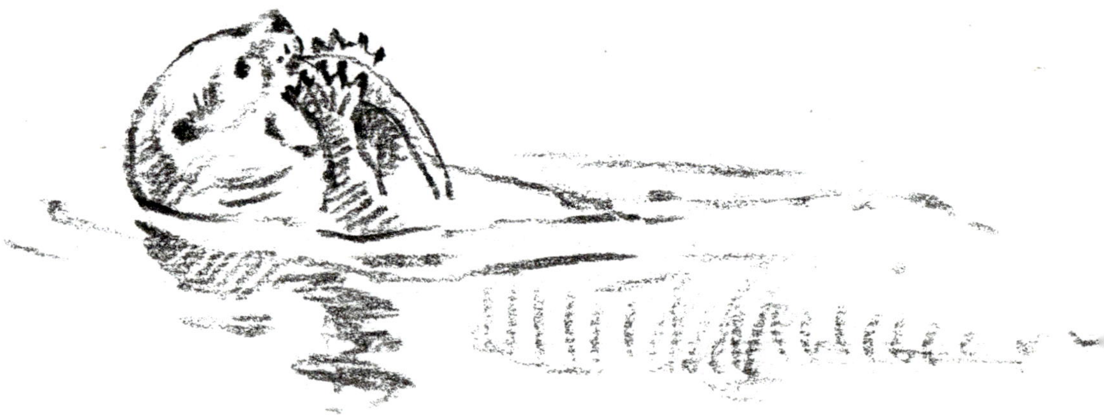

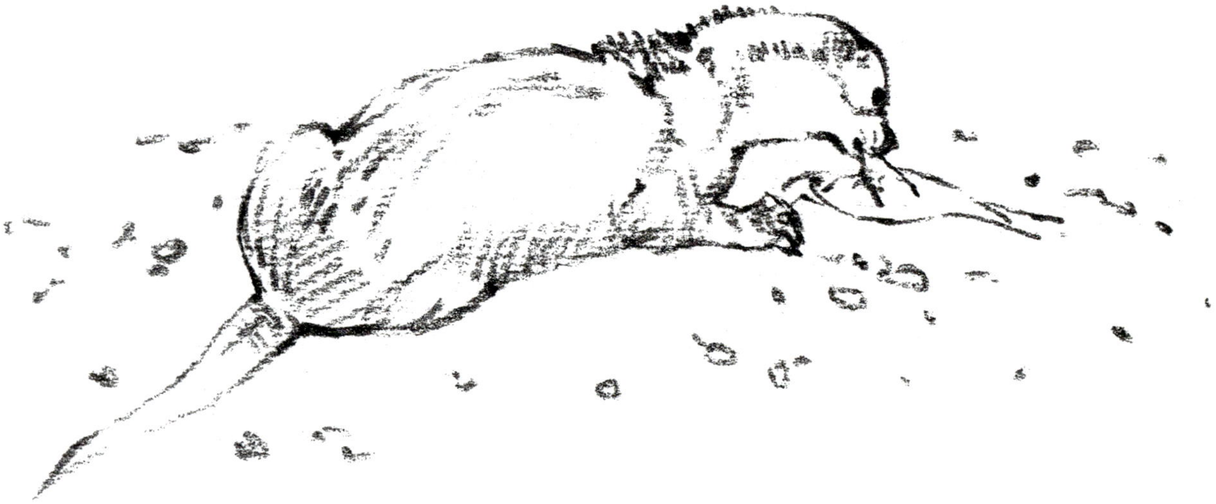

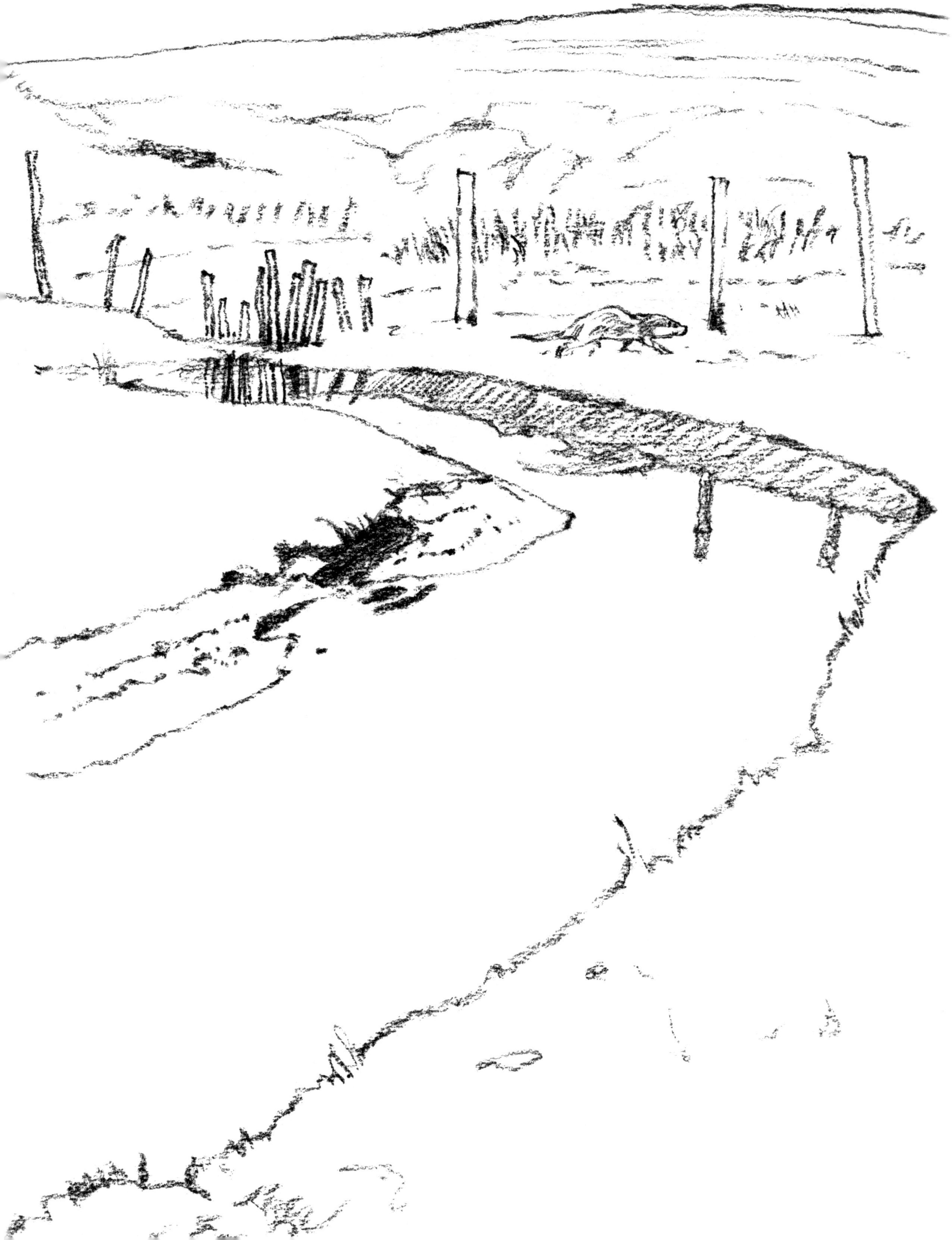

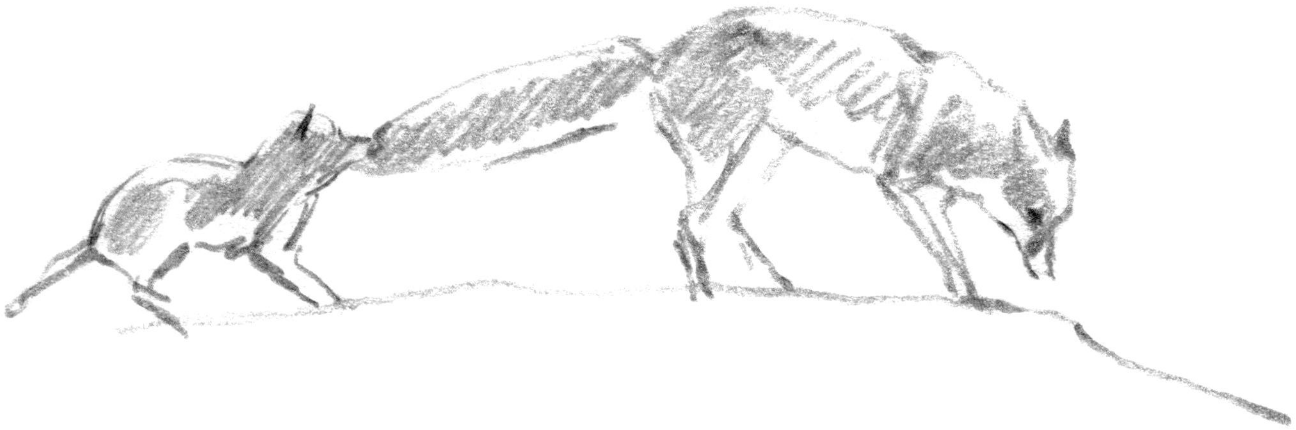

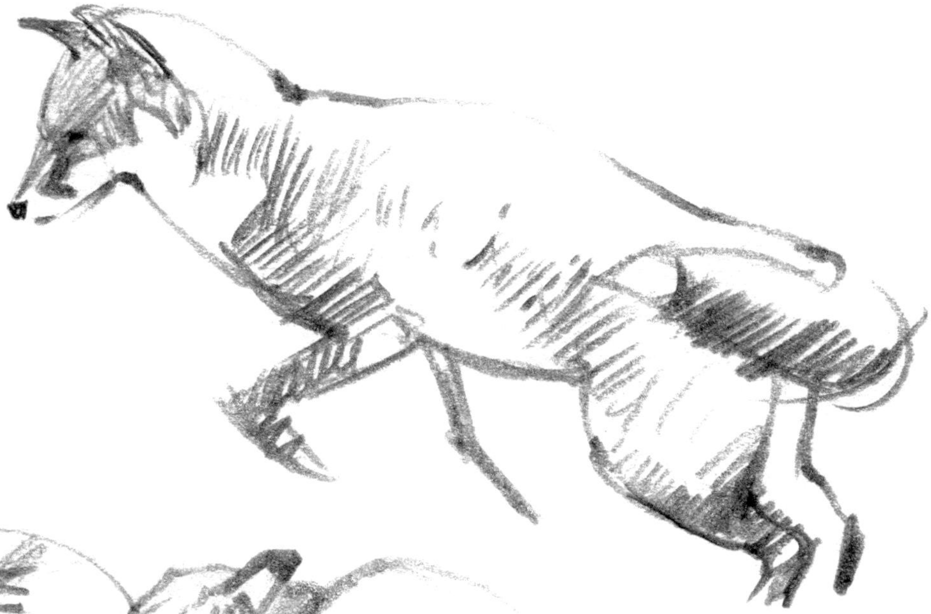

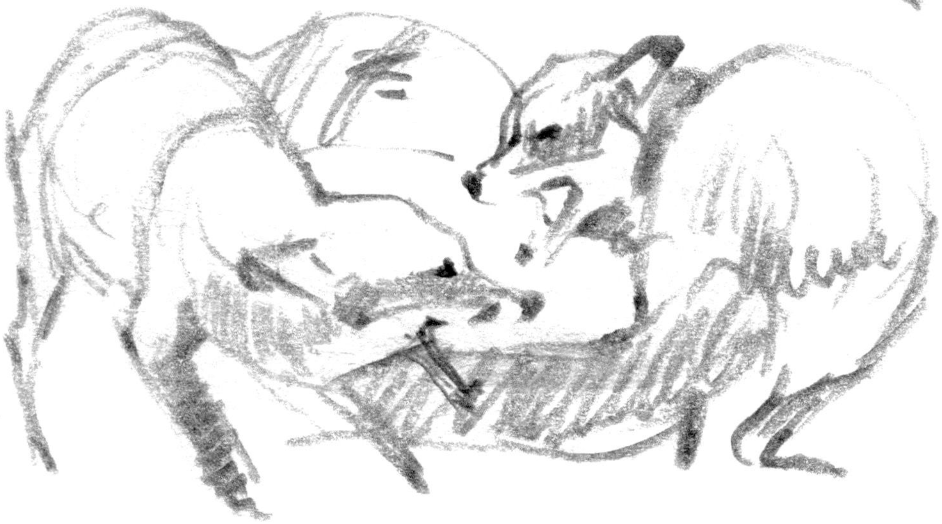

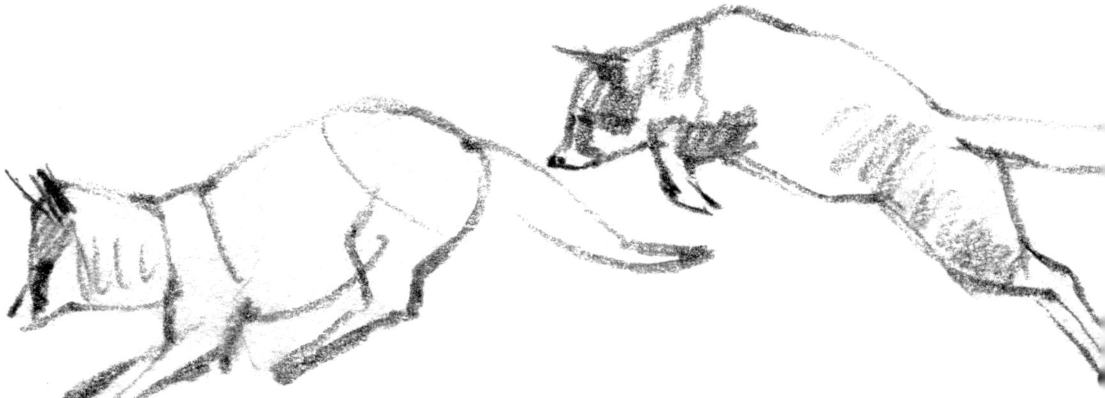

Playful fox cubs

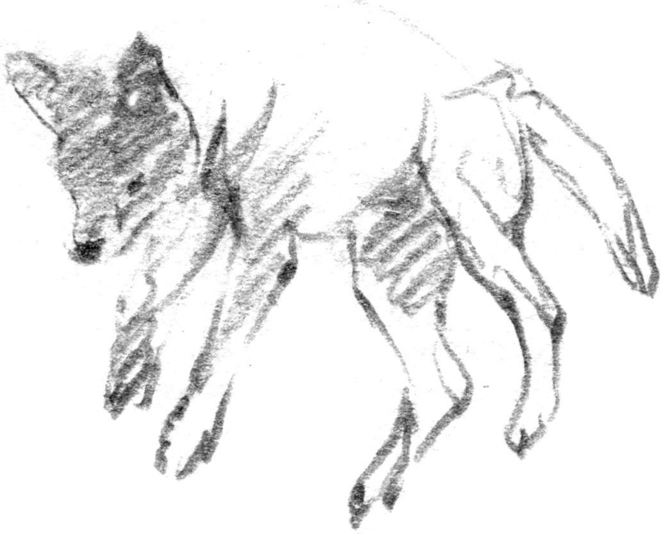

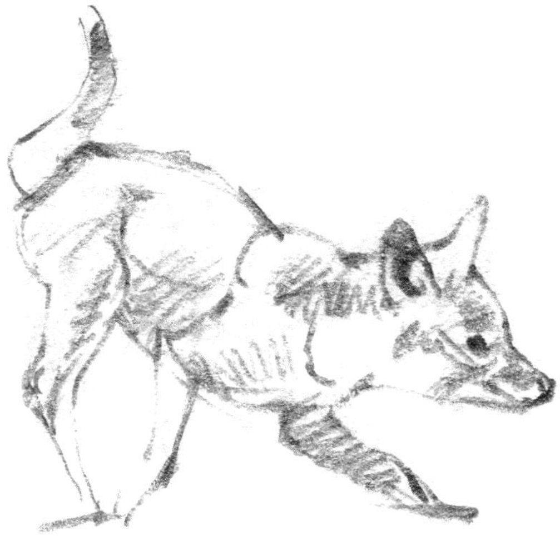

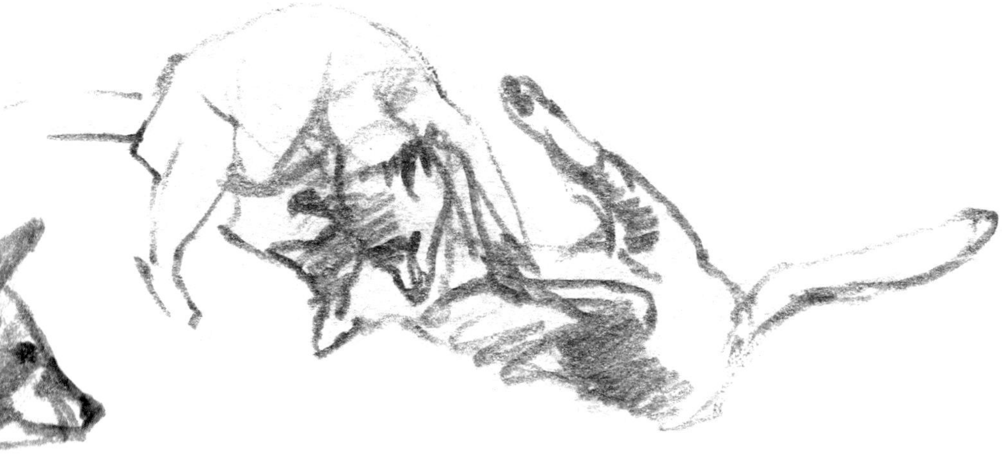

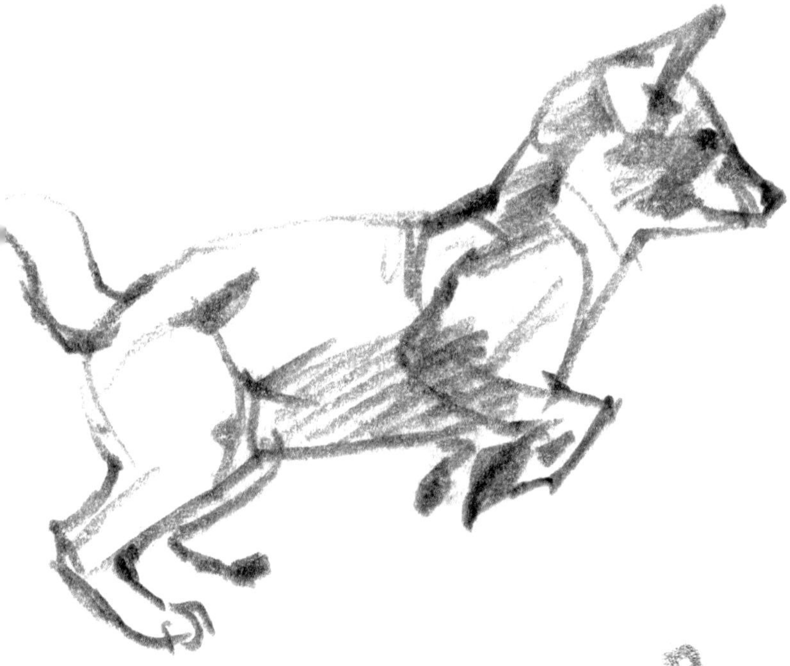

It is especially delightful to see interactions between adults and juveniles which can be playful at times. Here are some fox family drawings from a farm in Gloucestershire.

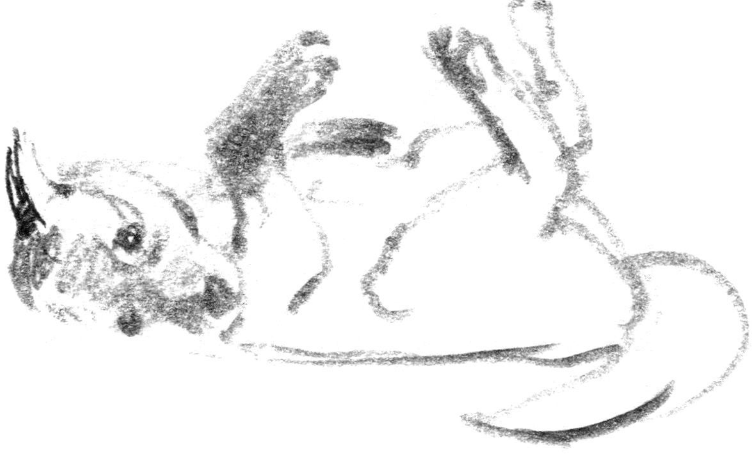

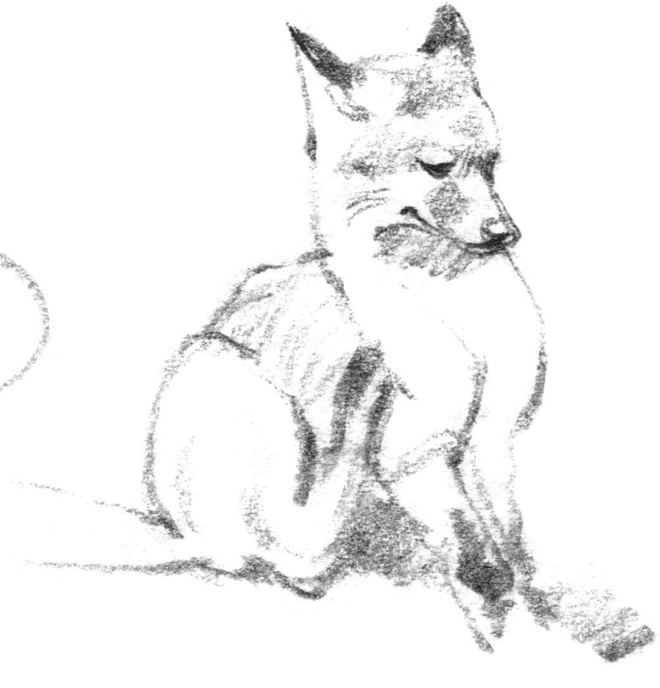

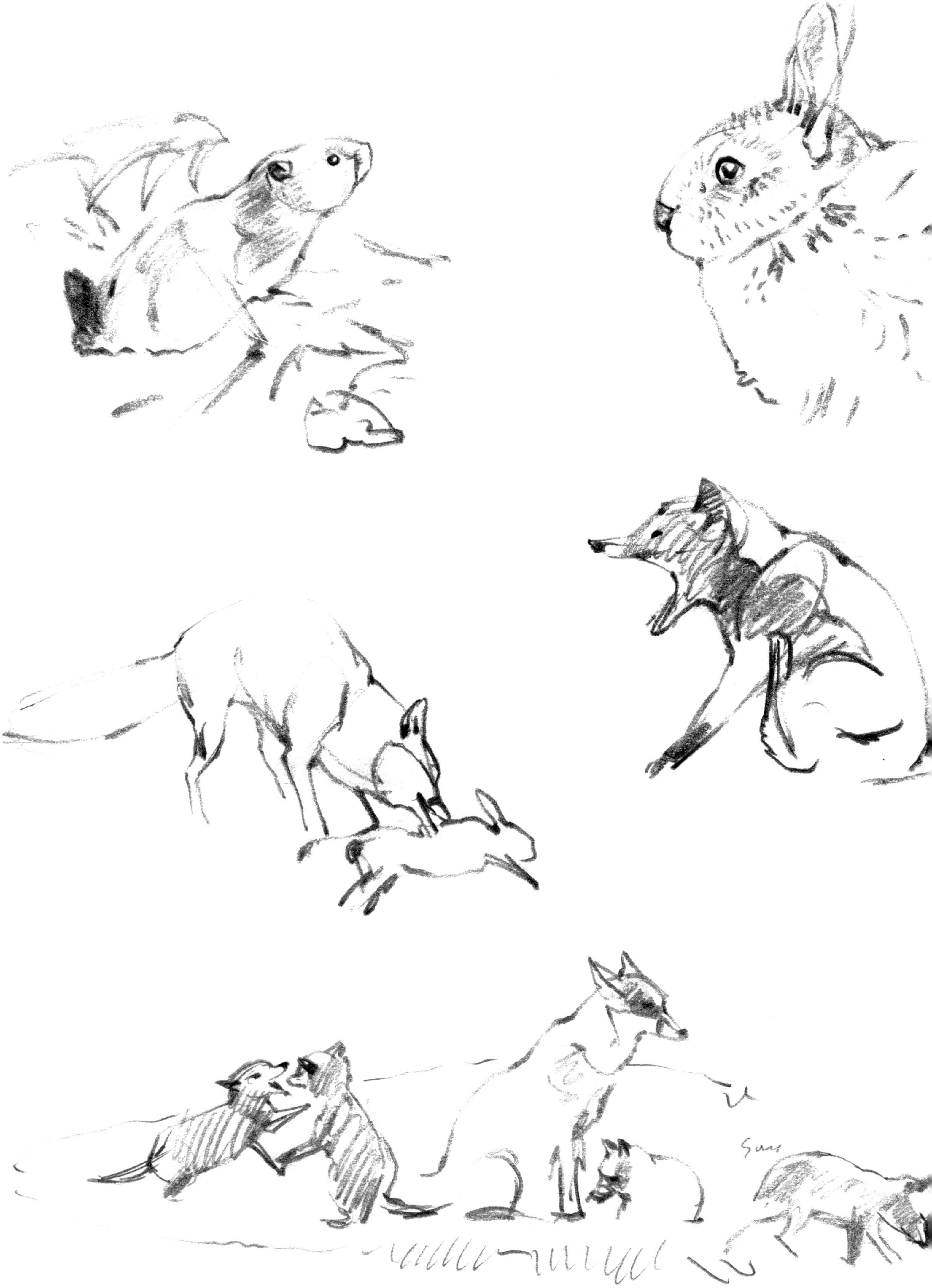

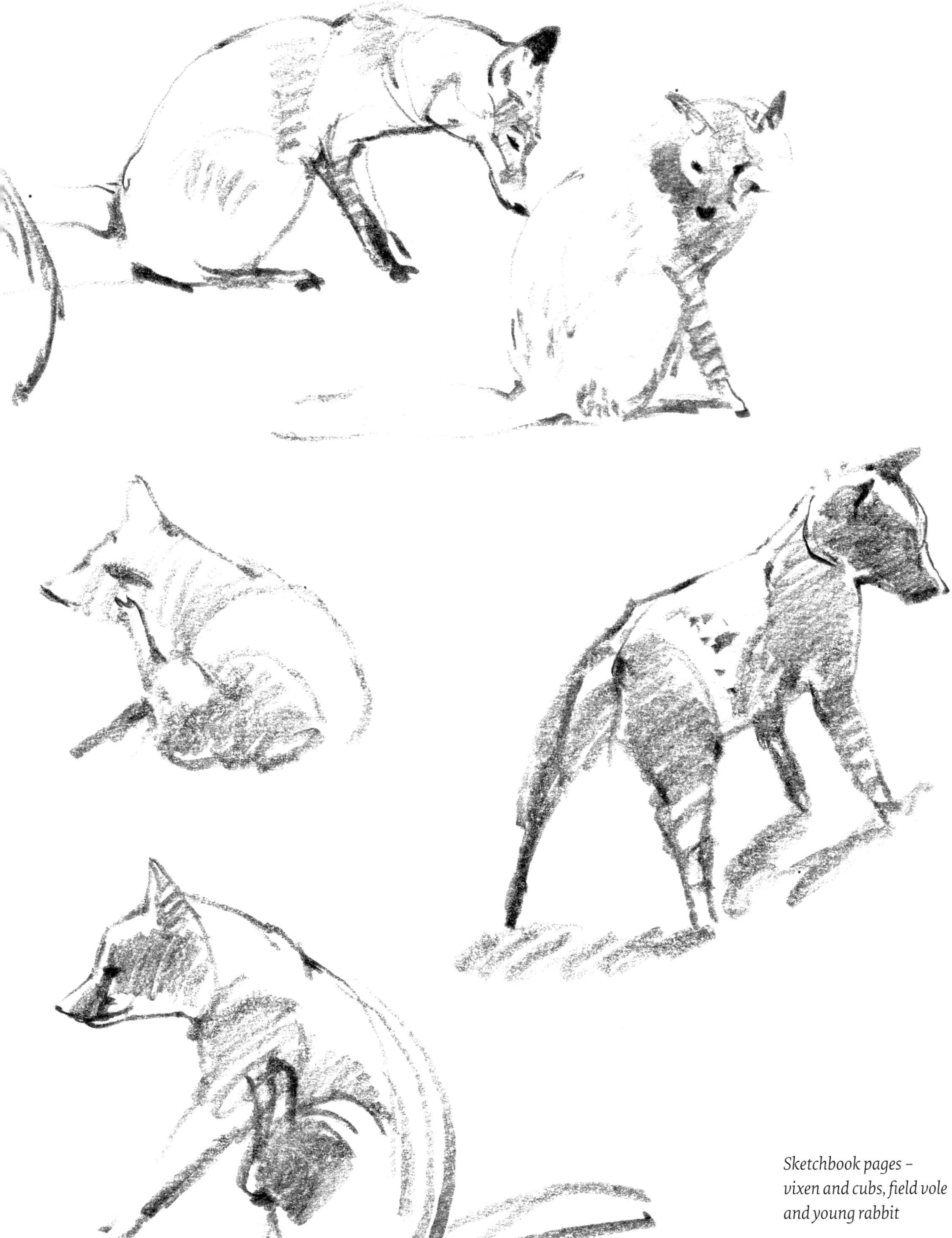

Sketchbook pages – vixen and cubs, field vole and young rabbit

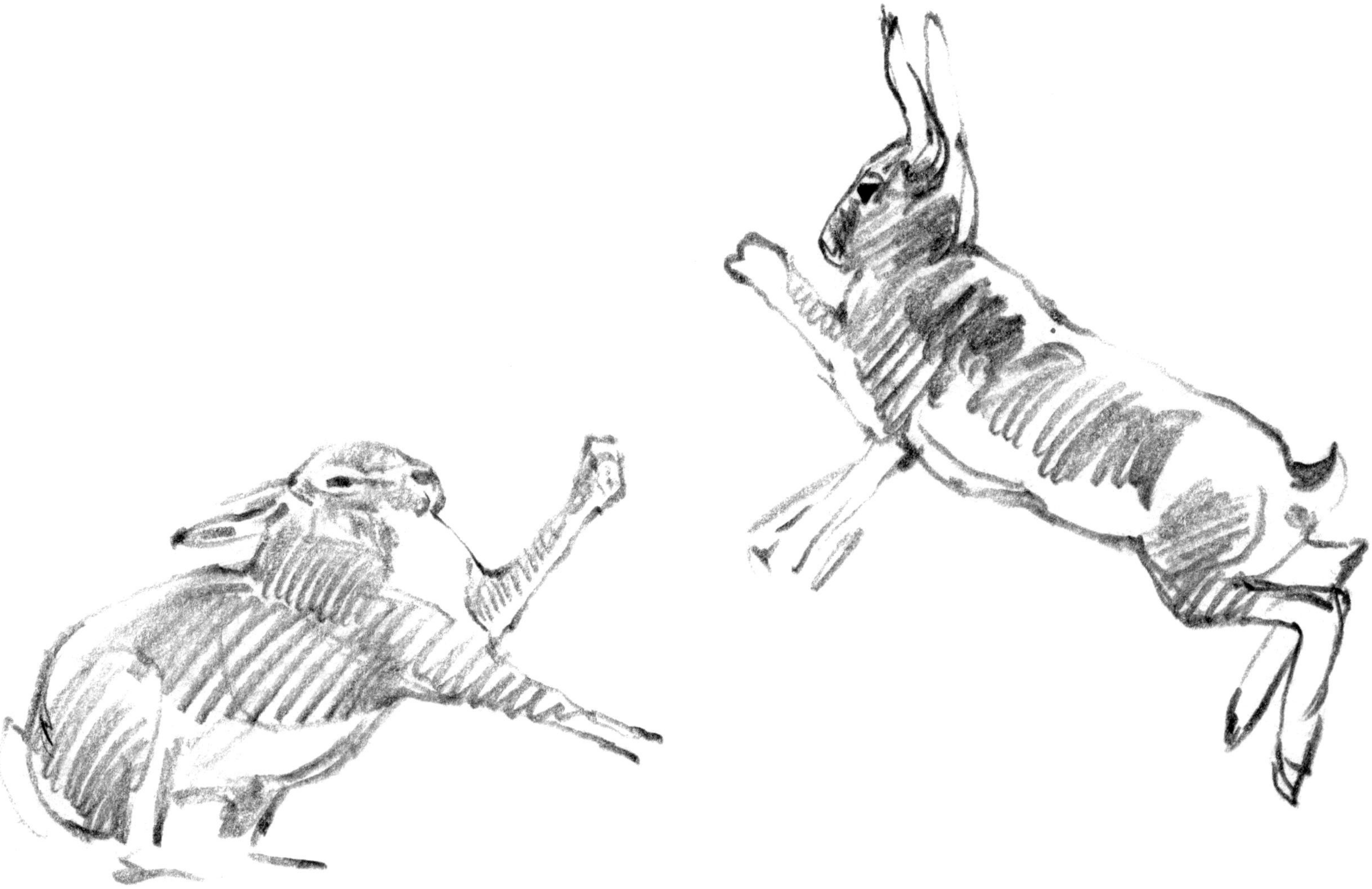

Boxing hares in spring present a challenge to catch the movement. Often they are too engrossed in their rivalry to be alarmed by a watcher. Hares seem so much more alive and intelligent than rabbits. Is that just my prejudice against the pests that invade our garden?

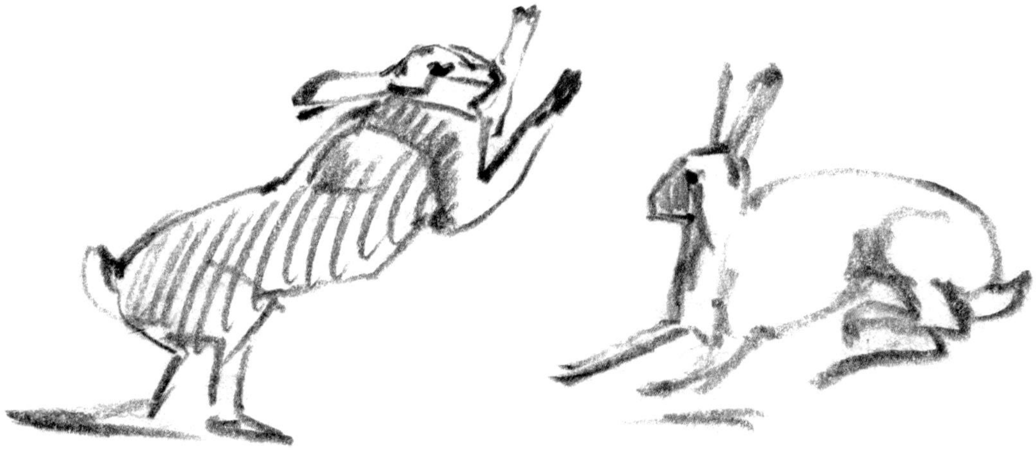

Boxing hares

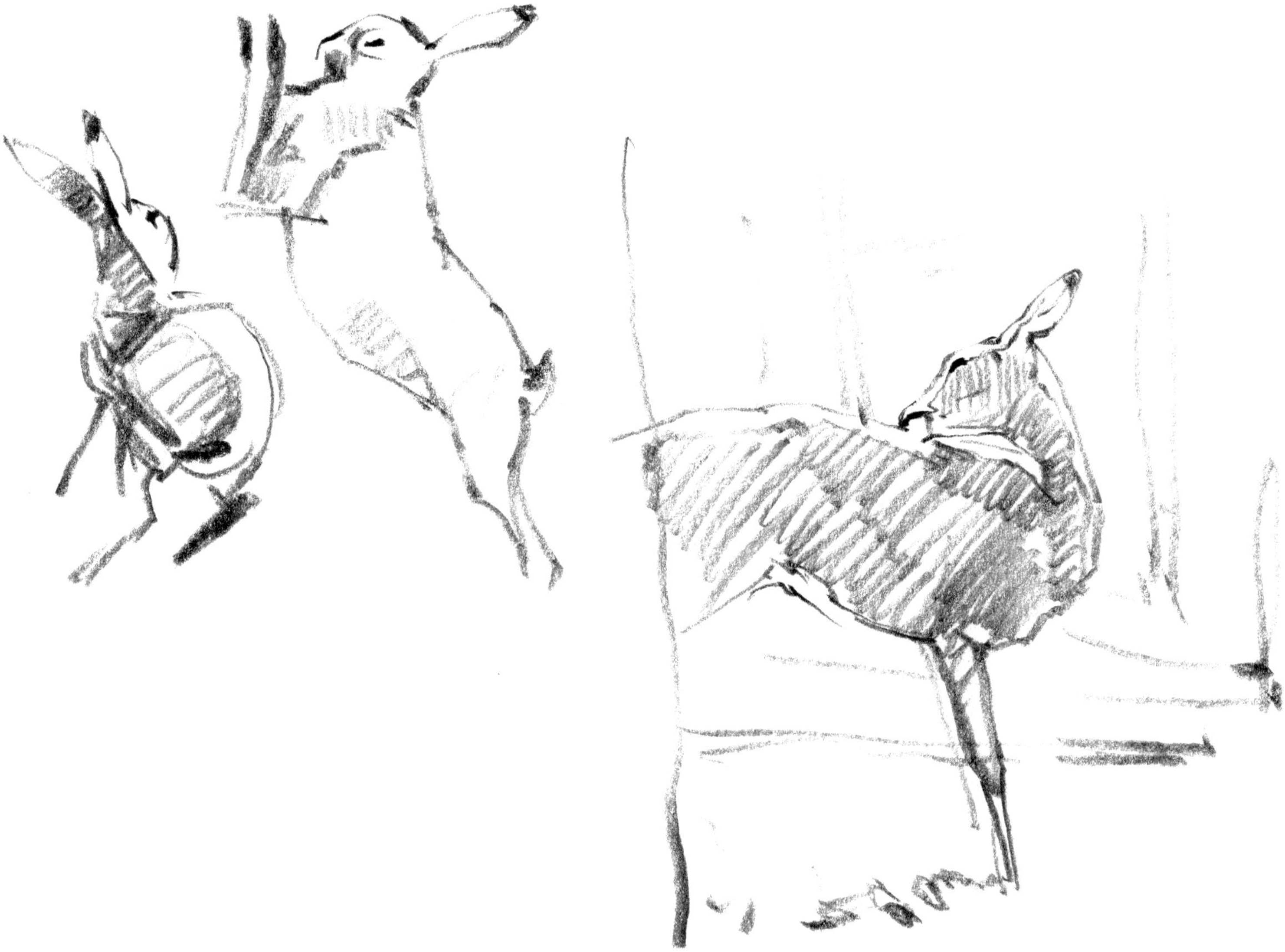

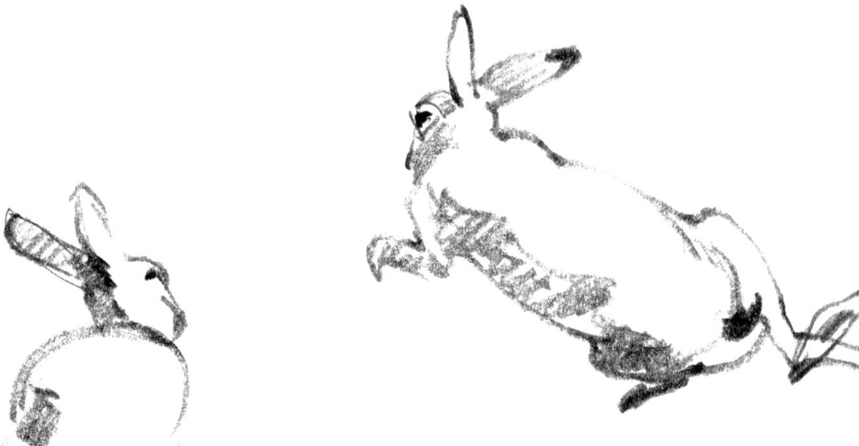

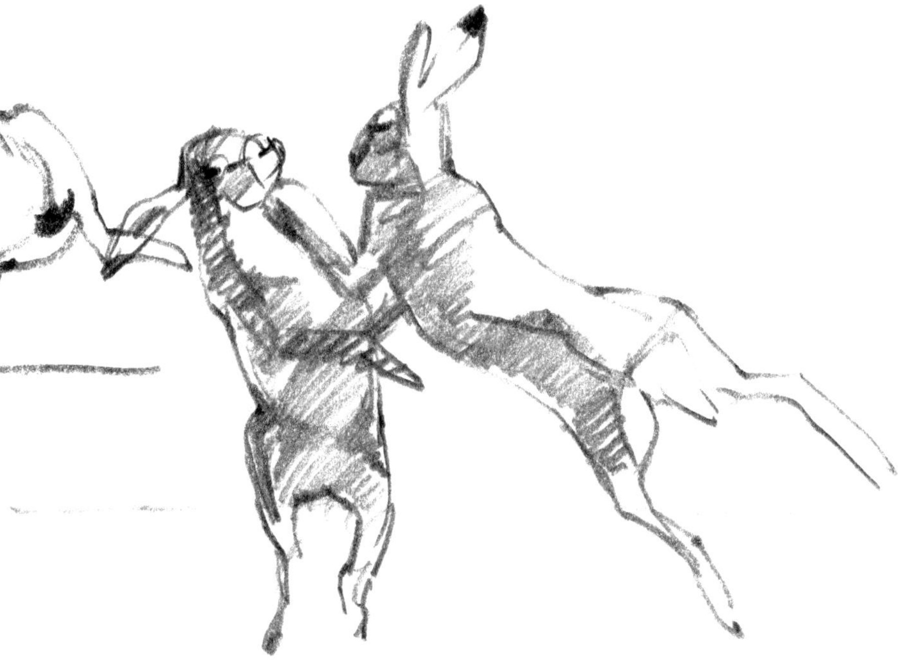

Boxing hares and roe deer

In the garden I watched a hedgehog which seemed to be spreading saliva across its back after licking something underneath it. When the hedgehog moved on, the 'something' turned out to be a toad, which, although somewhat stunned, showed no sign of having been harmed by the hedgehog's attention. Perhaps the toad's toxic skin coating can be lifted off to provide extra protective covering for the hedgehog and deter fleas or a predator even more than the spikes?

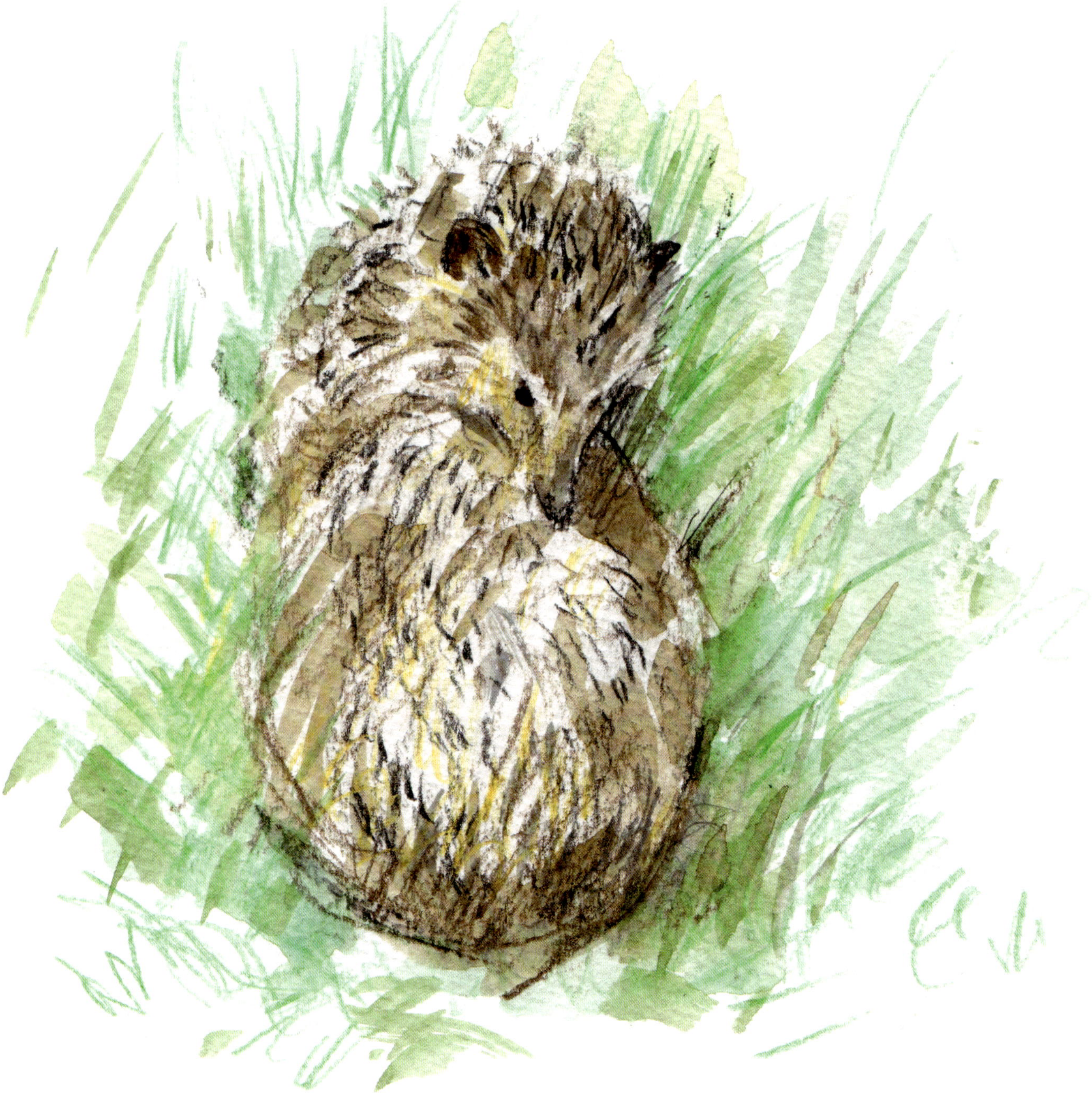

Hedgehog

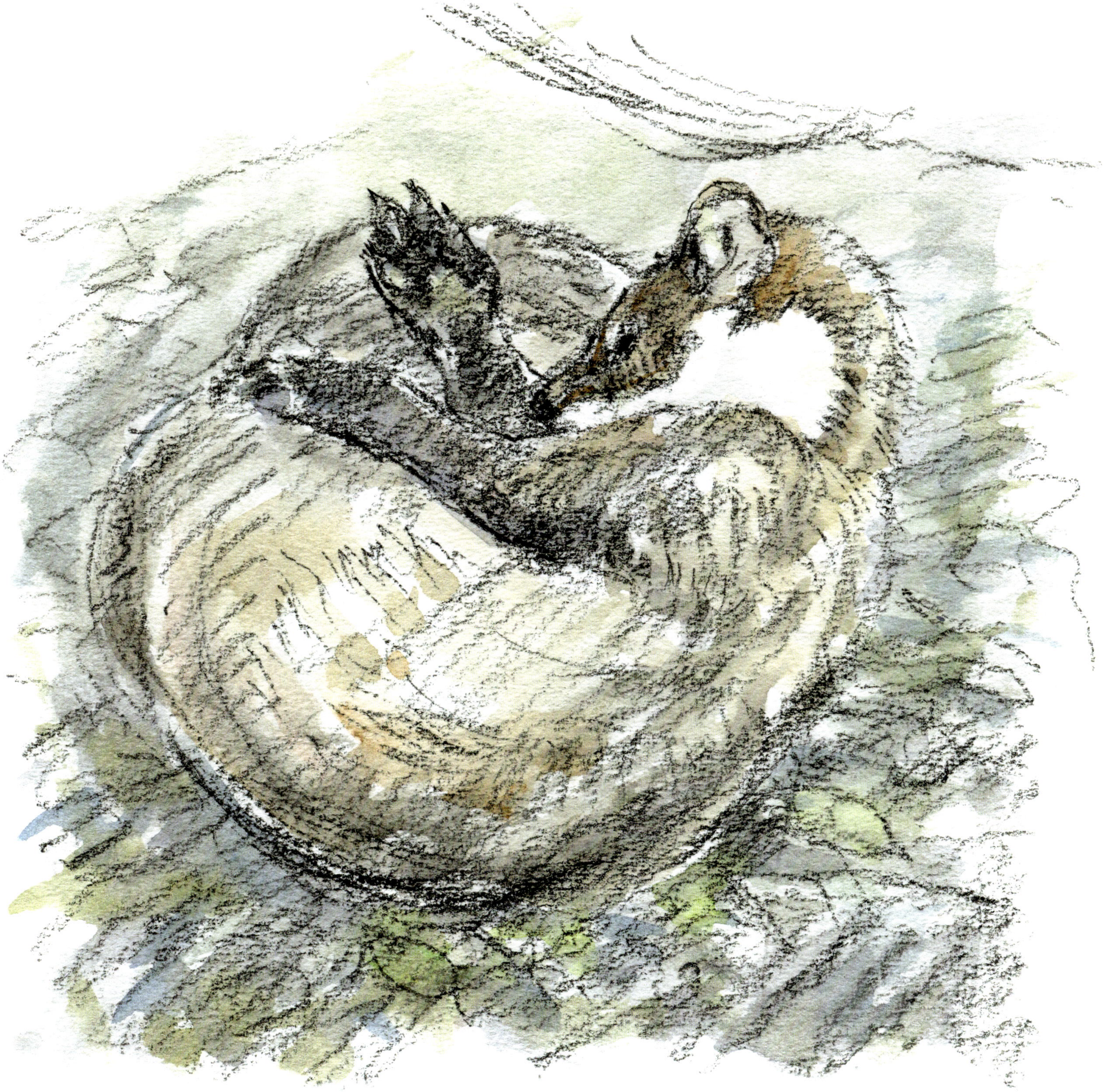

Pine marten asleep

At a Field Centre I visited in the Highlands, pine martens had a den under the floor, and from a small window above they could be watched. This marten was fast asleep while I draw it.

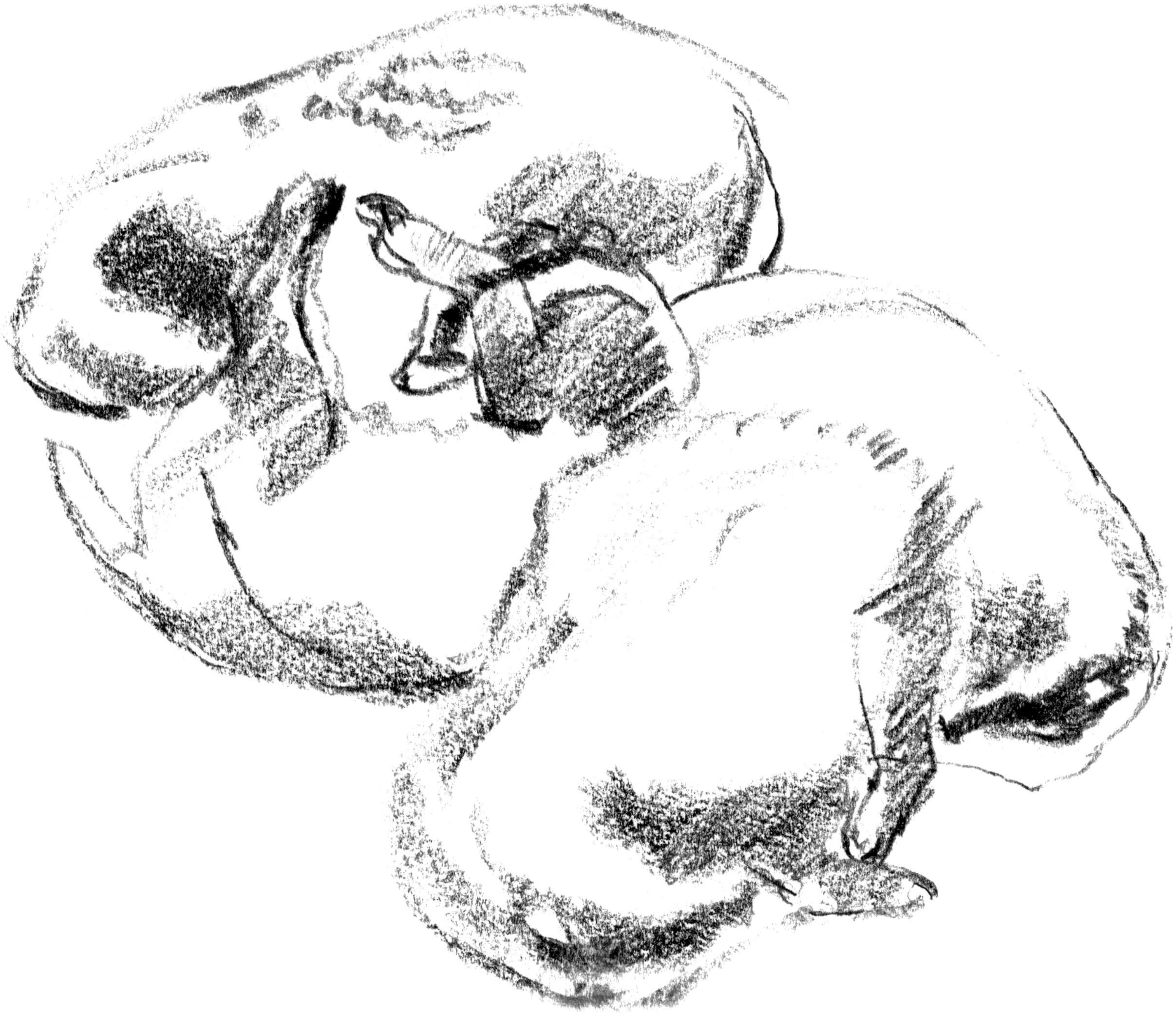

A family of badgers asleep in their set at a Scottish Nature Reserve

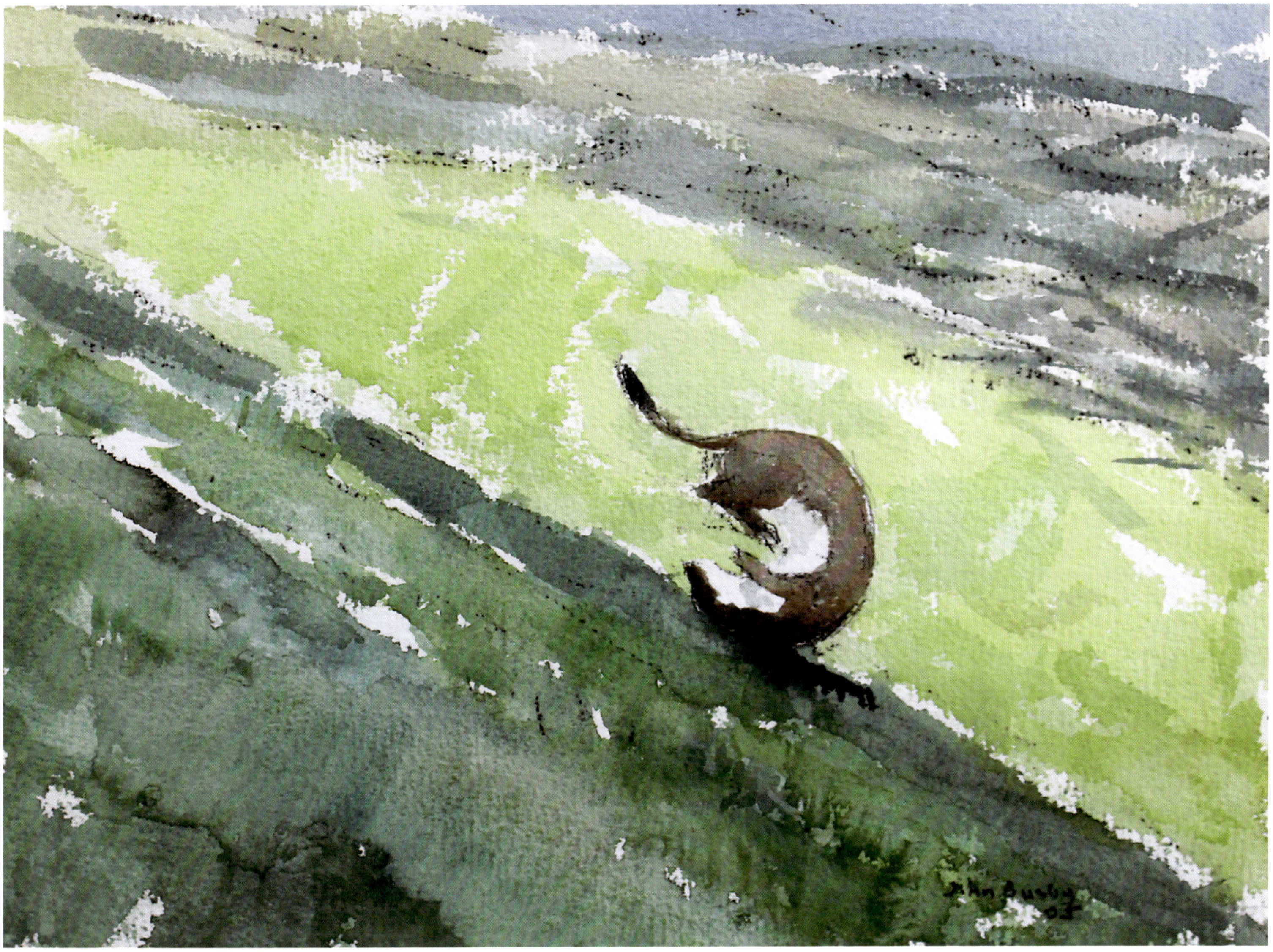

Stoat looping the loop

From our house window one day we saw a stoat running up and down a grassy bank in the garden, sometimes sliding down on its stomach, and twice descending in continuous somersaults! I could see no reason for this behaviour except play. There were no other stoats about or watching rabbits to mesmerize.

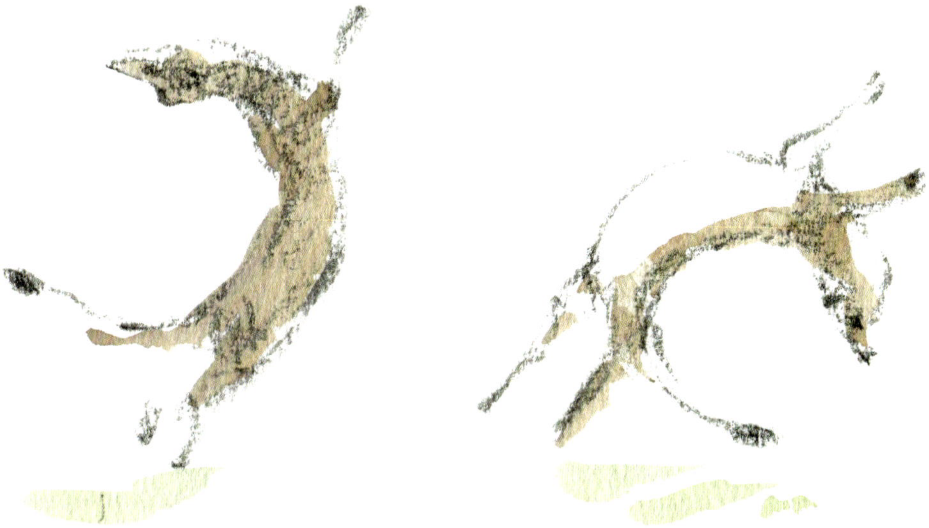

Red squirrels in our area of Lothian have nearly all been ousted by the imported greys. Of small rodents, here is a long-tailed field mouse and drawings of two British subspecies, an Orkney vole and shrew, as well as the usual British field vole. The Orkney vole is slightly larger.

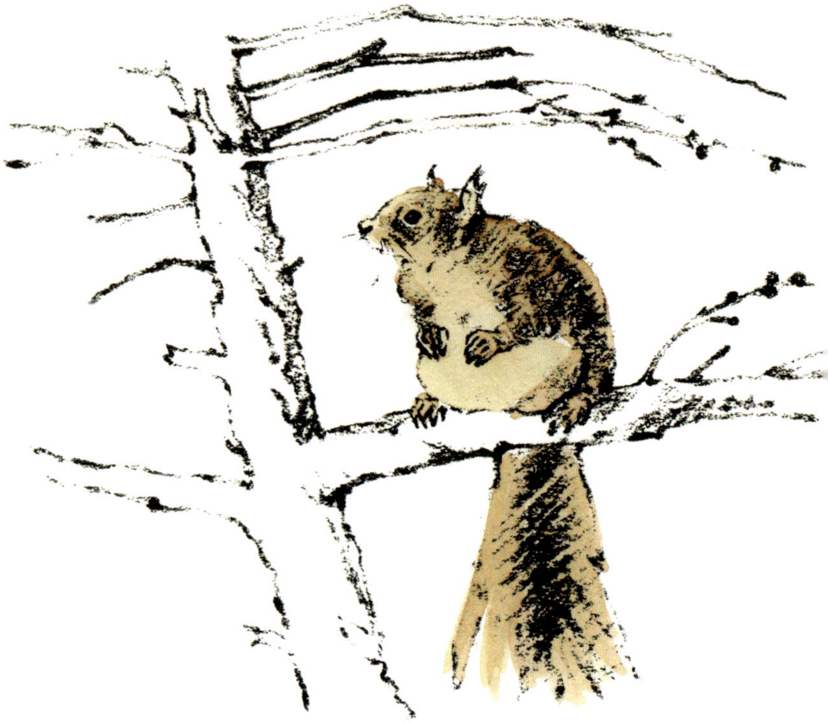

Red squirrel, long-tailed field mice and field vole.

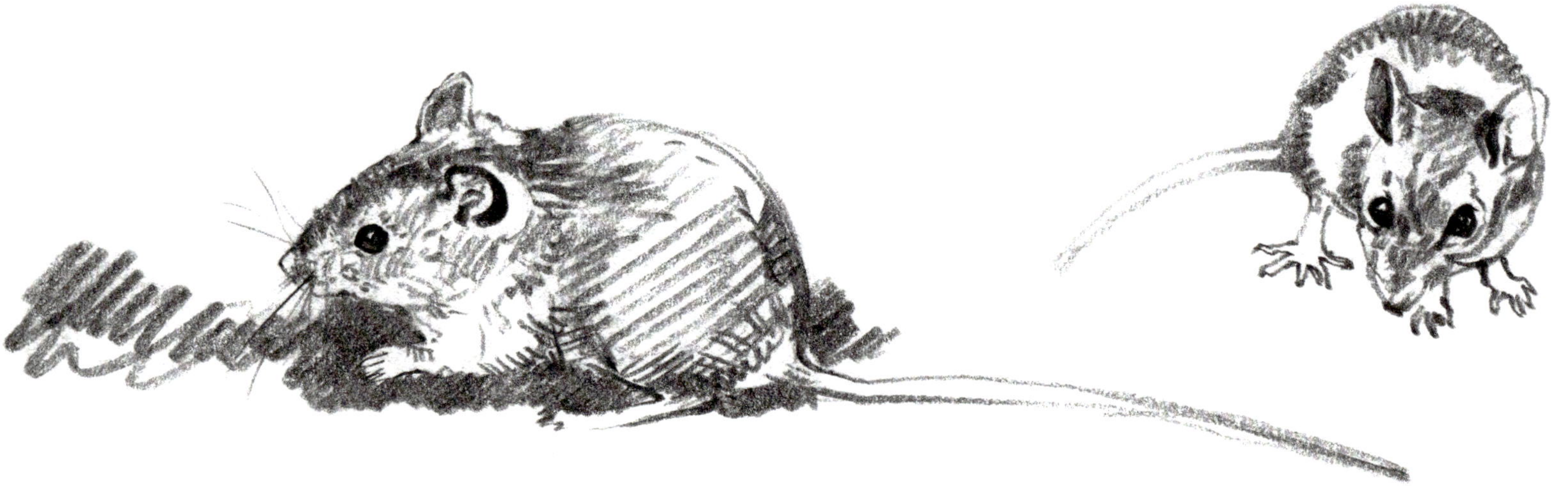

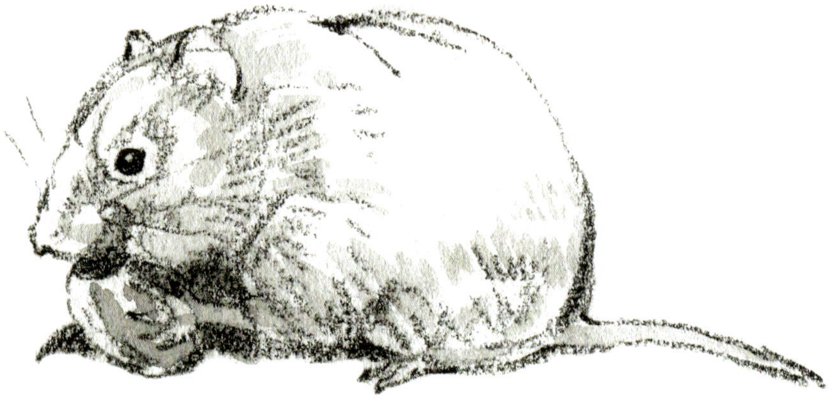

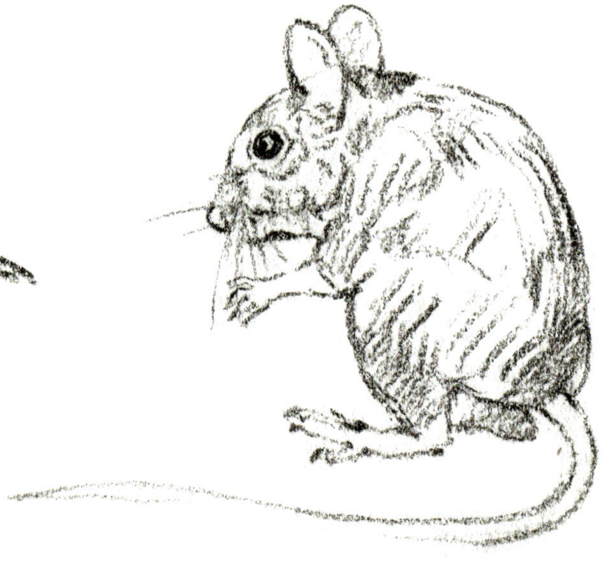

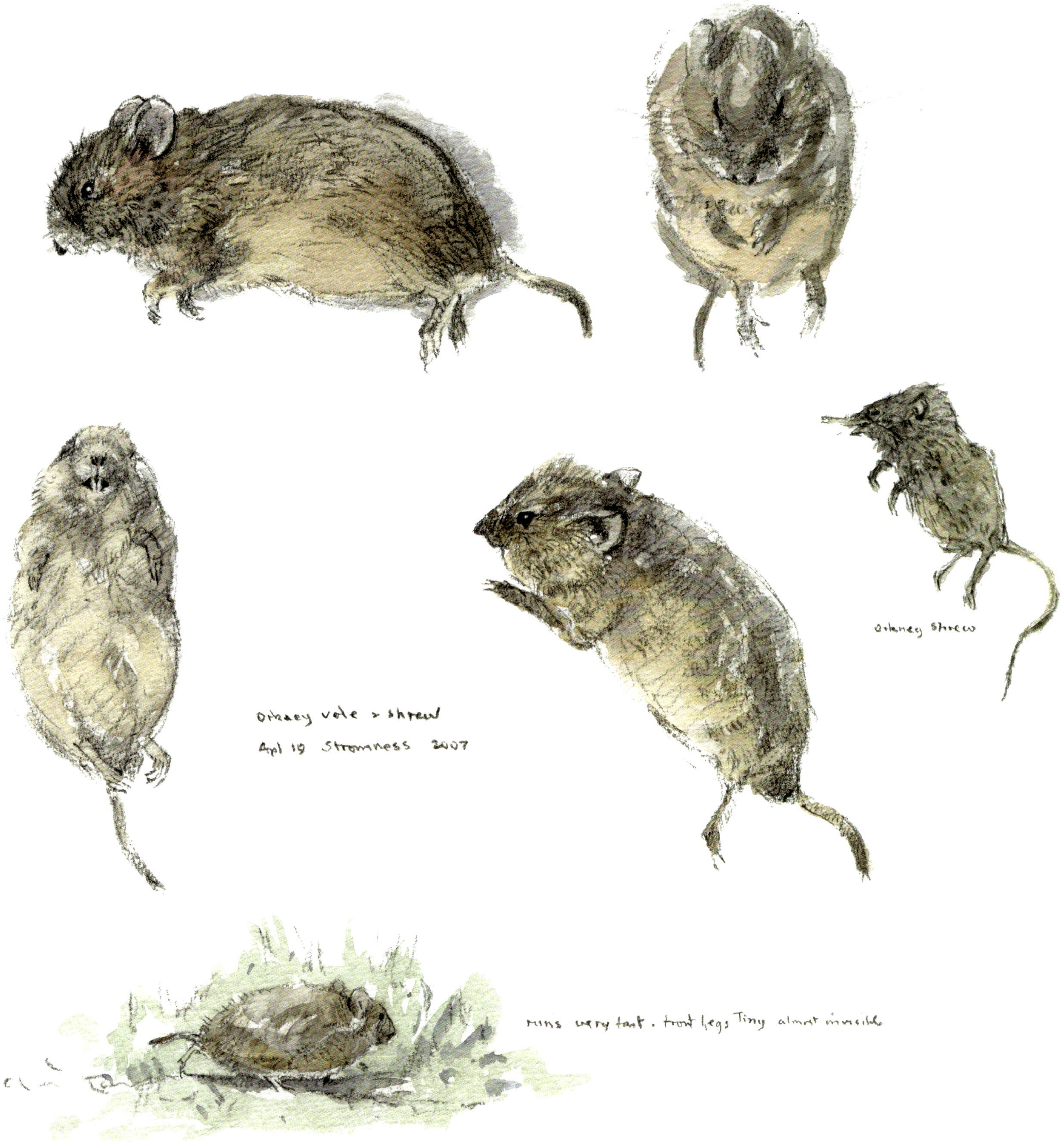

Orkney vole and shrew.

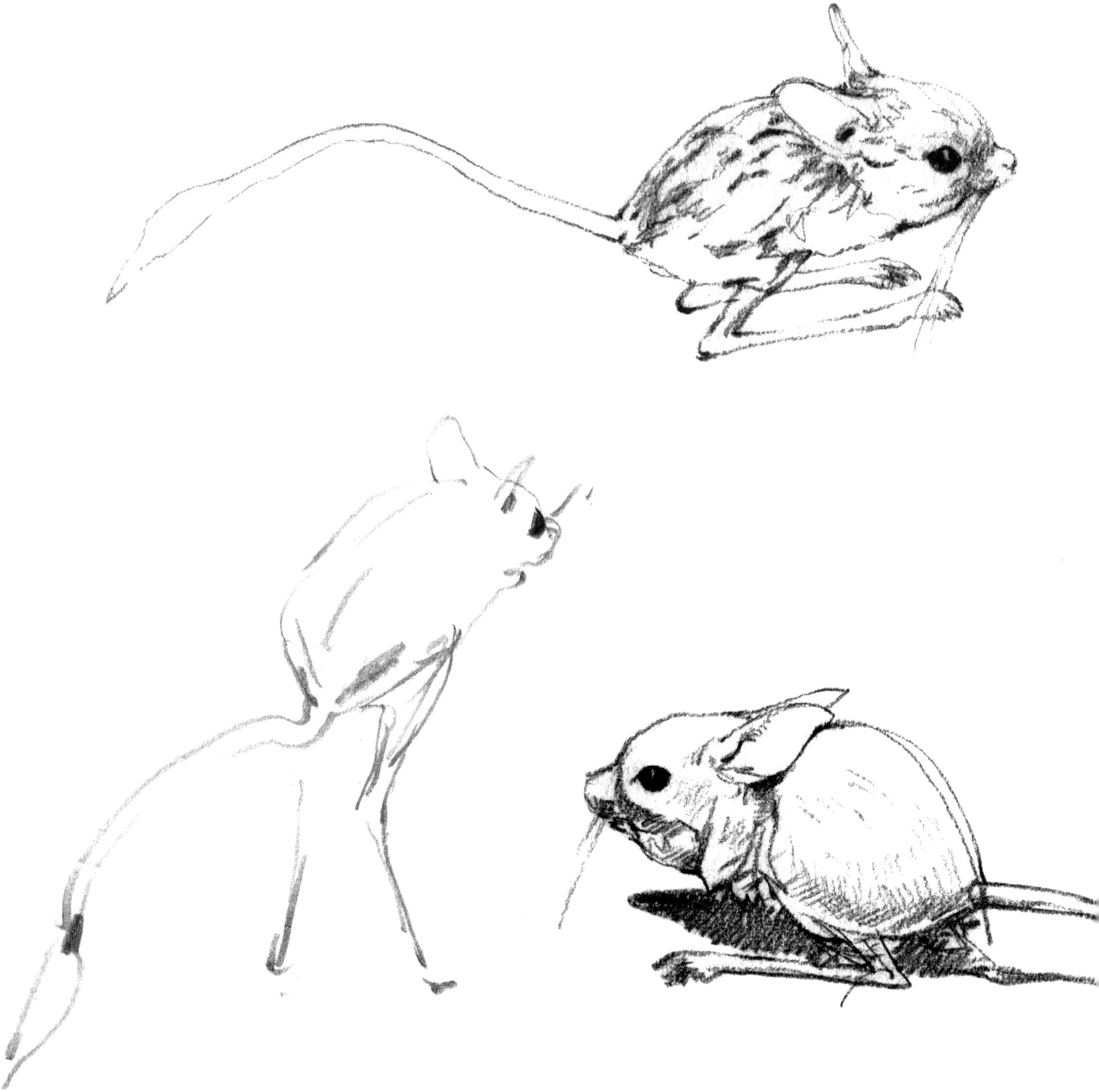

Jerboa studies

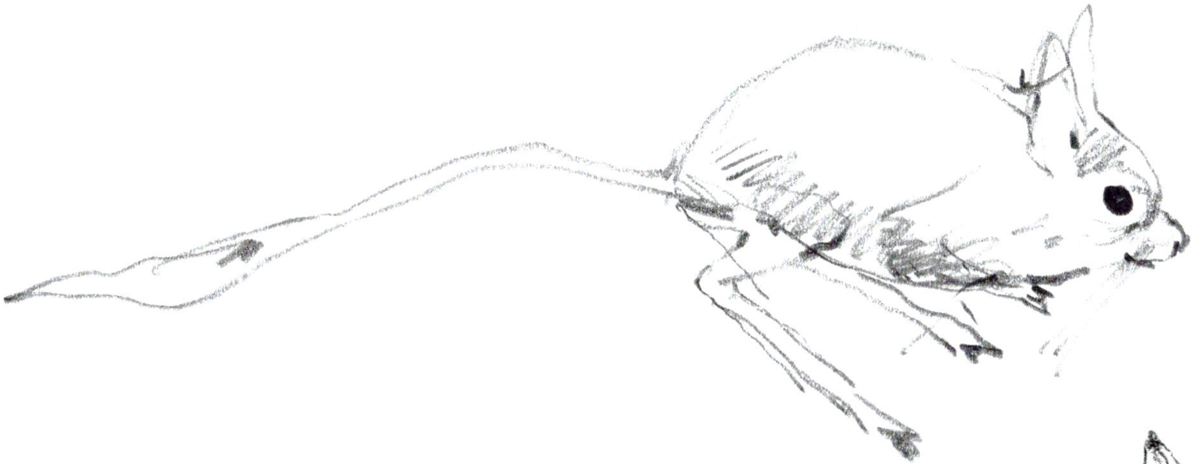

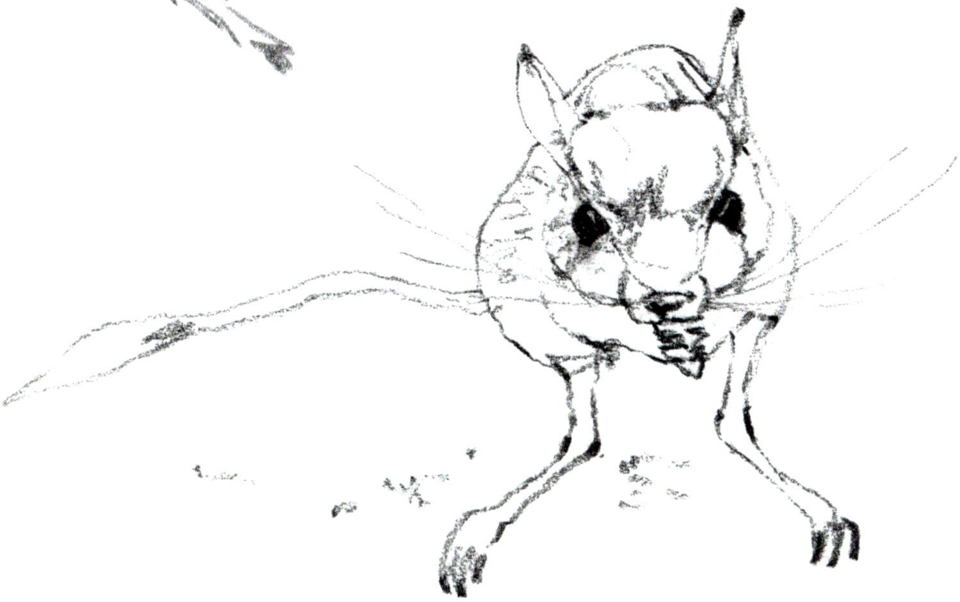

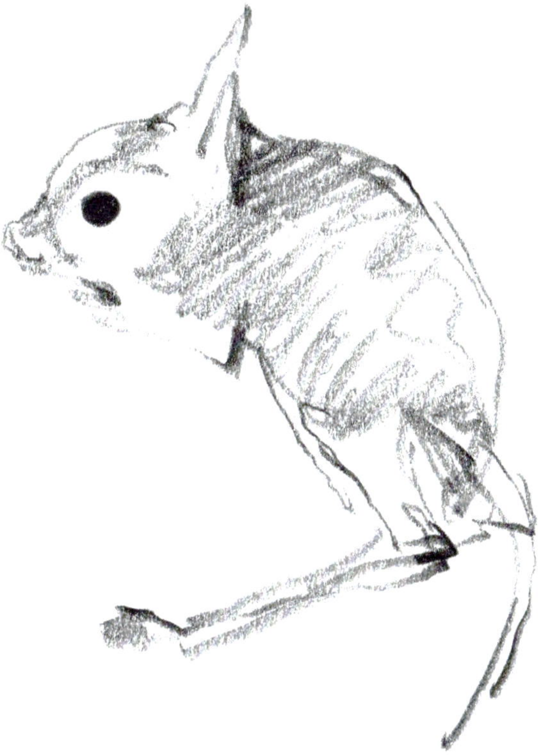

Non-native species

These strange creatures are jerboas, sometimes called kangaroo rats. They came from Azraq, an oasis in the Jordan desert which I visited when my naturalist friend Bryan Nelson was doing research there. I brought three back to Scotland for him to study, and they lived for a while in my studio. They were most active at night and needed space for two-metre high jumps.

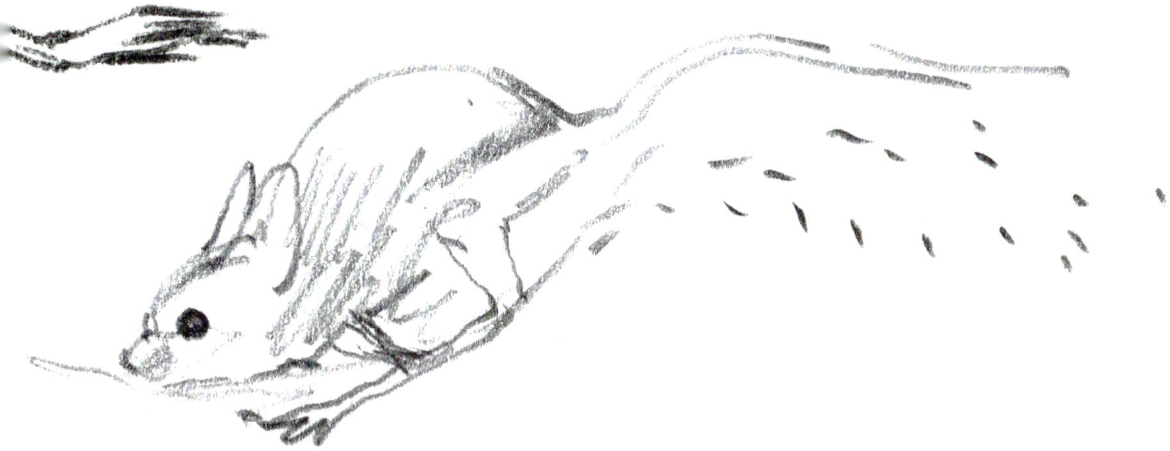

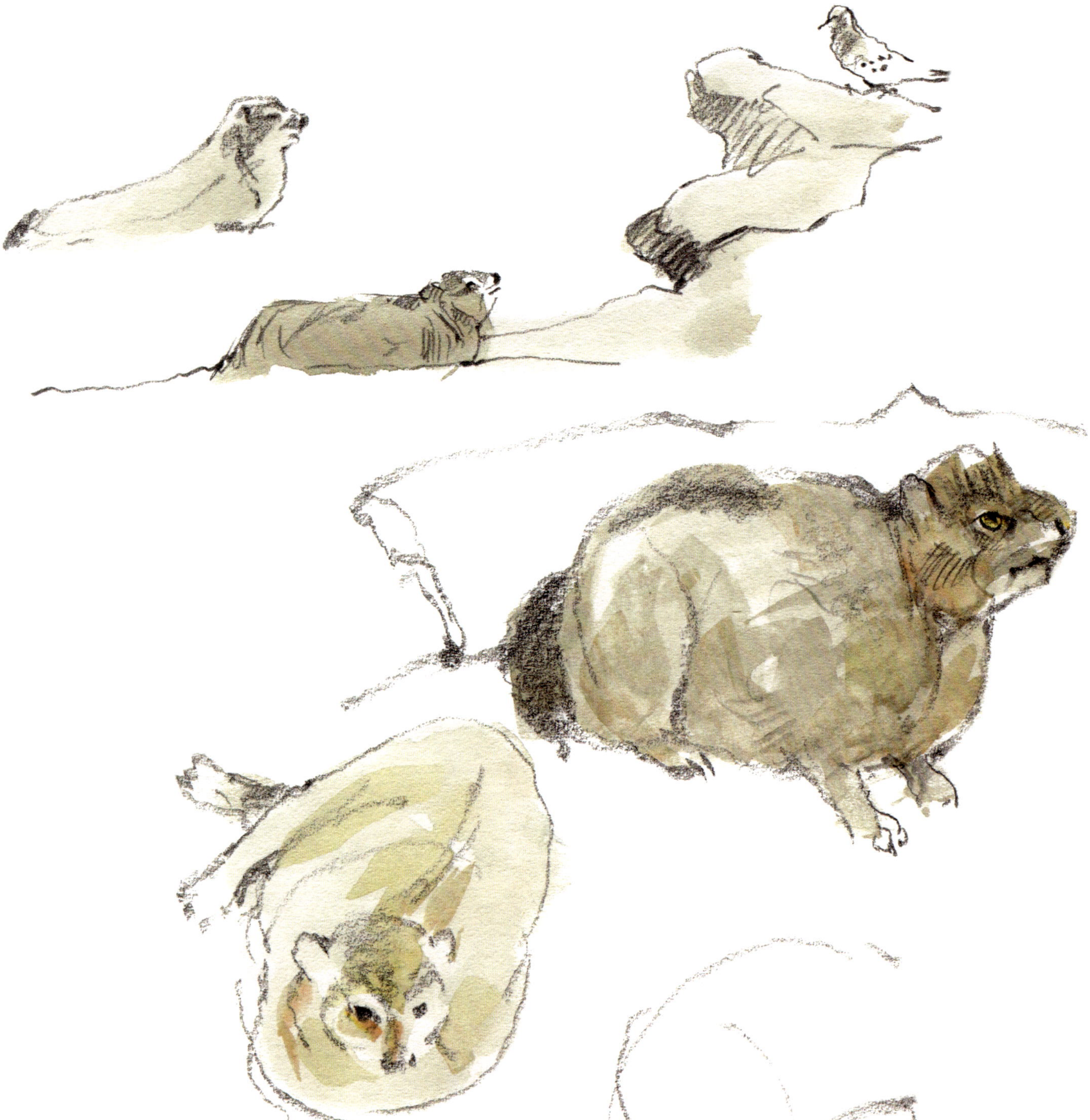

A rock hyrax from Table Mountain in South Africa

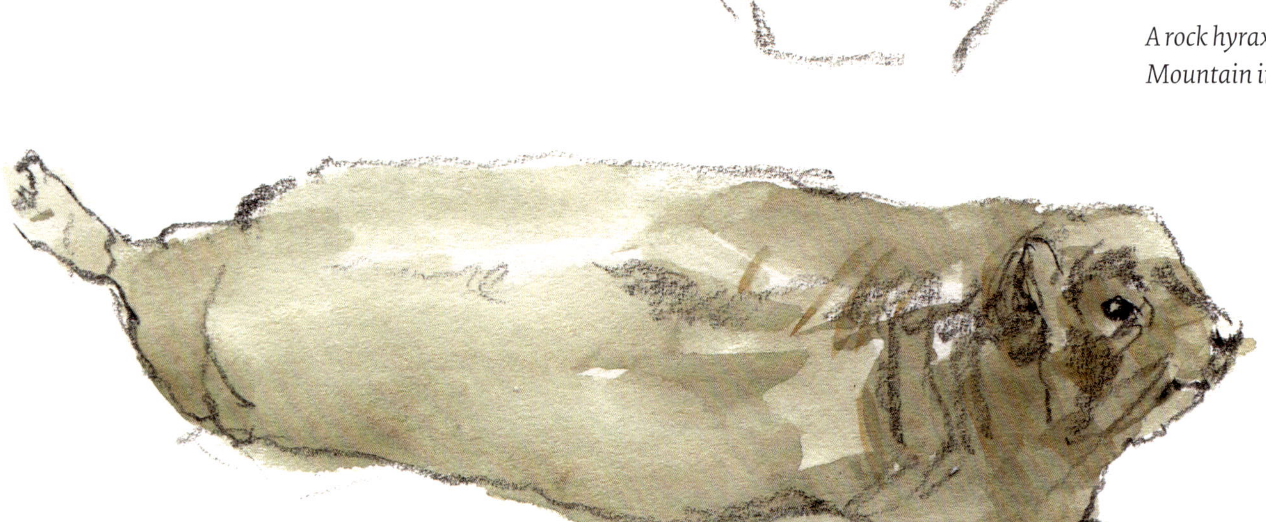

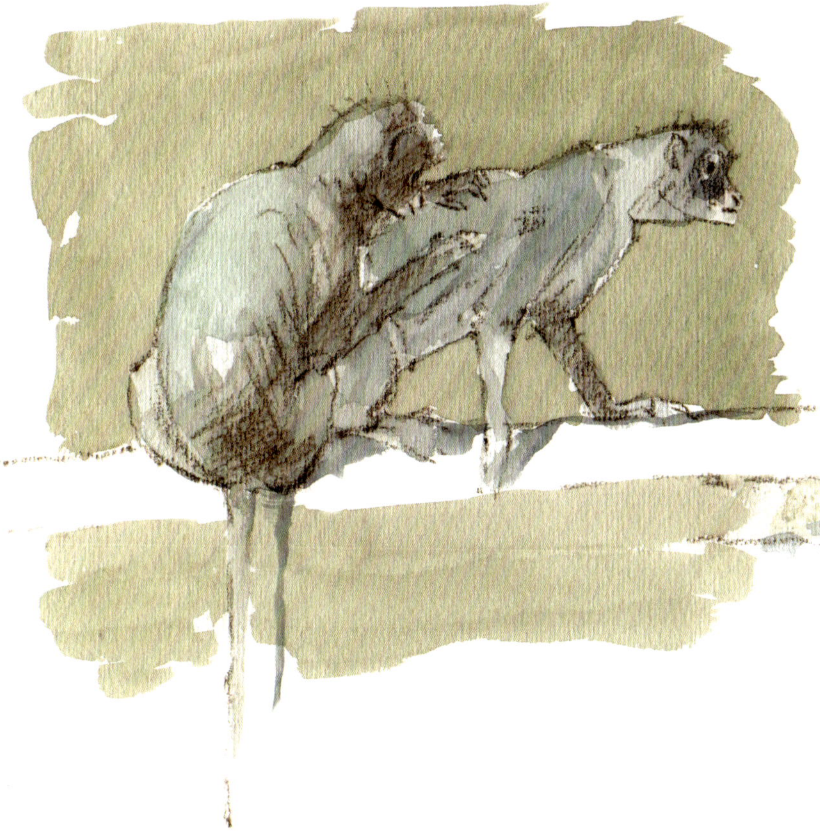

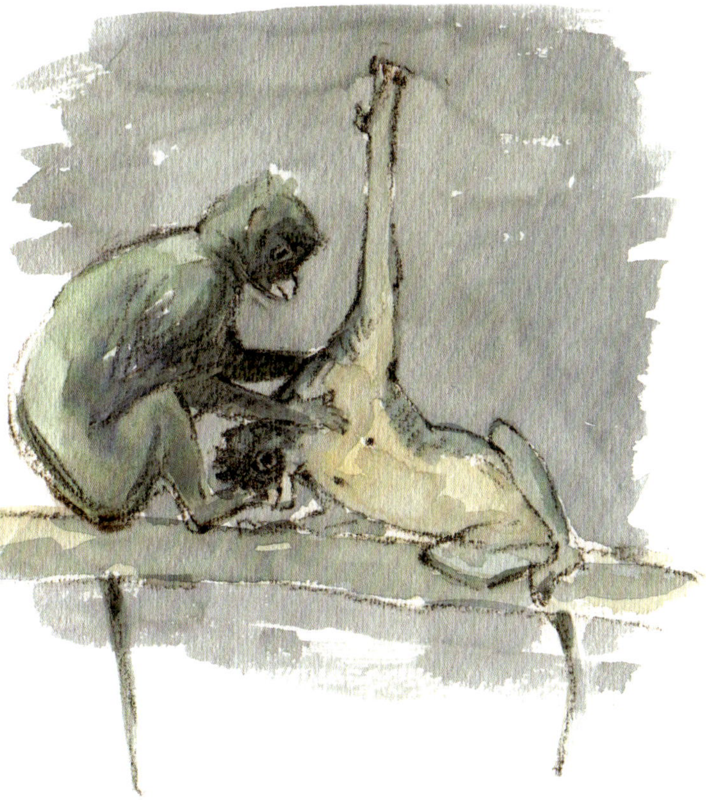

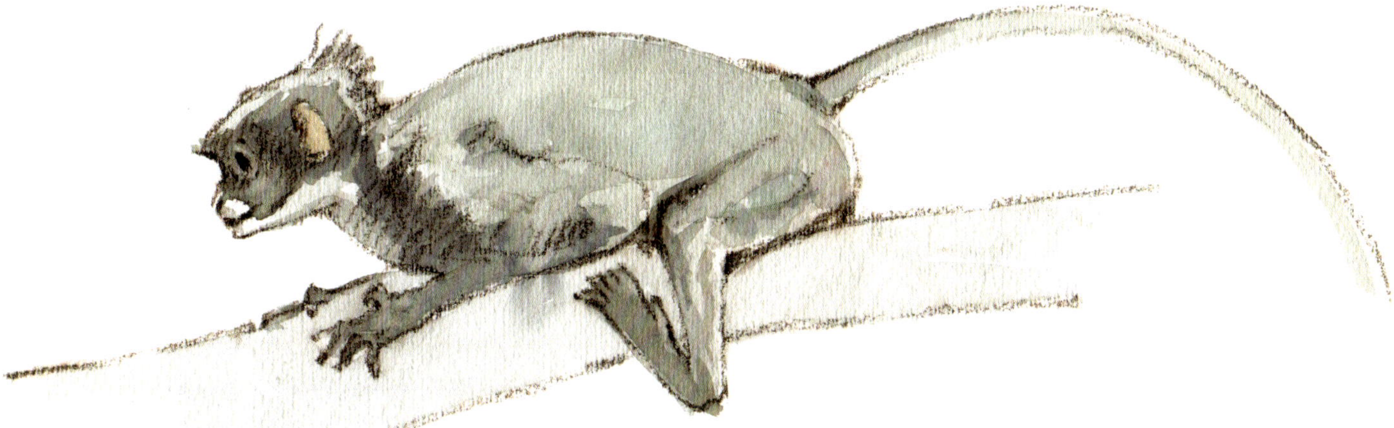

Spectacled langurs

This rock hyrax was drawn on the top of Table Mountain in South Africa.

I am told that the hyrax is a relative of the elephant, although it seems to have little in common with its vastly larger cousin, and more closely resembles a marmot.

When I go to a zoo I usually spend some time in the Monkey House. Monkeys are wonderful to draw as their body language so resembles our own. There are drawings of wild langurs at Bandhavgarh in the section on India. And here; some monkeys from Edinburgh and Chester Zoos – De Brasso's, spectacled langurs, and ring-tailed lemurs.

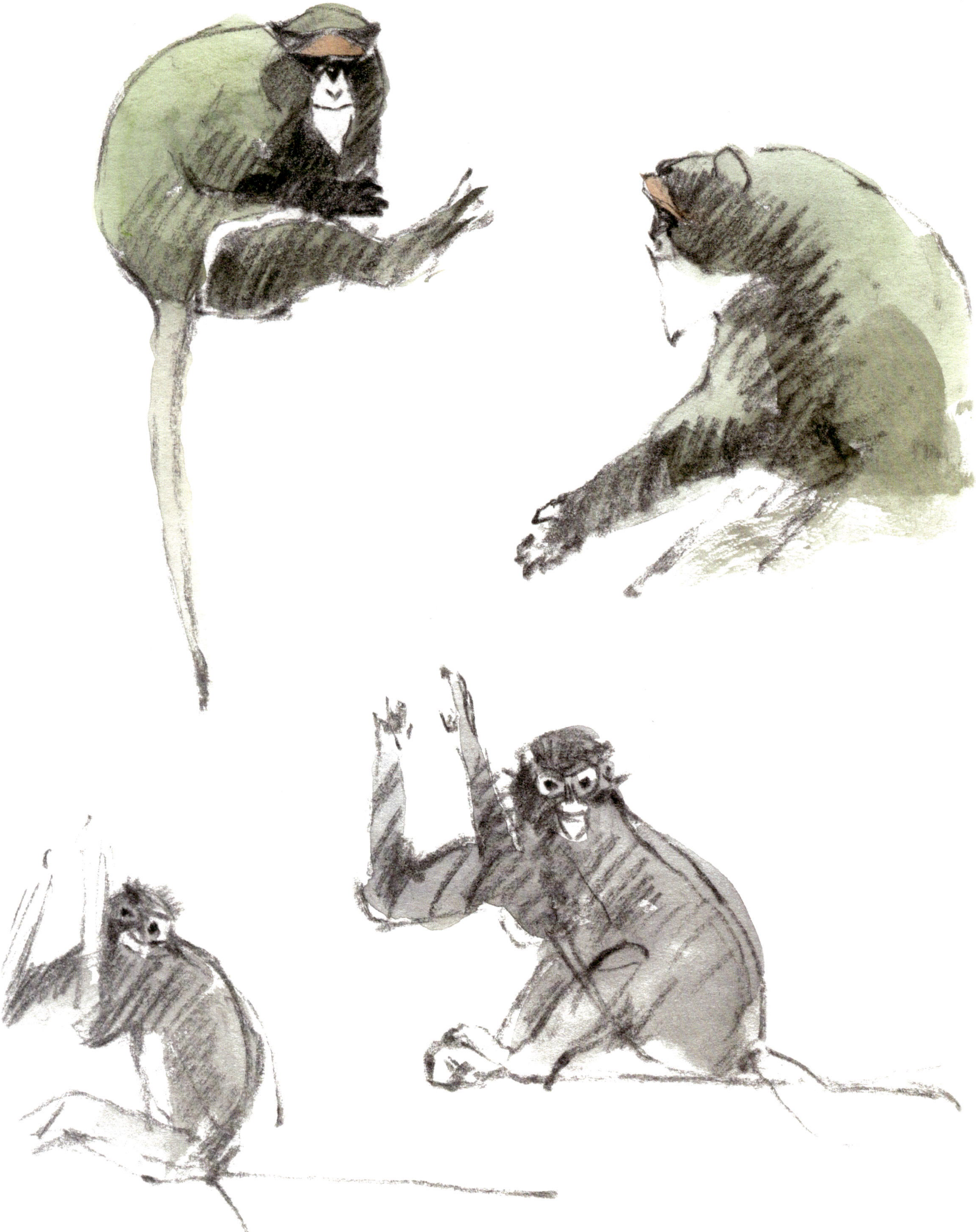

De Brasso's and spectacled Langur monkeys at Edinburgh Zoo

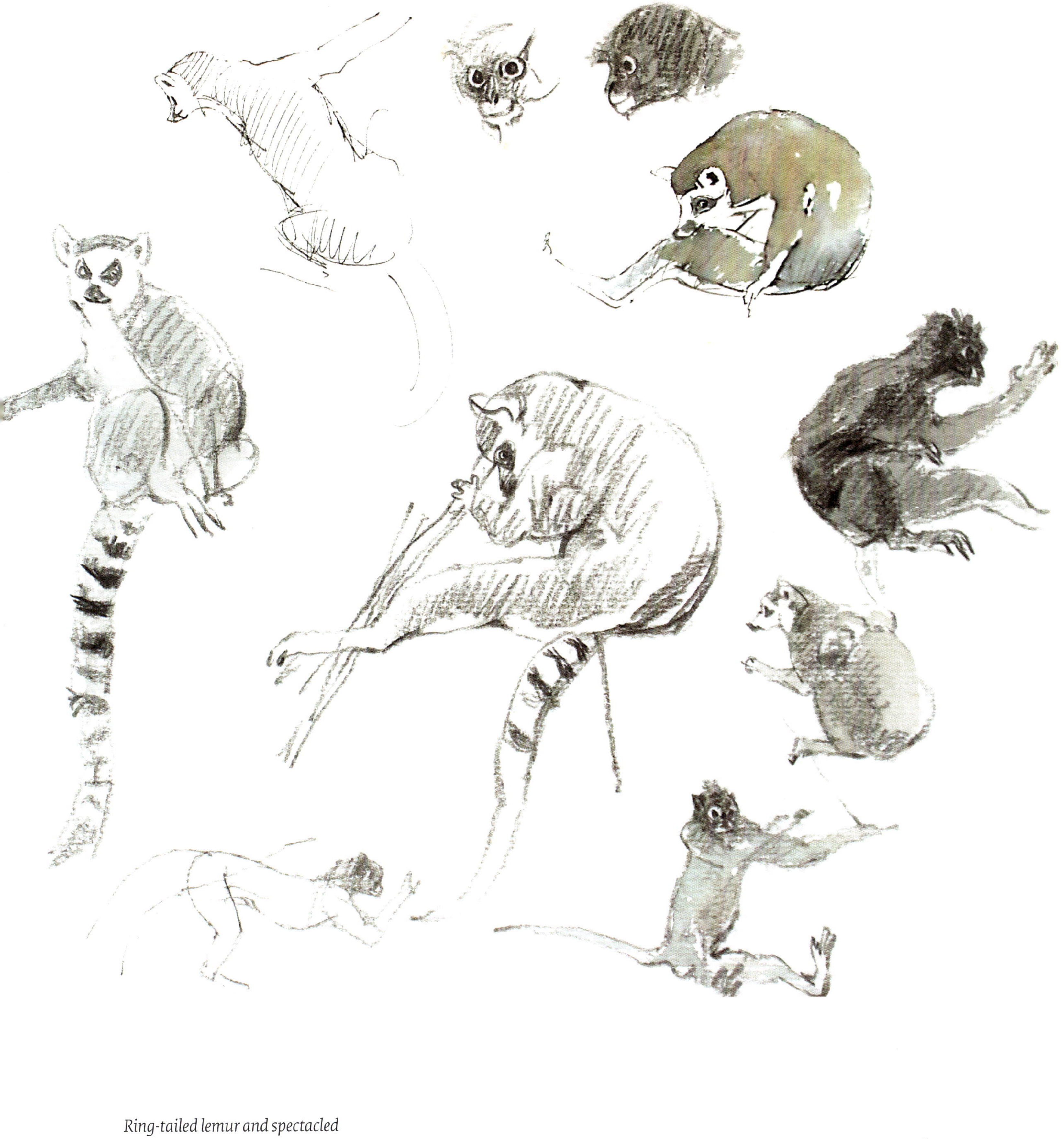

Ring-tailed lemur and spectacled Langur monkeys at Edinburgh Zoo

Grebes

Grebes are among my favourite species. Their lives are the embodiment of grace and buoyant movement, and coloured by the lights in surrounding water they are always a delight to paint.

The fluid courtship ritual of a great crested grebe is a joy to watch.

Whether in summer plumage, reflected in the quiet surface of lake, loch and river, or slimmed down in its winter plumage on a grey sea, these grebes epitomise elegance at all times.

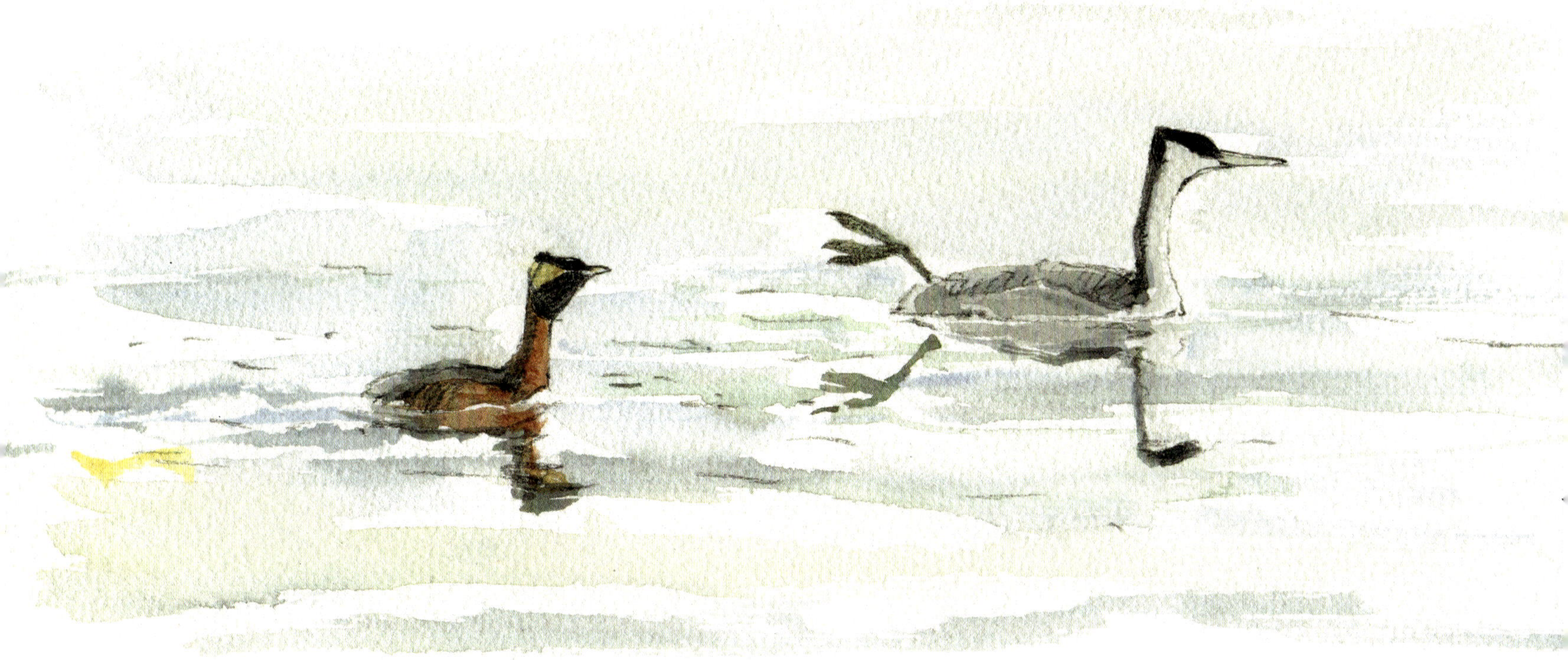

Horned (Slavonian) and Western grebes, USA

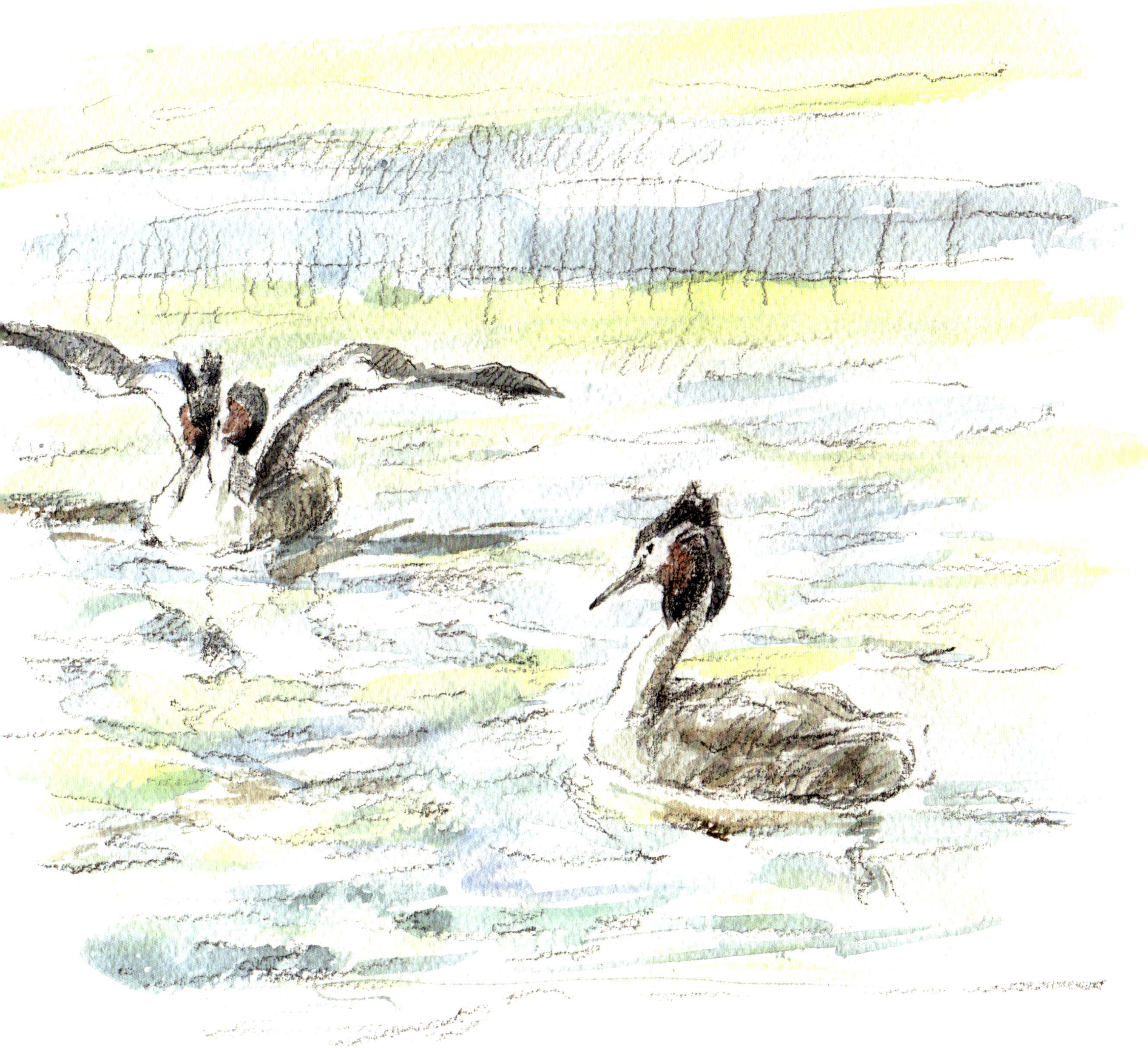

Great crested grebe pair in Oxfordshire

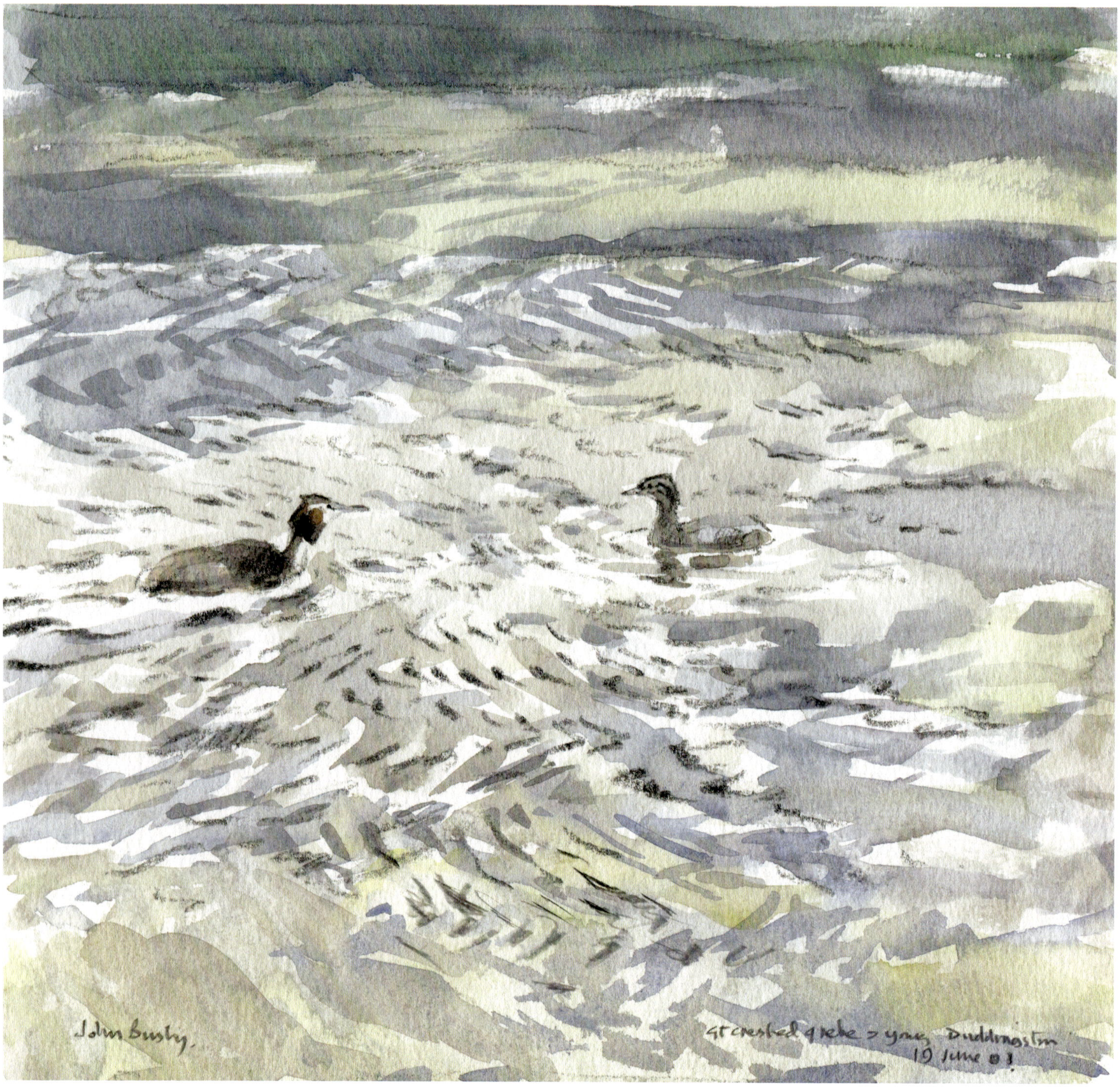

Great crested grebe and young, Duddingston Loch, Edinburgh

Mute swan with great crested grebe feeding young >

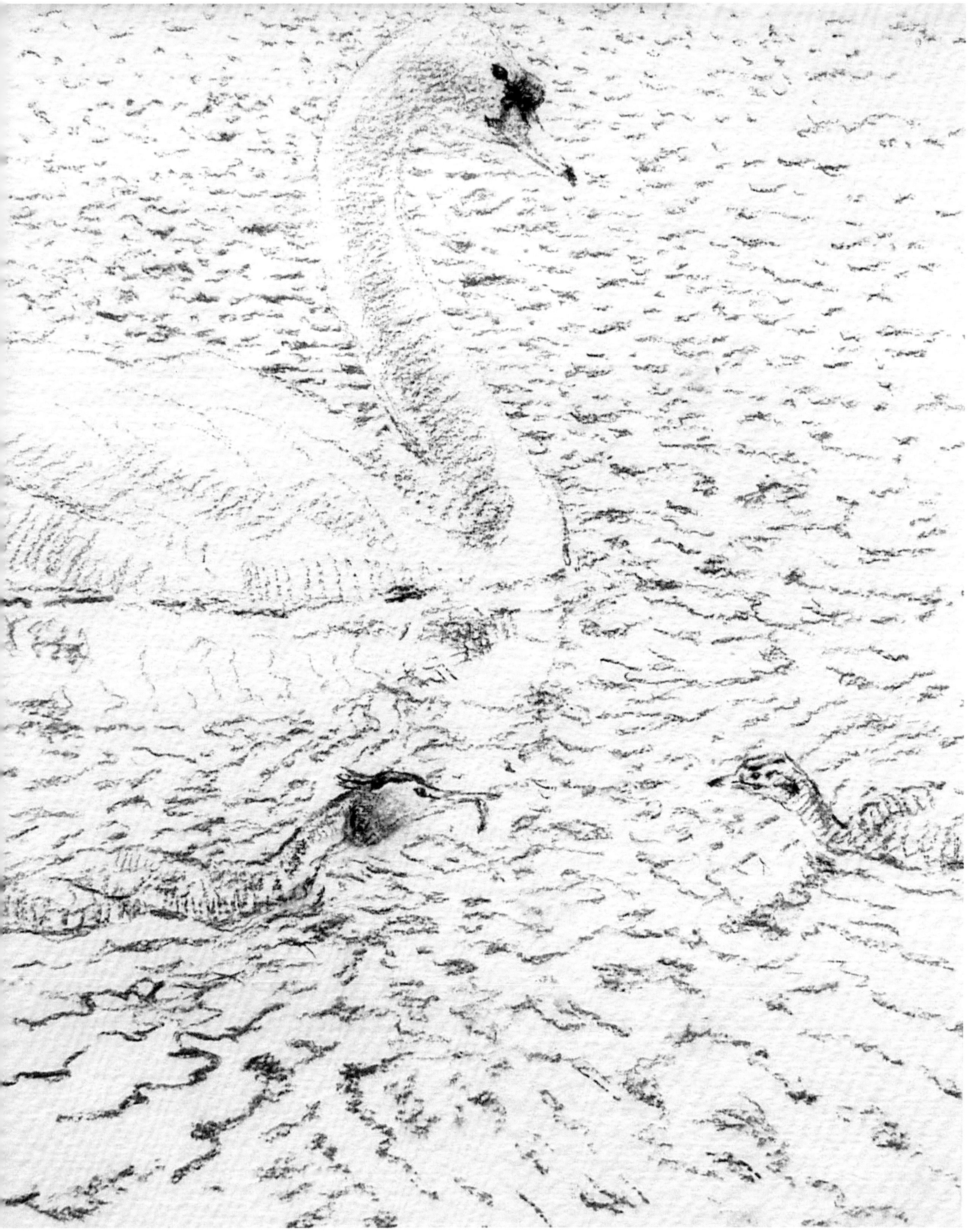

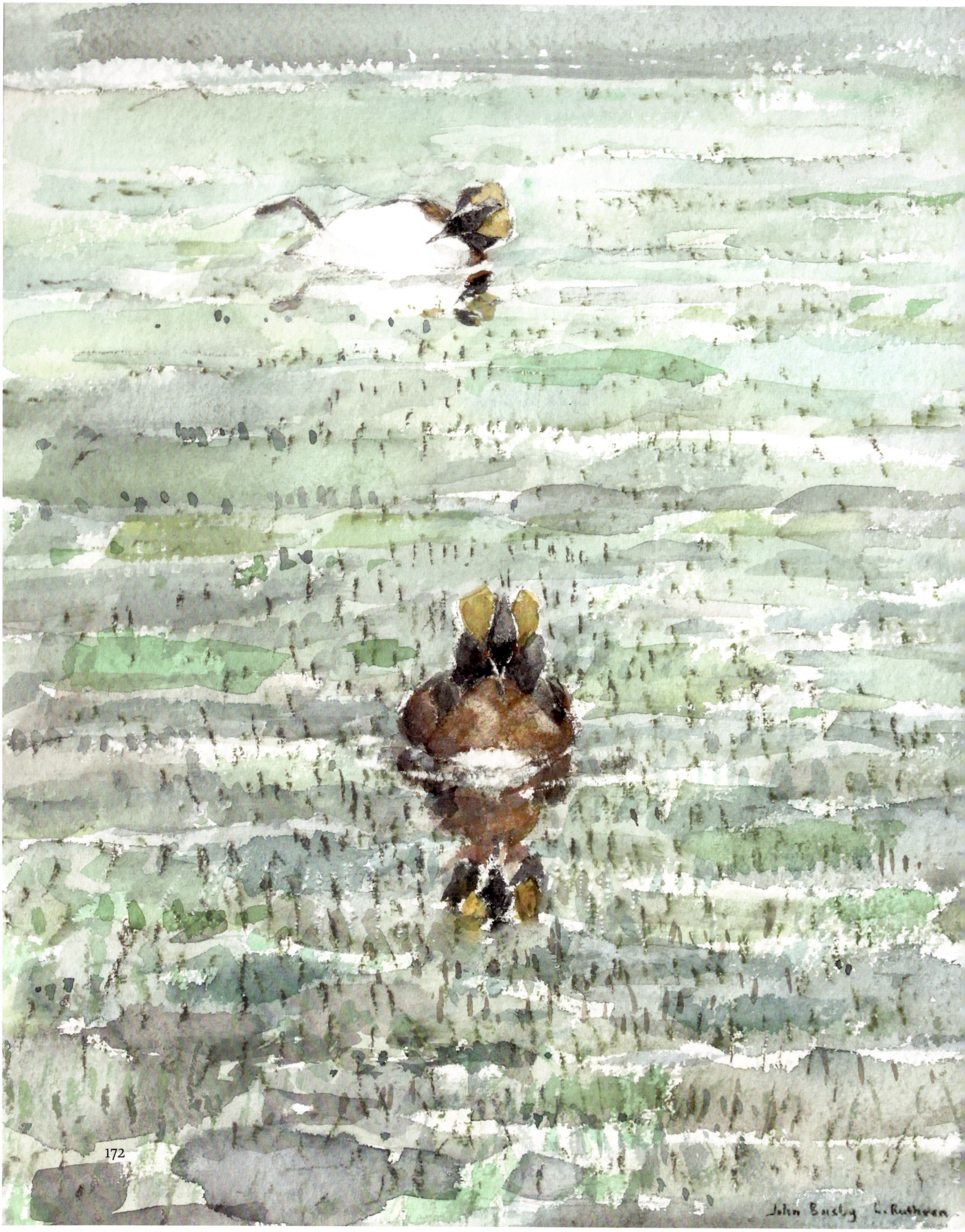
John Busby L. Ruthven

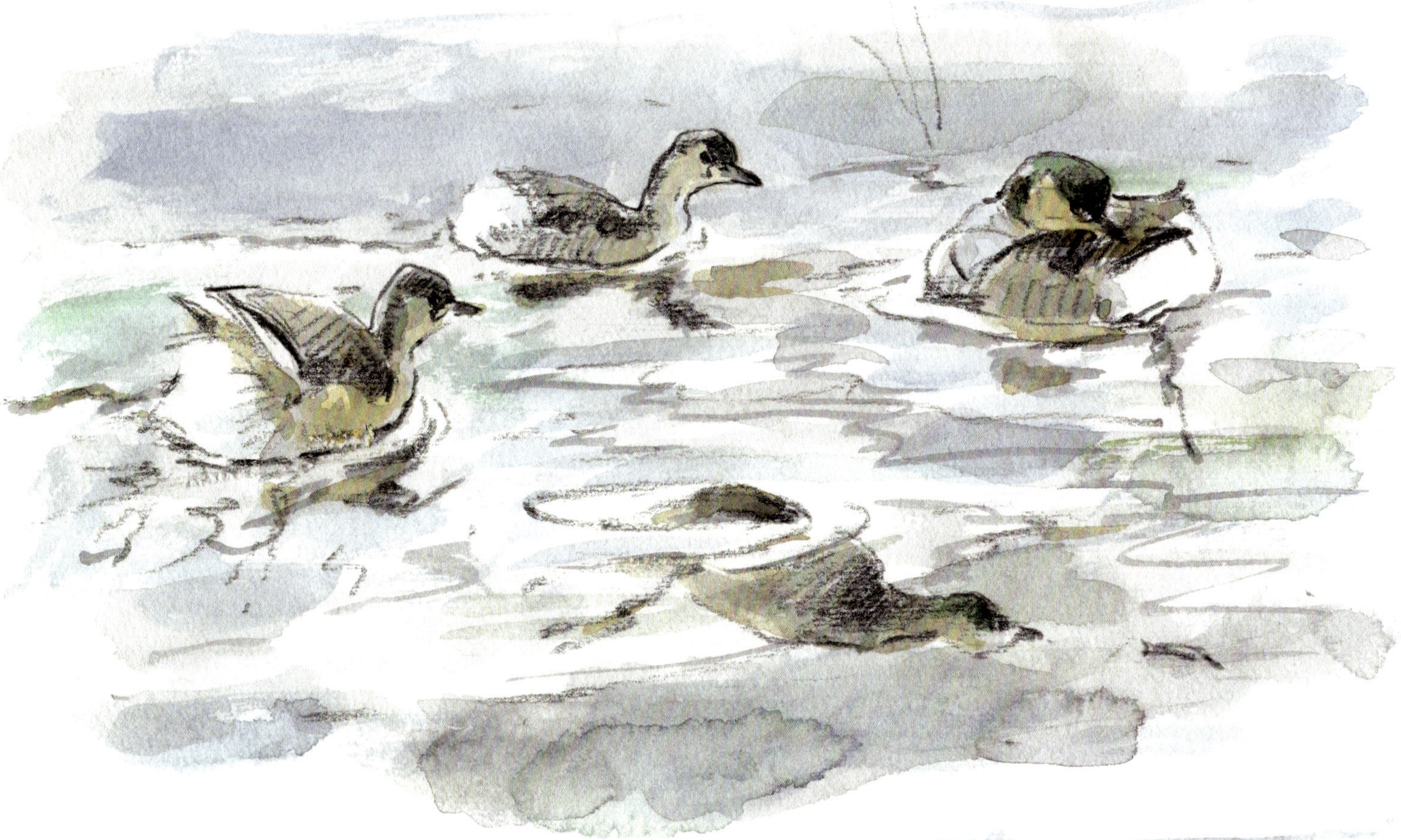

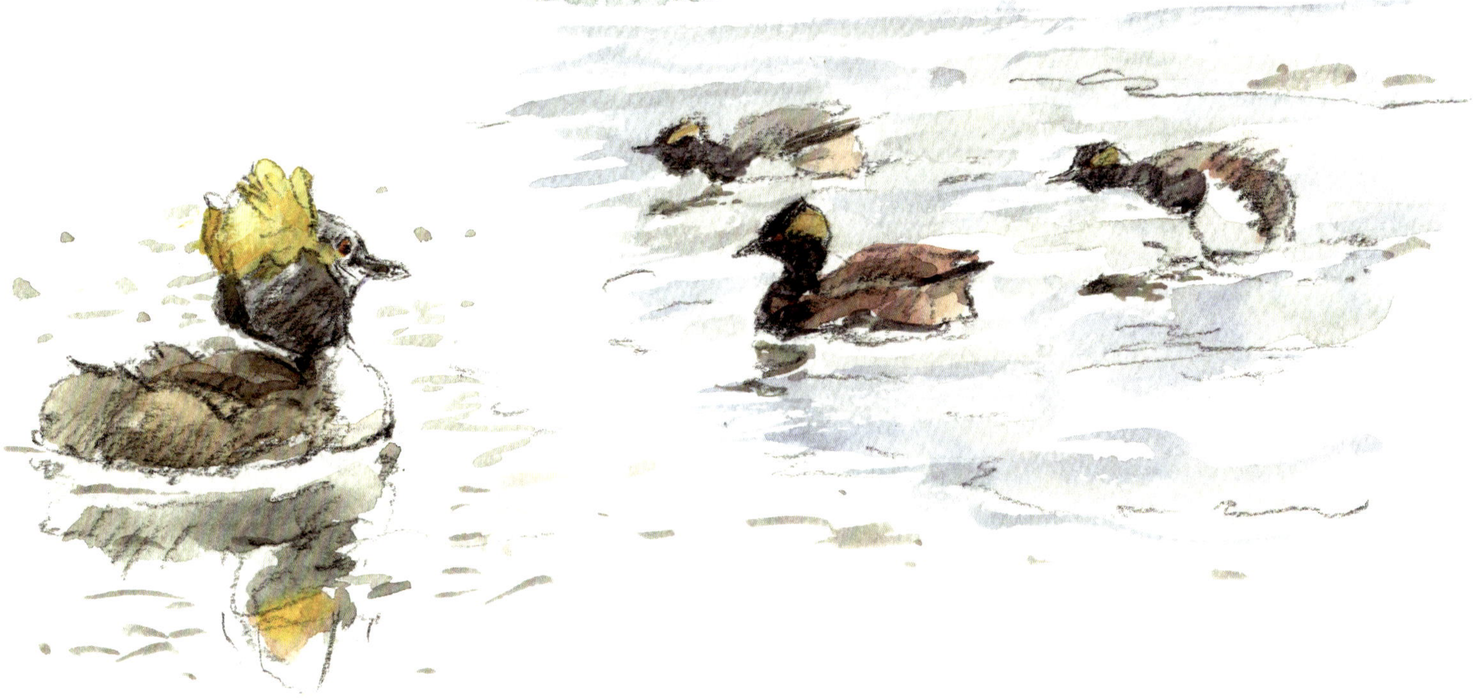

Top: Dabchicks

Slavonian and black-necked grebes

< *Slavonian grebes on Loch Ruthven in spring*

I love to see Slavonian and black-necked grebes, which breed on Scottish lochs and are also seen on the sea in winter, and the character-full little grebe, always busy above and below water. I have only seen the red-necked grebe in its summer plumage in Holland. In the Firth of Forth it is more often seen in transitional plumage, somewhere between summer and winter.

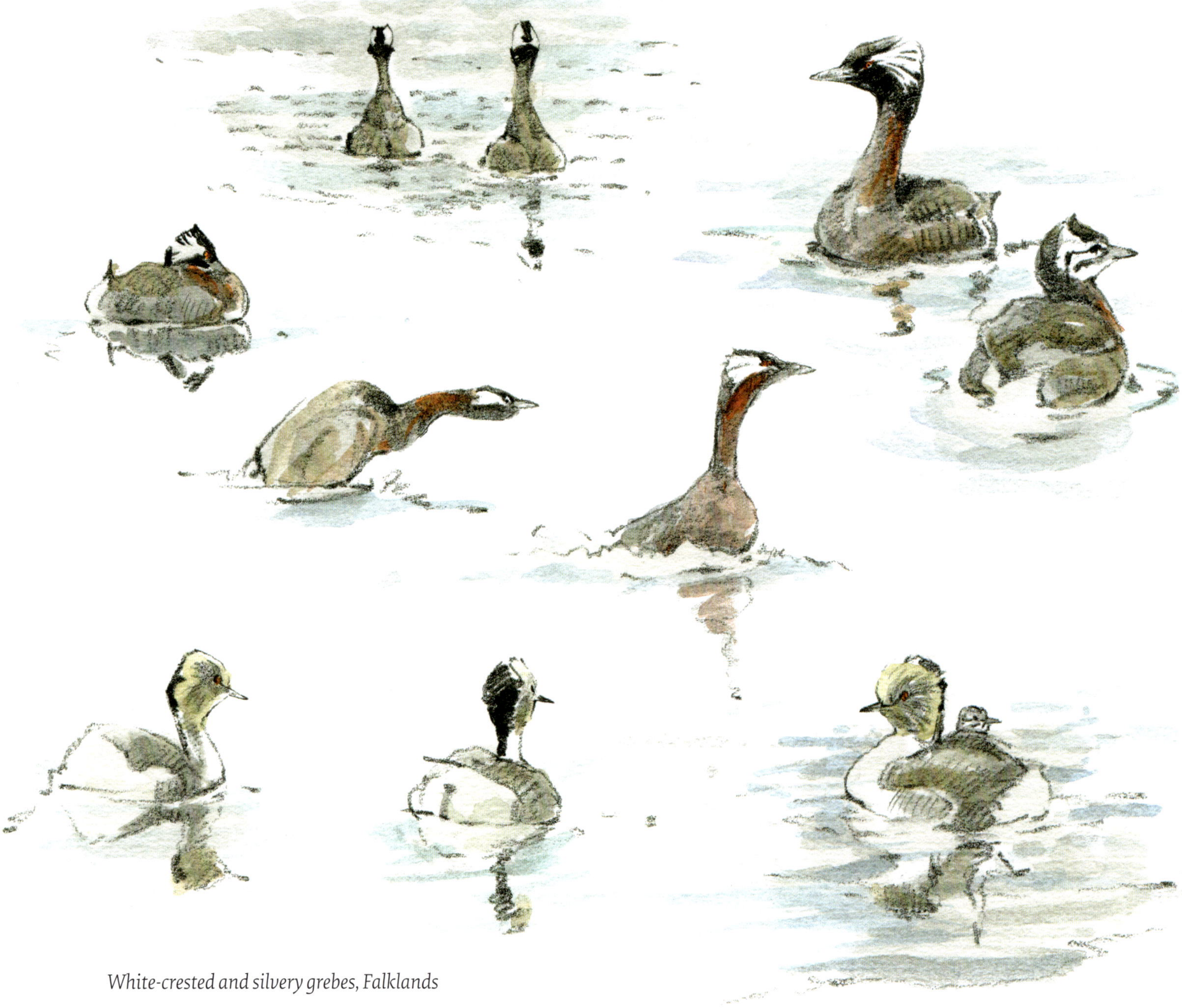

White-crested and silvery grebes, Falklands

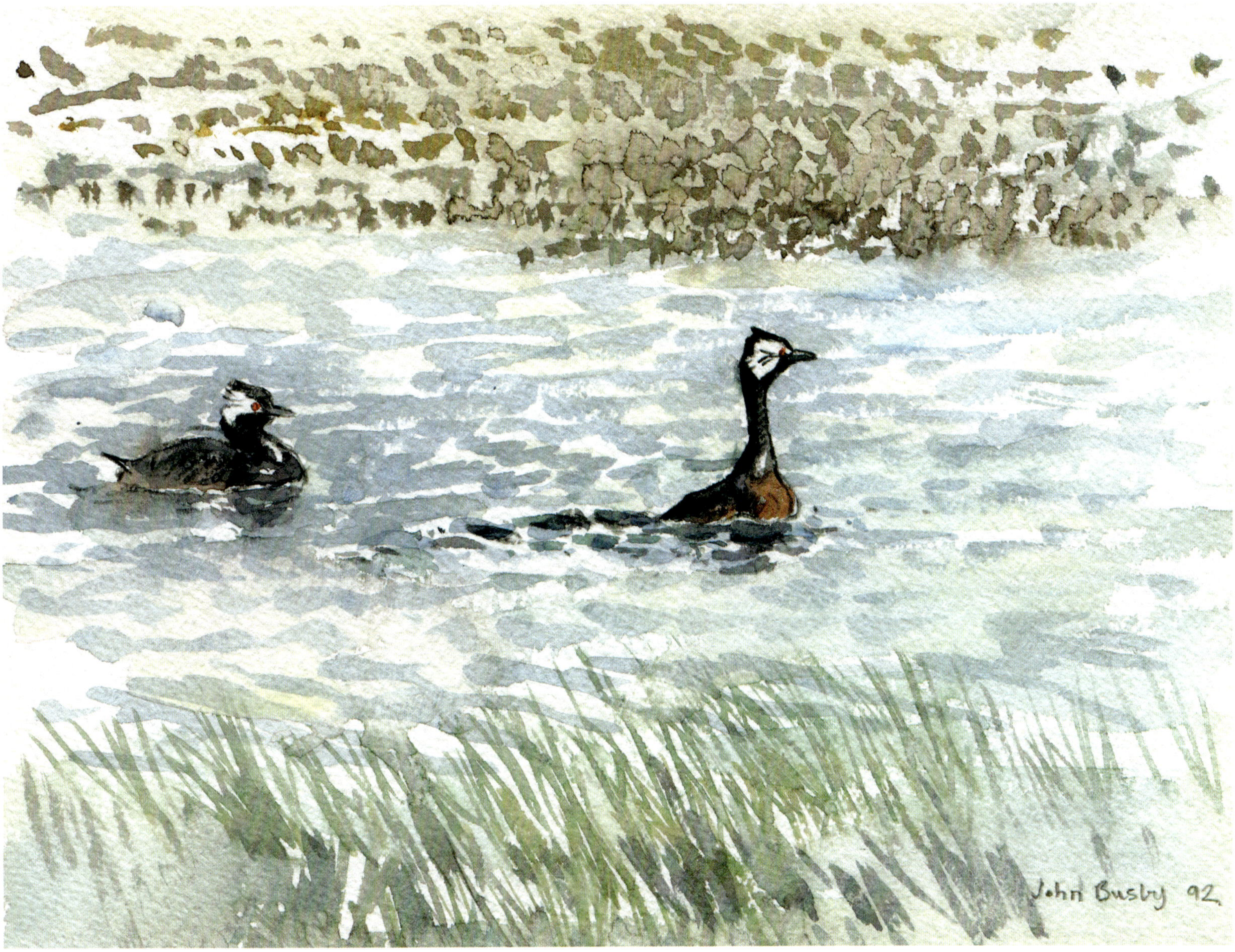

White-crested grebes, Sealion Island, Falklands

The western grebe of the USA is another splendid creature, especially in courtship action.

Two other delightful grebes are the white-crested and silvery grebes of the Falkland Islands. They are found nesting together on some inland waters and can be watched at close quarters as they show no fear of people. The silvery is even smaller than a little grebe and the white-crested resembles our black-necked in size and shape. Both have bright red eyes.

Like ballet dancers, grebes leave you with lasting memories of poise and movement to treasure.

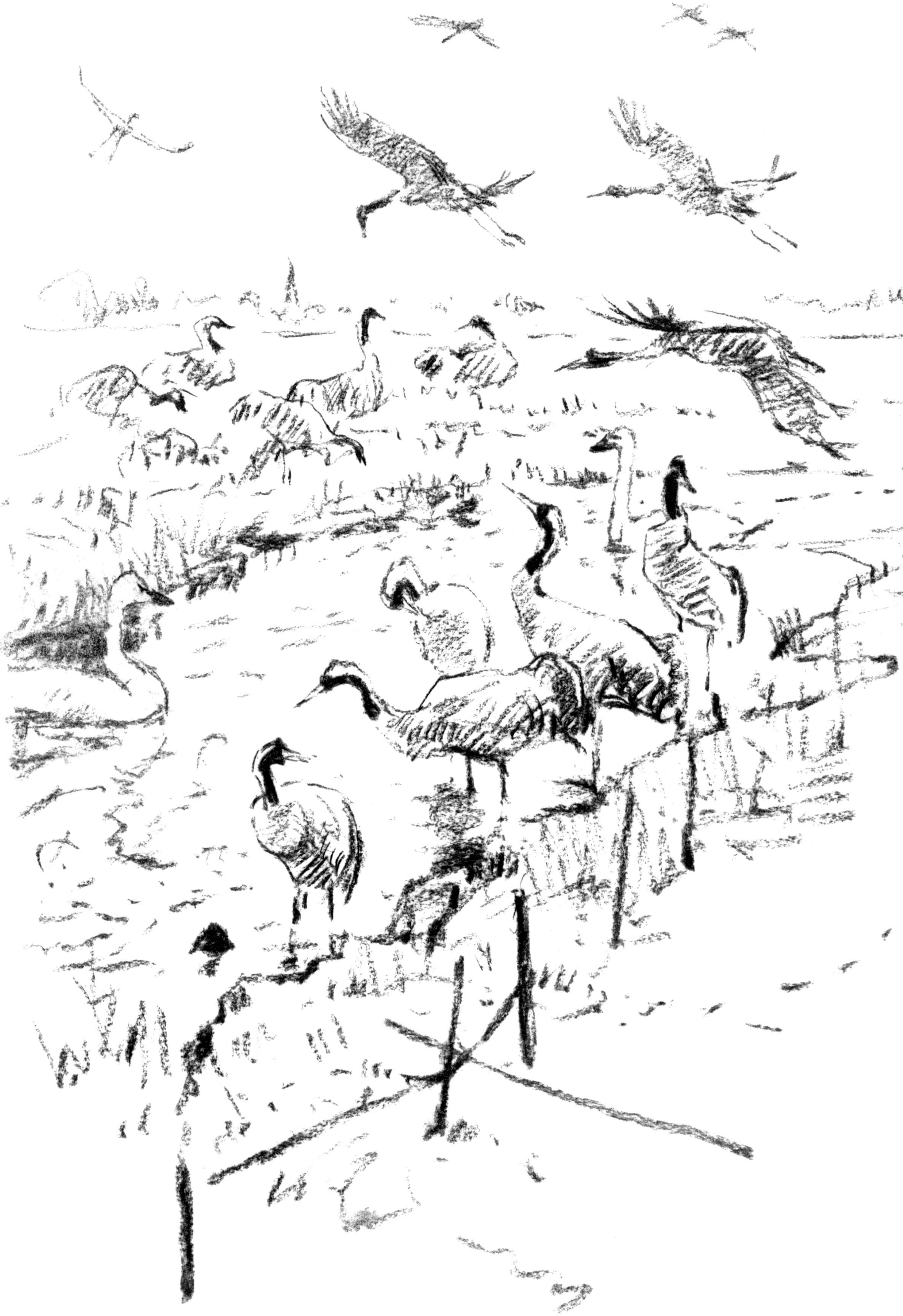

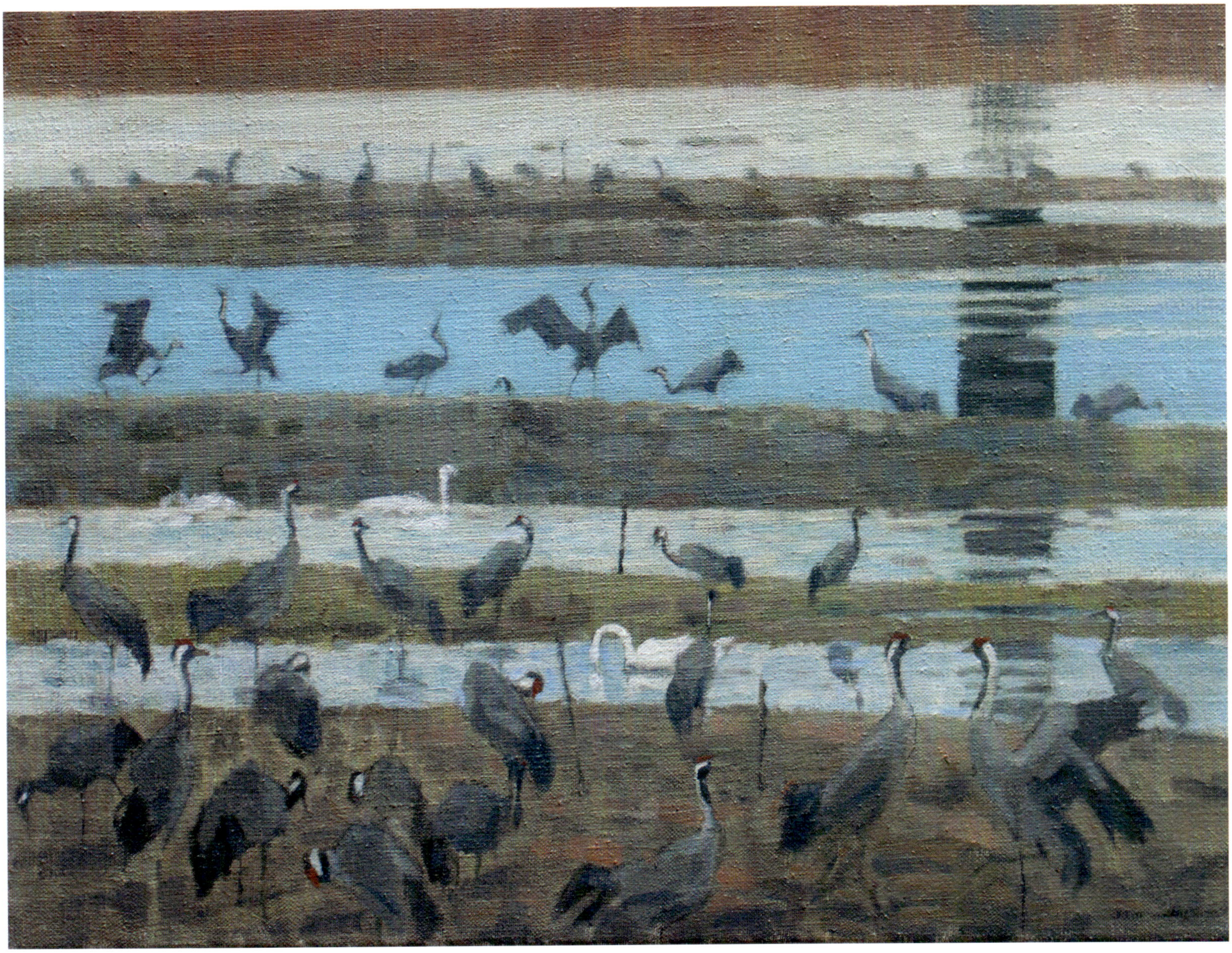

Cranes

It is small wonder that cranes stir human imagination. They are held in awe in parts of the world as almost divine symbols of faithfulness. The clarion voices of cranes, heard again over the still frozen lakes of Sweden, herald the arrival of spring. European cranes are tall elegant birds with a bustle of extended tertiary feathers at the base of their wings. They mate for life and breed in isolated pairs in the northern marshlands, only coming together again as their families join others for the migration to warmer climes and the acorn-rich Dehesas of Spain and Portugal, where they forage in family groups

European cranes, Hornborgasjön

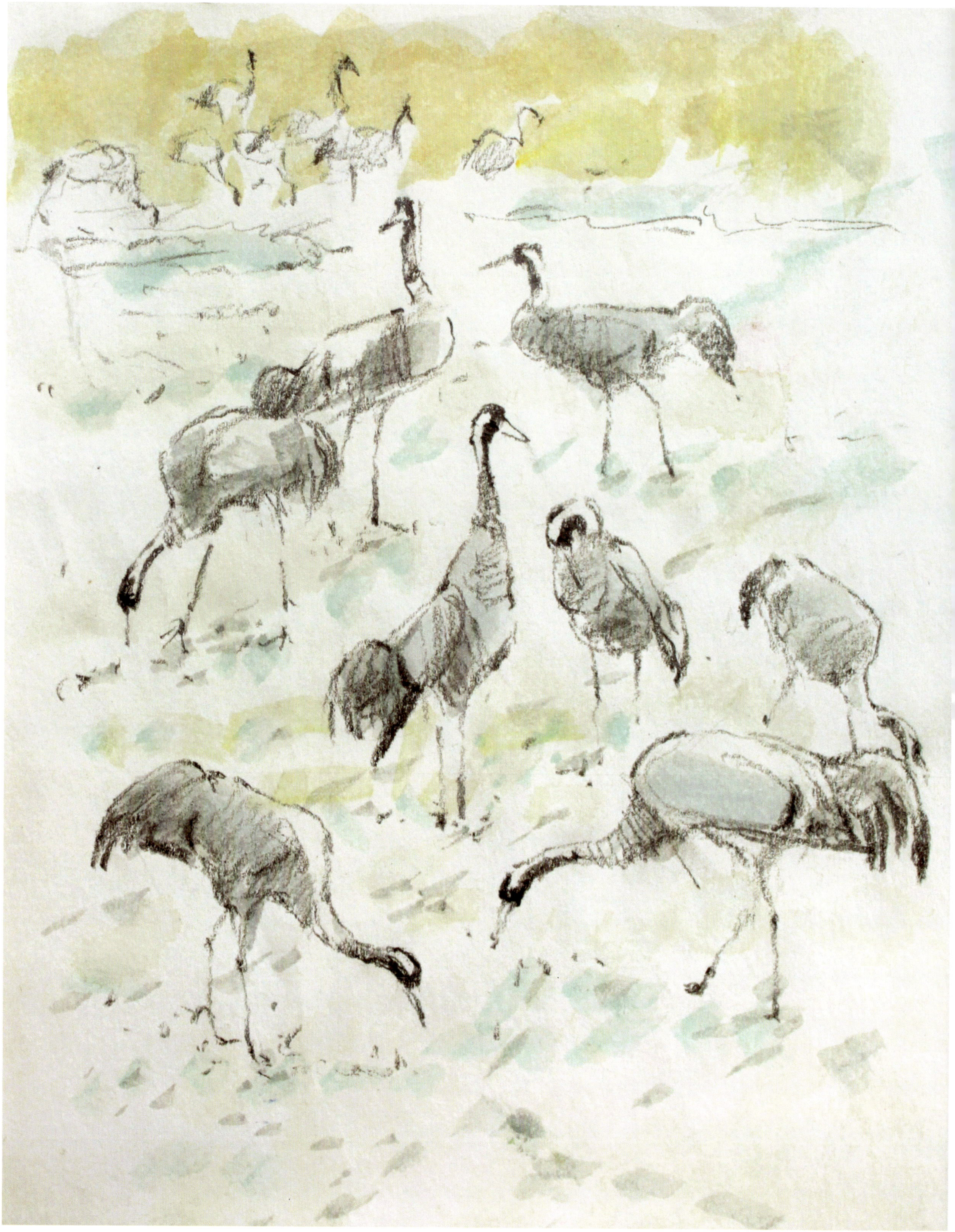

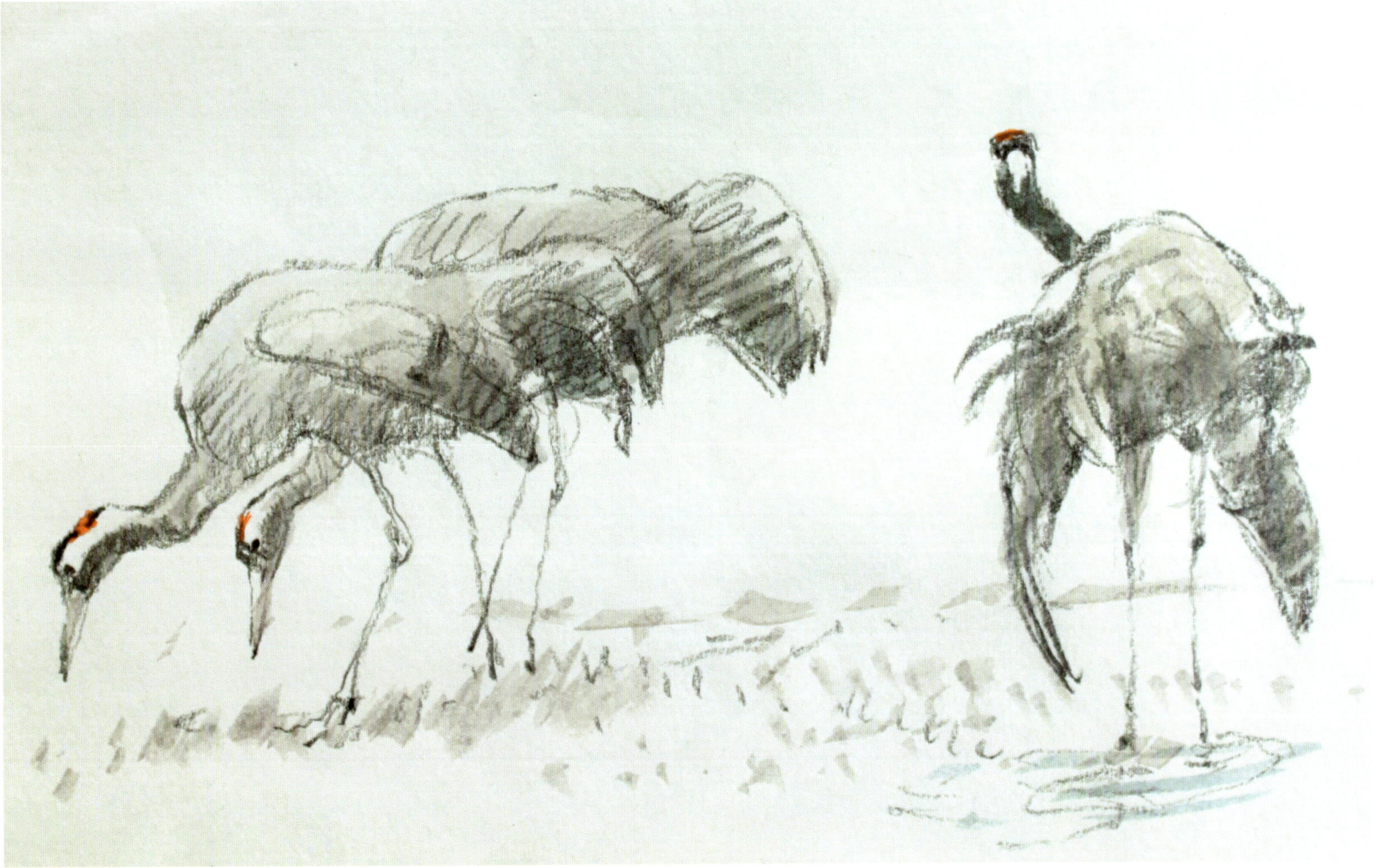

European cranes

among the cork oak trees, flying to communal roosts in the evening. Their skeins weave patterns in the sky and fill the air with their music. It is said that their flight figurations gave rise to written language in ancient Greece.

Their journey north in spring follows ancestral routes with well defined stopping places in Spain, France and Germany. They arrive in Sweden in early April and are greeted by hundreds of people enjoying the uplift of spirit they bring. At Hornborgasjön, where surplus potatoes are left out for their nourishment, they gather in their thousands. It is one of the great bird events of the world – birds feeding, preening, bathing, dancing, leaping into the air, picking up and throwing sticks and calling in great excitement. No wonder cranes are favourites with artists throughout the world. They were especially loved by the old Chinese artists, who matched their rhythmic elegance with beautiful brush strokes. I tried to touch this deep ancestral link between bird and man in my Crane Dance paintings.

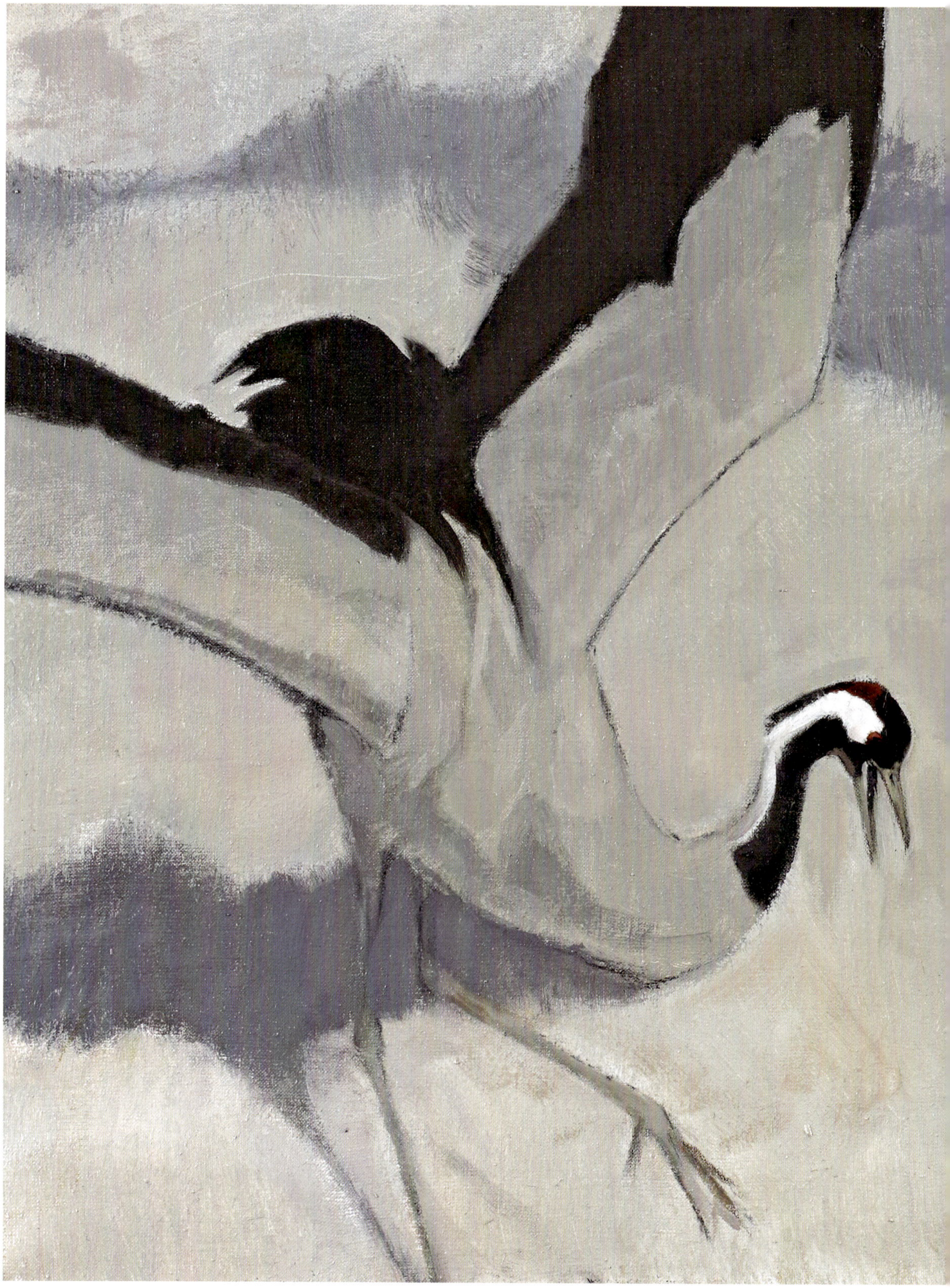

Crane
Arabesque

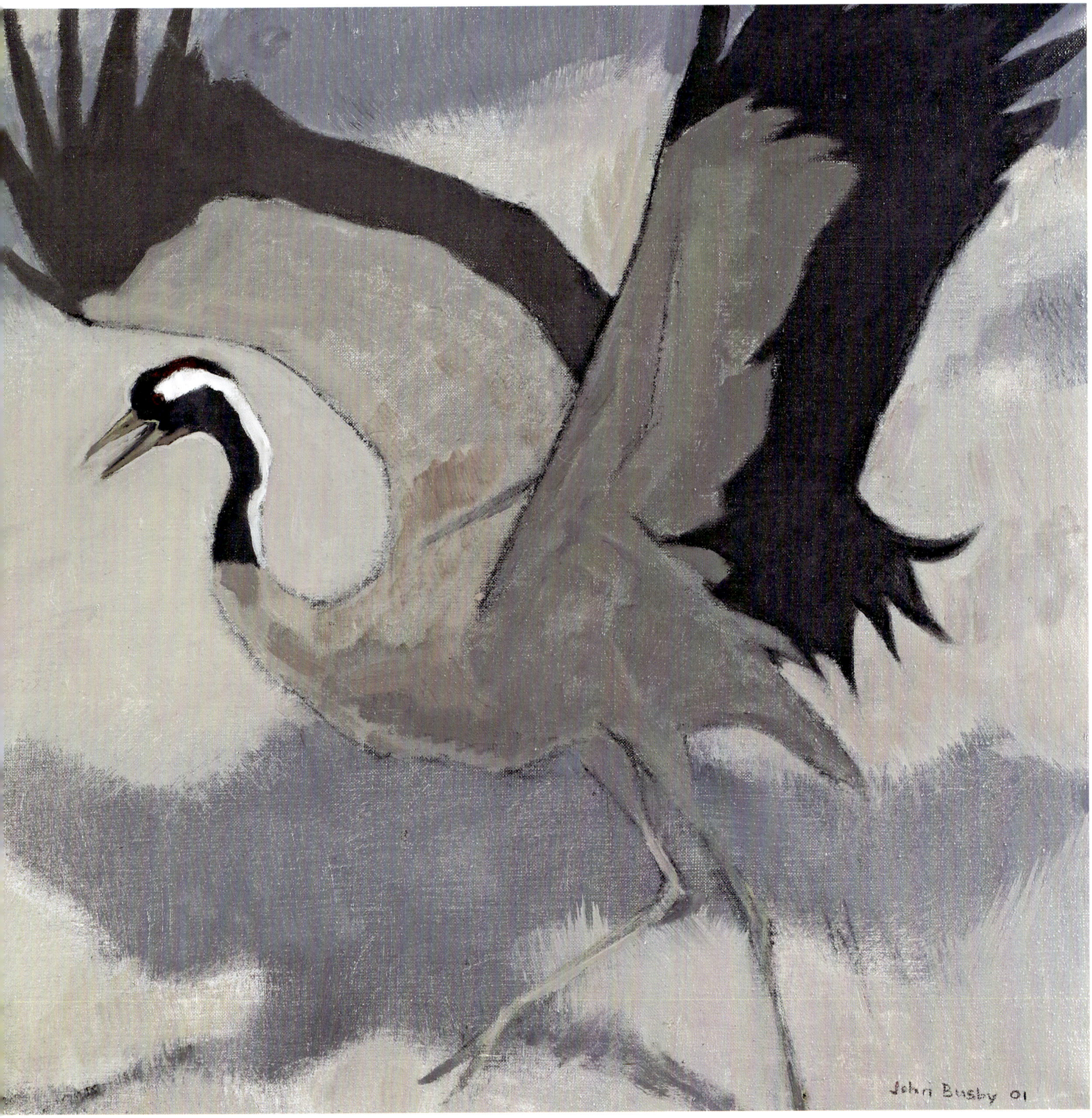
John Busby 01

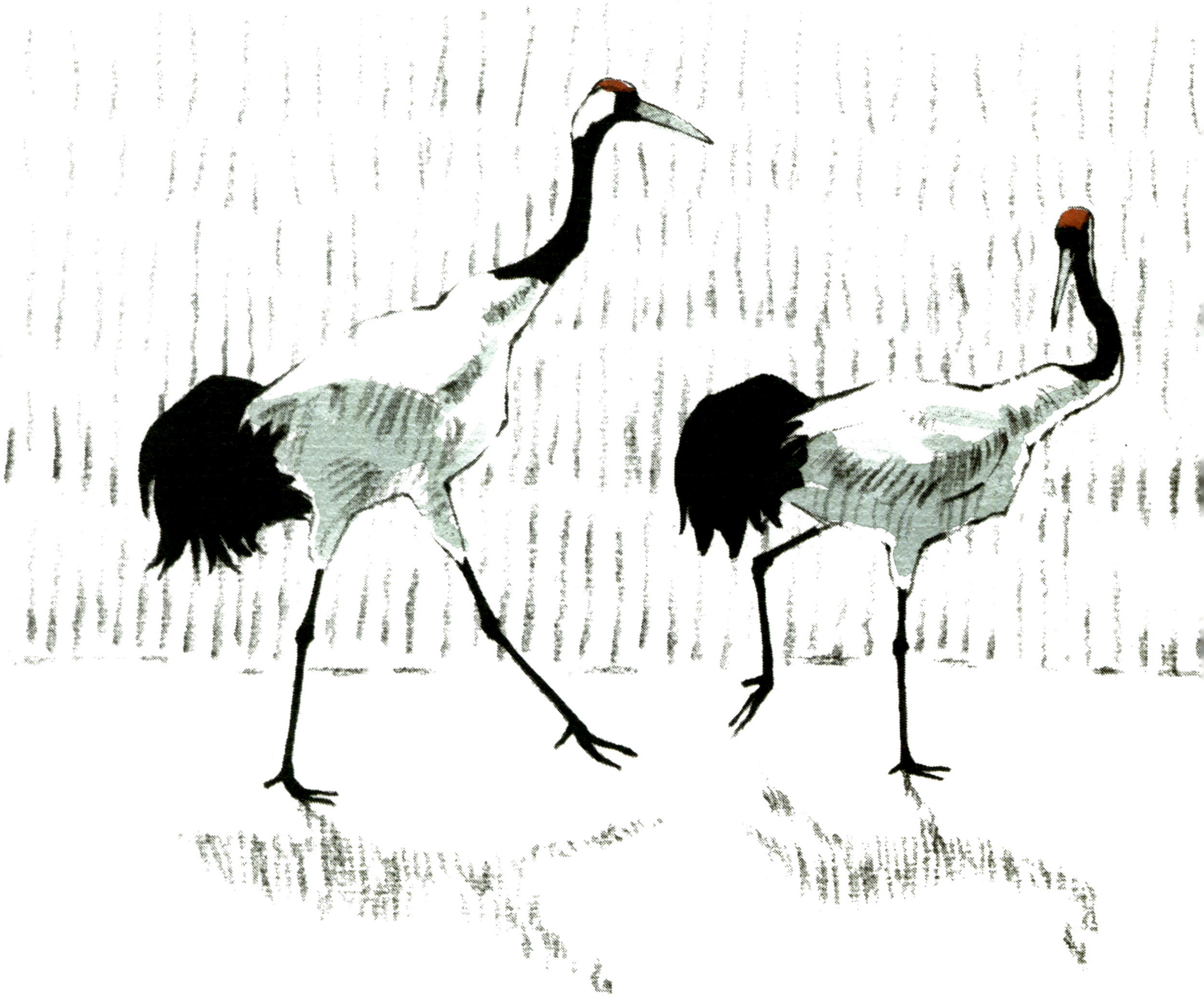

Imperial cranes

What a loss that there is no route still in a crane's consciousness that includes Britain: and few places left wild enough for them to breed. New experiments with captive bred cranes are encouraging and a small number now breed in England, so in time perhaps their vagrant visits to the wild places of the British Isles may have renewed purpose.

If you ever visit Wisconsin in the USA, be sure to call at the Crane Foundation. It has a live collection of all the cranes of the world, and George Archibald, its founder, has bred and cared for cranes for many years, and reintroduced them in parts of the world where they have previously been under threat.

The Foundation is quite near the Leigh Yawkey Woodson Art Museum at Wausau, which is a major centre for wildlife art in the States, so you could combine the joys of real and painted birds and enjoy the welcome hospitality of both.

One of my unfulfilled ambitions is to visit Hokkaido Island in Japan to see the magnificent Imperial crane in all its glory amid the snow.

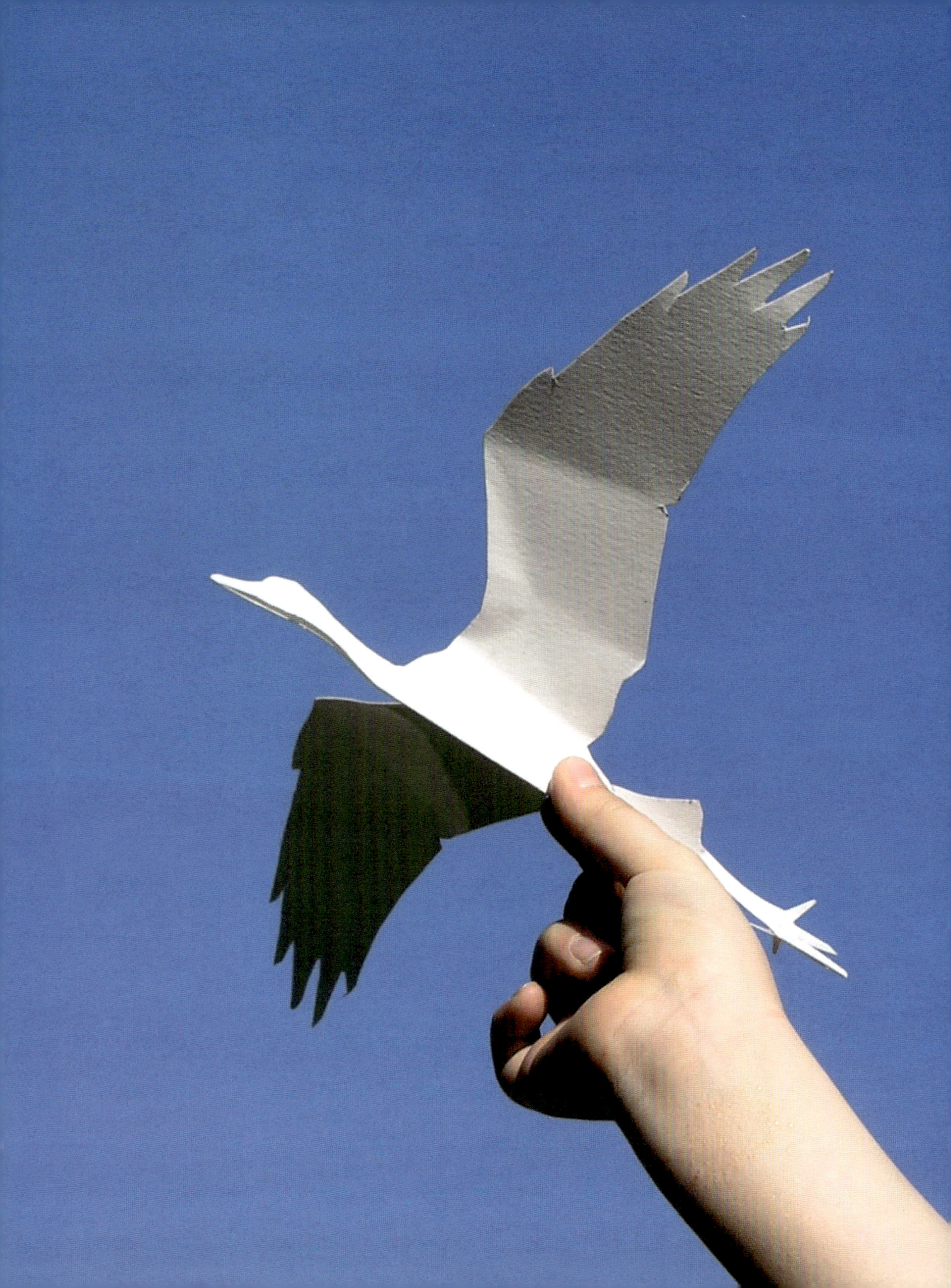

A visit to the Hula Nature Reserve in Israel 2009

The artists from 'Artists for Nature' arrive at Hula in the spring as the cranes are moving north. Crane voices fill the air with music.

Children from schools in Israel, Jordan, and Palestine, sit together near the marsh to hear stories about cranes, told by Amir Barabam.

I cut out flying cranes from folded paper, and the children wave them, making the wings beat. In imagination they become cranes.

What is music to our ears is not so to nearby farmers, who sound klaxons to keep the cranes away from their crops.

Artists try to discover patterns and meanings.

The restored marsh shimmers with water patterns as the wind plays over the surface. The drained areas are unmoving.

Cloud shadows make patterns on the slopes of the Golan Heights. As they change shapes, they reveal subtle contours on the escarpment and seem to dance.

A troubled past daring to change into joyful hope?

Cranes make slow patterns in the sky as they circle on rising thermals.

Birds have patterns of behaviour learned over millennia; people are still learning. Cranes communicate and act together. When the moment comes to go, they all know it. Where do our patterns lead?

Can we see the good things in nature before we destroy them?

Will the thunder and lightning pass, and will we listen to the still small voice that speaks love to our hearts?

Questions and Answers can be part of the same pattern.

Cut-out paper crane, Hula reserve, Israel

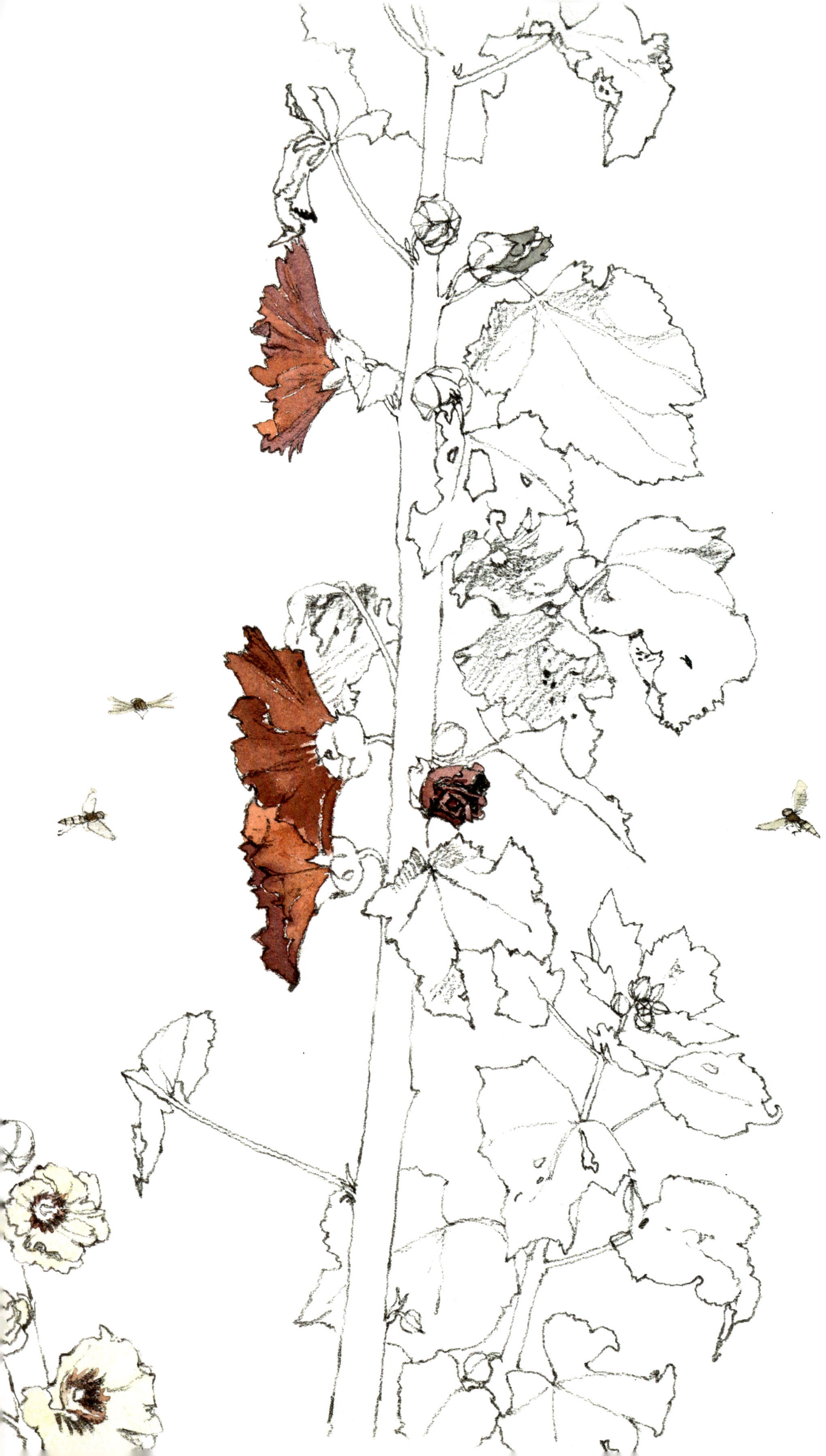

Acknowledgements

I owe a great debt to a number of artists who inspired me with their unique vision of wildlife and landscape: Eric Ennion, R.B. Talbot Kelly, J.A. Shepherd, David Measures, and to the exciting younger generation of today's wildlife artists. To my lifelong friend and fellow artist Derek Hyatt for his creative vision of landscape, and to that of the late Norman Adams.

To my time as a student at Leeds and Edinburgh Colleges of Art and the experience of teaching at Edinburgh with fine artists and exciting students.

To many colleagues at the Society of Wildlife Artists, and at the Royal Scottish Academy.

To the Artists for Nature Foundation who invited me to join a number of overseas projects, and particularly to Ysbrand Brouwers, its Dutch director.

To zoologist friends who commissioned illustrations for their work, especially to Dr Bryan Nelson, the 'Gannet man', and Trevor Poyser, the publisher.

To Sir Hew Dalrymple for allowing me to visit the Bass Rock.

To Hugh Miles, wildlife photographer, for including me in his work with otters.

To the Wildlife Art Gallery, Lavenham, the Scottish Ornithologists Club, and other places where I have shown my work, and to Ian Langford for publishing this, a second book from me.

To my wife Joan for many years of loving support and shared experiences, especially of music; and to the insights which my family, friends, children and grandchildren have brought me.

John Busby, Ormiston, March 2015

All the work for this book was completed by my husband, John, just before he died. I am indebted to Ian Langford for pressing on with publication, to Nye Hughes for realising the design so beautifully, and to John's friend and fellow-artist Darren Woodhead for his words on the cover and for his advice and support. Thanks to you all.

Joan Busby, Ormiston, November 2015

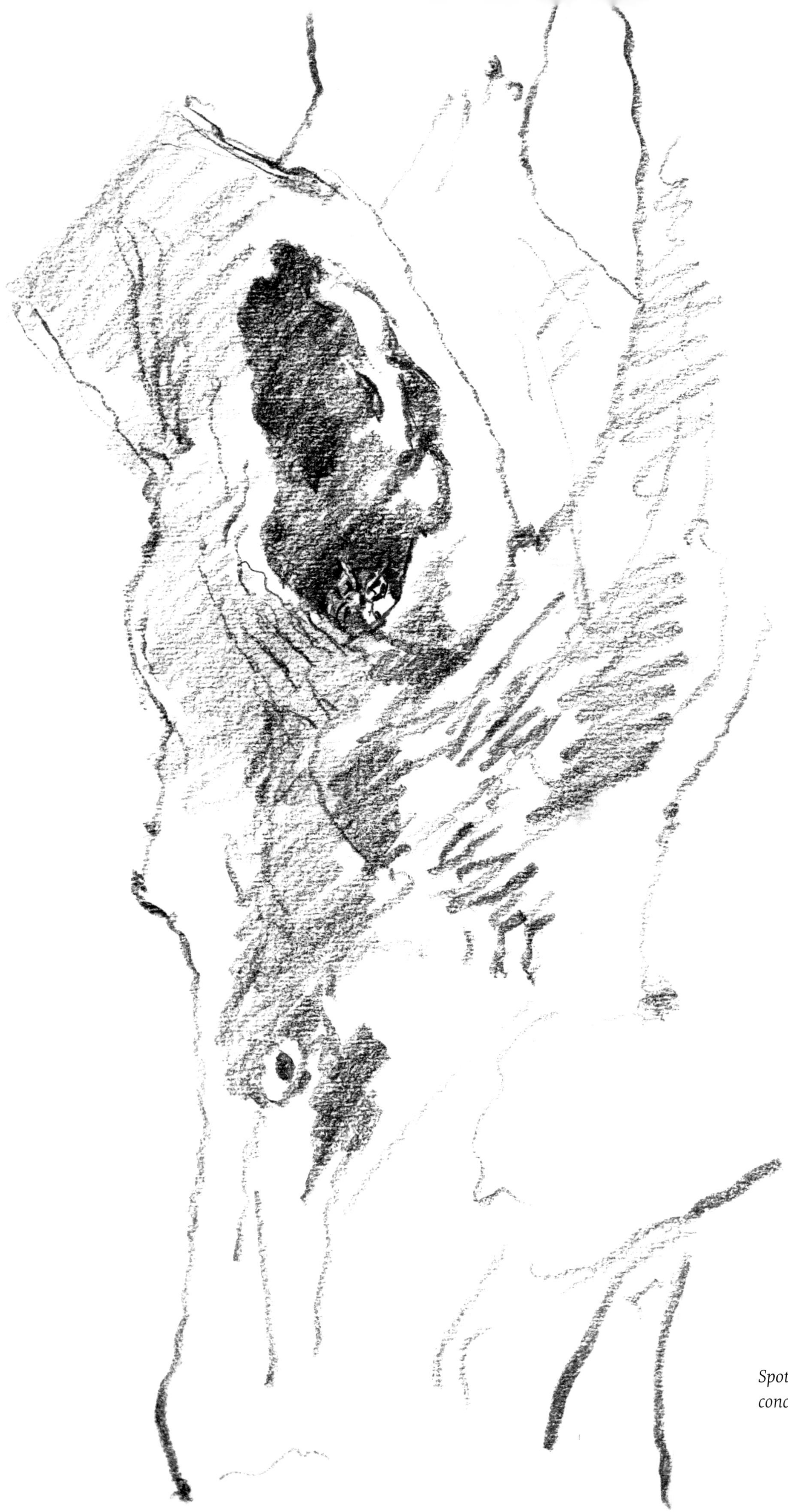

Spotted eagle owl concealed in an oak tree

Biography

John Busby was born in Bradford in 1928 and attended Ilkley Grammar School. After National Service, he studied at Leeds College of Art and then at Edinburgh College of Art (ECA) where he was awarded post-graduate and major travel scholarships. On return from France and Italy he was invited to join the staff of ECA, where he taught drawing and painting from 1956 until 1988.

A member of the Royal Scottish Academy (RSA) and the Royal Scottish Society of Painters in Watercolour (RSW), he became President of the Society of Scottish Artists, 1976–79. A lifelong bird watcher and naturalist, he was a Founder member of the Society of Wildlife Artists (SWLA).

Having led courses in Switzerland, Crete, the Falklands and Galapagos, and at Nature in Art in Gloucestershire, in 1989 he began a Seabird Drawing course based at North Berwick which has continued each year since, attracting participants from many parts of the world. He took part in projects with the Artists for Nature Foundation (ANF) in Holland, Poland, Spain, Ireland, India, Portugal, and Israel, and in SWLA/Forestry Commission projects in the New Forest and in the oak woods in the west of Scotland.

John illustrated over 35 books about birds and animals, mostly about behaviour, ranging from seabirds to tigers, garden birds to otters, and also a book of poems by Kenneth Steven called *Wild Horses*. His own books are:- *The Living Birds of Eric Ennion* (Gollanz 1982); the classic *Drawing Birds*, produced for the RSPB in 1986, with a second edition in 2004; *Birds in Mallorca* (Christopher Helm 1988); *Nature Drawings* (Arlequin Press 1993); *Land Marks & Sea Wings* (Lavenham 2005); *Looking at Birds* (Langford Press 2013) plus a booklet *Landscapes at the Edge of the Sea* in 2010, and another for *The Curious Eye* exhibition which he curated at the RSA in 2007.

In 2009 he was declared 'Master Wildlife Artist' by the Leigh Yawkey Woodson Art Museum in Wisconsin USA.

He lived near Ormiston in East Lothian, married to Joan, a renowned singing teacher. Music was an abiding passion and he was a lifelong Christian. He died in Edinburgh in June 2015.

Tailpiece

When our daughter Rachel came home from her first 'big' school, we asked her what was different to the old one. "Well," she said, after a moment's thought, "They call drawing Art".

The familiar action word had turned into something with a big question mark, needing explanation.

We are lucky if we carry our childhood love of making pictures through to adult life, and can escape from pretentiousness, keeping experiences clear from the merely artful.

A child immersed in creativity does not stop to ask whether the colours and shapes they are using express their inner being; nor are they terribly worried about accuracy, yet the result is usually true to both the inner and outer experience.

The child has not learned to divorce the eye from the hand – both are in action together, and the 'true likeness' is in the understanding of the eye and hand together, not something first seen, copied by hand, and held up to match the original.

For the child artist, the marks he or she is making become in imagination the very thing seen. When this happens, the drawing or painting truly becomes a language passed through its 'art' to another's understanding. It is as simple and as profound as that.

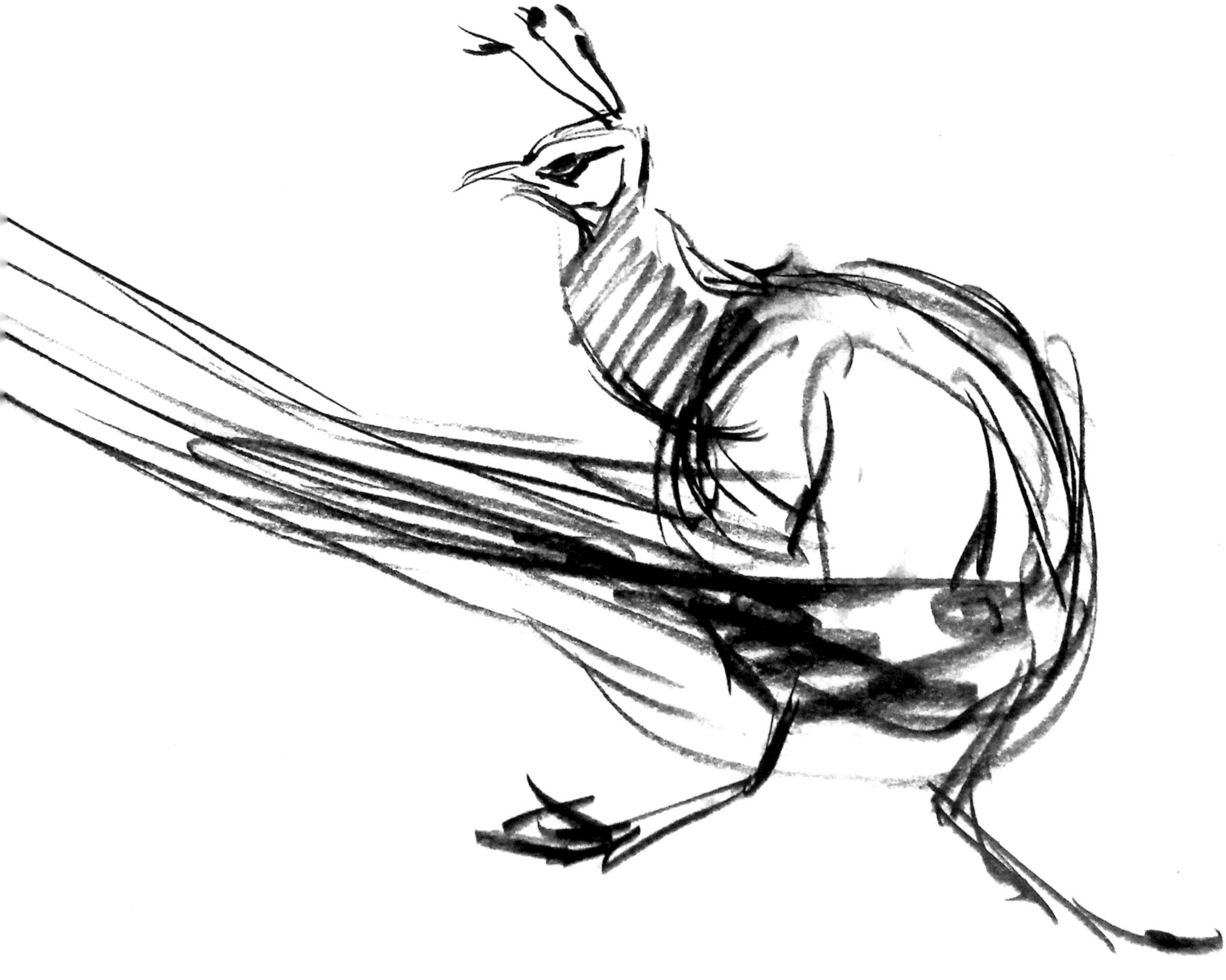

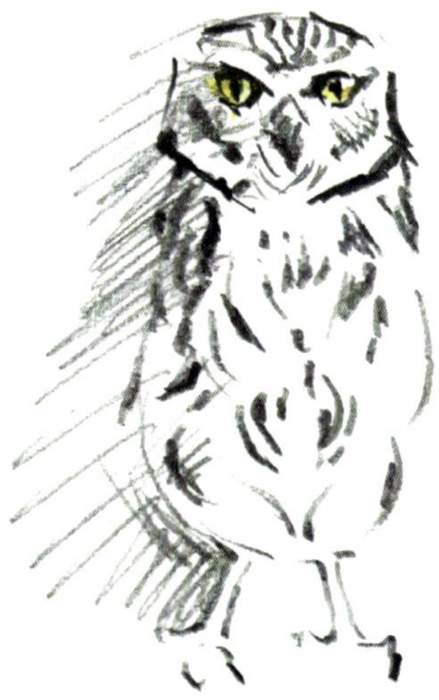

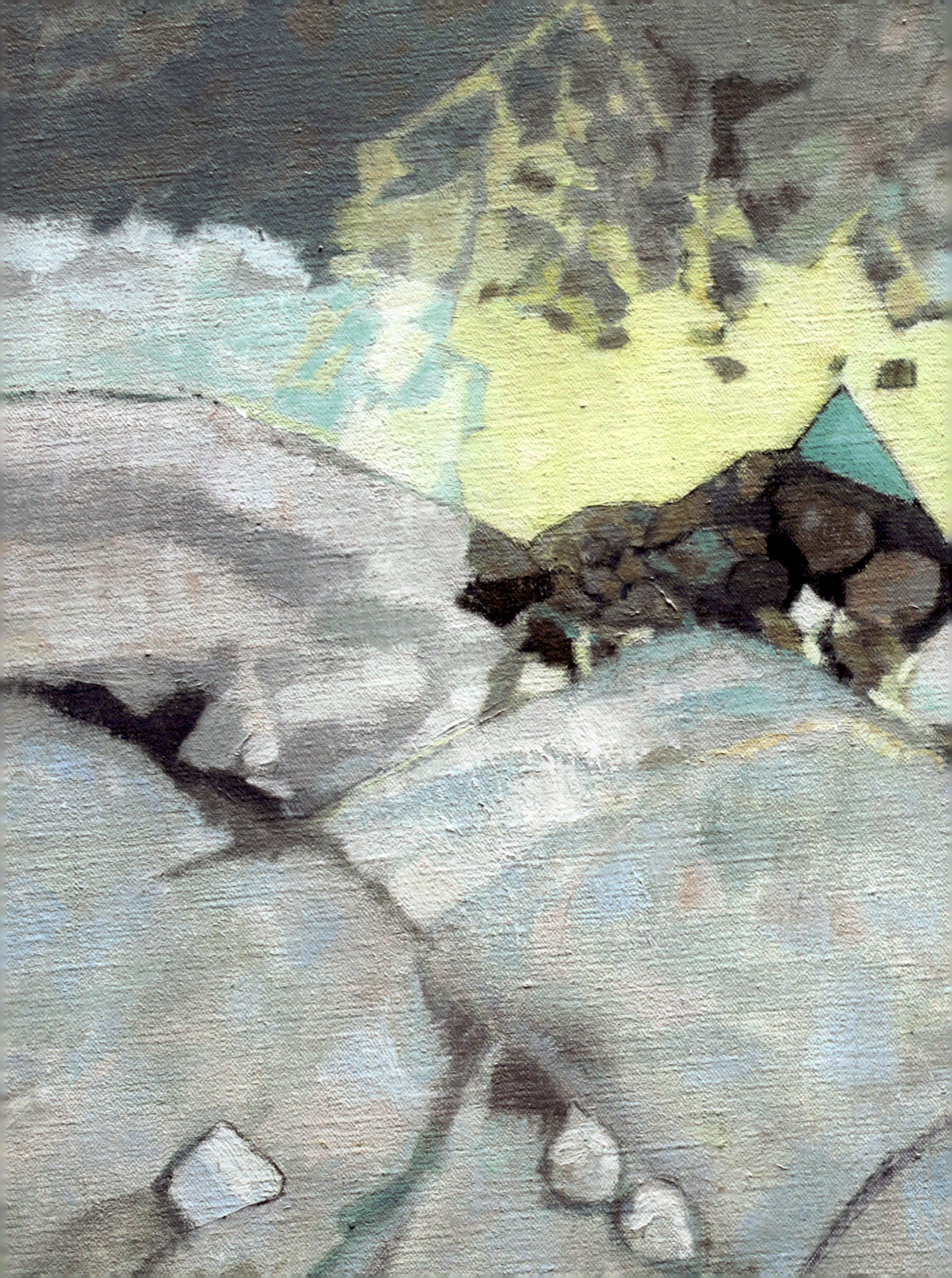